SOUL GARDEN

SOUL GARDEN

A CATHOLIC MOTHERS' COLLECTIVE

Edited by Hope Schneir and Sia Hoyt

IGNATIUS PRESS   SAN FRANCISCO

Cover design by Margaret Ryland
Cover and chapter art by Mary Pemberton
Interior illustrations by Sia Hoyt and Mary Pemberton

© 2024 by Ignatius Press, San Francisco
All rights reserved
ISBN 978-1-62164-685-3 (PB)
ISBN 978-1-64229-304-3 (eBook)
Library of Congress Control Number 2024942791
Printed in Canada ∞

To Our Lady of Nazareth,
and to our own mothers and daughters,
with gratitude for who you are
and what you gave us.

CONTENTS

PREFACE

Dear Sisters,

In 2010, a few mothers began to sense the budding implications of tech distractions on domestic life and took a little blog forward (or maybe backward) from the busy screen frontier to a pen-and-ink publication. *Soul Gardening Journal* was born, and with it a community of over two thousand readers and contributors worldwide. What you hold in your hands is a compilation of some of our favorite pieces from a decade of journaling. This book was written by an array of women (with a few pastoral additions): some lovers and dreamers, some poets and thinkers, some "Marthas", some "Marys"—but all of them mothers and all of them disciples of Christ.

We would like to thank all our contributors who breathed such life and variety into these pages. We especially thank our dear friend Mary Pemberton, who is both an artist and a writer. Her years of journal ministry and hard work on this book project from start to finish have been invaluable, including her uniquely beautiful chapter art. We also thank Ellie Nickelsen, writer, friend, and cofounder of the journal. She stepped away from the journal ministry years ago, but many of the thoughts she had as a young mother are memorialized here. We also thank Ursula Crowell for her undying support and bookkeeping gifts that have kept our tiny vessel afloat. We would have capsized without her! Likewise, we thank layout and brand designer Margaret Ryland, who has generously dedicated more hours than any of us can count toward this uniquely designed book. Finally, we thank all our family members who, through their encouragement, counsel, and patience, supported this project happening on the sidelines of busy family life.

Soul Garden is not meant to be read cover to cover but to function more as a resource manual for a mother's interior and exterior life. Flip through the pages to find what speaks to you and look for inspiration where you need it most. Whatever your life's circumstances, we hope you may find rest in the pages of this book. We are each humbled through the trials, the gifts, the joys, the pains, and the lessons motherhood and femininity bring; we are all united in the sisterhood of these experiences.

Truly, the work of a mother is that of a *soul gardener*. A woman cannot tend gardens all around the world; she can tend only one garden, the one she has been given, commending her work to the Author of creation, of which she is a part. Let us be confident that the Master Gardener is at work in our homes, our souls, and our families, welcoming his slow and wonderful work in us so often accomplished at the organic and sometimes imperceptible pace of nature. Here's to the journey: the sprouting, budding, blossoming, fruit bearing, thriving, and dying. May our lives be lived according to his good pleasure, and may we find comfort in one another as we grow.

Love,

Hope and Sia

NURTURE

THE CROWN

Peace of mind is important. At home laughter and energy and fighting and wrestling and emotional breakdowns happen all at the same time. I get tired. It's easy for me to snap when the toddlers tell me they're starving, and the teenage girl wants to talk something out, and the boy is begging me to intervene so his little brother stops wrecking his LEGO® creations. That's when I should mentally go to a happy place of riding a unicorn on the clouds, but I don't even have the energy to do that.

So I put on the Crown. Yes, I have a crown. It's my leave-me-alone-to-think crown. My mom-crown. And this crown has a story.

My husband used to work with an elementary school teacher who would sometimes wear a glittery dollar-store crown at her desk. One day when he asked her why, she said that her students knew not to approach her when she was wearing her crown. She didn't wear it for long, but it was long enough to give her time to grade or plan or just gather her thoughts. He suggested one evening, after I vented and cried about hating myself for snapping at the children, that I should

acquire just such a crown for moments of mayhem.

Because of our Greek heritage, I made a crown out of fake laurel leaves and gold ribbon, and I put it on when I'm writing or sewing, and sometimes when I'm cooking. Here's the great part: because I'm available most of the day, it actually works. I don't wear it for long, but almost once a day it goes on my head. The kids think it's funny. All I have to do is point to the crown and they turn around.

Maybe your thing is a hat. Or a scarf. Or a funny wig—that would be hysterical. Whatever it is, it doesn't get personal and doesn't require yelling or losing one's patience (which I still manage to do); it's just a visual reminder to the kids that Mom needs a little quiet time, a little peace of mind.

— Lindsay Younce Tsohantaridis, Oregon

WOMAN, RECLAIM YOUR RIGHTS

One thing I've noticed in our generation is a rapid decline of parents who understand what it actually means to parent, and a corresponding increase of parents who seem to be born into parenthood with invisible handcuffs. I don't want to be snarky toward these people; most sincerely love their children and mean well, I'm sure. It's just that I repeatedly see a cultural shift away from strong, confident mothers who sleep with one eye open and know the value of fresh air and hard work, toward indulgent, shoulder-shrugging, weak women who are too busy scrolling their own Instagram accounts to pay attention to what their teenage daughters may be posting on theirs.

I'm here to tell you: *Woman, you can do better.* We all can. And it's not too late.

The culture is *strong* (don't we know it), and we are in uncharted waters with iPhones in almost every pocket (young and old), which at worst brings sexual addictions and horribly inappropriate conduct, and at best a ferocious dopamine addiction. Divorce rates are high, parents are busy, kids are lonely, and most kids have unlimited Internet at their fingertips. This is having a devastating effect on our youth. It's time we muster a bit of a militant mindset regarding the fact that our most precious jewels are on a sinking ship, and it may take heavy infantry to reclaim them.

The reality is stark, and the future is bleak—it's enough to make me want to drink a whole bottle of wine and blow my nose and go to bed. Yet it has dawned on me: I can't change the world, and I can't change the culture at large, but I can change *my* world. The only thing I can control in life is that which I am obliged to, namely, to make my four walls the best they can be, protect my family, and raise them as well as I am able. Yes, the only thing a woman can change is her kingdom.

You know you are a queen, right? God chose *you*—with your mind, abilities (and lack of abilities), messy house, love handles, pretty lips, no time—to be the stand-in for him, the shepherdess, if you will, who will lead these precious souls to him. That is your first and ultimate goal, and you've got to give it all you got. You are the queen of your 1,200-square-foot apartment, or farmhouse, or wigwam, and you need to fashion yourself a scepter from a leftover paper towel roll and begin

your reign. Do not let the culture dictate the rules of your house and compromise the dignity of your family. Read up. Think about the families you admire, and work toward creating your own purposeful family culture. Every family is unique, of course. Your job is not to look like the "perfect" Catholic family next door but to be the best version of what you (and your husband) can offer. We need to lead by example but also to try to form our children to be *better* than we are. So, it's time to reclaim your rights, while you still have them. A few things to note:

1. You may need to take away things that you had previously granted your kids. *This is okay.* The *Catechism of the Catholic Church* states that parents are the primary educators of their children. Anything that is a threat to you, as the primary educator of your children, deserves death by hanging. Or at least a four-week vacation on a desert island. It is your right, and your duty, to correct any wrongful practices that have sprung up (even if you consented to them for a time). Remember this corny bumper sticker? *A woman is allowed to change her mind!* Keep that phrase in your back pocket. Your people may not like it, but they will eventually get over it.

2. The best defense is a solid offense. Work to create a positive and unique family culture, and do this with your husband. Discuss with him what kind of family you want to have; think back on the things you loved to do together when you first met, before life slapped you in the face. (If you are a single mother, brainstorm with the Lord!) Maybe you have new ideas about things to share with each other and your children; either way,

As little birds learn to sing by listening to their parents, so children learn the science of the virtues, the sublime song of *Divine Love* from souls responsible for forming them.

— Saint Thérèse of Lisieux
Story of a Soul

create a family identity that is known for its positivity, not its restrictions. *We are a beach family … We are a musical family … We read a lot … We like to play sports … We go camping every summer … We like to cook …* fill in the blank. But above all: *We are a Catholic family. We partake of the sacraments whenever possible. We know how to apologize to one another and to God. We celebrate the feasts, wear scapulars, love babies and the less fortunate. We look for the glory of God everywhere, and we find it. We use our gifts to serve others, we try to make sacrifices, and we labor to store up treasure in heaven, knowing that only there will our happiness be complete.*

3. Talk to your kids about this family culture and also about the restrictions you need to make for their good. One line I stole from my own father is "When I go before God, I will be judged for how I did my best to raise you, during the short eighteen years I had you under my roof. This is not about you; this is about me and getting myself to heaven." I love this because not only is it true, but it also shifts your identity from that of a power-hungry dictator to that of just another sinner doing your best, in need of the mercy of God. Another great line I learned from the headmaster at our school is "It's not that I don't trust you; it's that I don't trust human nature." The beloved disciple at the Last Supper asked "Surely, not I, Lord?" when Christ spoke of the one who would betray him. John shows that in his humility, he knew he was capable of the worst act he could imagine, as we all are. Given the right set of circumstances, all of us are prone to ruin, and it's foolish to think we are somehow above normal human temptation.

Many of these thoughts came about because of a situation I ran into with my oldest son, over my rule of optional "dumb" phones at sixteen (which he would have to pay for) and no phone that has Internet until after college, or until he is fully financially independent. I realize many amazing families have varying opinions on this, and

several families I know balance earlier smartphone use seemingly well enough, so nothing against that per se; I've just given it lots of thought and decided I don't want to let my high schoolers have them (and I don't think they are good for college kids either), and darn it, I'm allowed to have that rule if I want to, regardless of what the rest of the world is doing.

I love that my teenage sons fawn over their baby sisters and not their Instagram feed, and I love that they can make friends with all sorts of cute girls without my having to worry about who they are with or whether they are going to text them sexy photos later that day. I have too much going on in my life to take on babysitting underage iPhone users, so I'm opting out, because that's what my gut tells me to do and because I've had such a difficult time navigating appropriate phone use in my own life that I can't expect a person without a fully developed brain to be capable of this near-impossible task.

Naturally, my kids want smartphones, particularly my oldest son, not for any mal-intent but because that is the way most of his peers communicate. So we've had several intense conversations debating phone use, and my favorite one climaxed at "Well, if you want to give *your* kids iPhones at age fifteen, you totally can." His reply: "But I don't want them to have smartphones! I want them to have dumb phones! But I still want an iPhone." He smiled though he was frustrated, and I was grateful for a moment of victory in our conflict.

This conversation reoccurs every couple of months, and it continues to be a point of struggle at times. But in a weird way it's made us closer, and it's been an empowering reminder to me that it is okay to raise your family against the status quo. Maybe you are against sleepovers. Maybe you want people to take off their shoes when they come into your house. Those things are not my things, but I am in favor of parents who have rules, for God himself has rules with us, and it's only out of love. I think appropriate and reasonable rules will, surprisingly, make kids feel more loved.

Keeping teenage girls modest is hard to do. Caring about how kids spend their free time and what they watch, read, and do takes work. And interactions with your pouting, hormonal pre-teens and teens can be daunting. It's not a stretch to say the world is against you. But let me remind you, Jesus Christ is for you, and so is human nature. Deep down, the ties that bind parent and child are stronger than any worldly inducement. And why? Because even deeper down, more than anything else, we all want to be loved, especially by our parents. The natural love that exists between parent and child (albeit at times strained or awkward) is true and is the original and most primal of human loves. Even if it begets some strife, setting restrictions and guidelines sends a message that you care, and, conscious or subliminal, this message will eventually get through.

If your kids do have smartphones, make sure you and your spouse are forming their souls more than their phones are. If you are worried that's not the case, it's your right and duty as a parent to rectify the situation, and by that I mean take the phone away (and not just for an hour) while they still live under your roof and eat your food. One woman I know was so mad about an incident of deceit concerning her son's phone that she threw it out the car window into a snowbank as they were driving on the freeway. Isn't that radical?

It's easy for a woman to march for "women's rights" in a country with every freedom; it's harder for a woman to rebel against a culture that is pulling her family apart and her children into the dark. Whatever the direction you discern your family is called to go, be daring and strong enough to follow, regardless of the cultural tide. Women like this are the ones with real edge, spunk, and rebellion. The rest are just posers.

— Hope

WHIPPING UP A FEAST DAY

When I was growing up, my mother had a charming book by Helen McLoughlin called *My Nameday: Come for Dessert*. Published in 1962, it was full of ideas, like how to cover a cardboard basket with tiny icing rosettes and how to combine white cake, pink icing, and packaged Jell-O in various ways. It certainly was an interesting curio from that era! (What were the kids *doing* while mother was decorating cakes? That's what I want to know. Probably riding bikes all around town, climbing trees, and other dangerous activities.) In theory, each high-heeled, pin-curled, frilly-aproned mother would call her sweet brood of scrubbed, smiling children to a table covered with a white cloth and a vase of carnations. They would say a prayer, listen to a story of the saint or feast, and have dessert on a piece of Granny's tea set.

It's a pretty picture, and yet the modern family doesn't look quite like this. For one thing, our many wheat and sugar and dairy intolerances make our desserts look a little … funny. Our timetables are different, what with all the time spent in the car taking our kids to sports practices, music lessons, and such. We mothers don't spend our best hours in the kitchen. (Although sometimes it feels we spend *all* our hours in the kitchen.) Our tastes are different too. We rarely use fine table linen anymore. (It was a lovely custom, and perhaps our children would eat more tidily if they were eating over something *white*—but I doubt it.) As for the modern family, well, if you're anything like my family, you are the only big family in the neighborhood. You are probably loud, fun, and messy. You probably don't line up like ducklings in a row, and perhaps, like me, you have only three pieces of Granny's tea set left and they're up on a high shelf being saved for posterity. Parties are boisterous, not sedate.

My own childhood memories are filled with experiences similar to those encouraged by Helen McLoughlin, though less "Betty Crocker" in nature. My mother was a Charlotte Mason–inspired homeschooler. Her seasonal and liturgical celebrations were handmade and delicious. Her materials were imaginatively crafted from outdoors, thrift stores, or whatever raw materials were lying around. One of my favorites was her box of small statues and fine art prints of Mary, Jesus, and various saints. On a saint's feast day, she would take out the statue or picture of the saint and make a beautiful centerpiece on the breakfast table together with candles, flowers, or whatever was in season outdoors. When we came downstairs in the morning, a feast was awaiting us. She also had hanging centerpieces, like the hoop of dangling red ribbons with gold "tongues of flame" sewn on for Pentecost. It would sway gently in the heat from the candles, and to us kids, it was magical!

Now that I have a family of my own, I am overwhelmed by the lavishness of Holy Mother Church in giving us so many feast days (a different one each day of the year, for heaven's sake!), not to mention my mother's artistic example, Waldorf homeschooling books, Pinterest boards, and my mental picture of that impossible scenario: happy children quietly awaiting dessert. With all these lovely things calling out for attention, where do I start? Do I celebrate 365 days of holy men and women? It's too much! And yet I feel the need to go beyond Christmas stockings and the Easter bunny.

This has been an organic process for our family, and we are definitely starting small. If you are a newbie mother, or if you've been on this parenting journey for years and, like me, never felt you were organized or energetic enough to celebrate a liturgical feast, I want to encourage you. It can be done!

Just don't do it all. Choose one feast, whether a major solemnity like Pentecost or an obscure saint's day for your sweet little Walburga or Gondolphus. Or you could choose something significant to your family background, like a fiesta for Our Lady of Guadalupe (December 12)—a piñata and tequila in the middle of December? Yes, please!—or Irish soda bread on Saint Patrick's Day (March 17), with Irish coffee for the grown-ups. The only rule is to keep it very, very simple.

Here's an example. The night before the feast day, go to your supply cupboard and pull out the largest piece of paper you can find. (Resist the temptation to reorganize your cupboard.) Write the name of the feast day in big letters using your best handwriting—calligraphy or bubble letters in pink highlighter, it doesn't matter. It's not about doing it right; it's just about doing it. Tape it to the wall or window near your breakfast table. This is your feast day banner. Find a candle and put it on the table. A candle means "festive", and it makes the table special. Then open a recipe book or go online and choose something to bake that is easy and doesn't require a trip to the grocery store. Most people can scrounge up four ingredients for fabulous peanut butter cookies (which happen to be gluten- and dairy-free too): one cup peanut butter, one cup sugar, one egg, one teaspoon baking soda, baked at 375° F for nine minutes.

Resist the temptation to make a monthly meal plan or finally learn to make meringues. You can do that tomorrow night. And whatever you do, don't clean the house! When everything is ready, go to bed early and sleep the sleep of the righteous, because at the table where your family will gather in the morning, you have art, candle flame, and something special to eat. Don't worry about not having flowers or special songs (kids get all squirmy and embarrassed when you make them sing) or crafts or even a printout to color. Just mark it on the calendar and remember that you can always bling it up next year.

You're doing it! You're celebrating! Our homes are "domestic churches",[1] which means we pray, work, and celebrate along with our Holy Mother Church. The Church calendar intersects with the calendar of nature as it changes outside our windows. It puts us in touch with the whole history of salvation, from the mysteries of our Lord's life to the lives of holy men and women

---

[1] *Catechism of the Catholic Church*, no. 2685.

who have borne witness for the past two thousand years. It connects our present lives to eternal things. What a privilege to be part of it!

Even when our children are grown up and no longer celebrating their childhood feasts, the changing calendar will evoke a feeling of rhythm and celebration. For example, December 8, the feast of the Immaculate Conception, was made special for me by a white tablecloth and white frosted cake, and, occasionally, white roses. The date never passes without a special "Today is a birthday!" feeling. On the other hand, Lent always comes around with a faint odor of bland vegetarian cooking and the popular saying at my house, "Putting the *Lent* back in *lentils*."

— Mary

CREATING A PEACEFUL HOME

A cookie is divided in half—one for each child. Whoever did the dividing accidentally broke one of the halves, and that half is now crumbly. Uh-oh … here comes the argument over who has to have the crumbly half of a cookie (what an insight into the pettiness of our own complaints!). Nevertheless, to the children it is a big deal. You, a busy mother, have far too many things to do today, but you do your best to police the situation and make a decision, trying to recall who was the last one to eat a crumbly half of a cookie and who should therefore get a noncrumbly half this time. Or maybe you should make the one who broke the cookie suffer through the crumbles. But perhaps that child will get upset and wake a sleeping baby. *Ay yi yi!* See where I am going with this?

I really wanted to title this article "No More Fighting" or "Stop the Insanity", but there is really no magic wand (at least none that I have found) to get rid of kids' squabbles altogether; children are just little people with fallen natures. But our homes should be peaceful and harmonious more often than they are chaotic and quarrelsome, and thankfully there are a few solutions that work most of the time with ages four and up.

The first one involves teaching our children about sacrifice. If your children know what a sacrifice is—that it is a present to God, that it is so beautiful to him, so pleasing, like a secret package wrapped up in the prettiest paper and brought to the Lord by their guardian angels—then you can pose this question: "We need someone to make a sacrifice and give a present to God. Who wants to do it?" A few seconds may go by while your children weigh the sacrifice against the good of the desired item or perhaps while the Holy Spirit nudges one of them. It may take a moment, but you will find that one of them will take the challenge, if not both of them. Praise is due, of course, to the little one who has done something wonderful, and that praise combined with the knowledge that he has pleased the Lord is often enough to make a crumbly little half of a cookie taste even better than its counterpart.

Do you need some help in schooling your children about sacrificing? I recommend *Catholic Children's Treasure Box Stories*, particularly numbers 5 and 6. They show Saint Thérèse learning this very lesson and making sacrifices with her siblings. "Sacrifice beads" (a string of beads that fits into a pocket, on which the owner moves a bead whenever a sacrifice is made) may also be a help when starting out; they are available from religious goods catalogs, and there are even kits you can purchase so the kids can make their own.

But don't feel like you need to buy a bead kit (I never have) to implement this practice in your children's lives. All they really need is a good conversation with Mom or Dad, in which you explain how noble and precious sacrifices are, give them examples of what kinds of sacrifices they could make, and then praise them sincerely when they make them. It is beautiful to see the contrast: if you *make* children go without or get the short end of the stick in a given situation, they will sit and pout, but if, instead, you let them *choose* to suffer that same deprivation, they will do so happily. For they are no longer judging the world on the impossible scale of equity but instead with mercy and with the knowledge that they are powerful, that their small decisions can save souls, and that likely those souls will thank them someday in heaven.

Thérèse's mother, Saint Zelie Martin, had a cabinet drawer in her home, with little wooden discs nearby. She instructed young Thérèse to put a disc in the drawer each time she made a sacrifice, and at the end of the day they would count them together and see how many "presents for God" she had accumulated. With my plethora of children and sanguine personality, I can't imagine being this organized! Even if I did have enough drawers and discs for each child, I just know some little person would come along with a stool, climb up, and mess up the whole system, filling one person's drawer and emptying out the others in playful imitation. Tears would then commence from the sacrificer whose drawer was empty, and I would need to try to help the kids remember how many were in each drawer. No thanks, I'll pass on that one! But we can implement this point of practice without the accidentals, and the spirit of Thérèse and her mother can be alive in our homes with our daily (or almost daily) attention to our children's spiritual growth.

Although lessons and opportunities for sacrifice can help in many situations, they won't solve everything; sometimes kids just fight. They come running in a fit of tears with a "he said, she said, so I did this, then he did that" argument. No sacrifice to be made here, just two kids who are mad at each other. When children are small, or if there is a very obvious victim or perpetrator, it is necessary for a parent to get involved. But as kids grow older (perhaps older than five or six), there is no need for mothers to police these situations more than once in a while. And how difficult it is to do because, let's face it, kids are lawyers and each will present a persuasive case, until you are stuck in another impossible battle of wits.

So, what is to be done? I think the answer is simple. Families I have seen that have the most sibling harmony simply don't put up with fighting. It's just not allowed. I have heard of mothers giving the adorable consequence of making the arguers comb each other's hair or make each other's beds, but I personally have had the most success with the simple response, "We don't fight in this family, and since you aren't getting along, I will put you to work." In a busy household there is always something to be done, and each child can be assigned an age-appropriate task (e.g., empty the dishwasher, sweep the kitchen, tidy up the outdoor toys). This will both lighten your load (you can inspect their work or just tell yourself that a five-year-old's job is better than nothing) and give the children good reason to avoid arguing.

Of course, children also need to be taught how to speak kindly to each other, and occasionally (on a good day) you can make them reenact the scene appropriately. For instance, "Let's try doing this again. If you would like a turn on the swing, ask for one nicely and I am sure Aidan would be happy to give you a turn when he is finished, in about one minute. He is a nice boy, and he is good at sharing. Right, Aidan?"

The best preparation for loving the world at large is to cultivate an intimate friendship and affection toward those who are immediately about us.... By trying to love our relations and friends, by submitting to their wishes though contrary to our own, by bearing with their infirmities, by overcoming their occasional waywardness with kindness, by dwelling on their excellences and trying to copy them, thus it is that we form in our hearts that root of charity which, though small at first, may, like the mustard seed, at last even overshadow the earth.

—John Henry Newman

One of the things that was so surprising to me when I started to homeschool my children was that I actually had to teach them (shocking, I know). I guess I thought I would just give them workbooks at the kitchen table and remind them to practice piano. But it doesn't work that way for academics or for behavior. They need to be taught how to capitalize their names as well as wipe down a table. All that teaching means effort, investment, and sometimes exhaustion. Yet, in terms of teaching children how to get along, the amount of work is minimal compared with the years of kinship and harmony that will ensue.

I recently went to a museum with my kids, and on the way in, my eight- and ten-year-old boys were walking ahead, chatting together, hand in hand with their fingers interlaced. I looked on with amusement and didn't have the heart to tell them to break it up because they looked like weirdos. That was unusual for them, of course, but they are very good friends; not only does their relationship set a good example for their younger siblings, but it will also hopefully be a treasure for them throughout their lives.

Are there bad habits of fighting in your home that feel impossible to tackle? Don't lose hope! The good news is that kids are malleable and adjustable. It will take work, but they are still young dogs and can learn new tricks, with your consistent effort.

Another thing we can do to encourage peace in our homes is to cultivate appreciation within the family. My husband and I used to run a youth group where we would regularly have "affirmation stations": we would write each person's name on a separate piece of paper, and then we would all go around the room and write nice things about each person on his paper. If your kids can't write well, you can do this at the dinner table, picking a different person each night to affirm, with each member of the family finding something nice to say about the chosen person. If you are trying to end habitual fighting, this is a good place to start and can build camaraderie. When kids are recognized for their good attributes, they feel encouraged to develop them.

Perhaps the hardest and most effective way to create peace in our homes is to set a good example in our own speech. It is easy for any of us to let our frustrations take over and burst out at our children in impatience. Yet if we don't exercise restraint and patience especially in our own difficulties, it is unreasonable to expect it of our children. Now, don't get me wrong. I cringe when I see a child being awful to his parent, and the parent just responding in a sugary voice, "Now, now, that wasn't very nice!" If you can keep your cool effectively, that is the best scenario, but I actually think it is okay for a parent to yell every once in a while. Just be careful; if it is any more than once in a while, it becomes completely ineffective and sets a bad example. My dad would rarely get mad, but when he did, we all knew he meant business. Let's try to be good examples of peaceful people, for our children will profit from our efforts.

Finally, keep in mind these factors that may or may not be obvious to some: good nutrition and adequate sleep keep all of us in a state of mental and physical health, better equipping us and our children to confront life with charity, so be mindful of bodily health. Low blood sugar and unenforced bedtimes are sure to breed irritability, and then the discord is not so much the kids' fault as our own.

Here's to parents who don't holler too much, siblings who are the best of friends and not the worst of enemies, and homes that may be generating lots of messes and noise but are also havens of peace (at least most of the time!).

— Hope

A JUG OF OIL AND A SACK OF MEAL

The warm weather is here, and there are birds everywhere—birds our dog, Brynn, cannot resist chasing. She's never going to catch one, of course. The birds, secure in their power of flight, will happily hop around the grass as long as Brynn stays in her watchful crouch a few meters away. But the second Brynn begins to race over, they fly up to the security of the sky, only to alight again on the ground a few meters farther on.

It reminds me of my own younger pursuit of the ideal state of "happiness", which, like the birds, always seemed to stay just out of my reach. I knew I was empty, and I thought unhappiness was like a hunger that could be sated if I could just find the right thing to consume. Even God, when I found him, was one more thing I thought might fill the gnawing hole that lay between me and the goal of happiness.

A while ago I felt that there just wasn't enough of me to go around. I was feeling like the weary old Bilbo Baggins: "sort of stretched, like butter scraped over too much bread". The world's advice for overworked moms is to take "me-time", pamper yourself, indulge more—consume more.

I felt stretched, and the first day I consumed—I ate chocolate and sweets, napped, cut the bedtime routine short and devoured a novel, read funny articles on the Internet, slacked off in my work, and watched TV while doing the least demanding of my household chores.

Was I full, after all that? Was there more of me now? I felt crankier, fuzzier, and even less capable of giving and doing than before. Consuming more didn't fill me or make me happier.

What if instead I had thrown myself into work, brainstorming for fresh ways to help my clients meet their goals? What if I had completed my chores with extra care? Tried a new recipe? Written to a friend, instead of surfing the Net? Spent an extra half hour settling my children down instead of rushing off to kill more empty time on my own?

So that's what I did the next two days. I wasn't sure I could. I felt I had nothing left to give. I was afraid to loosen my grip on the little bit of "me" I thought I had left. But being miserly with myself had only bred resentment that I couldn't get even more space, more sleep, more time. My kids deserved better than that, and so did my clients and friends. The least I could do was give them what little I had to give.

I poured myself out, and as I did, I found that, like the widow at Zarephath, my jug of oil didn't run empty and my bag of meal was sufficient for each day. It runs counter to the laws of conservation that govern the physical world, doesn't it? Energy in, energy out. Did I really ever think I could become a great soul by consuming more, the way I become larger by eating more?

I should know better by now. I have been happy while in pain, happy in the midst of grief, happy and struggling to keep up with life's demands. Motherhood and marriage have demanded so much from me, so much more than I would have ever thought I had in me, and yet I've looked up from years when life's challenges demanded everything I had and found more *me* at the end than there was to begin with.

The soul is not a finite resource.

Have you ever fed birds from your hand? Up here in the north, if you stand very still near a bird feeder in midwinter with birdseed in your outstretched hand, sometimes a particularly bold chickadee or nuthatch will approach, cocking its head watchfully as it cautiously hops closer. Once, I stood motionless for nearly twenty minutes, watching a chickadee with my peripheral vision as it clung to my mittened fingers and ate from my palm.

Happiness flies from me when I chase it. But sometimes, if I still myself and set my sights on other things, it rests with a chickadee's lightness in my open hands.

— Kate Cousino, Ontario

ON DATING YOUR HUSBAND

I have the horrible habit of not seeing outside the present moment. Whether it is babies waking in the night, a head cold, an impossible toddler, or chaotic dinner prep, I all too often forget these wise words: "This, too, shall pass." I have, however, lately been applying this saying to my relationship with my husband. Not necessarily that he will pass, which he will, but that this time of child rearing will pass, and when the nest is empty (although it is hard to imagine now), we will be left staring at each other. What will that feel like? Will he be my best friend and familiar companion or an estranged bed partner? We have all heard the wise words of women before us, who encourage couples with busy families to make regular time for each other, and for the first time in our ten years of marriage, my husband and I are taking that advice.

I recently heard the phrase "become your husband's girlfriend", and it stuck with me. When I think of my husband's wife, I think of a tired, irritated, rather dull woman who needs to take a bath. When I think of my husband's girlfriend, I picture a peppy, flirtatious female with shimmery lip gloss, a ponytail flipping with the turn of her head, and a wild sense of adventure. Girlfriends laugh at jokes, listen intently, and overlook faults because they are blinded by love. I am not trying to degrade the beloved title of wife; I am just trying to remember how to be passionate about the things I'm passionate about, and dating my husband has definitely helped. Not every woman has the financial means or care-taking help to go on regular dates with her husband, but we can all make an evening at home special if we try: a glass of wine by candlelight, a pint of ice cream by the fire, stargazing on a blanket in the backyard. Let's try to get back to thinking romantically, the way we did when we were girlfriends. You may have heard stories of women who have sadly gotten swept up in some scandalous Internet relationship. Your real Internet boyfriend is only a text away! While I'm at it, girlfriends, I think now is a good time to share with you my parents' favorite marital tool, composed by an unknown psychologist.

Top Five Needs of a Man and a Woman in Marriage

For Men:

1. You know what it is
2. An attractive spouse
3. Admiration
4. Domestic order
5. Recreational companionship

For Women:

1. Affection
2. Conversation
3. Appreciation
4. Financial stability
5. Commitment to the family

Write these down and put them on your fridge (or bathroom mirror). Make sure to discuss them with your husband; it is important for him to know how women work. Likewise, when we view loving men according to their very different needs, we are bound to be better lovers. And what do real lovers do? They love according to the object of affection. A baby needs cuddling, a toddler needs play, a teenager needs conversation, and a husband needs, well, you know.

— Hope

AN OPEN LETTER TO VESTIBULE MOTHERS

Dear vestibule mothers,

Your arms are tired, your blood sugar is sinking, and poor Oswald just won't stop squirming and screaming. So there you are in the vestibule at Mass. As usual. You'd invite others to your pity party but frankly, everyone is rather relieved you left with your whining child. So, besides a couple of other long-suffering parents, you're on your own. You sigh with the resignation of a reluctant saint. "Well, at least I'm here, right?" And you wonder just how far away is the day when you'll get to experience a peaceful Mass in your life. You can just imagine how wonderful it will be: you can hear the bells of Consecration; you can even smell the incense if you're lucky. But for now, you wait in the vestibule, gritting your teeth in disbelief or shame at just how naughty your child is acting.

Don't lose heart! Those peaceful days of quiet worship will come before you know it. But in the meantime, the attitude of "at least I showed up" can be so much greater. In truth, the sacrifices given to us that we accept lovingly are worth a thousand times more than any self-imposed sacrifices. So don't squander this cross. The graces of Mass are real and vibrant and present even in the vestibule or cry room. We may not feel them, but thank God our religion isn't one based on subjective feelings anyway. Jesus promised that our lives would be hard; the sweet glory of a peaceful Mass would really be just an extra consolation. The vestibule is like purgatory, fellow sojourners. Devote your time there for those forgotten souls in purgatory. Every time you walk to the back of the church with an unruly child, think of it as a gift, and smile on the inside for the offering you get to present to Jesus on behalf of these poor souls. For they are like you: waiting and suffering just outside the doors of the heavenly banquet.

Yours truly,
— Ellie

BABIES

Babies are made on cold winter nights.
They are made from birthday presents, and
   everyday presents
And looks, and nods,
And patience, and peaks,
And flushed cheeks.
So that when the sun rises, and summer comes,
They might kiss our skin with their touch.

Gentle, and thrilling,
Holy, and light,
While daylight dances in a wood far away.

— Hope

WHATEVER YOU DO

"Jesus has a Facebook page!" our archbishop declared from the pulpit last May at a Confirmation Mass. "You can see what he likes, what he doesn't like, who his friends are … It's all right there! If you want to get to know Jesus, check out his Facebook page. It's called … the Gospels."

The older I get, the more I appreciate Sacred Scripture as the Living Word of God and the most important thing we can put our eyes on each day—more than the news or novels or social media. Saint Thérèse of Lisieux made a decision to read only *The Imitation of Christ* and the Bible, politely declining all other spiritual works because she knew that Christ himself would be her teacher, and so he was; Pope Pius XI declared that she "rediscovered the heart of the Gospels". A veritable spiritual feast is sitting on our bookshelves or nightstands, and despite our busy lives, we should make it a point to sit down at this banquet every day, even if just for a moment.

This spring I found a distinct word in the Gospel of Matthew that I believe is a particular invitation and gift to mothers, and it should ring clear as a bell to us. Though we are used to hearing it as a modern, apathetic catchphrase, it's this little word "whatever".

> "Lord, when did we see you hungry and feed you, or thirsty and give you something to drink? When did we see you a stranger and invite you in, or needing clothes and clothe you? When did we see you sick or in prison and go to visit you?"
>
> The King will reply, "Truly I tell you, whatever you did for one of the least of these brothers and sisters of mine, you did for me." (Mt 25:37–40)[2]

It almost seems as if Jesus is speaking directly to women who care for small children, and we can be sure that he *is* speaking to us, though not exclusively.

[2] NIV.

We welcome children into our lives, we feed them, we give them drinks, and more food, and more drinks. We care for them when they are ill, we clothe them, we pick up after their messes, we discipline and comfort them (sometimes acting as jailer, judge, and rescuer!). We defend them when necessary and help repair damage done when the forces of life deal them a blow.

Yet it goes beyond this. Jesus knew when he was speaking these words that a mother's work is never done. If you were to try to write down all the things you've done for your family *just today*, you wouldn't be able to, because it's impossible to keep track. Knowing this, Jesus went beyond the description of basic human care to include the word "whatever". So when you are sweating bullets and running late, but you pull off the freeway to find a sketchy gas station bathroom because your two-year-old keeps screaming "Need to go potty!", and when she finally sits down and nothing comes out, and she smiles and says "All done!", you can be okay with that. Because you did it for Jesus. When your newborn is crying in the night and your body feels nailed to your bed, let the words "Baby Jesus" be enough to get you on your feet and tending to our Lord in his lesser brethren. When you clean out a disgusting car seat or fridge, change your little girl into her fifth outfit of the day, spend half a day trying to find a lost stuffed animal, deal with a toddler's tantrum, monitor your teenager's pop music choices—seriously, *whatever* you did today and will do the rest of the day, tomorrow, and the next—*know who you are caring for*. We have, in the word "whatever", a golden ticket to a life of intimacy with Jesus.

Children are poor. They own nothing that has not been given to them. My kids have to beg me for weeks before I get my act together to buy them new socks, a necessary belt, or shoes that aren't falling apart. Not only are they tangibly poor, but they are also born ignorant, unwise, and lacking independence, ability, and experience. Christ makes it so clear in this passage that when we love these children of ours, these "least brothers" of his, we are loving him. He wants to walk intimately with us each day and each moment. He wants to be right there in the center of the love you have for your baby, your toddler, your adolescent. And he wants you to be right in the center of his living intimacy with the Father. This always blows my mind, but it's what our faith teaches: "I in them and you in me, that they may become perfectly one, so that the world may know that you have sent me and have loved them even as you have loved me" (Jn 17:23).

Let that sink in for a moment. The Father loves us as he loves Jesus. It's unbelievable, yet we must believe it. Can you imagine sacrificing the life of your own child for the sake of another child? You would have to love that child as much as, if not more, than your own. And in this case, it sometimes seems like even that is true. The Father often treats us, his adopted daughters and sons, with more privilege in this life than he did his own beloved Son. We lie down at the end of the day on soft pillows, but "the Son of man [had] nowhere to lay his head" (Mt 8:20).

We are princesses in the kingdom of God—not the Disney kind, but the Narnian kind—and the closer we follow the life and lessons of our brother and teacher, the more we will share in the riches of that kingdom. The lessons of our "Rabboni" are closer to us than we think. I suggest we go back to the basics: the schoolbook is the Bible, and the classroom is our homes. As long as we live with children, with the "least of these", we live with Jesus himself, and the invitation to abide with him finds its reality in a little person with cold feet climbing into your bed at the break of dawn.

We are walking with him, dear mothers, and abiding with him through the beauty and messiness of family life. Find him today where you least expect him, in the ways you are needed, for he himself promised us that he would meet us in these little things, *whatever* they happen to be.

— Hope

MORNING PRAYER FOR A CHILD

My family loves this consecration prayer. It's short and easy to memorize, and it helps habituate children to both a morning offering and Marian devotion. Little ones particularly enjoy the motion of blessing various parts of the face and body. As a young child, Saint Josemaría Escrivá learned this prayer from his parents, and he prayed it regularly his entire life. The best part: it takes less than thirty seconds, perfect for your busy life!

My Queen and my Mother, I give myself entirely
   to thee,
And to show my devotion to thee, I consecrate to
   thee this day

My eyes + + (*make small
   crosses over each eye with
   your right thumb*),
My ears + + (*repeat with
   the ears*),
My mouth + (*repeat with
   the mouth*),
My heart + (*repeat with the heart*),
My entire being without reserve + (*make the full sign
   of the cross while saying this line*).
Wherefore good Mother, as I am thine own, keep
   me and guard me as thy child forever.

— Hope

TOUCH

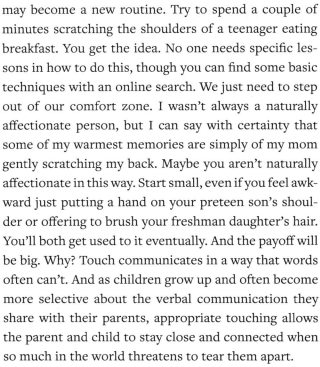

Ten years ago I became certified as an instructor in infant massage. At the time, I was simply looking to qualify for a family-support or education job on the military base where we were located. So I paid the hundreds of dollars and drove my pregnant self the 120-mile round trip every day for the length of the class with dreams of starting my own little business on the side. In and of itself, I had no extraordinary interest in infant massage; I just thought it would be a cool qualification in my back pocket for the flexible side-job potential it offered.

What I learned from that class is priceless beyond compare. It's fairly common knowledge that the benefits of infant massage are fantastic for both parent and baby. It increases bonding, decreases cortisol levels, increases serotonin, reduces pain, and has amazing effects on preterm babies' ability to thrive and gain weight.[3] What is less well-known is how the practice of infant massage pays off huge dividends in the long-term relationship between a parent and child.

In our culture, it seems the chasm between healthy and unhealthy touching is ever widening. North Americans, in particular, are not physically affectionate when compared to our European, Middle Eastern, or Hispanic counterparts. But we are starving for touch. We pay for professionals to massage us. There is something missing in how we communicate with one another. Part of the problem this reality presents is that many children grow up uncomfortable with physical affection or are taught so strictly about privacy and protection that they fear it. Infant massage builds a bridge of healthy touch communication that can remedy this.

My babies are grown, you may be thinking, but it's not too late. Touch communication doesn't have to end when a baby becomes a toddler or a toddler becomes a big kid. It just changes. The rhythmic music, dim lighting, and soft surroundings your baby loved may give way to a simple shoulder rub while a child reads a book report to you. Doing a nightly foot rub with essential oils before bedtime may become a new routine. Try to spend a couple of minutes scratching the shoulders of a teenager eating breakfast. You get the idea. No one needs specific lessons in how to do this, though you can find some basic techniques with an online search. We just need to step out of our comfort zone. I wasn't always a naturally affectionate person, but I can say with certainty that some of my warmest memories are simply of my mom gently scratching my back. Maybe you aren't naturally affectionate in this way. Start small, even if you feel awkward just putting a hand on your preteen son's shoulder or offering to brush your freshman daughter's hair. You'll both get used to it eventually. And the payoff will be big. Why? Touch communicates in a way that words often can't. And as children grow up and often become more selective about the verbal communication they share with their parents, appropriate touching allows the parent and child to stay close and connected when so much in the world threatens to tear them apart.

I am so thankful I took those classes when my oldest child was just two years old. Today, I enjoy being able to put my arm on his shoulders at Mass without either of us feeling weird about it. He still comes and snuggles up to my side when we read together. I admit, the last thing in the world I want sometimes is to instigate or accept physical contact when I've had babies nursing and toddlers crawling on me all day. I'm tired, and believe me, introverts value their personal space. But I have to keep telling myself how important it is to be intentional about creating and maintaining communication with my children.

I remember one moment in particular when my son's feelings were crushed by one of his buddies a couple of years ago. He came in the house fighting back tears of resentment and hurt. I didn't say anything, even though my Mama Bear heart wanted to protect

---

[3] Rebecca Mrljak et al., "Effects of Infant Massage: A Systematic Review", National Library of Medicine, May 24, 2022, https://www.ncbi.nlm.nih.gov/pmc/articles/PMC9179989/.

> Would you like to know a secret to happiness? Give yourself to others and serve them, without waiting to be thanked.
>
> — Saint Josemaría Escrivá

him from all the evil in the world and go chew the kid out and talk to my son about how people sometimes let you down. Somehow, I had the (regrettably rare) sense to keep my mouth shut. I just sat by him and let him cry, scratching his back in support and saying a silent prayer. I felt very close to him then, and I know he felt it too. After the tears subsided, he stood up, wiped his face, and said in his best gruff ten-year-old voice, "Thanks, Mom." And that's all we've ever said about that … but it was enough.

I have known many kids who feel uncomfortable with touch, even to the point of obviously tensing up if they are hugged. Some children have suffered grievous abuses, and their aversion to touch is understandable and sad. Prayer and compassion are the best we can offer in those cases. But on the whole, we can still do more to promote healthy touching for the next generation. Mother Teresa said, "We think sometimes that poverty is only being hungry, naked, and homeless. The poverty of being unwanted, unloved, and uncared for is the greatest poverty. We must start in our own homes to remedy this kind of poverty."

Words aren't enough to convince children that we love them, especially as they go through the awkward, finding-their-identity, self-doubting phase. Neither is it enough simply to feed them, buy them stylish clothes, or show up to every soccer game. Love communicated through touch is unique, and its message is unmistakable. It's not something we should skip just because it's not our love language. Authentic, appropriate touch says, "You are worthy. You are wanted. You are loved." And that's a message we all need.

— Ellie

FOR CHARITY'S SAKE

I want to write a little about the glories of siesta. Nap time. Quiet time. Leave-mom-alone time. Call it what you will, I love it and I am going to tell you why. But first a story:

When I was a girl, some of my most favorite memories were made at a summer camp run by the Sisters of Mercy when they still wore their habits (bless them!). The setting, on Lake Champlain, is probably still my favorite place on earth. I wish you could see it—a three-story hotel built in the 1920s, enormous and white, with a wraparound porch, creaky wooden floors and stairs, windows galore, and old-fashioned sinks in the bedrooms. It was just dripping with charm and surrounded by an expansive green lakeside property (how the Church got its hands on that place I'd love to know). It was called Camp MaryCrest. A big statue of the Sacred Heart looked over the lake and all the little girls trampled around, swam, canoed, played tennis, put on plays, shot bows and arrows, sang songs around campfires, fought, cried, made up, rolled down the hills, and basically had the time of their lives. Amid all this activity, however, rigorous order was enforced. Each morning we awoke to the sound of a bugle over the loudspeaker, and after tidying our rooms for inspection, we gathered for morning prayer. The bugle would continue to sound throughout the day to direct us to our next activity. After breakfast we met at the flag-pole and raised the flag with some patriotic song, then departed to our age-appropriate daily chores. The flag would be taken down again after dinner (with meticulous folding), and after lunch we would all, perhaps one hundred girls, four to a bedroom, for one full hour, have … rest time.

The rules for rest time were as follows: you could sleep, read, write in your journal, write a letter, or listen to music on headphones, but you had to stay on your bed and could not talk to others. Counselors or sisters patrolled the halls, and we had enough fear, most of the time, to behave ourselves.

An hour is a long time for a kid to keep quiet, and, yes, it was boring, but it was good. I ended up reading my friend's vampire mystery books (high class, I know), writing letters to family members back home, and braiding more friendship bracelets than I had friends. But, like I said, it was good. And now I find myself with my own set of permanent campers, wondering how those nuns did it. If they could get one hundred girls who were too old to sleep during the day to be quiet for an hour, I should be able to get four smaller ones to do so. But I won't lie to you … it takes work.

I've got some tricks to share, as well as some motives to enforce a daily siesta. Let's start with the motives. First, it gives our children a regular experience of silence, which in this world we too often run away from. How can we expect to hear God if we are uncomfortable with periods of silence? To learn to be quiet, to learn to calm oneself, is a good practice from which we all could benefit. Second, it gives siblings a break from each other. For one hour in the day, no one is able to argue, and guess what? I find that when that hour has ended, children are more excited to play with one another and more able to play well. Third, it gives the mother a chance to rest. She can nap, pray quietly, pay bills, accomplish something or nothing at all. It is her time to recoup and nourish herself before the chaos

of afternoon activities and evening duties bombard her. The fourth and last reason is along the same lines. My dear friend is a Carmelite sister in Los Angeles, and her order practices a daily siesta because their beloved Mother Regina says it *preserves charity*. Need I say more?

I should mention that I am not advocating putting quiet time above all else. If you go out for the day, go out for the day, but on the days when your family is at home, enjoy a siesta.

I'll share some tips that work in my household. It usually works best to make everyone be quiet when the baby (if you've got one) is sleeping in the afternoon. Set a timer in the kitchen for one hour. It will not wake up a baby, but the other children who are listening for it (and they will) can hear it.

Make the rules known and adjust them to your preferences (stay in bed, on the couch, in their rooms, etc.), but be clear. If possible, give kids their own space. Put one in the laundry room with a pillow and blanket, one in the living room, and, if some have to be together, let it be the older ones who have more self-control and ability to keep quiet. Provide books, LEGO® bricks, or coloring supplies for younger children to occupy the time. For older ones, require some silent reading or letter writing. When the timer goes off, reward good behavior with a popsicle, a small piece of chocolate, a star on a chart, or another privilege. Heck, a gummy vitamin could work as long as they have something to look forward to.

I've had friends ask for more details about implementing this daily rhythm. With caution and keeping in mind varying discipline standards, I will share what has worked for me and offer a step-by-step strategy. Different families have different methods, of course; this just works for my family.

I love this Charlotte Mason–inspired maxim: *Teach a child obedience and everything else will follow*.[4] In our home, we have established that nap time is mandatory, not optional. If you really want to implement it, be

---

[4] Charlotte Mason, "Authority and Docility", in *Towards a Philosophy of Education* (Radford, Va.: Wilder Publications, 2008), 57–65.

prepared for a battle and do not accept defeat. Be sure to separate noncompliant children however you have to, and if spanking is not your thing, set yourself up in the hallway with a book and be on patrol. You can enjoy naps later, in a week or two when the routine is established. Read a book (don't look at a screen; for some reason it just doesn't work as well) for an hour in the hallway, or pray for the grace to endure. When a child comes out of his room the first time, kindly but sternly remind him of the rules and send him back. The second time, no more reminding and no arguing; just silently send him back. You will have to put up with some crying, but that is to be expected when he is having to do something he doesn't want to do. You may have to send him back twenty times or more, and it may be the same amount of mayhem the next day. You will probably end rest time feeling anything but rested, but eventually his dear little stubborn tenacity will give way and he will realize that it is pointless to fight anymore. Rewarding good behavior at the end is critical, especially when establishing the new afternoon ritual. Make the treats really good (especially in the beginning), and if the children don't deserve any, enjoy one yourself right in front of them when it is over, reminding them that tomorrow they will have another chance to earn it. Note: I've often lain down in the same room as the three-year-old. Everyone else seems to get the drill, but sometimes children that age will do best when they know they are under constant supervision.

Perhaps it seems like too much work for you, and if it does, I don't blame you. But if you follow the principles and don't engage in yelling fights, it should be over in five days. Taming the will of man or beast can be done with persistence. Good thing God is persistent with us.

Whenever I have a hard time being tough on my children, I think of my sister, who is so good she should write books on the subject. She is loads of fun and treats her children with so much respect. They laugh together and talk about everything under the sun. She plays games and is creative, and her children adore her. However, when she says to do something, she expects it to be done, and she will easily turn from fun to business. She is really strict with them about obedience and good behavior, and I think they love her all the more for it.

— Hope

METANOIA: A REFLECTION ON ADOPTION

I have to be honest from the get-go: what I have to say here has nothing to do with how to make a mean granola or how to re-create a fab outfit from *Vogue* (you seriously don't want my recipes or my fashion advice). But it does have everything to do with our role as Jesus followers. As a mother of adopted and biological children, I've been forced to examine what it means when we speak of "our own children"—and whether we might need a little change of heart when it comes to how we view adoption.

Our two older children, Gabriella and Isaac, are adopted. I cannot put into words what an amazingly beautiful experience it is when another woman gives you a piece of her heart, trusting you to love and cherish that new life. But I will say that from the day we brought them home, Gabriella and Isaac have been our children, our beautiful gifts from God.

Our church community and all our Catholic friends were very supportive of the path to parenthood that we took. Yet oftentimes curious remarks accompanied their profuse congratulations: "Wow, I could never take in someone else's child." "That's great, but I'd be too scared to go through the process." "I'm glad you guys adopted; it's such a good thing, but I don't think God would ever call me to do that." "I'd be too nervous to adopt, not knowing where the baby came from."

In my joy, I don't think I took these comments to heart. In fact, I think I rather pitied those who had never experienced the adoption process. That began to change when, much to my surprise, I became pregnant when Isaac was eight months old. Our Catholic friends were so happy for us—which was great—but their comments were hurtful. "We've been praying for years that you'd have a baby!" "Isn't it so exciting to be having a baby of your own!" "See, God is rewarding you for taking in those two orphans!"

⁵NIV.

For the first time in my life, I didn't have anything to say. I felt like I had been pierced through the heart, by friends no less. I began to wonder, *Do they really not believe Gabriella and Isaac are my children? When my biological child is born, will my adopted children be less my children in the eyes of others? How can all these wonderful pro-life Catholics think adoption is second best?* Then I reached a rather sad conclusion: many people in our community considered the adoptive path to parenthood to be somehow defective. Yes, they thought we had done a wonderful thing, but they did not think Ella and Isaac were truly ours. Apparently, only biological children would be our "own".

One more biological child down the road, and I think I have arrived at the heart of the matter: none of our children are our own. God has entrusted them to us, to love them, to nurture them, to bring them closer to him. Whether God brings us children through adoption or through biological means, he expects us to take them to the same place: the foot of the Cross, to gaze upon his Son.

I love the Scripture passage that talks about how in Christ, there is neither Jew nor Greek—God loves all his children. Why? Because we are made in his image and likeness. "He chose us in him before the creation of the world to be holy and blameless in his sight. In love he predestined us for adoption to sonship through Jesus Christ, in accordance with his pleasure and will.... In him we were also chosen, having been predestined according to the plan of him who works out everything in conformity with the purpose of his will (Eph 1:4–5, 11).⁵

Obviously, these verses speak to me in a particular way, but these words should be a reminder to all of us as we consider our vocation as Jesus followers, called to defend and protect those babes in the womb that the world preys upon.

Does this mean we're all called to adopt? Of course not. Most Catholic families have a full complement of

> Who of us is mature enough for offspring before the offspring themselves arrive? … The value of marriage is not that adults produce children but that children produce adults.
>
> —Peter De Vries
> *The Tunnel of Love*

lovely biological children. That is their calling. Does this mean that I don't appreciate the beauty of procreation within marriage—the natural desire of husband and wife to produce an expression of their love? Not at all.

My only real point here is that as Jesus followers we must be open to all new life. For most of us, that means examining our views about love and family, stepping out and making friends with an adoptive family (though it might take us out of our comfort zones), and educating ourselves about the process of adoption—the beauty and the complicated realities. We should look beyond pro-life slogans to see the grace of God working in hearts through adoption.

For some of us, being open to life does mean embracing the reality that God is leading us to adopt—to give over our natural desire to a loving God who desires to give us something beyond it. To transform our hearts and lives, to choose love over fear, to fill our hearts and arms with children who don't share our DNA, to embrace the ache and beauty of another family, to make their story part of ours.

— Rose Decaen, California

GAME OVER

Why do you spend your money for that which is
    not bread,
    and your labor for that which does not satisfy?
Listen diligently to me, and eat what is good,
    and delight yourselves in rich food. (Is 55:2)

Not long ago I went to a homeschooling talk by a very inspiring mother. She was using all the phrases that I love and that keep me schooling at home: fostering a love of learning, a culture of the family, and so on. On the topic of nature study, a mother from the audience raised her hand and said, "My son never wants to do nature study. He will only do the bare minimum of his schoolwork, and whenever I suggest going to the

meadow, he never wants to go." The gifted speaker spent some time troubleshooting with her, but she finally got to the meat when she asked the question "Well, what is he passionate about?", to which the poor mother innocently answered back, "Gaming." All of a sudden, it was clear to me (and I presume to many others) why dear little homeschooled boy shunned time with his mother in the meadow. It is the same reason that a child who is offered an endless supply of junk food will lose the taste for nutritious things like hummus or Asian pears. I find that in our generation, we parents desire to give our children everything we can to

> The computer can, of course, tell us who worked at which task for how many hours yesterday, and therefore whose turn it is today. But it cannot tell us why a man should leave his father and mother and cleave to his wife, nor why that man should push that plow year after year, nor why his wife should stagger about for nine months every couple of years bearing the fruit of his momentary pleasure, nor why she should get up a hundred nights in a row to suckle his infant and hers; nor why this ridiculous treadmill is spoken of in a holy Book as being a picture of the mystery of Christ and the Church. The computer and its programmers will smell a plot and set about to rip it all up. They will demolish the sanctuary and tear down the veils that hide the holy things. But there will be some people who will want to get on with the rite on the belief that it does in fact have something to do with self-giving, which has something to do with Charity, which has something to do with Joy.
>
> —Thomas Howard
> *Hallowed Be This House*

make them smile, to please them. Yet if we do so to the extent of turning off the button that says "parental authority", we end up doing them a disservice. Most of this is not our fault; the baby boomers were the first to use contraception widely and to have both parents working outside the home. Thus, with only two kids to love and a limited time to love them, the rules were bound to be bent. Over time, the art and science of rearing children has been lost, as we have yielded our God-given right of authority to so-called experts, institutions, and, even worse, commercial media. Going back to the story about the mother and son, I find that it is commonly thought, even among good families, that video gaming is a valid interest or hobby. This type of mentality really bothers me. I am not entirely against video games; I know they can be an avenue of bonding for males. What I am against is this problem of parents not seeing them for what they are or at least what they should be: an indulgence.

If you are happy with your child's primary hobby being gaming, then you may as well be happy if your own list of interests comprises sitting on the couch watching TV, surfing the web, and checking your cell phone. As for me, I think we are called to a life richer than that. God has placed both us and our children in this world during this particular time in history, and most of us are not called to shut out modern technology from our homes completely, as it becomes more and more the way of communication, business, and even evangelization. Yet we must be sure not to let it replace the finer things in life and those things that nurture real joy and communion. When my boys question our restrictions on video games (and TV, for that matter) I sometimes tell them that one of the problems is not what they are doing but what they are *not* doing. They are not reading something of interest. They are not having a true interaction with another live person. They are not experimenting in the kitchen, getting muddy outside, or learning how to care for an animal. They are not becoming better athletes, musicians, or artists, and they most certainly are not improving their prayer lives. I have gotten to know a family whose parents were the strictest possible regarding television; all television shows and movies were forbidden, even in the homes of others. I am sure there were some difficulties along the way and the grown-up children attest to this, but what they have ended up with is a family of some of the most incredible musicians I have ever known, not to mention artists, photographers, horse ranchers, farmers,

Latin scholars, and who knows what else as they continue to leave the nest and make their way.

Monitoring of television and video games is a delicate matter, and for every family it will look a little different. For my family, it looks like this (for now): no cable, very limited computer usage and movies, and no video games (but they are free to play them at their cousins' or approved friends' houses). We do have chickens, a dog, big climbing trees, a temperate climate, and a generous-sized home and property to have adventures in. I feel less guilty about withholding video games when we have so much with which to replace them. For those who live in more urban settings with less space to roam around (or with more inclement weather), I can understand further lenience regarding media. Yet whatever your situation, do not be fooled by the lie that gaming and television will make your life easier. Often they don't. A friend of mine bought the popular Nintendo Wii gaming console with excitement, thinking it would be fun for her four older children to play together after school. But instead of resulting in a quieter house, the kids actually fought more about whose turn it was, with the older children monopolizing the playing time and the younger children being driven to tears. In a fit of frustration, the mother packed it up and said, "Enough!" Within a few days, imaginative play reentered her home and sibling harmony greatly improved.

Some argue there is little difference between video games and a movie, but I disagree. A movie or television program has a beginning and an end, if carefully chosen tells a story with a positive message, and is in its very nature less addicting than a video game. Gaming requires more involvement, ensuring the never-ending pursuit of beating the next level and moving on to the next hot game. Additionally, unlike movies, gaming seems to stimulate self-serving aggression, manifested by players who frantically yell things like, "Get out of my way! I can't see!" or, "It's my turn. I only had one turn!" Even worse, conversing with those playing a video game is nearly impossible: after several minutes of trying to tell them something, you receive a blank look accompanied by "What did you say?" Finally, video games are harder to grow out of. While a dude who still has a soft spot for *A Charlie Brown Christmas* is seen as endearing, an adult man who still spends hours a day playing video games risks being seen as unattractive and juvenile.

We mothers should make thoughtful decisions for our families to the extent we feel called. I have had to argue pretty hard to keep video games out of our house, and I can only hope that our kids don't resent me for it when they grow up and that what they miss out on in popular gaming skills they will gain in their ability to converse and to thrive in true pursuits of intellectual and artistic endeavors. I pray that when all is quiet, the noise in their heads will not be as loud as the voice of Jesus and his gentle call.

Postscript: We mothers are constantly revamping our routines and rules as our family's ideals and circumstances change. If you are at all inspired to limit your media use, here are a few ideas I have picked up from other families:

- Schedule a media-free day. "Screen Free Sunday" is a great way to intentionally unplug and reconnect over the weekend, or choose another day that is more convenient for your family. No screens (that includes you, Mom and Dad) for the entire day. You'll be surprised how freeing it is!
- Use gaming or movies strictly as rewards for chores or good behavior. Making them work for it can give kids not only a sense of pride and accomplishment but can keep them from feeling like it is something they are entitled to.
- Limit gaming or movies to times when you and your husband could use some in-house babysitting. Remember to choose *quality* films that edify and are not just mindless entertainment.
- When I was a child, my parents used to cover the television with a lace tablecloth during the season of Lent, as a reminder that it is a time of quiet, prayer, and sacrifice. Both Lent and Advent (traditionally penitential times) are good seasons to take a break from screen time, or at least reduce it. Limiting movies to topics of spirituality and the saints can be a nice way to enjoy family films during Lent.
- Remember, whenever you take something away from your children, it is always good to replace

it with something else. "We are going to be doing less gaming for a while. But we will be taking more hikes (or bike rides, reading aloud, art classes, card games). Why don't you look online with me and help me pick out some fun board games? Or let's look into those classes we've been talking about."

Post-postscript: If you are reading this and you have just had a baby or have moved or are in the midst of a difficult pregnancy, please flag this article and read it in six months. Now is not your time!

— Hope

WANT LESS

There's a sticker on the back of our van that has gathered a few undeserved gushes of praise. It simply says, "Want Less." I thought it was about time to set the record straight. Wanting less is more the ideal for our family and not so much the reality. Of course we want. We want all kinds of stuff. My Amazon wish list is in the triple digits! Robert Louis Stevenson said, "The world is so full of a number of things, I'm sure we should all be as happy as kings!" And yet we're not.

Due to the economy, our family has been forced to uproot and move off our remote island to a bigger, busier area to find work. Long gone are my free-spirited meanderings through forest trails and along island bluffs; now we watch the digital billboard across the traffic-filled highway and try not to step in broken glass as we walk past the friendly neighborhood tavern. We live in a smaller house, without any attic or garage. The line in the sand has been drawn: minimize your belongings or drown in stuff. Oh, how therapeutic to rip the barnacles off! The initial pain was real: "But I'll use that food dehydrator someday" or "But I have such fond memories of playing the original Super Nintendo." With time, the pain has dulled, and like a freshly polished rock, the shine is starting to come through. Four fully loaded trips to the good St. Vincent's and a run to the city dump later, we are making progress on our little domestic monastery. We are trying to want less. There is a very real benefit to minimizing the stuff in our lives, other than the practical need for it: the less one has in material things, the more one is able to center the home on God. Each

of us is called to different stations in life and financial states, but all of us are called to be poor in spirit. And an excess of unnecessary things too often dulls our minds. How can we hear that eternal voice beckoning if we have a constant flow of background noise and a constant presence of clothes, makeup, toys, electronics, gadgets, and knickknacks filling up our lives? The truth is we can't. Like the saints we strive to emulate, our goal should simply be heaven. And this true treasure is immeasurably more in focus when the path is clear and the space open wide.

A simple home isn't just about aesthetics. It's about reaching deep to the roots of what is good, noble, beautiful, and true. As far as I am able, I hope to surround myself with natural materials and handcrafted items because it helps me focus on the work of human hands and the dignity of artisanship, values that seem to be vanishing in the era of Tickle Me Elmos and sixty-inch plasma TVs. Now, we all have families, and the reality is that we have accumulated LEGO® bricks and plastic tumbler cups and countless Hot Wheels. But we are trying to keep these things to a minimum, to keep our eyes and ears open to the simple joys of basic, God-given materials. Furthermore, none of us is going to pack up and move to a one-room sod house, Laura Ingalls style. I don't think that's what God calls most of us to do. I'm okay with using space for camping gear, sleds, bikes, and items that aren't strictly necessary. I also enjoy hanging lovely art or photos on my walls. But moderation in all things; plain walls or clear counters can serve to calm our eyes. I am enjoying not only the liberating feeling of purging stuff from our lives but also the spiritual fruits we harvest because of it. We no longer have a TV in our main living space. My eyes are able to put more emphasis on the crucifix on the wall. My ears are able to hear the rain more clearly. I can call the children to a noontime Angelus more easily. Everything seems more real in a way. Time seems more precious, and God seems more evident.

So don't imagine that we've achieved a blissful state of minimalism when you see the sticker on the back of my vehicle. (I may be on my way to a fresh crop of garage sales, after all—the spirit is willing, but the flesh is weak!) The challenge "Want Less" serves as a powerful reminder to this oft-tempted family. We want to hunger not after things to fill us up but deeply and wholly after God alone. Like Saint Augustine, I want to be able to say with an honest heart, "You, my Father, supremely good, beauty of all things beautiful. O Truth, Truth! How inwardly even then did the marrow of my soul pant after You."[6]

For more thoughts to this end, I highly recommend Thomas Dubay's book *Happy Are You Poor: The Simple Life and Spiritual Freedom*. I try to read it every few years.

— Ellie

THE MARTYR'S FOLLY

This is directed to all you martyr types. You know who you are. You are the kind of woman who takes pride in being capable, industrious, and pulled together. Yes, you can admit you have your off days—like the rest of us—but you do your best to keep those to yourself for the most part. After all, you wouldn't want to burden anyone with your problems or put anyone out. If you do an honest self-examination, you may even detect a bit of an ego involved there. You may want to appear organized, confident, and strong, or, worse, you may let others know (directly or indirectly) that you are struggling but stalwartly refuse any offers of help. You may sigh and say with a weary smile, "God has certainly blessed me with a lot of crosses right now." Pity. Now, don't get me wrong—the life of a Christian is destined to be filled with trials. There's no doubt about it; we are called to take up our cross and follow him. But I'm convinced that Christ didn't intend for all of us to live independently of each other's sorrows.

It seems to me that many women are trying too hard to live up to the Superwoman identity. They think that they should be able to do it all and that they are failures if they cannot. I know because I've been there. We are the types who don't allow the "something's got to give" mentality in our homes. We think we should be able to be excellent housekeepers, gourmet chefs, master educators, attentive nurses, efficient chauffeurs, doting wives, nurturing mothers, and prayerful Christians all at the same time.

Even if I were missing a couple of fingers, I could count on one hand the number of times when I've achieved all those titles in one day in almost ten years of married life. Usually, the reality is that something's got to give. And I'd wager that most of you agree it's unreasonable to expect a woman to be able to do everything. We all know what it's like to struggle with wearing many hats. The trouble is that so many of us are reluctant to—or flat out refuse to—ask for help or even accept help that is genuinely offered. We are

[6] Augustine, *Confessions*, 3, 6, 10, trans. J.G. Pilkington, from *Nicene and Post-Nicene Fathers, First Series*, vol. 1, ed. Philip Schaff (Buffalo, N.Y.: Christian Literature Publishing Co., 1887). Rev. and ed. for New Advent by Kevin Knight, https://www.newadvent.org/fathers/110103.htm.

martyrs! We're working off our purgatory time! No one can take our crosses away from us! We may not be able to do it all, but we sure aren't going to dump our problems on anyone else. Yes, my child is sick and clingy, and I've got a fever myself, and the dishes are backed up, and there's no food in the fridge for dinner, and Billy needs help with a science project that's due in the morning, and my husband has no clean clothes to wear to work tomorrow, but I do *not* need any help from you! No way, no how!

I can count three distinct tragedies that result from this mindset:

1. We don't receive any help. We allow the full weight of our trials to crush us when it could be greatly alleviated by allowing someone to make us a meal, watch our children for an hour, or run to the grocery store to fetch a gallon of milk and some cough drops.

2. We deprive another person the opportunity for grace. Why is it okay for us to practice the works of mercy but not to allow ourselves to be on the receiving end? Most of us think people aren't being sincere when they say "Well, let me know if there's anything I can do to help" or "Call me if you need anything." And truthfully, while the sincerity is there, I do think many people say these things not expecting that you'll take them up on it, because most of us would rather suffer silently than burden anyone else. There is certainly some merit to that. But it is good for our own humility to allow others the opportunity to be charitable. Their own lives are sanctified by the actions they perform, and we allow a moment of self-mortification to temper our pride. Our children also see firsthand what it means to be a friend and to practice a corporal work of mercy. It's a win-win-win situation that we should allow more often.

3. We close a door to bonding. One thing the entire human race has in common is suffering. In one way or another, we all face hurdles in our lives, and I believe that allowing others into an element of our suffering draws us close to each other. Think of the people in your life who are the nearest and dearest to your heart. These are the ones with whom you can share your heart. These are the ones from whom you will accept an offer for supper or babysitting. These are the ones with whom you are comfortable when they see that you hurt and that you struggle and that you can't do it all. While discretion is important in all our relationships and we certainly shouldn't be vulnerable with everyone we meet, we do need to let down our guard, overcome our pride, and set aside our image once in a while to let others share in our sufferings. These are the spiritual works of mercy, and true-blue friendships are built on these rocks. Women feel a connection with other women when they share their struggles. We find encouragement knowing that Superwoman is just a character from a comic book. It is reaffirming and consoling to be able to let our hair down and admit we do need help every now and again.

We are all sojourning together toward heaven. When we are strong, we would do well to reach out to those who are weak. When we are weak, we would do well to allow the strong to help us. A dear friend once said a wise thing that has comforted me greatly in many different situations: "Even Jesus needed help carrying his Cross." We cannot pretend to be greater than our Master.

— Ellie

SPRING BULBS
TALKING ABOUT DEATH WITH YOUNG CHILDREN

My eldest, four years old, has recently become fascinated with Great-Grandma Elaine: her great age, her wrinkles, her frailty, the way her false teeth move in and out when she talks, and all the parts of her body that don't work. As you can imagine, it has led to a lot of interesting questions about aging and the end of life. It is a sad time for me, partly because of the imminent parting with my sweet grandmother, and partly because it is the close of an innocent age when my little boy believes that life just goes on and on. I find myself hesitant to give him the facts of death straight out. I want to do it right. I don't want to scare him. Maybe I'm a bit cowardly about the harshness of death myself. I find myself saying in a loud and cheerful voice, "Oh, little boys don't have to worry about dying, because you have a long, long life ahead of you. Dying happens when you come to the end of your life." Yes, I am a chicken. But sooner or later Grandma Elaine is going to pass into the next life, and my job is to prepare my little ones gently.

Eventually I decided to tell my son that dying is a little bit like falling asleep, only you wake up in heaven with everyone you love. I told him that your body goes into the ground and turns back into soil, just like compost. It seemed a straightforward explanation to me, but he was still getting details mixed up and asking questions like, "Will it be dark underground?" and "Will you be in heaven, Mama?"

I found inspiration the other day when I was nursing the baby and idly picked out a book from the shelf beside me. It was a collection of Longfellow's poems that I had bought more for its beautiful old leather binding than a desire to read Longfellow. I opened it to a poem called "God's-Acre" and read the first line: "I like that ancient Saxon phrase, which calls/the burial-ground God's-Acre!" The poet drew a connection between the graveyard, or "God's Acre", and the ploughed field.

> Into its furrows shall we all be cast,
>   In the sure faith, that we shall rise again
> At the great harvest, when the archangel's blast
>   Shall winnow, like a fan, the chaff and grain.

It was February, and I was attracted to the thought of green, growing things. I resolved to buy some bulbs for my kitchen table. I chose paperwhites because they can be planted in soil. (Many bulbs can be forced in a glass vase or dish full of rocks, which is pretty, but I needed soil for my purposes.) I bought a little potting soil and, with my son, spooned it into a flowerpot. We felt the soil with our fingers and talked about how bulbs sleep in the cold, frozen soil all winter, but when the sun shines on them they put down roots and start to grow. We looked at the dry brown bulbs. We felt how "dead" they were, not at all like a nice green plant.

Then we put the bulbs to bed. "They're going to have a little sleep, and then what do you think is going to happen?" We discussed our various hopes for

the bulbs. (*No, Hugh, I don't think they will grow into dinosaurs. But you never know.*) We said "Good night! Good night!" to the bulbs. Then I told him that when Grandma Elaine dies, we are going to put her body into the ground just like the bulbs. Her soul will not be there. Her soul will be happy with Jesus, and her body will be waiting in the ground like a peaceful bulb. And then, when it is the right time, there will be a wonderful resurrection, just like Easter, and all the bodies will rise up, shiny and beautiful. He gave me a disbelieving look. He still had no idea what I was talking about. But he will in a few weeks when our paperwhites pop up.

> With thy rude ploughshare, Death, turn up the sod,
> And spread the furrow for the seed we sow;
> This is the field and Acre of our God,
> This is the place where human harvests grow!

— Mary

CHILD OF MINE, CHILD OF GOD

My son is out in the garden. He is now plucking peas from their vines and tasting their sweetness—*crunch, crunch.* There is a tooth missing in his mouth. The baby tooth fell out this week, so he bites off to the side. He notices a plane passing overhead and turns upward to look. Then he runs away and finds a shovel for the dirt. He digs away. It's the young age of innocent discovery.

Another child of mine is catching a yellow balloon. His arms are outstretched as it falls into his sweet, chubby, little hands. When it falls into a vase of flowers out of his reach, he runs off to strum the banjo and the guitar, then twirls around like a top in the middle of the living room. This one is always running, always moving—he's our little wiggle worm. He sings his own little song.

My third son is eagerly helping me with dishes, shirt off at the sink, sitting on a little stool. So happy to be by my side. He could be content with water for hours. Fill up the cup, pour it out; again, again, again.

And my baby, well, she's just lying on a cotton blanket in the kitchen with me while smiling at the air or at the shadows or at the whirring of the fan. She has the complete luxury of just *being.* She is enveloped in my love and depends completely on me. She is alive, alert, full of life and Light.

These little ones don't have emails to answer, dinner to cook, or a house to clean. They are so free. (Oh, to be little again!) I am reminded that their spirit is the spirit I must have in my journey toward heaven. I desire to have their trust, their dependence, their simplicity of heart and mind. In the words of Catherine Doherty, "Lord, give me the heart of a child."[7]

There is a candle on my windowsill, burning in front of an icon of Mary. There is a flower there too, in bloom. Outside, the sun is shining. The birds are flying from tree to tree. They, like my children, are so free and well provided for by their Maker.

How did I come to be so blessed? But of course! My children are not my own. They are God's very own little plants, and they were created for him—growing upward, stretching up to the sun, putting out branches, and becoming strong in his Love. I'm just here to help them along their little paths. I'm their gardener, here to provide fertile soil and a nurturing environment. I'm here to temper their little diverse personalities. Every little plant needs a different amount of sun and water. *They are yours, God, not mine. Take them and mold them. Water them and feed them. Give them plenty of sun. Thank you for the honor of being their gardener.*

— Sia

[7] Catherine Doherty, *Season of Mercy: Lent and Easter* (Combermere, Ontario: Madonna House Publications, 1996), 25–26.

WATERMELON

Ripe watermelon,
how easily your rind yields
to the heft of my knife,
your crimson flesh—
intricate matrix of membranes—
to our teeth.
My son, at three, sits still only
   long enough
to consume a slice
and streak his bare chest
with juice.

Heavy fruit,
to think you began
a weightless seedling
we watched and watered,

flourishing slowly behind
a soft spoken
yellow flower,
swelling until
our gentle tapping told us
you were ready.

Is nothing constant
in this verdant August garden?
I recall—
the summer of 1989, my father
and his video camera.
A few shots of my sisters and me
amid hours and hours of film
of the backyard garden.
Close-ups of sweet corn,

squash plants,
beans.

And I understand:
after dinner, bathing my son,
I marvel at his pink skin,
his round cheeks,
the sureness of his young being.
He is a seamless vessel of growth
stopping not even
to let me
watch.

— Emily Donegan, Vermont

A NEW KIND OF LIST

Over the last few years, my house has been *very* messy. I am finally feeling that the hardest time in my life as a mother (well, the most chaotic, anyway) has passed. Before now, all my children were little. They were all babies. They needed every part of me, all the time. But my boys are self-sufficient now, and my oldest is actually making a visible mark on my house: he helps me clean, unloads the dishwasher, and even carries his one-year-old brother around, taking him down the slide at the park and sitting with him on the picnic blanket. It really is a monumental time in family life. Where does the time go? Despite the independence of my boys, most of the week I am on my feet much of the day, trying to keep the house clean and orderly. Some days I don't even sit down. Even if each child is picking up after himself, the counters are kept clear, and the floors are swept, I find more to do. I write more lists, I sweep the closet, I wash the bathroom floors … the list goes on. Housework is *never* done. It is always in progress, always moving. But I *will* complete something and check one more thing off my list! What kind of list? Well, I mean the everyday, crazy, million-things-to-do list: the various stuff that just piles up in our mama brains. You know, the one that reads like this:

- Sweep cobwebs out of high windows
- Roast squash for soup
- Pay bills
- Thaw chicken for tomorrow
- Fill out atrium class forms
- Send out email for parish meal needs
- Organize boys' new bookshelf
- Bake leftover-oatmeal muffins
- Wash bathroom floor
- Scrub upstairs bathtub
- Wash diapers and rags
- Make card for baby shower

- Make bean dip
- Find recipe for candied almonds

Oh, it can be mentally and physically overwhelming.

But we can't keep up with every little thing. The important thing is to have order and peace in the home and a sense of purpose and love of God while doing each little task the home requires. The risk we run in continually moving, working, and thinking about checking things off our lists is losing the joy of the passing moments. Of missing out on little things like those light-bulb moments in our children's development. Even a new word or skill one of them learns can be miraculous and beautiful to behold. Sometimes I wake up and think, *I haven't tickled or cuddled my boys in three days. I haven't taken them to the park all week.* So, I find that sometimes the best thing I can do is just sit and be, savoring my baby's smile and the little conversations that my three- and five-year-old are having nearby. Especially in winter it is such a treat to get cozy in one's own home, when outside it is pouring rain, snowing, or just plain freezing.

Some mornings it would be wise if I wrote a new kind of list for myself:

- Make tea
- Read tons of stories to the boys
- Build a block castle or a marble run
- Take a nap or lie down to read during quiet time
- Get cozy on the couch and read some articles while the boys play; let them drive trucks all over my legs and arms
- Light candles
- Write a letter
- Sit
- Make the boys laugh their heads off
- Say a decade of the Rosary together
- Play on the floor with the baby
- Spend an hour at the park with a thermos of hot cocoa
- Go puddle stomping

Let's savor the moments. Breathe. Find the bits of amazing life and joy that our days are so full of. Be. Stop to smell the roses. Pray for joy in the ordinary. Sure, our children can be needy and tiresome—but they are *so* fun and so darling too! Isn't it an *honor* that we are needed and tugged and pulled in so many directions? And having a messy house really isn't the end of the world. It's more important for us, as Catherine Doherty says, to catch the smile of a baby and hug it close to our hearts. After all, as my friend Hope once said, "Kisses from baby are kisses from Christ, I think."

— Sia

How do I show my girls I love them on a morning in June? I pick them wild strawberries. On a February afternoon we build snowmen and then sit by the fire. In March we make maple syrup. We pick violets in May and go swimming in July. On an August night we lay out blankets and watch meteor showers. In November, that great teacher the woodpile comes into our lives. That's just the beginning. How do we show our children our love? Each in our own way by a shower of gifts and a heavy rain of lessons.

— Robin Wall Kimmerer
Braiding Sweetgrass

PONDER

ALL SHALL BE WELL

It is mid-March as I write. The full weight of an Atlantic storm is hitting the side of the house—hurricane-force winds over a hundred miles per hour. The southeasters are called *les suêtes* here in French Acadia. We have taken to calling our toddler Les Suêtes because she can do as much damage as a hurricane in half the time.

I am banking ashes over our fire, prodding it with the poker to wake up the coals, laying on the still-green hardwood, raking ashes over the lot to keep it alive until morning. Wood fires take tending, and it's gradually becoming part of the rhythm of life. Spring soon!

There are many metaphors in this task. My husband and I spend so much of our life tending fires: tending our marriage, tending gardens, turning over the laundry, feeding the sourdough starter, tending animals, tending the spiritual life, caring for ourselves. It all needs upkeep.

"If you have peace in your heart, then thousands of souls around you will be saved", said Saint Seraphim of Sarov.[1] Some translations say, "Thousands will be *healed*." It's probably true. I know that the opposite is certainly true. "*Don't* cultivate peace, and thousands around you will feel miserable" could be an aphorism at our house. I've seen this to be true. We have the capacity to send our partner into paroxysms of self-doubt and misery and our darling children scampering to therapists for decades to talk about their mother.

In my more cynical moments when I feel scowl-y about the state of the world—the exploitation, bloodshed, misery, displacement, pollution, homelessness, and violence in the daily news—I sometimes think about the Christian martyrs. (I know, cheerful, right?) The martyrs of Eastern Europe under the Communist regime hit particularly close to home. In Romania under Ceausescu, political and religious prisoners were kept in underground cells, in total darkness and solitude, for years on end. Imagine never seeing daylight or breathing fresh air, day after day, month after month, the only human contact being daily visits from prison guards who came to beat you or subject you to psychological torture.

What blows my mind is that some individuals, barely alive in this environment, grew not only in prayer but also in kindness and peace. News of them spread to other prisoners, and they became a sign of hope in a hopeless situation. Stories abound of sudden conversions, miracles, powerful forgiveness, and changes of heart. In complete darkness and deprivation, they kept the image of God shining.

What a privilege to call these people our sisters and brothers! It reminds me of the words of Dmitri Karamazov in Dostoevsky's *The Brothers Karamazov* written eighty years earlier: "If God is driven from the earth, we'll meet him underground! … And then from the depths of the earth, we, the men underground, will start singing a tragic hymn to God, in whom there is joy!"[2]

I often think of these men and women. It's a reminder that we are part of a bigger picture. Whatever our daily struggles, we are in the company of heroic men and women who have already run the race. Some of us are struggling every day in our jobs, marriages, and health. Our society is more depressed, in debt, medicated, incarcerated, obese, divorced, and anxious than ever before. These are real struggles. Even those of us with stability and health have days when nothing goes our way.

Yet we profess a faith that offers a way of spiritual healing. It changes people. According to tradition, the early martyrs went to their deaths joyfully, singing hymns. This is humbling—I, for one, can barely say a civil word if I'm not properly caffeinated or have missed a night's sleep. Yet all around us men and women quietly live the Christian life, singing hymns

---

[1] Matthew Lewis Sutton, *Compassionate Presence: The Trinitarian Spirituality of Adrienne Von Speyr* (Brooklyn, N.Y.: Angelico Press, 2022), 86.
[2] Fyodor Dostoevsky, *The Brothers Karamazov*, trans. Richard Pevear and Larissa Volokhonsky (New York: Alfred A. Knopf, 1992), 592.

in the kitchen or factory line or while mucking out the barn or typing in the office. Christian mothers sing to soothe cranky children, and Christian fathers persevere cheerfully in dreary workplaces. Long nights of caring for babies bring parents to the outer edges of mental stamina. Yet they continue without complaining while giving up their lives for others. These are acts of real heroism. If I have any faith at all, I'd say it's due to saints such as these.

As someone who sees myself as rather a mediocre Christian, I've struggled to understand what sets us apart from the world. Jesus said, "You are the light of the world" (Mt 5:14). Well, most days I don't feel like a light. So, what does it mean to be Christian? Is Christianity just a philosophy or a set of ethics? Or is our faith a living conviction, cultivated deep in our hearts? I believe that we can be part of the healing of this world, that we can cultivate peace and build up a generation of peacemakers. But our conviction has to be kept alive. It needs tending, like a hearth fire. It has to be built and rebuilt, raked out and started again. Our faith teaches us not to be afraid, as Julian of Norwich professed: "All shall be well, and all shall be well, and all manner of thing shall be well."

— Mary

RICE IN THE POT

The rice grains scatter rhythmically onto the floor of my aluminum pot with each flick of my wrist and the metal cup. I place my pot in the sink and let the faucet fill it up. I plunge both hands into the bed of heavy wet grains and work my fingers around the bottom, loosening the white starch and clouding the water. Swish, drain, rinse, swish, drain, rinse.

Once, a woman from Thailand told me, "I love rice! I could eat it at every meal." I was appalled. *What kind of pallid diet does she have that she prefers rice to all other foods?* I thought. At the time, my idea of rice was the stuff that comes packaged so that it cooks in the microwave in five minutes. So accustomed was I to machine-cleaned, ready-to-cook rice that it took almost a year of living in Tanzania—and a chipped molar—for me to realize that I should be picking out the tiny rocks and sorting the rice into long and broken grains before I even cooked it.

Now I have tasted the perfect pot of rice eaten in the cool of the new evening in a mud hut, steaming hot, and I am ruined. Here rice is a special treat like pizza or dessert for American families—you don't get to eat it every day.

Straight off the wood-cooking fire, it is piled into a cloudy white mountain on a large circular metal plate.

The whole family sits around the plate, which is ceremoniously placed in the middle of a grass rug, and they eat politely with their right hands. Here are the rules: don't hold more than you can eat in one bite, take turns, don't scoop into your neighbor's part of the pile, and don't let your fingers touch your lips or tongue (that would be rude). To eat rice with one hand, first scoop a handful into the finger-part of your hand. Then squeeze the ball against your palm, squishing the grains into sort of a ball, roll the ball loosely back to the tips of your fingers in one motion, and finally tip your head back ever so slightly as you flick the morsel onto your tongue.

Each bite tastes nutty and toasted, with a tinge of salt and the aftertaste of soothing coconut. Each grain is separate and slightly chewy, *al dente*. I have grown to love this stuff more than bread. The wonderful taste, I assume, comes from the fact that it is hand gathered from the field, hand pounded (to remove the hull), hand sorted, hand washed, and finally cooked in a family-sized portion over an open wood fire, all usually within the same day.

I am very much a novice at making (and eating) rice, but the soothing, tactile motions of cleaning, pouring, and washing in the quiet of the afternoon links me, I know, with my Tanzanian women friends as well as the worlds of other women with whom I long to be joined. At times, I feel that there is so much cultural distance and so many differences between us that simple acts like food preparation grow increasingly sacred to me. In this respect, we are the same: there is rice in the pot, and we mothers are the ones to cook it.

— Heather Kellis, South Carolina

ALL YOU EDUCATORS

With the last of our five children soon going off to (in all likelihood) major in classical music, the perennial question arises: Does the fruit fall far from the tree? How common is it for an Einstein or a da Vinci to drop in on the world? Or how often does a giant arise from humble origins (e.g., an Abraham Lincoln)? On the other hand, how many times have I heard an interview with published authors and learned that they are themselves the children of English professors, writers, playwrights, or poets? Why do the children of directors, producers, or actors so often go into that industry? How often do professional athletes beget athletes? We all know "military families" or "musical families" or "artistic families".

When I was in the thick of the homeschooling years, I was all too aware of my shortcomings in science and math. I simply could not summon up the same enthusiasm (or time) for science and math that I did for fine arts, nature logs, literature, and history. Yes, I berated myself once in a while, but gradually I made peace with the pitfalls of home education and reassured myself that if one of my children was meant to be an Einstein or a Lincoln, there would be no holding him back. He would be sure to find his gifts and aptitudes on his own at home or after he went off to college or whichever path he chose. So far though, not one of them has surprised us in that way. If we had had an interloper, we would have recognized him right off, and I would have been happy to find a mentor. The conclusion I've reached, however, is that the apple really does not fall terribly far from the tree and that the ingredients you put in really will affect how these little cooking projects come out. Of course, these are not just cooking projects or experiments. They are flesh-and-bone humans with souls that through your blood, sweat, tears, and prayers—and through their blood, sweat, tears, and the grace of God—will metamorphose into adults and will (hopefully) better the world in some small way. Your family milieu is your family milieu, and it's time to be proud of it!

I point this out for two reasons. First, so you mothers out there who are in the thick of your homeschooling years can stop castigating yourselves for not being the best science or math teacher (or, for you science and math lovers, for not being the best art, music, or literature teachers). You are giving your children something distinct to your family that no other set of parents can give them. Second, to encourage you simply to give them what you know best, what you do best, and what excites you the most, and above all, not to feel guilty about it. If they turn out quite a bit like you, what's wrong with that? If you have shared your love of art and they become art history majors—great! We need more of those. If you just love reading and thinking, that's okay; the world is already chock full of ambitious, busy people. Praise be to the thinkers, the readers, the contemplatives. If all you manage to do is impart your knowledge of and love for music— wonderful! Maybe your child will become a music critic (you gave them a love of reading and writing, remember?) or a musician, and the world can never have too much music. Musicians and writers and religious and artists all know that they may not make a fortune, but they are doing what their heart is calling them to do and helping to put good into the world. As a bonus, your children will be familiar to you.

— Dru Hoyt, Ohio

OUR PLACE IN THE KINGDOM

It's easy to feel entitled. In this diverse country, it's the one sentiment most Americans have in common. It's especially easy for a mother, I think, because we've been robbed (robbed!) of some basic human props. Is it too much to ask that I not be woken up by a kick in the face from a two-year-old in my bed? I'm supposed to be Catholic, so could I actually pray at Mass every once in a while, instead of roping kids down in the foyer? Can't a woman just take a shower or use the restroom for two minutes in peace?

We live in a society where the Golden Rule is no longer "Do unto others" but "Follow your dreams." Gone are the days of thousands of young men eager to fight for their country and the freedom of others; the only duty we see now is to "treat yo'self" and to hold on to youth as long as possible. (YOLO!) I think it's hard to be a Christian in a post-Christian era. It's hard to grow up, to take on duty, and to admit that it is someone else's turn to be served and your turn to serve.

What's a girl to do? Well, what did Mary of Nazareth do? It's funny to think of a normal female's response to the knowledge that she was to be the mother of God. "Wait! If I'm going to be the mother of the King of the Universe, that means that I get to be the Quee—" Stop. *Handmaid.* She knew that *all generations* would call her blessed. But she gave herself the title of handmaid.

I watched my daughter Indigo receive the Precious Blood for the first time at Mass this morning, on the feast of the Sacred Heart. And I knew that God *delighted* in entering her. She didn't need to have deep, profound thoughts. She didn't even need to pray all that well afterward; she just needed to believe and

The ego-drama is the play that I'm writing, I'm producing, I'm directing, and I'm starring in. We see this absolutely everywhere in our culture....

The theo-drama is the great story being told by God, the great play being directed by God. What makes life thrilling is to discover your role in it.

—Bishop Robert Barron

receive. And I knew that God was happy with me. There is nothing more satisfying and pleasurable to him than entering a new soul, and if it wasn't for me waking up and doing what I do every day, he would have one less soul to enter and delight in. And paradise is there now, inside her.

My sons and daughters, and your sons and daughters, are princes and princesses in the kingdom of God. There are none dearer to him than these precious souls, these lilies. Don't forget that you're a princess too, my friend. But it will behoove us to follow Mary's example and associate ourselves with her title of handmaid.

It's like this: God the King has some royal children, and he's looking for a nanny. It is a really good job with really good pay, and he could have chosen any number of highly qualified people, but you were lucky enough to land the job. You just have to show up and serve. And you are serving royalty. You cook and clean, smile and teach, give them time-outs, and all the while you echo in your heart, *I am the handmaid.* Or even, *I am the nanny of the Lord.* God has no grandchildren—they are all his, and we are lucky to be on the payroll.

– Hope

CORAGGIO

Some of us may be tempted to feel like we are "bad Catholics" if we aren't feeling over the moon when we see those double pink lines indicating a new pregnancy. Then when we get around to announcing the expectation of a new baby, and people say "Congratulations!" we are thinking cynically, *Yeah, really.* But we can't express our misgivings. We smile politely and make some joke about God's sense of humor while inwardly feeling devastated. Our fears may revolve around physical, mental, financial, or emotional concerns. Whatever the case may be, we do not want to admit to our good Catholic friends—much less to our hostile non-Catholic family—that the idea of having more children is gut-wrenching.

So we move along in this faux reality of a Catholicism where being open to life means everyone is giddy about being pregnant when it happens. But I think many of us live in this reality where we constantly have to do some serious internal wrestling as we try to accept God's will and love yet another baby on the way. The fear is sometimes crippling. We can't talk about it. Will people think we don't love our children? That we have a weak faith? That we're bad moms? What about the duty to bear witness to the truth, to set a positive example of the Church's teaching on openness to life? As the weeks of pregnancy go on, we eventually become reconciled to the idea. By the time baby is born, or shortly thereafter, we are in love all over again with this new creation and we can't imagine our lives any other way. Being horrified at the idea of a nameless, faceless pregnancy is a completely different story than being horrified at having another child in your family.

But I often wonder how helpful it would be if we were a little more honest or vulnerable with our true feelings? How many of us can raise our hands and say that we are testimonies to the fact that an "unwanted pregnancy" does *not* equal an "unwanted child"? I know I can. When I became pregnant with my fifth child, I had just gone through two back-to-back miscarriages. I was in a dark place, mentally. The pregnancy was fairly rough on me physically. I didn't feel a sense of bonding with the baby the entire time. I confessed to my midwife toward the end that I was feeling "*prepartum* depression" if there was such a thing. She said there was. I was terrified to go through labor again, and I honestly dreaded the birth. Whom could I talk to about this? My husband knew but didn't really understand. And I think one or two of my closest girlfriends knew. While I wouldn't think it appropriate to dump all this on the general public, I also made sure not to share the misgivings, dread, or fear I had with my friends and certainly not with family members who disapproved of my family size already. I felt guilty. I felt like I was a bad person for feeling such awful things. Who dreads her child's birth, after all? I didn't want people to think I was crazy, depressed, or faithless.

When the time came, I prayed to God *not* to let the baby be born just yet. All the kids had coxsackievirus, and my husband and I were on different communication wavelengths. It was a bad time. Yet he was ready, right on his due date. I labored silently alone for a couple of hours. I had just read something by Pope Saint John Paul II where he kept encouraging his readers with the word *coraggio* (courage). For some reason, that became my prayer, my petition. I whispered it to myself over and over. It was an awful, intense labor with lots of back pain, lots of emotional blockage. When our son finally entered the world, in that last push of courage, agony, blood, and water, I finally cried. But it wasn't over the joy of my new baby. I was weeping in relief that it was over. I couldn't look at my son. The midwife put him on my chest, and I felt his warm, wet body breathing in his first gasps of air. But I couldn't look at him. I was just thanking God that the labor was over. I wasn't ready to see him. I didn't feel ready to love him. But I did. I knew I did, even if I didn't feel it immediately.

Eventually, of course, we bonded. And in all honesty—despite it sounding trite—that child became the absolute joy of my life. He is the most amazing, lovable baby, and both my husband and I truly can't remember enjoying the babyhood of any of our children quite this much. What miracles God can work on hearts! Who would have guessed that this little one was once just a dreaded theory—a "pregnancy" for so long? Others would be ashamed to admit it; it is scary to be vulnerable. It takes *coraggio* to admit the truth. But I want to have that courage. I want people to know

All our life is sown, so to speak, with these tiny thorns which produce in our hearts a thousand involuntary movements of hatred, envy, fear, impatience, a thousand little fleeting disappointments, a thousand slight worries, a thousand disturbances, which for a moment at least alter our peace of soul. For example, a word escapes which should have not been spoken, or some one utters another that offends us;… a child inconveniences you, a bore stops you,… you don't like the weather, your work is not proceeding according to your plan; a piece of furniture is broken, a dress is stained or torn.… This is no occasion for practicing very heroic virtue, but I do say that this would be enough to acquire it without fail, if we really wished to.

—Saint Claude La Colombière

the amazing graces showered on my unworthy heart. How can people know the goodness God is capable of if we can't reveal a little bit of just how far he's brought us? How can we testify to women who are experiencing fear or doubt over an unwanted pregnancy if we are afraid to empathize with them? So often women just want to feel like they aren't alone. They want to have hope that it will indeed be okay. How can they know that if we aren't open about living it? As far as they can tell, if you aren't thrilled about a pregnancy, you will never want your child. What a pity! What a lie! The transformation of the heart isn't just some spiritual assumption people talk about. It's a living and breathing presence that I believe many open-to-life Catholics experience all the time. We have to be more willing to share that glorious hope in our culture of death.

We are now expecting our sixth child. This is the very first time, in all my pregnancies, that I have felt such an immediate sense of delight, hope, joy, and wonder at the life inside me. (Usually my pregnancies were met with resignation or some such emotion; I always wished for—but never had—that Hollywood-portrayed instant excitement.) A friend pointed out that I learned of this pregnancy right after I finished making a consecration to the Blessed Mother, on the feast day of Our Lady of Fatima. I'd like to think it was her gift to me—that I can know such an overwhelming sense of happiness at being a cocreator with God. My love for God may be weak. But every now and then, I look at my flock of children and think of the ways each of them has brought me closer to him. Each pregnancy may be a temporary test of faith, but the story always ends the same: each baby born stretches my willingness to surrender a little bit more. Each baby born stretches my capacity to love a little bit more. And each baby born has carved out new dimensions of joy that I never knew existed before. In that, there is truly nothing to fear.

—Ellie

RAINBOWS AND THE STORMS THAT PRECEDE THEM

Driving down a familiar road on the way to a lecture at a local community center, I suddenly saw a car headed directly toward me. With no time to think, I swerved to avoid a major crash and, as a result, clipped the car next to me. While there was some minor damage to both cars in the form of broken headlights, I had avoided what could have been a serious accident. I was doubly grateful for this because my one-month-old, Bridget Rose, was in her car seat right where the impact would have occurred.

This is not the first time I've felt Bridget's guardian angel protecting us. Miraculously, when she was born by induction, we discovered that her umbilical cord was disintegrating and only holding on by a thread. Had we waited for me to go into labor naturally, the cord might have come off in the meantime, threatening her life. And just a few weeks ago, a big brother (who shall remain nameless) climbed up on the changing table and toppled it—and Bridget!—onto the floor. Bridget was quite frightened but completely unharmed.

These three incidents have served as tangible reminders to me of God's hand in our lives. When my two preschool-aged boys sing "He's got the whole world in his hands", I might be tempted to think it trite, until I realize how true it really is. I know that the Lord has some major issues to be concerned about—violence, starvation, and unbelief, to name just a few. Yet he still cares for me and my children here in Richmond, Virginia. How easily we can forget that miracles happen every day.

Bridget's survival is already a trend at a mere five weeks old—even her survival until birth was in question. When I got a positive pregnancy test last year, I was a bit excited, but mostly scared. My husband and I had lost three babies before she was conceived. Three souls I knew only from their beating hearts on the monitor and the plans I had for their entrance into our families. Even returning to the hospital for my first prenatal appointment was tinged with stress—the last time I had been there I was in the Emergency Room for the loss of a baby.

But little Bridget thrived in the womb, thanks in great part to bio-identical progesterone supplements I received biweekly. I joked that Bridget better know how much I loved her, since I was getting shots twice per week with an instrument that made an epidural needle look like a thumbtack. Yet as I, and many other parents, have discovered, these trials were small compared to the joy of being able to carry a baby to term.

When I first heard the term "rainbow baby", I thought it was kind of silly. I associated rainbows with illustrations in children's books: happy, cheery, silly signs of sunshine after the rain. Yet, of course, babies born after previous miscarriages are called rainbow babies because they are signs of hope. Like a rainbow, these babies are signs of joy after a storm.

The seasons of motherhood, as so many of us know, are far from easy. Every six months there seems to be a new challenge. Some moms are experiencing rough pregnancies, where "morning sickness" is a nine-month event. Others are struggling with infertility or miscarriage. Still more are dealing with postpartum anxiety, depression, or other surges of emotion. Perhaps you've experienced all these things. The truth is that motherhood can knock you to your knees. Over and over again.

But if there is anything that all these losses, struggles, and joys have reminded me of, it is how utterly dependent I am on God. No one really wants to echo these words of Job, and yet it is the complete truth: "The LORD gave, and the LORD has taken away; blessed be the name of the LORD" (Job 1:21). Yet as I look at my Bridget (currently sleeping and ensconced in a warm bear suit) and think of all we have already been through together, I cannot help but know that God's goodness is everlasting and that there is always hope after the storm.

—Caitlin Bootsma, Virginia

LET'S TALK ABOUT YOUR SMARTPHONE

Every modern invention, every step forward in the progress of man, has a corresponding loss. With the advent of the telephone came a decline in frequent neighborly visits. With the arrival of radio and television, we lost some of our habits of reading and study. As a result of a shared Hollywood influence, localized identity of towns and states was lessened, and, perhaps even graver, our ability to quiet ourselves was severely compromised. The Internet has made undesirable images available to practically everyone and has isolated us to our own homes and screens even further, to be content with community found through social media. This is not to say we should not progress (we hope the benefits of technology outweigh the drawbacks), but I think it is important to note what is being lost and to try hard to hold on to what we can of it. The culture of the smartphone is a fascinating and dangerous one. It poses a constant distraction and presents a great temptation—to make technology our most needed friend and our god.

Who and what do you reach for when you have questions about life? What's the last thing you do before you go to bed and the first thing you do when you wake up? Do you catch yourself blankly staring at your phone wondering what you should do next, indicating that your habit of looking at it is stronger than your ability to use it as a tool that serves a purpose? Computers are addicting enough. Combine that with your telephone, calendar, shopping list, and a few dozen convenient apps, and the aliens looking down won't have to say "take me to your leader"; it will already be evident.

I was the last in my circle of friends to join the smartphone culture. I used to get annoyed when other people laughed at private texts in the presence of others, or checked their social media at a party when conversation grew dull, or scrolled while in line at the bank or post office, seemingly avoiding friendly conversation with their community members. I judged them. Now I get it. I know now that when another person is on his phone, it can seem annoying and unnecessary, but when I have something to do on mine, it always seems worthy and completely necessary.

Miss Manners of old was always on top of propriety and charity understood within the social norms of the day, but somehow our love for convenience and technology has caused us to bypass any critical analysis of our use of these devices. I think we've got to slow down and look at how cutting-edge technology in a handheld device can both help us and harm us. Let's come up with some rough guidelines for appropriate usage of these devices (especially within the family), even if we occasionally fail to follow them.

I'd like to address two things here: first, smartphone etiquette, and second, how we can use this technology to our spiritual advantage.

Side note: I am addressing adult use of smartphones specifically, as I haven't given my kids phones yet and don't intend to for a long while. This is a totally personal call that is relative to each family; the only blanket statement I can say about kids and phones is what I hope is already obvious: *kids should not have unlimited access to the Internet on a phone. Especially boys.* The end.

My older children attend Cotillion, a formal dancing and manners club for young people. Six times a year they get all dressed up and act like ladies and gentlemen. The rest of the time, well, we're working on it. At each meeting, the leaders address some issue of charity through manners. Last month the leader posed the question "How many of you have a handheld device that you carry with you, be it a phone or an iPod or something

of the sort?" Most of the hands shot up. Her next question was "How many of you have ever been in the middle of talking with a friend and all of a sudden your friend is looking at his device and not at you?" About half the hands went up. Now for the clincher: "Okay, boys and girls, how many of you have had that happen when you were speaking with an adult?" Every single hand went up, and the watching crowd of parents blushed with embarrassment.

We might try to mind our manners around our peers, whether out of charity or out of vanity, not wanting to appear like a phone junkie. But how easy it is to deny our children the same respect! Will our children grow up with more memories of us smiling down at them or down at our phones while they are trying to get our attention? Granted, we live with our children; we spend almost every waking moment with some of them, and we have things to do. We have messages to respond to, shopping lists to create, phone calls to return, and other relationships to maintain, and texting can be less disruptive than a phone call in a busy home. But somehow, we have to quantify it. The *Cotillion* leader went on to say this: "If you are in the middle of a conversation and you hear the little ding of a text, it can feel like it is very urgent, but you must remember it is not. The person you are conversing with might even say, 'Aren't you going to get that?' But how much more of a leader you will be in this world when you reply, 'I can get to it later. I'm talking with you right now, and you are more important.'"

Your children watch you. And my children watch me. They see me text and drive. They see me ignoring the baby so I can reply to an email. Our mothers did not have to navigate this new terrain, which is both a blessing and a curse. I think it will serve us well to devise a few practices that will both reign us in and model to the next generation this delicate balance.

1. **People in the room are more important than people out of the room.** We need to keep this in mind with our husbands, our children, and any person that is in our physical presence. A good way to do this is to power off your phone for a few

hours at a time during the day and then again for a few hours in the afternoon or evening. If you are homeschooling your children in the morning, then something like 9:00 to 12:00 might be wise. If your kids are at school but come home at 3:00, perhaps you could turn your phone off then so you can be the fully present mother your children need you to be. If you work outside the home and don't get home until 5:00 or 6:00, try to keep those last few hours of the day phone-free, until the kids are in bed. I often remind myself, *Everyone I am responsible for is here with me; therefore, any text or call or voicemail can wait a bit.* If you go on a date or a hike or to the beach, try leaving your phone in the car. Connect with your spouse, your children, your friend having tea with you, the moment, and God. You can connect with your Facebook friends later.

2. **Set aside time for your phone or your computer.** It's okay to say, "Mom needs half an hour to reply to some phone calls and messages; why don't you go play outside?" Or you can wait for the natural lulls in the day to check your phone and return calls. We can offer up these little sacrifices, these "waiting" periods, for those who struggle with chastity or addiction. Want another challenge? Set the timer for half an hour or however long you think checking your phone will take you, and then you will be less tempted to waste away an entire afternoon. A final thing I've tried at the advice of a priest is to allow myself three daily check-ins with my phone. Ask yourself, *What's a reasonable number of times to check messages in a day? Email? Social media?* And then try to create some boundaries or rules around those things. A handwritten list of phone to-dos can get those tasks out of your brain and into a safe waiting place until your next check-in time.

3. **Interrupt conversation or time with others only for something that cannot wait.** And in that case, treat children with the same respect as you would adults. Politely excuse yourself and say, "Dad needs me to send him an important phone number right away—just a moment!" We are all happy to wait if we know the person has an urgent matter to deal with and is not just zoning out due to boredom.

4. **All time on the phone or the Internet should point to, serve, and be subordinate to the beautiful physical world God made.** *Matter is good,* as is noted in Genesis. We must rightly order our habits, our hearts, and our minds to prioritize the corporal and the created world instead of the man-made Internet and metaverse.

I've heard it said, "What if we began to treat our Bibles the way we treat our cell phones? What if we turned back to get it if we forgot it? Checked it for messages throughout the day? Used it in case of emergency? Spent an hour or more using it each day?" It is sobering to realize how we often cannot find the time to crack open Scripture or spiritual reading, but we can manage to check our phones a dozen times a day. The good news is this: if we are that comfortable staring at screens, we should be comfortable with praying from them too, and the resources available are numerous. A wonderful priest encouraged me by pointing out that with all the technology out there, it is easier than ever to find spiritual resources. I still prefer reading print, but I love the audio Rosary and Bible apps that I can enjoy from my phone, plugged into the speaker in our van or at home. Of course, I would love a candle-lit family Rosary in the evenings, but lately on weeknights, the best I can do is play a YouTube Rosary on my laptop while we do the dishes. My little ones stare at the holy images, and they understand that we're praying while we work. There are countless wonderful apps and podcasts that can aid us in the spiritual life. YouTube is also full of old Latin hymns with the words to follow along, accompanied by beautiful images. What a great way to recover some of our lost Catholic culture and learn liturgical songs with our children!

Yet even with all these holy resources, we must carve out time for silence. It is so important to demonstrate to our children that the smartphone is not a toy or a way to escape dull moments but a tool to be used for certain purposes and put down to embrace the present moment. Sometimes the present moment means silence or boredom, and that's okay. We must become comfortable with ourselves and one another and rediscover our humanity in these moments. I've recently purchased a dumb phone for myself, and I'm praying that when it arrives, I'm brave enough to make the swap. See, despite all the spiritual resources and convenient tools the smartphone has to offer me, with all its distractions I feel less in touch with my humanity, and my family, than I did before I had one. Sometimes stepping backward is actually stepping forward.

Lately I've been thinking about it in this light: Who will you want beside you when you are at the end of your life and lie in pain? Who will bring comfort to your bedside when you die? We are body and soul, we will die someday, and we will die the way we lived. We will likely want to reach for the same people and the same things that brought us comfort and joy when we were healthy and vibrant. Let's use our phones, but not love them. Let's get comfortable with them not being constantly in our hands and try to spend equal amounts of time holding the hand of a little child or an aging person instead. Because the aging hands will soon be gone, and the little hands will soon be grown and holding another's before we know it.

— Hope

TEDIUM, TIREDNESS, AND GREENER GRASS

I secretly envy the lives of some of my single, globe-trotting, sailboat-voyaging, theater-going, scuba-diving, music-gigging, wine-testing, and skinny family members. "Remember the days", I lament to my husband, "when we didn't age five years in one night by dealing with a sleepless toddler? When we simply went to our room and shut the door when we needed private time? When our spare time was devoted to culture and the arts instead of dirty dishes and wet firewood?"

Occasionally, I get phone calls from these beloved family members who gush enthusiastically over my life. Ah, the beautiful children! Ah, the adorable animals! (We live on a hobby farm.) Ah, the settledness and contentedness!

Ah, the irony. Ah, human nature. I live on a homestead in Cape Breton, very picturesque and close to the ocean. My kids step dance and carve bows and arrows, and we plaster our house with art. My husband milks cows, logs with horses, and raises bees, sheep, and goats. I post pictures on my blog of adorable children and baby goats. But beyond the green pastures of Raventree Farm? Pretty shabby. We yell a lot. Complain a lot. Every day is a marathon of chores, repentance of basic human sin, and fresh

Have regular hours for work and play, make each day both useful and pleasant, and prove that you understand the worth of time by employing it well. Then youth will be delightful, old age will bring few regrets, and life become a beautiful success.

— Louisa May Alcott
Marmee, *Little Women*

starts. Not so glamorous and sometimes downright discouraging.

I once heard about a woman, a friend of a friend, whose professional job was chocolate tasting—no, I'm serious. She was actually paid by food companies to fly around the world and grade chocolate by taste-testing. Romanced by handsome men, spending her workweek in beautiful resorts and exotic cities, she was, according to my friend, a bitter, unhappy woman. We had a good laugh over this, but seriously, isn't there a touch of irony? That yes, even lives that seem improbably wonderful can become tedious?

Envy is my inner animal, the primitive, instinctual enemy of my peace. I struggle with it so badly that I have to turn off social media for months at a time just to get a break from envying other people. My thinking brain, of course, tells me that Facebook and Instagram and Pinterest are unrealistic, that people crop their pictures and glorify the trivial while ignoring the real. And of course, I know that every life has struggle, even the lives of gainfully employed, globe-trotting people. But you see, I'm easily swayed by cropped pictures.

Some days, my unthinking brain feels that I'm a prisoner to routine, that my kitchen is a cell, that our compost toilet buckets are a terrible retribution for past sins, and that my children are simply wild animals in human disguise. I want to be anywhere else but here. Not because my life is so awful, but because I am so restless, because there are greener pastures out there.

But are there, really? The maligned compost toilet is just a piece of the big picture of soil renewal and preserving our water. Our children are becoming our friends. My husband gave up a career in order to steward a little patch of earth and build a cleaner, better life for his family—I'm proud of him for that. We have organic meat in the freezer, milk and eggs in the fridge, clean water in our taps, clean air in our lungs. No small gift. The big picture is beautiful, even if the details are a bit scruffy.

In everyone's life, there is a big picture. Your life might not encompass the same details as mine. It will have other tasks, big and small, other challenges, other joys. You know that by virtue of your motherhood,

you are doing good every day. And, ultimately, we're all headed toward the same end: a life of abundance in God.

The real struggle is sanity. We have to fight to keep perspective, to keep the big picture in mind at all times. Our faith has an ascetic practice called the "remembrance of death"—not as macabre as it might sound—which is a very practical way of keeping perspective. The truth is, we are all headed for glory, and this little life of ours is passing quickly.

We need to remember that we're training ourselves and our children for the long term. The little disobediences, emotional meltdowns, infractions, and arguments are not the end of the story; they're just bumps along the way. Let's give ourselves the grace to smile a bit more, at them and ourselves.

It's not the external struggles (for us: cash poverty, power outages, a badly insulated farmhouse, coyote kills, and hard work) that are important. It's the attitude we bring to them. It takes rocks and gravel, baby, to build a solid road (says Bob Dylan). We absolutely can be doing the right thing with the wrong attitude. Don't you think this is true for every life? Chocolate tasters and homesteaders alike?

If we want to keep perspective, we need to cultivate stillness, to set aside time to descend into the monastic cell of our hearts, to be still with God. It might mean meditating or carving out adult time at night to spend in reflection, to bring to mind the good we are doing, the good we need to strive for, and the good that's been done for us.

— Mary

TO LIVE DELIBERATELY

My favorite professor in college had an extremely dry sense of humor, and he was utterly brilliant. He was a professor of American Literature, and as that was always an area where I lacked knowledge—and to be honest, interest—I knew I wouldn't regret taking a class from him. He was a Quaker in the old tradition from Ohio, complete with a bushy beard and suspenders. As a published poet and diabetic, he would joke about his secret poems about doughnuts—all with a straight face, of course.

When it came time to discuss Henry David Thoreau, the famous transcendentalist who lived independently in the woods around Walden Pond and wrote of his experiences, he slipped a print of Thoreau's cabin onto one of those old-school overhead projectors. In his usual dry tone, he described the dimensions of the tiny cabin, the raw materials used by Thoreau, and so forth. Then he said, "And people were shocked to discover nude photographs of Emily Dickinson tucked away among his things." So deadpan was his delivery, none of us knew whether to giggle or gasp until he followed it with, "Just wanted to make sure you were listening."

A few years ago when we moved our little family to New England, just a half hour from Concord where Walden Pond sparkles in its splendor, the site of Thoreau's cabin was at the top of my places-to-go list. This past summer we finally went with backpacks and sketchbooks in tow. It was captivatingly beautiful and, in spite of the many tourists and locals taking a swim, peaceful too. At the site of Thoreau's tiny cabin now sits a plaque that reads, "I went to the woods because I wished to live deliberately, to front only the essential facts of life, and see if I could not learn what it had to teach, and not, when I came to die, discover that I had not lived."

As we meandered over the trails through the woods, picking up acorns and sketching plants, I contemplated this quote. I kept thinking of the phrase "to live deliberately". It was not so foreign an idea. Though I have never secluded myself in the wilderness for a long period of time, I have come to understand what it means to choose to "live deliberately". Isn't that what we do as mothers? Otherwise, motherhood can become a drag, a bore, a leech on our lives.

In any vocation, to "live deliberately" becomes a daily commitment, a daily prayer. If a man who works at a job he hates for the sake of his family does not begin each day deliberately, the dull hours will poison his spirit. For a priest, a sister, a brother, I am sure it's no different. I find that on the mornings when I wake up begrudgingly, my lack of charity threatens to darken the whole day, not just for me but for my whole family. To "live deliberately" is to live thoughtfully and carefully. It's finding the beauty in life. It's making a daily choice and knowing that every action of each day is worth something significant—or rather, something eternal. And in those many thoughtless moments of weakness and failure, our apologies and reception of God's mercy can be a beautifully deliberate action.

Thoreau's noble goal to "front only the essential facts of life" has become clearer to me during these years of motherhood. As a child, I lived in a world full of distractions. Daily motherhood drained me in a most bizarre way—I was exhausted by boredom because I didn't understand the beauty in the "essential facts of life". Nurturing the essential facts of life in my children has helped me nurture those essential facts in my own life. The daily nothings are no longer trivial, but so very significant in their simplicity, something Thoreau knew he wouldn't see until the rest of life had been stripped away.

The last part touches me the most deeply: "and not, when I came to die, discover that I had not lived". The loud, blaring voices of any age insist that to live fully is to chase constantly after one's goals, never to stop pursuing, gaining, getting on top. Here in the constant hustle-bustle of the greater Boston area, it seems like no one ever slows down. No one can come to dinner or meet for coffee because the busyness of life is all-consuming. We are surrounded by a sparkling coastline, stunning fall leaves, feet of adventure-filled snow, and I wonder how much it can be appreciated when life is made such a maze. It's so refreshing to see Thoreau's thought immortalized at Walden, one of the gems of this beautiful area, hopefully inspiring more rest and contemplation. My hope is that my children will experience the riches of life and the beauty of God through our walks to the beach, our treasure-hunting walks, our liturgical feasts and daily family prayer, and the imaginative worlds my children create together within the reliable walls of our home.

Now that I've lived through a few bitter New England winters and mosquito-infested summers, I think it couldn't have been easy for Thoreau to live in a tiny cabin in the woods. But he did so to reach another level of understanding about the meaning of life. We mothers don't have to look very far to see the meaning of life, though it's all too easy to miss it in the wear and tear. God leads us in the life of motherhood so that we might learn to "live deliberately". We are given only the "essential facts of life" to rely on: God's patience, strength, and grace. And the great purpose is to learn what life has to teach—which seems to be boundless—and not, when we come to die, to realize we "have not lived". For to spend oneself nurturing life—in any vocation—is what God has called us all to.

— Lindsay Younce Tsohantaridis, Oregon

DOROTHY DAY AND THE CHALLENGE OF MERCY

"We Are All Responsible for All"

In his address to the U.S. Congress in 2015, Pope Francis highlighted Servant of God Dorothy Day among three other key figures in American history: Abraham Lincoln, Martin Luther King, Jr., and Thomas Merton. Each lived during difficult, dark, and pivotal chapters in our nation's history: the Civil War (Lincoln), the Great Depression (Day), legalized segregation and discrimination (King), and the Cold War (Merton). In the face of injustice and conflict, the pope tells us, their social action shaped "fundamental values which will endure forever in the spirit of the American people".[3]

The pope interwove the actions of these Americans with a litany of issues that our world faces today: violent religious conflict, modern slavery, a refugee crisis of historic proportions, the continuing practice of the death penalty, harm to the environment, and the identity of the family, among others. In the midst of chaos and disarray in a world that seems to grow ever distant from God, Christians may feel the temptation to retreat in fear into their families and parish communities, leaving the troubles of the public square to others.

According to Pope Francis, Christians, more than any other group in our world, must respond to the call to work actively in the public sphere in order to promote and secure the common good. As Pope Saint John Paul II reminds us, we have a moral duty to commit "to the good of all and of each individual, because we are *all* really responsible *for all*".[4] Thus, as lay Catholics especially, due to our unique place within the world, it is not enough for us merely to feel compassion for

[3] Francis, Visit to the Joint Session of the United States Congress (Washington, D.C., September 24, 2015).
[4] John Paul II, encyclical letter *Sollicitudo rei socialis* (December 30, 1987), no. 38, emphasis added.

> Love in action is harsh and dreadful when compared to love in dreams.
>
> — Fyodor Dostoevsky
>
> Zosima, *The Brothers Karamazov*

others and their misfortunes. We have to *commit* ourselves to improving the conditions of our neighbors because we are *responsible* for the well-being of *all* without exception. To involve ourselves in this way is not an option but an obligation issuing from our Christian identity. Given our place in the Jubilee of Mercy, as well as the Holy Father's reminder of Dorothy Day's importance to America, it is worth turning our attention to the works of mercy as the foundation of the call to serve our neighbors, especially the most vulnerable.

Reclaiming Social Justice: Conforming to God's Will

Pope Francis recalls the important, yet neglected values that Dorothy Day promoted: "social justice and the rights of persons".[5] In some Catholic circles, the term "social justice" has sadly become a negative and controversial term—a politically charged notion that strikes some as associated with secular social activism rather than with the fundamental call to live the gospel. Some American Catholics seem to have unwittingly excised from their conception of Catholicism the "inseparable bond between our faith and the poor",[6] perhaps due to the highly divisive and polarized political rhetoric in our country. Accordingly, many of us have left our poor—to whom "the Gospel is addressed in a special way"[7]—out of our faith, our hearts, our families, our churches, and our votes. This is nothing short of a scandal.

True justice, Pope Francis tells us, is "faithful abandonment of oneself to God's will".[8] Social justice, then, is nothing other than integrating God's will into our civic lives. What does this involve? Following his will that we care for the most vulnerable among us: the orphan, the widow, the poor. Jesus himself told us that it was by our love for one another that all would recognize us as his disciples (see Jn 13:35). This love is not abstract but is instead lived daily through *concrete* intentions, attitudes, and behaviors toward one another, such as feeding the hungry, sheltering the homeless, clothing the naked, and visiting the sick and the imprisoned (see Mt 25:31–46). It is by the corporal works of mercy that we Christians show our love for God, and they will be the basis on which we will be judged: "At the evening of life, we shall be judged on our love."[9] Hence, there is urgency for Catholics to reclaim social justice.

Works of Mercy as a Rule of Life

The Catholic Worker Movement was founded in 1933 by Dorothy Day and Peter Maurin in the midst of the Great Depression. In their houses of hospitality, they provided food, shelter, and clothing to the poor. Through their *Catholic Worker* newspaper, they shared ideas about many issues ranging from the works of mercy and the tradition of the saints to the evils of war. Day wrote that the works of mercy are "our program, our rule of life.... We must consider our daily occupation in the light of a work of mercy."[10] When Pope Francis announced the Jubilee of Mercy, he called on all to reflect on the corporal and spiritual works of mercy so as to "reawaken our conscience, too often grown dull in the face of poverty", as a way to "enter more deeply into the heart of the Gospel where the poor have a special experience of God's mercy".[11]

For some of us, the works of mercy are familiar. I have previously listed the corporal works of mercy.

[5] Francis, Visit to the Joint Session of the United States Congress.

[6] Francis, apostolic exhortation *Evangelii gaudium* (November 24, 2013), no. 48.

[7] Benedict XVI, Address to the Bishops of Brazil (May 11, 2007), no. 3.

[8] Francis, apostolic letter *Misericordiae vultus* (April 11, 2015), no. 20.

[9] *Catechism of the Catholic Church* 1022, quoting St. John of the Cross, *Dichos* 64.

[10] Dorothy Day, "On Pilgrimage", *The Catholic Worker*, May 1, 1946, https://catholicworker.org/424-html/.

[11] Francis, *Misericordiae vultus*, no. 15.

The spiritual works of mercy are to counsel the doubtful, instruct the ignorant, correct sinners, comfort the sorrowful, forgive all injuries, bear wrongs with patience, and pray for the living and the dead. But familiarity with a list makes it no less difficult to enact its items. Notice that all the works of mercy are directed toward *the other*. They cannot be done to or for oneself. They push us out of ourselves. Without them, Dorothy Day writes, our religion becomes "for ourselves alone, for our comfort or for our individual safety or indifferent custom".[12] Our faith, then, becomes devoid of meaning, because when we reject loving and serving one another, we reject loving and serving Christ (see Mt 25:31–46). Let us understand this plainly: our *salvation* hinges on the works of mercy. But we do not perform them so that we can be saved, as if they are a means to an end; rather, they are the faith that saves.

Works of Mercy for Busy Mothers

For us mothers, though, who is *the other* whom we should serve? As we serve our families, practicing the works of mercy may seem to be something that other people must do. We might worry that we don't have time for them. But the very first recipients of our mercy are with us on a daily basis: spouses who need to be forgiven, constant hurts that need to be borne, children who need to be corrected, aging parents who need to be cared for, distanced family members who need a phone call. We see the face and hear the voice of vulnerability

each day. Responding is no less difficult, yet it is required for our sanctification and theirs. It is perhaps harder to practice the works of mercy with those closest to us. Maybe we find it easier to dismiss them with our families, since it seems less heroic than serving the stranger. Or perhaps it is because the hurt and vulnerability—ours and theirs—is so near. Let us take courage from Pope Francis, who urges those families in which life is "imperfect or lacks peace and joy" to be "a sign of mercy and closeness",[13] to make a *daily* intention to practice the works of mercy in our homes.

Our busy homes, however, should not hinder us from serving others outside our families. We can still practice the works of mercy in creative ways. I have learned from and been inspired by the resourcefulness of other mothers who have found ways to serve those in need in their communities. They cook meals for families who have just welcomed babies, are recovering from surgery, or have lost a loved one. They organize drives to collect baby clothes and items for mothers-to-be who are in need. They counsel couples grieving the loss of a newborn child. Their ministry is vast, and the lives they

---

[12] Dorothy Day, "Aims and Purposes", *Catholic Worker*, February 1, 1940.
[13] Francis, apostolic exhortation *Amoris lætitia* (March 19, 2016), no. 5.

> We're called to speak to people to whom we often don't feel like speaking; to refrain from surrounding ourselves with people "just like us" whose thoughts, ideas, and actions we can more or less manage and control; to share not just with the poor, but with the rich, the mediocre, the irritating, the Republicans, the Democrats, because we never know who the poor are. We never know whose heart is hemorrhaging. We never know who needs a kind word, a smile, a helping hand.
>
> — Heather King
> *Shirt of Flame: A Year with Saint Thérèse of Lisieux*

have touched are countless. I have been deeply humbled by the service these women have given and continue to give to those in need around them. As channels of God's love and mercy, they show that a faith that serves extends well beyond one's home.

Let me conclude with a quote from Dorothy Day, which beautifully reflects this point:

I found out so many times, over and over again, that women especially are social beings, who are not content with just husband and family, but must have a community, a group, an exchange with others.... Young and old, even in the busiest years of our lives, we women especially are victims of the long loneliness....

We have all known the long loneliness and we have learned that the only solution is love and that love comes with community.[14]

— Katerina Deem, Pennsylvania

THE ECONOMY OF EMOTION

Some years ago, a friend told me she had given up her opinion for Lent. That's it: her opinion. I laughed at the simple absurdity of it at the time, but it didn't take more than a few minutes for it to really hit me how profoundly difficult that must have been. To refrain from offering one's thoughts on Facebook articles. To withhold one's two cents at dinner parties. To defer to another's preference on whether to get take-out Chinese or Mexican food. And on. I don't know about all of you, but opinions buzz around in my mind like fruit flies on a spotty banana. I used to think that not offering my opinion (solicited or not) would make me a terribly boring person.

But life has a way of broadening my perspective, and enough stupid things have come out of my mouth by now that I realize more and more how much wisdom and solace there is in simply remaining silent. It's taken a long time, but I've also realized that I don't need to jump into every conversation that I know a fair bit about. Unless directly asked, I no longer go on and on to people about which baby carrier is the best or which homeschooling curriculum I liked the most. Or even about liturgical discussions or faith debates I see happening. Do I have things to say? Sure. Ought I say them? Usually ... no.

However, just as I began to appreciate the value of keeping quiet on things, humbling myself enough to recognize that I don't have all the answers for all the people all the time (Sheesh, what a burden that would be!), I spent a lot of time with a friend who simply had no opinion. And that changed me.

I know this sounds strange because I was suspicious at first too. "What do you mean you don't care whether people come over or not? Whether we grill chicken or have soup for dinner? Whether you go to this party or not?" As someone whose natural temperament includes having strong opinions on nearly everything, I didn't understand. Was this her pious way of deferring to others just to be agreeable? Of being a martyr by dying to her own preferences? I tried fishing around, asking whether she was *sure*, whether she *truly* meant that she didn't have an opinion. And, more often than not, she was. It wasn't just a holy gimmick. This was unreal to me. After reflecting for some time on this, I pressed further to understand. She explained that she has trained herself not to have opinions on things deemed to be small matters in her mind. The goal wasn't to be a floppy, thin doormat. The goal was to save up her emotional energy for the things that were really important to her. She said, "It's just too much work to care about everything."

[14]Dorothy Day, *The Long Loneliness: The Autobiography of the Legendary Catholic Social Activist* (New York: Harper & Brothers, 1952), 157–58, 286.

Living an authentic Christian life requires fighting a lot of battles. It requires men and women to stand their ground and form strong convictions concerning what kind of spiritual, educational, medical, and social lives they want for their families. By not investing her mental energy in trivial things, my friend forged a cast-iron moral compass. She's as easygoing and accommodating as can be on what's for lunch or where to go on vacation. But she turns into a mother bear you don't want to meet if you cross her on something important. Adding wonder to all this, my friend also happens to have a heart for ministering to others that is practically unparalleled.

From her and my friend of Lenten silence (even if not giving an opinion comes with a wry, Cheshire Cat smile), I've learned something about economizing emotions. One of the beautiful side effects of this came unexpectedly to me. Being selective about where to invest my energy and attention not only has relieved mental stress but also offers something essential to others in my life.

By virtue of our baptism, we are mandated to respond to the call to evangelize others. *Evangelization is not optional.* For most of us, this is accomplished not by serving in foreign missions but by simply living an authentic life rich in the works of mercy. And do you know what the primary thing people in today's post-Christian world are starving for, after genuine love? Peace. We are a culture drowning in anxiety and chaos and arguments and noise. God cannot be heard, seen, or encountered in this climate. So few people have the calm, collected mental state necessary to minister to the emotional needs of others. Increasingly, so many of us are busy investing our emotional energy in everything else under the sun. When we practice a healthy economy of emotion by surrendering large parts of our opinion, we free up space in our minds for others. If we are so busy putting our energy into trivial things, we have no room at the inn of our hearts for others.

We don't have to care about everything. We can fulfill our essential duties of evangelization by caring primarily for others *and freeing up some space in our hearts to make a resting place for them.* Then, in that still, small space, Jesus Christ can be found.

— Ellie

THE VIRTUE OF MAIL

Who doesn't like getting mail? When I was younger, I picked up pen pals at every opportunity and tried to be a dutiful niece to my great-aunt, only to lag in my correspondence after a few months. It wasn't until after college that one of my friends molded me into a real letter writer. Jamie is one of those utterly dependable and orderly people—she goes to bed at a reasonable hour, exercises consistently, and writes to both grandmas every month.

When she left for grad school, Jamie sent back charming, well-crafted letters about her life, the books she was reading, and the social debates she was having with her roommates. It was all very different from my life as a new mom, and I was hooked. At first, I wrote to her so that she would write to me and so that I could hold forth on my philosophical opinions and the books I had read. After a few years, I decided to reach out to others. I started writing again to my great-aunt, now ninety-four and even happier to receive letters than she was twenty years ago. Another friend who moved away and married has started writing every other month, and I'm trying to keep up. And a few other people I write to every few months.

It's not a lot, really, but it does mean a great deal to the people who receive my letters. My great-aunt has said more than once that I am the only person who remembers to write, and since she broke her hip, she doesn't get out much.

Our visits to the nursing home have been spotty at best, in part because I don't want to bring any kid illnesses to those who are frail. Letter writing has become a very practical way for me to "visit" the sick and far away and to preserve some continuity with friends who have moved.

Not every relationship is the letter-writing kind. I call some friends a few times a year for a good long chat. But older people, and those in my generation who are more old-fashioned, really enjoy something they can keep and see.

I've noticed that the prettier the stationery is, the more eager I am to write, and the best time to do it is just after I open a new letter. If that doesn't work, I try to leave it out where I will notice it (i.e., have to pick it up).

I might spend an hour on several pages to a friend or ten minutes on a quick note to an honorary grandpa.

It's a spiritual work of mercy that doesn't require putting the kids in the car, and it works well even if the weather is bad. Of course, the kids are watching and developing the habit of writing to their grandparents, who love getting mail and writing back.

This is not meant to be another burden, another item for the list. But if this speaks to you, perhaps you know people feeling cut off from the world, and a letter would make their day.

— Jen Dunlap, California

HOLDING THE BLACKBIRD

One Lenten season, when Kevin … knelt with his hands outstretched and lifted up to heaven through the window of his hut, a blackbird settled in [his hand], as in her nest, and laid an egg. And so moved was the saint that in all patience … he remained, neither closing nor withdrawing his hand, but until the young ones were hatched, he held it out unwearied, shaping it for the purpose.[15]

Long ago—before I entered the land of Motherhood—I traveled through the bracken-coated hills of Wicklow, Ireland, with my husband. We stopped at wayside shrines as gypsy caravans passed us by, and we beheld the stone tower of Glendalough rising just over the crest of the wooded mountains. Slowly we traced our pilgrim's way through ruined chapels and uplands edged with hawthorn and fern, until we came

to a spot called Saint Kevin's Cell. These few ancient rocks, supposedly once forming the base of Saint Kevin's hermitage, lie deep in sylvan solitude overlooking the crystalline expanse of the lough, or lake, from which Saint Kevin's monastic settlement took its name. It was here that, as Seamus Heaney writes, Saint Kevin found himself "linked into the network of eternal life" as "in agony all the time" he held his hand "like a branch out in the sun and rain for weeks", "stiff as a crossbeam", as the blackbird made a nest out of his upturned palm.[16]

The imagery of the "crossbeam" and "branch", bringing to mind Christ, is deliberate. Through the gentle agony and monumental endurance of Kevin, life is given—the fledgling takes flight. God's very plan of creation is somehow consummated in the prayer of Kevin. In Kevin, we find a self-giving man fully participating in God's saving action, an efficacious prayer that

---

[15] Benedicta Ward, S.L.G., ed., trans., and comp., *Christ Within Me: Prayers and Meditations from the Anglo-Saxon Tradition* (Collegeville, Minn.: Liturgical Press, 2008), 67.

[16] Seamus Heaney, "St. Kevin and the Blackbird", *Opened Ground: Selected Poems 1966–1996* (New York: Farrar, Straus and Giroux, 1998), 384.

finds its fruition in its potential to give life, and life that descends (as in the blackbird nesting) and then reascends heavenward in the fledgling's flight, mirroring the action of the Divine Word itself. What a beautiful idyll of the spiritual life.

But now, back to reality. The life of a mother: toilet-training issues that don't seem to resolve, behavioral problems that show few signs of improvement, the everyday battles, the child who just doesn't seem to listen when we speak or seek to explain, the hard work that just doesn't seem to pay off, the hopeless endurance of a mother who can see no future beyond the endless child-rearing trials of the present. It is easy to feel our work will never come to fruition. Our patience alone cannot overcome the challenges we face. Motherhood seems, at times, an agonizing, prolonged toil that can only promise—perhaps rather emptily—the far-off fruits of its labor.

I feel this kind of hopeless impatience several times every day. Perhaps several times every minute.

But at such moments, I remember that I am holding the blackbird. My hands are weary, but it is God who shaped them for this purpose. My patience cannot see beyond the agony of my labor, however transient it may be. Yet patience is my prayer: patience with my child, with myself, and with the work God puts before me. There may be pain in this prayer of endurance, but it is exactly through such a prayer that life comes to fruition in us. Who, more than a mother, is "linked into the network of eternal life"? She will find her prayer of patient labor at last realized in an ascension—the ascension of the soul of her child as it takes flight into life, into the eternal sphere of life.

Alone and mirrored clear in love's deep river,
"To labour and not to seek reward," he prays,
A prayer his body makes entirely
For he has forgotten self.[17]

— Erin Brierley, Georgia

LIFE IN WATER

Through water we are made new.

My children splash in the warm pool I have filled for them by the blueberry bushes. Nearby there are tubs of water for peach washing and sorting. I like to watch the sunshine on the surface; the water bounces off the peach fuzz. My boys water the potted plants while my little one-and-a-half-year-old patters around the room, bringing me items for the kitchen, rearranging the magnets on the fridge, carrying her baby, singing her happy songs. We make pot after pot of tea, boiling the water, pouring the water, drinking the water.

We jump, ankle deep, into the waves of the ocean. We watch the canoes glide soundlessly across a lake. The boys collect driftwood from the shores of the Columbia and make rafts, singing sailor songs. Once my friends and I all headed up to Mount Hood with our children and drove up dirt roads just to go swimming in a crystal-clear alpine lake mirroring the blue of the sky.

We come from our mother's womb filled with water.

Hiking through the woods, my children and I cross over bridges above waterfalls. We run along the little trails finding sticks to take to the lake. The boys attach little ropes to the ends of their sticks and sit on the shore to pretend they are fishing, watching with admiration the nearby fishermen who sometimes kindly give them some bait, hooks, and tackle. We wade in the swimming holes, making paper boats.

"Mama, why is it raining?" "Because the clouds are full of water." The skies … they are grays and whites and sometimes a pale heron blue. Then the rain comes

[17] Heaney, "St. Kevin and the Blackbird", *Opened Ground*, 384.

down to water the soil; the lupines and daisies burst from the ground in color and strength. Water nourishes, it sustains; it's essential for life: life in our souls and life on our earth.

In the beginning, God created a roaring ocean … The spirit of God was moving over the water. It is in us, it is around us; it makes up more than half our planet.

The shoreline is made up of river stones in blues, greens, and grays. Little hands toss them into the moving water. Wading into the swirling, clear waters with our boots on, we are looking for beautiful stones and pebbles underfoot. Redwing blackbirds and finches are singing over in the blackberry hedges along the shore, and we build cairns marking our river adventure.

We're making little boats out of walnut shells: a toothpick for the mast and a birch leaf for the sail. The children throw sticks and leaves into the currents, watching them bob along downstream, chattering about where they will end up. Will they make it all the way to the Columbia, which travels over a thousand miles through desert and mountains, draining nearly all of Idaho; large portions of Oregon, Washington, and British Columbia; almost all of Montana west of the Continental Divide; and small portions of Wyoming?

Perhaps our sticks will even make it all the way to the Pacific Ocean! I wonder!

We cradle hot mugs in our hands, cozying up in coffee-shop armchairs, looking out the windows into the world of gray, watching a train pass by or the occasional barge transporting sawdust or lumber make its way down the Columbia River.

People confessed their sins and were baptized by Saint John in the Jordan River. Entering into our churches, we bless ourselves with holy water, a reminder of our own baptism.

There is the washing of the floors. Homemade broth simmers on the stovetop; the kettle boils, the lentils are bubbling, and steam fills the room, fogging up the windows. I fill up my kitchen sink with warm water, giving my babies cozy baths while I do my steam ironing on cold mornings. Candles flicker on the windowsill, and beyond this window birds alight on the dripping branches of trees; raindrops splash on the window. There is the washing of laundry and warm, heavy quilts after a hot bath. "Mama, I am thirsty". I give them water to drink.

Rest on us, Holy Spirit, for you are the Heavenly Dew.

— Sia

PLANTING CHRIST

Cheerful bird songs herald the onset of spring: a time of renewal, new growth, and returning migrators. Gardeners till, amend, plant, and wait. What do we plant in the garden of our minds and souls and in the minds and souls of our families? Do we wait patiently for the fruit, as Mary did? Mary waited patiently, hopefully—without doubt, despair, or question for the manifestation of God's promises—as she washed the next dish, changed the next diaper, prepared the next meal.

Do we embrace the growth that comes in darkness through brokenness?

We see tender green shoots peek up from black soil. Eventually, a daffodil blooms. A tomato ripens. Growth that began in darkness. Hidden. Mysterious.

Miraculous. The seed pod broken, split by the press of new life, erupts forth into our field of view.

We humans begin with a joining of simple cells in complex beings. Many divisions and multiplications later, new life emerges from the darkness of the womb. Even our spiritual growth can be borne from the darkness of brokenness and suffering. God's light shines through our fractures, leading to the abundance of harvest. So, too, the brokenness of Christ's body, hanging bloodied and spent on the Cross, leads to the everlasting abundance of salvation.

What was Mary thinking, looking at her Son lifeless on the Cross? Was she able to anticipate with joy the glory that was to come? And if not, still she waited patiently in darkness, and "kept all these things, pondering them in her heart" (Lk 2:19).

I want to plant seeds of bounty in my own heart and mind and in the hearts and minds of my children, moment by moment, decision by decision. I often think of Christ's generosity and graciousness, even as his body stumbled, responding in gratitude to Veronica's kindness, exuding power and grace even as he was dying. Veronica's simple act of charity elicited a miracle: Christ's image in cloth, another lasting reminder of glory shining in the midst of brokenness.

How do we manifest Christ's glory as we stumble through our days? Are we able to respond with patience and generosity to seemingly unending interruptions and requests while we try to multitask? Can we draw near in our hearts to our loved ones, even as the dishes remain undone, the toilets yet unscrubbed? Can we practice the Ignatian way of spiritual detachment, recognizing that we can serve God in all moments and circumstances, acknowledging with peaceful spirits that it matters not whether we serve God in quiet prayer or when our quiet prayer is interrupted?

How are we living out the Eucharist in our own lives, and how can we pour more of the Risen Christ into our world?

We can carve out time with our Savior. Perhaps we can implement an order to our days that begins with prayer, tithing the first moments of our day to our Lord. We can lace the day with prayer: a decade of the Rosary here, a decade of the Rosary there, the

> To believe yourself brave is to *be* brave; it is the one only essential thing.
>
> —Mark Twain
> Louis de Conte, *Joan of Arc*

Chaplet of Divine Mercy, prayer instead of music on a commute, Adoration. We cannot encounter Christ without becoming transformed by him. Little by little, we may realize some tendencies softening. A tendency to respond to interruptions with frustration evolves into tenderness that creates a moment of connected grace. As we lose ourselves in Christ, we find our truest being—one created for communion with our Lord, created for communion with others, created for love, peace, joy, and hope. Let us encourage one another in prayer, dear sisters, so we can shine Christ's light to those around us, despite our imperfections. Because we know, from the lives of many of the saints, that sometimes Christ's light shines most brightly through fractures—brilliantly displaying his healing and redemptive power. Come, sisters, together let us be salt of the earth, spiritual bread for the world, physical manifestations of God to those around us.

— Michelle M. Montalbano, Oklahoma

THE HIDDEN SAINT

BEFORE·THY· CROSS· WE BOW

She walked into the nearly empty church wearing some heavily worn, solid-colored comfort sneakers that are all the rage in elderly circles. She was a tiny Filipino woman in her late sixties or so, and she slowly shuffled down the aisle with an obvious pain in her hip. I watched with curiosity; it was later in the evening, and I was glad to be jolted awake during my Adoration hour. This woman was a welcome distraction from

my feeble and failed attempts at deep thought and prayer.

She bowed reverently toward the tabernacle before heading toward the side altar with a statue of Mary. Once there, she didn't do what I expected (light a candle, kneel down and pray fervently, perhaps for some wayward child, as I often see many other women do). She pulled out a plastic grocery bag from her sweater. *Why the sweater?* I wondered; it had been a hot day and was muggy in the church. (There was no hope of dutifully attempting a prayerful state now; she had all my attention.) She very delicately peeled back the plastic bag to reveal a cheap spritzer bottle filled with water. And then what she did nearly brought me to tears. She misted Our Lady's roses. A few vases of flowers in front of the statue contained flowers that were not quite in their prime, and this woman brought them a drink. She very gently moved the blooms and sprayed each flower in a determined but incredibly tender way.

When finished, she conscientiously put the spray bottle back in the plastic bag, trying to minimize the crinkling sound, and moved back toward the center aisle. After bowing again to our Lord, she tottered back out of the church and left me alone with my thoughts. I was fully awake now.

I don't know what this woman's home life is like, what relationships she has, or anything else about her. In fact, I don't remember ever seeing her again at our church. But I haven't been able to stop thinking about her. She is how I envision so many saints—living hidden lives of holiness. It wasn't the greatness of her act that left me floored (How hard is it to wet some roses?); it was the apparent and abundant love with which she did it. This beautiful woman taught me something very valuable in that hour as she embodied a quotation from Saint Teresa of Avila that I'd heard before but struggled to internalize in a meaningful way: "The important thing [in prayer] is not to think much but to love much." So many of my efforts in dedicated prayer have felt so dry, distracted, and fruitless. But God is not measuring the amount of profound reflections and beautiful sentiments we have—far from it. He is simply measuring our love. In seeing that little, nameless bit-of-a-woman offer what she did, *how she did*, I am certain I witnessed one of the greatest acts of love I had seen in a long time.

— Ellie

THE LITTLE WAY OF ENVIRONMENTALISM

Today, I grabbed lunch out. I wanted something healthier than a drive-through burger, so I parked, got my four little kids out of the van, and *actually went inside to eat* at a fast-casual local franchise known for its high-quality ingredients and healthy menu. I ordered at the counter, and when my order came up, I was brought five plastic plates with covers and five full sets of plastic utensils (even though I was dining in) to toss in the garbage when we were finished. The food was delicious, but the whole time I felt a knot in the pit of my stomach because of the plastic waste I'm responsible for, not only for that lunch, but pretty much every day.

If you're tempted to shrug your shoulders, give me a minute. We Catholics promote an anti-contraception model of sexuality that leads to children—often many children. If the whole world were to live a Catholic lifestyle (as we wish it would), it wouldn't take long for our population numbers to explode exponentially, which was in fact the very design of our Creator: that we *go forth and multiply and fill the face of the earth*. Does our planet have room for many more of us? Yes. Does our Western disposable way of life? No. Those in the overpopulation camp want to make us believe the problem is the number of people, but at least for now—and most honest people acknowledge this—the problem is sustainability. People managed to leave barely a trace for the first 5,800 years of civilization; it's only recently that our lives on earth have been in contest with the health of the planet. It seems obvious to me that Catholics, *because* of our anti-contraceptive worldview, along with our love for God and understanding of stewardship, bear a responsibility for leadership in the space of environmental dialogue and practice. Yet I've been surprised more than a few times to hear negative reactions from Catholics on this topic, as if somehow a passion for the environment means a lessening of the importance of the pro-life movement or a dangerous flirtation with liberal politics. On the contrary, properly ordered environmentalism is an extension of pro-life ideology and can serve as a "shared good", a wonderful bridge to unite us to those with whom we differ on other political matters. It's a shame to let the liberals own the cause of stewardship—all people should be stewards, members of the Church first and foremost.

The Catholic Church is the greatest nonpolitical institution with global influence that exists. Individual countries have their own economic interests to lobby, but the Church is able to care for the whole world with a freedom and godly freshness that political institutions lack. Joel Staliton, acclaimed sustainable pig farmer, holds that if Christians could support the environmental movement, they would "own the moral high ground". This is true, though making thoughtful changes in our lives is worth doing for its own sake, whether our liberal friends see it as us taking the "moral high ground" or not. It's worth doing because God loves this place even more than we do. Through the Incarnation, God dignified mankind, and in turn all of creation—in fact *all matter*. So we can say with theological confidence that "matter matters". And even though this world is destined to pass away, I'd like the Weaver to be the one to sever the last thread, in his time, and not rend the beautiful tapestry prematurely due to our selfish habits.

To change our culture from one that is indulgent and wasteful to one that is thoughtful and sustainable feels only slightly more impossible than changing those very same qualities in myself. This is where the Little Way of Saint Thérèse can come to the rescue. Saint Thérèse pioneered the thought that for many "little souls", it can feel impossible to climb the mountain of holiness. The answer she provided to this impossibility is to remain little; she said it is our *very littleness* that keeps us close to Christ and allows us to be picked up by him, letting his arms act as an elevator to draw us to himself. If we remain little and confident and trusting, he fixes the brokenness that we cannot fix, and he solves the problem that we cannot solve, namely the problem of our holiness. But here's the catch: just because we have an impossible task before us and we desperately need God's help, that doesn't mean we can sit back and do nothing. We must continually attempt to climb the first step of the mountain, even though we fail repeatedly. Father Michael Gaitley boils down the method of Saint Thérèse in this simple phrase: "Keep trying, and keep trusting."

Living a modern, sustainable life feels nearly impossible to many of us. Our society's constructs for daily living are set up to benefit the marketplace, not the environment. Yet despite the seeming impossibility, we must keep trying, in small ways every day, to reduce our consumption and waste. And though we fail, we must always begin again, praying that God will help us, trusting that he will bless our humble efforts and come to our aid to fix this problem that we cannot fix ourselves. This is the little way of environmentalism. Our world is God's world. Our problems are his problems. If we remain docile, humble, and eager, in the end it is he who will save us; he always does.

With that in mind, let's now look at some ways we can try to make our households "greener". Please, as

I like trees because they seem more resigned to the way they have to live than other things do. I feel as if this tree knows everything I ever think of when I sit here. When I come back to it, I never have to remind it of anything; I begin just where I left off.

— Willa Cather
Marie, O Pioneers!

part of the little way, be content with small efforts. A friend of mine recently shared this phrase: *slow growth is sincere growth*. Try to work on one habit at a time, get it under your belt, and then move on to another.

(Disclaimer: I've created the following list as a nonprofessional earth resident. I don't claim to be an authority on the subject, so please forgive any underemphasis or omissions. I consider these practices among the most doable steps for a busy mother, and they reflect the changes I'd like to make in my own life.)

1. *Start seeing plastic as the enemy.* You may not think about this often, but plastic is a major problem. Yes, it's durable, convenient, and cheap, but the problem is that *it doesn't go away*. Think of it as forever-waste. Aluminum, paper, and glass, tossed in the sea or buried in a landfill, will eventually rust or erode, but the lifespan of plastic is almost endless.[18]

Last summer I took my baby to the beach for the first time; she had just started to walk, and I was excited for her to discover the sand and the waves and to feel the wind tickle her face. As I sat on the sand, I looked around and saw a gorgeous horizon of ocean—and … trash. It wasn't just a piece; about every square foot or two there was something: a bread tag, a juice box straw, a granola bar wrapper, a gum wrapper. And most of it was plastic. I realized that this was part of my one-year-old's landscape and that she would likely never know an unpolluted beach.

Virtually every piece of plastic that has ever been made still exists in some shape or form, and most of it has been made in the past twenty years.[19] You might think recycling somehow absolves us of our plastic addiction, but according to *National Geographic*, 82 percent of plastic isn't even recycled.[20] Think about it: How many things do you buy that are made of recycled plastic compared to first-generation plastic? Exactly.

Miles of garbage patches exist in every major ocean, wildlife is suffering, and plastic has even made its way into the human bloodstream. Bisphenol A, or BPA, a chemical used in the manufacture of plastics with overwhelming links to poor health, is found in 95 percent of Americans, with children having the highest levels. It has even been found in breast milk.[21]

The answer to this growing problem is to try to phase this material out of our lives, as much as possible. So let's try to say no to single-use plastic, and a hard maybe to any other plastic. This is perhaps the most difficult thing to do, as plastic is the hallmark of convenience and it's hard to choose any lifestyle change that requires more time and effort. Here are some things to keep in mind:

- Pay attention to packaging. Whenever possible, choose products with paper or glass packaging instead of plastic. Ask for your meat wrapped in paper at the butcher counter; look for compostable garbage bags and produce bags, or use paper bags; and buy in bulk when you can.
- Prepare home-cooked meals. (The more we make from scratch, the less packaging we use.) When you do need to pick up convenience food, be on the lookout for options that use better packaging.
- Thrift an extra set of flatware for parties. (Occasional paper plates are forgivable, but plastic cutlery should be avoided.)
- Here's a hard one: curb your Amazon addiction. Sorry to say this, but until Amazon stops using the ridiculous plastic pillows for box packaging, they should be patronized only sparingly.

Lastly, kindly remember that the laws of human charity supersede the laws of good stewardship. If your host hands you an hors d'oeuvre on a plastic plate,

[18] Laura Parker, "We Made Plastic. We Depend on It. Now We're Drowning in It", *National Geographic* (June 2018): 46, https://www.nationalgeographic.com/magazine/article/plastic-planet-waste-pollution-trash-crisis.

[19] Ibid., 59.

[20] Ibid., 46.

[21] "BPA in Food", Environmental Defense Fund, April 17, 2024, https://www.edf.org/bpa-food#:~:text=BPA%20exposure%20is%20widespread.,amniotic%20fluid%2C%20and%20breast%20milk.

please be gracious. We are all, as Sia says, "blundering toward heaven", and people are always more important than things.

I should note that for years now I've been trying to eliminate plastic packaging from my life completely, but I still can't seem to do it. However, a 50 percent consumption decrease is still significant. So remember the Little Way, keep trying, and don't get discouraged.

2. *Buy used.* Whenever you buy a new product, it has to be manufactured somewhere. That manufacturing almost always creates pollution. Although it is often out of sight for us, others around the world suffer its effects. I have a friend who travels to China regularly, and his pictures of the permanent dismal industrial haze are enough to convert anyone who overconsumes. The people who live in Beijing are breathing air with small-particle pollution forty times over the international safety standard. These pollutants are now beginning to waft across the Pacific and harm the air quality in our own country. Advertisers don't want you to think about this, but try to see through the smoke and mirrors of the Target dollar aisle and just see the smokestacks. Let's be more resourceful by shopping Craigslist, eBay, and our local thrift stores before buying new.

3. *Regift without shame, even used items.* One thing I think we need to get over in social etiquette is this idea that unless something has a tag or is in new packaging, it is somehow not a real gift. We need to get past this unfortunate misconception and not apologize about it. Give a houseplant or inscribe a used book for a lovely, personal gift. A sweet thrifted baby quilt or used children's cowboy boots can make a darling present, or you can say, "I've always loved this framed picture; I thought you would like it too."

I love to reference the writings of the visionary Blessed Anne Catherine Emmerich,[22] and according to her, Our Lady was the ultimate regifter! In the first few weeks and months surrounding our Savior's infancy, many gifts were given by the shepherds, and later many more by the Wise Men (beyond gold, frankincense, and myrrh). With loving, perfect graciousness, Our Lady received each gift; and with humble charity, she gave many of them away to poor travelers who passed through. (This is especially true of the shepherds' gifts; the Wise Men's vestments, thuribles, and carpets were mostly saved by Saint Anne and used in the early Church Masses.) When someone gives you a gift, try to imitate Our Lady's graciousness and also her simplicity, keeping only what is necessary in the spirit of poverty.

Here are a few more ideas to consider:

- Use cloth diapers. It is not that bad, I promise! You'll save money and you might even learn to like it. Disposable diapers were invented not for daily use but as a diaper to use when traveling. We would do well if we could go back to using them sparingly, in times of sickness, travel, or family upheaval.

- Compost. Chickens are the best composting machines, but even without chickens, or gardens, composting is still totally doable. I knew a family that had a large crate box without a bottom in their yard. They threw in the food scraps, covered them with hay, and went about their lives. With decomposition, it never seemed to fill up all the way, and they were able to reduce their household waste significantly.

- Educate yourself about where your food comes from. Plenty of great documentaries reveal the evils of the practices employed in the corporate food industry. Whenever possible, buy local, shop organic, and support sustainable farming practices.

- Pick up trash. It's everywhere. I knew an old, dear, saintly farmer who when walking around town would quietly bend over, pick up litter, and put it in his pocket to throw away later. I sometimes try to imitate Mr. Stehly and imagine a plastic soda lid stuck in the bushes as a soul being rescued from purgatory. We can use any kind of sacrifice to save souls, and this little practice is a great way to labor for souls and make the earth more beautiful at the same time.

- Hike more. This might not have a direct impact on the environment, but it will on your perspective and on your spiritual life. First, it quietly reminds us that all our measly efforts are important because

[22] Specifically *The Complete Visions of Anne Catherine Emmerich*, vol. 2, part 7.

this planet is so darn beautiful (far better than Mars). Second, it brings us closer to the source of beauty, God himself: "I will allure her, and bring her into the wilderness, and speak tenderly to her" (Hos 2:14). Why were the Fatima children, Saint Bernadette, Saint Juan Diego, King David, the LaSalette children, and the Bethlehem shepherds chosen to bear messages to the world? Maybe because they were listening. Four out of the six groups of people were actual shepherds who spent most of their time in the hills, and six out of six were outdoors when they received their heavenly messages. God has good things in store for us if we take out the earbuds and listen for his voice in the wind and trees.

Mothers are busy. For many of us, survival mode is a regular state of life. We all have our days when our environmental transgressions are more than we can count. But despite this, we must not get discouraged. We must daily do what we can and keep trying. And when we fail, we must trust the loving power of God to turn all things, even our failings, to the good, as he has promised to do for those who love him.

— Hope

LESSONS OF SEABIRDS

I climbed over the sea break wall
Where rocks drop black and bare—
Seabirds are here with spreading sails
Riding the currents of the air.
The wind is bold enough to throw
Me off my feet and whips
My hair into my eyes.
One knee is bloody where wind and
    sands
Conspired to take me by surprise.
A seagull hangs overhead
On an invisible tether,
The only object standing still

In the wildness and wanton will
Of Atlantic weather.
She ascends the windy skies
By easing up. She stoops to rise.
The secret of all life
Is buried deep in seagull brains.
While I, evolved like-unto-god, am wife
To treacherous weather,
And strain against the currents of time,
And pump my arms against the wind,
And curse the sideways rains.

— Mary

DANCING FOR JOY

There are three things my daughter cannot live without: eating, breathing, and *dancing*. Sleeping is most definitely optional. While she was still in the womb, her legs were constantly in motion. As a newborn in her hospital bassinet, her limbs flew faster than a gerbil's wheel. I leaned over to my husband, whose makeshift bed sat next to mine in the recovery room, and said with satisfaction, "See! I *told* my mother it wasn't the hot sauce. *That* was why I had indigestion all this time! Those legs are never still!"

And it's true. My daughter has not kept still since she was born. Perhaps not since she was conceived.

The inmost significance of the exaggerated value which is set upon hard work appears to be this: man seems to mistrust everything that is effortless; he can only enjoy, with a good conscience, what he has acquired with toil and trouble; he refuses to have anything as a gift.

The vacancy left by absence of worship is filled by mere killing of time and by boredom, which is directly related to inability to enjoy leisure; for one can only be bored if the spiritual power to be leisurely has been lost. There is an entry in Baudelaire's Journal Intime that is fearful in the precision of its cynicism: "One must work, if not from taste then at least from despair. For, to reduce everything to a single truth: work is less boring than pleasure."

Leisure is only possible when a man is at one with himself, when he acquiesces in his own being.

—Josef Pieper
excerpts from *Leisure: The Basis of Culture*

I've always thought it would be rather useful if she could be hooked up to some kind of power station, her legs moving like windmills at double speed, solving the world's energy crisis. At nine months, she was walking, and a few months later, she was kicking and pointing along with the ballet dancers she saw on my workout video. One of her first words was "grand battement", and now at age two, her days are filled with emulating Jean Butler's *Riverdance* moves and practicing her own unique version of the *pas de deux* from Act 2 of *Giselle*. For my daughter, dance is the breath of life, and it's always been that way.

In celebration of her second birthday, we took our "Dancing Queen" on a trip to Orlando. The first port of call was the Basilica of the National Shrine of Mary, Queen of the Universe for evening Mass. The basilica was cast in shade. The candles were aglow inside, the dim lighting outside the church barely illuminated the palms that whispered on the breeze, and the exotic flowers whose sultry scent permeated the nighttime air were heavy with humidity. An imposing statue of Saint Michael spread his wings beneath the moon above, staunchly defending the cross he held, while nearby, a smaller statue was illuminated. It was a new installment, depicting the conversion of Saint Paul,

flinging up his arms in astonishment as he beheld the vision of Christ on the road to Damascus. My daughter approached the statue and flung up her arms too, and then she followed through with one of her legs curved gracefully behind in an *attitude derrière*. It was clear she thought Saint Paul was dancing.

As I watched her, joy manifesting in her movements, I reflected on my own conversion. If you saw Jesus and were converted, wouldn't you dance? Dance is joy. Joy is the obvious response to conversion. At least, it should be. As this all happened on the feast of Candlemas, the feast of the Presentation of the Lord in the Temple, I immediately thought of David, dancing and singing out his praise to God in the presence of the Ark of the Covenant. *If psalms can be danced as well as sung*, I thought to myself, *my daughter will never have trouble praying!*

In her joy and grace, my daughter offered me the inspiring example of what it means to offer ourselves to God, as Jesus was offered in the temple, as Mary offered herself as handmaiden, as David offered his praises. Offering is not an act of dismal piety, joyless in its resigned air of morbid self-sacrifice. Offering joyfully to God means being just what we are, just what he created us to be, "catching fire" like kingfishers in all their natural radiance. "Perfection", wrote Saint Thérèse, "consists in ... being what He wills us to be".[23] Beatitude is obtained not so much through the rejection of self but through the joyful realization of the truth of ourselves.

As a former atheist, I'm familiar with the arguments commonly used against Christianity and religion in general. One accusation is that religion makes martyrs out of sensible people. Another is that it sucks all the joy out of life. Yet another—which has indeed caused some of my Christian acquaintances to turn against the faith of their fathers—is that the Christian God is an Old Testament Titan, always demanding something from mortal men, expecting to be obeyed and served by human beings who relinquish both their freedom and dignity through that very act of divine service.

But what does service to God really mean? The God we proclaim—the God of love, the loving Creator—calls us to *serve* through the freedom of active participation in his creative work, rather than through the passivity of *servitude*. If God has joy in his work, shouldn't we, who are made in God's image, also be joyous?

Pope Francis has recently been at pains to reaffirm the joyful message of Christianity and to warn Christians against sour-faced self-righteousness. And who could be more sour-faced and self-righteous than mothers? Many of us, if my friends and I are any indication—at least once, twice, or a hundred times a day—bemoan the martyrdom of motherhood. As Christians and as mothers, we are constantly at odds with ourselves, strained with self-sacrifice and desirous of personal fulfillment. We want to serve God and do his will. But what does that mean? Is "I want" an ugly phrase, to be reserved only for vehement secularists? What happens to *my* will when I say "Thy will be done"? These questions ought to provoke further exploration and introspection in each of us.

I think again of my daughter, dancing because she must dance, joyful because she is dancing, happy to be exactly what God made her to be—herself. The self that you are is part of God's plan. The self does not have to get in the way of God but can be that coworker as well as that coheir who brings joy to the heart of God.

Following our instinct—prayerfully clinging to what is good and true and doing what gives us genuine joy—seems to me to be as near as we can get to serving God. While our God is the God who suffered on the Cross, he is also the God who loves to be proclaimed with the psalmist's dance and song. The apparent paradox is illusory when one considers that love feels joy in all its actions: it rejoices to suffer for the Lord as well as to praise the Lord in ever new and more radiant ways. The question we must ask ourselves is, What song is love leading *me* to sing? I ponder this question within myself as I pray with these words:

Joy is the Song of my Soul
My life is a canticle of Praise
To the One who fills all my being,
I sing out my happiness:
I am alive in God.

— Erin Brierley, Georgia

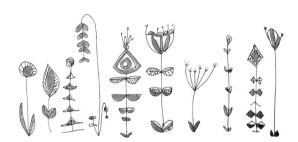

---

[23] Thérèse of Lisieux, *Story of a Soul: The Autobiography of Saint Thérèse of Lisieux*, trans. John Clarke, O.C.D, 3rd ed. (Washington, D.C.: ICS Publications, 1996), 14.

ONLY FOR TODAY

1. Only for today, I will seek to live the livelong day positively without wishing to solve the problems of my life all at once.

2. Only for today, I will take the greatest care of my appearance: I will dress modestly; I will not raise my voice; I will be courteous in my behavior; I will not criticize anyone; I will not claim to improve or to discipline anyone except myself.

3. Only for today, I will be happy in the certainty that I was created to be happy, not only in the other world but also in this one.

4. Only for today, I will adapt to circumstances, without requiring all circumstances to be adapted to my own wishes.

5. Only for today, I will devote ten minutes of my time to some good reading, remembering that just as food is necessary to the life of the body, so good reading is necessary to the life of the soul.

6. Only for today, I will do one good deed and not tell anyone about it.

7. Only for today, I will do at least one thing I do not like doing; and if my feelings are hurt, I will make sure that no one notices.

8. Only for today, I will make a plan for myself: I may not follow it to the letter, but I will make it. And I will be on guard against two evils: hastiness and indecision.

9. Only for today, I will firmly believe, despite appearances, that the good Providence of God cares for me as no one else who exists in this world.

10. Only for today, I will have no fears. In particular, I will not be afraid to enjoy what is beautiful and to believe in goodness. Indeed, for twelve hours I can certainly do what might cause me consternation were I to believe I had to do it all my life.

— Saint John XXIII
"The Decalogue of Pope Saint John XXIII"

GARGOYLES

I am a stone carver,
A woodworker
Building gargoyles in the night
Hand unseen but foretold
In facades that will proclaim
For ages untold
The glory of the one

Who made the hands
Who made the stone.
And I?
But a worker in the field
Ready to go
Upon the call
Of him who made me

Him who called the stones
To cry out
All is good
All is won.

— Margaret Ryland, Illinois

DWELL

MARTHA AND MARY

THE DIGNITY AND DRUDGERY OF HOUSEWORK

When we think about the big picture, it's easy to see how motherhood is a wonderful and worthy vocation: tending beautiful, fresh souls; forming responsible citizens; partaking in God's creativity through the conception of children. But it's so easy to get mired in the details. All that sleep deprivation. And the housework. How is it that dishes breed and multiply when your back is turned? And then there's my white plastic kitchen floor that has to be wiped and rewiped all day. (Ladies, why would anyone put white plastic flooring in a kitchen? Don't they know what people *do* in kitchens?) Sometimes these chores make me feel resentful because unlike, say, reading to a child or building something for the house, they don't have a permanent result. They don't seem to serve any purpose except maybe preventing dreadful diseases from breeding in my kitchen.

The endless rounds of dishes, the endless sweeping and wiping of floors: these are the chores that, like the poor, are always with us. If I am not careful, they can embitter my heart till I am grumbling like Martha in the Gospel, "It's just not fair! Why should I spend my precious hours and waste my expensive education standing in front of a sink, folding laundry, peeling vegetables?"

It is a first-world problem, I admit, especially in light of the more heroic and difficult things mothers do—like childbirth, for instance. But so many hours of our day go into these brainless tasks, and it's easy to lose sight of their importance. We need to know that our hours are not being wasted, that we are making a difference in the world!

The solution, of course, is very simple. It lies in converting our hearts so that we can be both Martha and Mary, sitting at the Master's feet *and* getting supper on the table. Serving, but serving with love. Putting on the toddler's shoes with sweet patience, rather than "Ack! Push your foot in! *Push* it!"

When I was sixteen, I stayed at Madonna House, a community of laypeople who live and work together while serving the (mostly inner-city) poor. Madonna House has built a whole spirituality around work, teaching that the "duty of the moment" is God's very will for a person, that work is a holy thing even if it's not personally fulfilling. I remember a lovely woman named Kathleen pinning back her long dark hair and rolling up her sleeves to work. "You know," she said, smiling, "I love cleaning. When we clean, we are literally transforming the world. We are helping to restore it to Christ." She began to wipe down the industrial kitchen so gracefully, so peacefully.

"Any work you do for a selfless purpose, without thought of profit, is actually a form of prayer.... Do we not hallow places by our very commitment to them?" These words might sound like they're from a modern saint, but they are from the secular vegetarian cookbook *The New Laurel's Kitchen*.[1] When I read these words, they sent a shiver down my spine, resonating with the very fibers of my Catholic soul. To "hallow a place", to make it holy. Surely we can make our homes holy by the attitude we bring to them, turning the sink and floors into altars, the food and laundry into sacramentals? This is the permanent gift we desire so much to give, the big picture.

Long after our children have forgotten whether the laundry got put away or whether supper was peanut butter sandwiches, they will remember their mother. Was she always fretting and anxious, grumpy and irritable? Or was she peaceful and kind because she knew that love was more important than laundry?

— Mary

[1] Laurel Robertson, Carol Flinders, and Brian Ruppenthal, *The New Laurel's Kitchen: A Handbook for Vegetarian Cookery and Nutrition* (Berkeley, Calif.: Ten Speed Press, 1976), 28, 30.

KITCHEN PRAYERS

These past couple of years, I have acutely felt that knock-you-down desperation for grace: *O God, I can't do this! I am frail, I am hurting, I am ill-equipped for the daily battles. I need you.* I am a weary pilgrim, and my need for God is on the forefront of my mind. Every day I feel that I am at the beginning of a long and very rocky—though beautiful—journey. Like an addict on his knees, or a man lost in his travels turning to a map, or a starving person begging for food, I am there too: genuflecting in my heart as I wash the dishes; kneeling at the tabernacle; bowing down in my soul as I bathe my children; saying novenas while I sip my herbal tea in bed at night, eyes closed. And my prayer becomes, *I cannot do this alone. I can do it only with your help. Give me the strength to bear my crosses. Give me the strength to become the woman you want me to become. I am nothing without you.*

I have been talking to God day in, day out, ever since I was a child, yet I am still just a baby—a mere beginner! One thing I have done over the course of all my years of adulthood (inspired by many others before me, to be sure) has been to jot down some notes on little pieces of paper, sticking them here and there about the house—especially in places where I stand for long periods of time, like at the sink as I wash the dishes. The writings may be little prayers, passages from Scripture, a lovely poem, something I must be reminded of each day, words that bring hope,

parts of a favorite litany—any phrases or word clusters that inspire, lift me up, and call me onward. I stick them to my bathroom mirror, the closet door, the kitchen sink window, all at eye level. I love these little reminders, these little bursts of life and hope in my busy days.

Another great thing about these inspiring words being visible throughout my home is that they may strike a chord at a family dinner or with friends who are over for coffee or Sunday brunch. They may end up taking home completely new food for thought, as I have often done when visiting my own friends. My daughter's godmother had, taped to her kitchen cupboard, a good quote from Pope Saint John Paul II: "Children must grow up with a correct attitude of freedom with regard to material goods, by adopting a simple and austere lifestyle and being fully convinced that 'man is more precious for what he is than for what he has.'"[2]

Another dear friend has an excerpt from Saint Faustina's diary taped to her wall right next to the window above the kitchen sink where she spends hours on end each week washing dishes (don't we all!) and watching her young children play outside. Do a Google search for the whole entry later, but sip your tea and let this little bit marinate in your heart for now: "Help me, O Lord, that my eyes may be merciful, so that I may never suspect or judge from appearances, but look

---

[2] John Paul II, apostolic exhortation *Familiaris consortio* (November 22, 1981), no. 37.

> Remember that the mind can quite well be elevated to God while the body attends to material matters. Therefore, don't distress yourself if you are unable to carry out your usual spiritual exercises due to a great deal of work. Endeavor, without wearying yourself, to do what you can, and Jesus, who looks into the depths of the heart, will be pleased with you.
>
> — Padre Pio

for what is beautiful in my neighbors' souls and come to their rescue."[3]

Taped to my kitchen window currently is this little prayer that I wrote one day when I needed to be reminded to see others as Christ sees them, to love them even more. It is taped directly above three holy card icons of Our Lady, Christ, and Saint Anne. The prayer reads, "Lord, give us good cheer and the strength to love each other as You have loved us."

Underneath a friend's tiny kitchen crucifix are three items: quotes from one of her favorite saints, Saint Francis de Sales; "SERVIAM!"; and the wise, famous words of Saint Teresa of Calcutta: "For love to be real, it must cost; it must hurt; it must empty us of self."

Age quod agis is one of Ursula Crowell's very favorite reminders. It is the motto of Portland's Jesuit High School, and it translates "Do well what you do." Since her introduction to Jesuit, a once-upon-a-time all-boys high school where many of her friends attended, it still strikes a chord and has resounded in her heart and mind throughout these many years. Also, she had the inside of her husband's wedding band engraved with *Ad Majorem Dei Gloriam*—"For the greater glory of God"—another beautiful reminder to keep our hearts fixed on God's glory.

A priest that was very formative in Hope's life had taped to his kitchen sink, "God is to be found among the pots and pans" (Saint Teresa of Avila). She doesn't even need to see the words anymore to remember that quote whenever she does the dishes.

Under Mary's icon of the Trinity is the Prayer of Saint Ephrem, taped above her sink: "O Lord and Master of my life, take from me the spirit of sloth, despair, lust of power, and idle talk. But give rather the spirit of chastity, humility, patience, and love to Thy servant. Yea, O Lord and King, grant me to see my own transgressions, and not to judge my brother, for blessed art Thou, unto ages of ages. Amen." And written on a stick of wood: "Seek peace and pursue it", which is her prayer and her goal for these homeschooling days.

These are some examples of our own current scribbles; what are yours? These prayers guide us, inspire us, keep our paths lit. They give us the affirmation we need on those hard days when so many things are going wrong or when we are weary. They also guide us on the good days as we savor the precious moments in a spirit of thanksgiving and gratefulness. After all, we are all pilgrims journeying to heaven.

— Sia

[3] *Diary of Saint Maria Faustina Kowalska: Divine Mercy in My Soul*, no. 163 (Stockbridge, Mass.: Marian Press, 2008), 92.

WHY I MAKE MY BED

So often I have been "too busy for that". Crazy Americans that we are, we fly into our days, on the go-go-go. Many cultures take life a little more slowly, and I think we would do well to pay attention. Brewing tea, walking, and making time for rest are expected in many countries. For us, they can feel like laughable luxuries. But this article isn't about Japan's tea ceremonies or Sweden's admirable work-life balance; it's about the value of doing one little thing that can create more order and peace in our days, even if it seems small or insignificant, or even if we don't feel we have the time.

Whether you're a stay-at-home mother or a professional woman, making a bed is a worthwhile thing to do. I don't know about you, but at the end of the day, especially now that I am the mother of a teen and am in midlife (wow!), I realize that the smallest, most hidden actions are often the loveliest: the stirring of the soup, the arranging of the flowers, the pouring of the coffee. And all of us mothers, no matter what our calling demands of us, can *find God* in these everyday moments.

Making one's bed is for anyone who wants true order in his mind and life. Visual order helps clear the mind. Order and everyday chores are essential and freeing, a cement in our days that keeps us thinking straight. My father said to me once, "You've got to keep a garden and plant some vegetables so that you don't lose your mind." This has resonated deeply with me as I have navigated my own path in life. Who knows, making your bed (or working in a garden) could be the saving moment in your life! (Indeed, it was for me; once, in the middle of a life crisis when my mental state was fragmented and confused, the act of making my bed gave me strength and a firm sense of belonging amid my own acute pain.) So as for me, I'm going to keep making my bed and folding my laundry and pulling weeds, because alongside the sacraments, these are the most grounding parts of my life and some of the secrets to true joy.

— Sia

STAYING HOME

I set fire to intolerance
    with a toddler's game,
Explode bigotry
    with careful diaper changes,
Drive out loneliness
    with my soft, warm breast,
Rebuke chaos
    with every washed dish,

Silence stupidity
    with a tender caress,
Blow up selfishness
    with a lullaby,
Chase away fear
    with the push of a swing,
Shake the house of poverty
    with every laundry load,

Fight doubt
    with nursery rhymes.
My motherhood
    sets a future ablaze.

— Heather Kellis,
South Carolina

> However many years she lived she should never forget that first morning when her garden began to grow.
>
> — Frances Hodgson Burnett
> *The Secret Garden*

GROW WHERE GOD THROWS YOU

A little more than a decade ago, I left my parents' house as a twenty-one-year-old and moved into my first apartment, situated in the upstairs story of the historic Craftsman-style house my sister and brother-in-law had just purchased in the heart of our downtown. It was a lovely place to live, airy and bright with a little rooftop balcony. The location was ideal. Our city adjoins to West Lafayette—home of Purdue University—and in part because of that, our area is rich in culture and holds the arts on a pedestal. Downtown Lafayette is a happening place. Festivals and open houses on Main Street throughout the summer with live music, vendors, and wine, along with various art exhibits and weekly farmers' markets held on the same brick road for a hundred years, are just a few of the attractions of the area. Living mere blocks from all the hubbub was a fantastic experience. I was among the artists along Main Street, as I played music regularly at a number of establishments and for various special events. Along with being a musician, I worked in two different small retail businesses—first a gift shop, followed by the neighboring fair trade store. Downtown quickly became home to me, a special little spot in a great big world.

My husband proposed to me on one of our long evening walks. We married at the church I could see from my apartment window. We didn't drive away from the church in a fancy car with a "Just Married" sign on the back and cans tied to the fender—the wedding party walked together across the street to the reception hall.

It made sense that when it came time to decide on a place to live as a newly married couple, we would remain downtown. We never really got around to apartment hunting, and my lease was being turned over to a new tenant. Chance would have it that a house just a few blocks from my apartment and around the corner from my husband's home was chosen to be fixed up as a decorator show home by a local housing organization that worked to supply affordable houses to people who may not otherwise be able to purchase a home. We took a sneak peek prior to the decorating and were intrigued by the house. It seemed like a great option, and family and friends urged us to buy. It was such a deal! And buying a house while we were young was a great financial move. We went for it.

After moving in, we went on to spend six and a half years in that house, growing our marriage and our family. We had three daughters there, became close friends with our neighbors, had a prosperous garden, lived a pedestrian lifestyle, and were happy. But toward the fifth or sixth year, we felt a shift, both in our surroundings and in our hearts. The neighborhood, which had always felt safe and friendly, was taking a downward turn. The sweet families who were our trusted neighbors began moving away, and in their places came less trustworthy tenants. Walks down Main Street at night were changing too. In the economic downturn of those years, we noticed the hit our area was taking. Storefronts that used to be lit up all night long now sat dark. While getting in and out of our car, people would approach us and ask us for money at any time of the day. One morning we woke up to find pills on our porch, right outside the front door, and a woman's ID on the sidewalk. Our car was robbed multiple times, as was my sister's house. I didn't feel comfortable going outside anymore. It was definitely not a place in which I wanted to be raising my children.

We had always had in our hearts a desire for the country life. As children, both my husband and I were drawn to animals, the woods, and a rustic lifestyle. It seemed reasonable to move on this seed of desire when we realized it was time to relocate our family. We spent a long time searching, but we finally found the perfect spot: a two-acre property about twenty miles from town. When I drove down the road to meet the Realtors at the house for the first time, I came over a small hill and saw it up ahead—a little white cottage with a weeping willow tree in the yard, surrounded by lush green fields. I knew it was the one. My heart sang out! This would be our home.

And indeed, it was our home for more than a year. Shortly after moving in that August, we found out we were expecting daughter number four. We named the place Possum Cottage and immediately set to work making it the homestead of our dreams. Some parts were easy—setting up for and acquiring chickens, for example. My husband went on to build a stall in the garage, and we became owners of a beautiful Alpine milk goat named Zelda. My girls learned to milk her and to gather eggs. We hatched baby turkeys and chicks, made improvements to the house, and eventually got ourselves a second milk goat and a bonus Dorset ewe! We had a bona fide homestead at this point, and it was a good life.

It did have its downsides. The house itself was old, and there seemed to be little to no insulation. Winters were very, very cold. We were far from a hospital, which always made me a little nervous, and our walking days, surprisingly, seemed to be over. We were literally in the middle of nowhere, which was great sometimes, but at other times, it was less great. Still, we loved the homestead life. We felt fulfilled and happy, thriving in our little pocket of the world, all by ourselves.

A little less than two years in, God intervened. Through a strange series of events, we found ourselves moving to yet a different homestead. It was a marvelously idyllic spot very close to town, right near where my sister and brother-in-law had moved just the year before. It was three acres instead of two, with a big barn and three other outbuildings, plus a small cabin overlooking a public pond. The farmhouse itself needed considerable work before it could even be lived in, but it had three upstairs bedrooms and two possible downstairs bedrooms. After being squeezed into our tiny cottage, the idea of all of us living in a one-room cabin for a summer seemed totally doable.

The purchase was complicated. It involved my parents being the actual buyers and us being the checkbook. At the time it seemed a perfect plan, while in retrospect it was a terrible idea. We moved into the cabin, and that summer was just as idyllic and carefree

as we imagined it would be. Our animals had an enormous green pasture and barn. Our rabbits, which had lived in cages inside a chicken coop, now were free-range and happy. Our beloved cat had a litter of kittens. We took on two more goats to breed and expand our herd. Everything was perfect, except for the financial aspect.

Details are unnecessary for this story; we simply ran out of money. It was terrible to have everything and to live so simply yet have the stress of money hanging over us constantly. Though we didn't recognize it as God's hand at the time, our downtown house was not selling. It wasn't even being rented. Nobody wanted to live there. We kept paying the mortgage for it, wishing and praying it would sell. I couldn't understand it! It was such a darling little house, warm and comfortable with plenty of room, a driveway, and a fenced-in yard. While it's true that the neighborhood wasn't ideal for raising children, for a single person or a group of college roommates, it would have been a great option at a bargain price.

We hung on for an unnecessarily long time. We would say, "Let's see what the next paycheck brings." At about the same time we ran out of money to pay our bills, all our major appliances started breaking. Both the cabin and the farmhouse had furnaces that needed full replacements. The well pump froze and burst. We couldn't afford any of the repairs. We called my parents—the technical owners of the property—and told them we felt it was best if they sold it.

While it was admittedly difficult to leave the cabin and our country lifestyle and to watch the place be renovated by a different couple, we found a distinct peace upon our return to our downtown house.

Life downtown is completely different from country life; that fact is undeniable. But in an age where so many people dream of and wish for a homestead in the country, I am here to tell you that city life can be *incredible*. In our time away, our neighborhood underwent changes and improvements. It isn't scary anymore! One positive change was that the city took over the warehouse across the street and remodeled it, allowing it to become a great coworking studio where people can work quietly, network, and form community, big and small. The city is also planning a sidewalk revamp in the coming years that will greatly enhance the pedestrian and small business life of Main Street and the surrounding districts. New groups are being formed to start and support community gardens, neighborhood associations, organic food co-ops, and urban foraging/homesteading programs for enthusiasts. The people of the area have pulled together to make this community really great, and we, by God's gentle nudge, have been given the opportunity to be a part of it. We were stewards of the country earth; now we are required to be stewards of a smaller plot, but one of equal importance.

God's call is not always what we want for ourselves. By stretching ourselves thin for what was truly an earthly desire, my husband and I see now how greedy we were being. We wanted more land, we wanted more animals, and we wanted to be independent of community. Our simple life was not as simple as we thought, though it's only in retrospect that we see how often our plans were punctuated with the word "more". And as soon as we gave up our greed and let God lead us, the dark clouds lifted. We felt the kind of peace that only he can give. And now, for the first time in many years, I feel that we are thriving. Yes, money is still tight and probably always will be. But we are again living within our means and embracing all the gifts God has laid before us, however different they may look from the life we envisioned for ourselves.

By living downtown, we can support small businesses and local agriculture almost exclusively. We can reduce our emissions by having one car and returning to our pedestrian way of life. We can tend the same sized garden in our backyard that we had ever planted in corners of our two-acre and three-acre properties. We can again embrace a lifestyle in which, when it's time to go somewhere, my daughters ask, "Are we driving or walking?" We have been called to bloom here, among a unique and wonderful slice of history and culture, and even though I would consider us to be in more of a crack in the sidewalk than a field of wildflowers, we can still bloom here. God plants his treasures all over the world in many different situations, and all of us can bloom.

— Annie Hatke Schap, Indiana

DECORATING ON THE CHEAP

Part of our vocation as mothers is making a home. That can mean many different things, but one of my favorite implications of that call is the literal tending to our physical home environment. As mothers, often with little children, it is an understatement to say that we spend a lot of our time in our homes. Creating a lovely and pleasing backdrop to our daily lives can serve as a reminder of the dignity and purpose of the vital work we are doing, provide a creative outlet, and be of real benefit to our entire family.

Of course, another part of our vocation is to be responsible and smart in the use of our resources. While working within a tight budget can feel like an unwelcome limitation, we can instead view it as an opportunity and a catalyst to be creative, which often results in a more individual and personal home.

Perhaps the most obvious way to be a resourceful decorator is buying secondhand. Over half my furniture is from Craigslist and thrift stores. The key is to be patient and discriminating; both will save you from the unnecessary "but it was a good deal" type of purchase. Bookmark Craigslist on your phone or computer and make a habit of skimming through it once or twice a day. There is a lot of junk out there, but if you're willing to be patient, you can often find quality furniture

that costs less and lasts longer than new assemble-it-yourself items from big-box stores. Keep your second-hand score as is or give it a new look with paint, stain, or new knobs. Think outside the box: an old-fashioned spindle bed can be painted in a vibrant color for a child's room. Or consider giving a living room accent piece a fresh look with a high-gloss red or a matte black paint.

Another important, but generally costly, piece is the rug. When you have a lot of kids, it can be hard to splurge on something precious. Jute rugs layered with neutral tan cowhides have worked well for us. The hide resists any and every stain and holds up incredibly well, even in our dining room!

Kids' art is a time-tested way to personalize your home. Limiting the palette to your preferred colors will give a cohesion to various works. Thrift stores are a marvelous treasure trove of inexpensive frames for your mini masterpieces. Spray-painting the frames the same color is one way to achieve unity from disparate shapes and styles. The contrast that ornate frames give children's work can be fun, but it is also lovely to have them all framed in simple, white, clean-lined modern frames and hung in a series.

Window treatments can be a big expense without thinking outside the box. Fabric on sale, simple Ikea canvas panels, or even drop cloths from the hardware store can work with a little thought and time. Even if you're not a seamstress, a simple set of rings and clips (and possibly hemming) can turn any of the above into a curtain with little effort. Pay attention to

rules about height and drape when hanging. There are also many ideas out there for customization, such as attaching accent-colored trim onto the leading edge with fabric glue or a simple stitch.

Most mothers I know crave simplicity in their homes. One way to achieve this is to foster functional beauty wherever possible. A chalkboard can be made from a piece of plywood and chalkboard paint. Lovely wood bowls are great for corralling keys and sunglasses. Baskets are more attractive than plastic bins. And because storage is always an issue with children, I'm also a big fan of using dressers in place of sofa tables, in entryways, as nightstands, or as servers. Proportion and visual weight are key here; pieces should align with the scale of the room, and visually heavy pieces should be balanced with lighter ones.

Finally, the thrifty wife must have patience when approaching the setup of her home. We used a couple of old chairs as nightstands for a year and a half before I found some great dresser-type nightstands at our local thrift store just waiting to be sanded and painted. There are several DIY projects that I have neither the time nor the energy to tackle now but will get to eventually.

It won't happen overnight, but with time and intention, your home will feel nurtured, collected, and personal—which is much more satisfying and stylish than an attempted replica of some catalogue.

— Noelle Mering, California

MARKETPLACE MANIFESTO

It all began one day, a few years back, when I read an article about forced sterilization in China. Shocked, I asked my husband, "When I buy something made in China, am I contributing to this gruesome practice?"

"Well," he said, "it's still a communist country, so, yes, money paid to Chinese companies is technically paid to the Chinese government."

I looked over at the pretty little bowls I had bought on a clearance shelf that morning—made in China, of course. "So my money is supporting Chinese government policies!"

We were both a little stunned—we hadn't thought of it like that before. In the big picture, trading with China means supporting horrendous abuses of human rights. But it also means living cheaply off their goods. I mean, what isn't made in China? Raising a large family on a student income, we appreciate good prices!

Thus began an ongoing conversation about how and where to spend our money. Should we boycott items made in China? What about other unjust labor? Should we limit our purchases to artisans and live like medieval peasants? Is it possible to live in modern times without living on the proceeds of slavery? What about the sweatshop workers? Would a boycott deprive them of their livelihood? Is it a moral obligation not to boycott sweatshops? Once you start asking questions, you realize it's complicated.

Yet all our resources come from God; our money, like our talents, beauty, intelligence, and time, is a gift from him, and we're going to be held accountable for it. When our Lord says, "I was hungry and you gave me no food, I was thirsty and you gave me no drink, I was a stranger and you did not welcome me, naked and you did not clothe me, sick and in prison and you did not visit me" (Mt 25:42–43), it won't be enough to say, "But, Lord, I didn't see you. You were over in Cambodia. All I did was swipe my credit card."

It's an uncomfortable subject, a controversial subject. It's one I'd rather not think about because nothing makes my eyes light up like the word "sale". I love going to Ikea and finding affordable and well-designed items. I love the discount superstore, which is the friend of the frugal family. I love the expensive health food market that makes me feel so responsible. In short, I'm the ideal consumer: I'm a glutton, I'm a sucker, and I believe I can have it all.

But perhaps we should be feeling a little uncomfortable. To offer these affordable goods, stores buy from companies that essentially use human beings—our brothers and sisters—as slaves. Slavery has been officially abolished in Canada since 1834, but I'm wearing makeup containing mica that was mined by little children in India. We can't pretend it isn't happening just because it isn't happening in our country. The world is indeed a "global village"—not in a nice, politically correct way, but in the reign of the Almighty Dollar. The question for my husband, Will, and me

was how to buy our necessities without being part of a person-damaging system.

After months of discussion, we eventually nailed down our priorities to a manifesto, which we printed and taped to the fridge. It helps us navigate choices, reminding us that since we are stewards of the earth, our choices aren't just for our families; they affect the workers and their families, the local economy, and our precious environment.

Our manifesto dictates that if we want to buy something, we have to obey the following rules:

1. *Do without.* This is the primary rule. Really, so much of what we buy ends up broken or forgotten or unused. We need to learn how to discern between a need and a want. Do I need another pair of jeans when the two I have will do (one to wear, one for the wash)? Are these toys really going to enrich my child's life, or am I buying them to please myself? (My kids usually want to play with toilet paper rolls anyway.) Do I need to own this book when I can borrow it from the library?

If we've decided that something is a genuine *need*, then we:

2. *Make it ourselves.* I must clarify that this does not mean driving to a store and purchasing new materials for the sake of making something by hand. That's what hobbies are for. I love to knit, and I would love to spend eighty dollars on yarn to knit a child's sweater, but I would swiftly drive my family into the poorhouse! This rule means using what you already have. If you look around your house, you'll be amazed at how you can repurpose old junk. Old sheets and blankets are a treasury for fabric. What about orange crates? What about covering the old cushions? What about spray-painting the ugly end table from Grandma? With a few simple tools, Will repurposes old wood into shelves, beds, and other furniture for our home.

This criterion forces you to become ingenious, like the poor of the world who can't just go out and buy what they need, and like our grandparents in the Great Depression who learned to fix their own radios (or do without), turn meal sacks into clothing, unravel old sweaters to save the yarn, and keep their tin cans and buttons. With the DIY (do it yourself) renaissance on the Internet, you can learn how to make or fix just about anything.

This winter, I somehow managed to run out of pants for the toddler. He was being potty trained, so I considered him pants-optional, but when the temperature dropped, he needed some emergency bottoms. With a few simple sewing skills, a needle and thread, and the washing machine, I made some little felted pants out of a shrunken wool sweater. They were cute, and they kept him warm!

From a capitalist point of view, it was a very expensive pair of pants, costing me two afternoons of work—a full day's wage. But when you are the mother of a household, your time is not your money, and it's yours to spend. You can spend it caring for your children and your home, recycling, reusing, and repurposing like a good steward. (Plus, who can put a price on job fulfillment?) In this case, an old sweater found a new use, my toddler found warmth, and no sweatshop labor was employed. (Other than my kids, who took orders while I sewed: "Bring me a diaper! Turn off the stove! Get outside and play! Finish your math!")

Of course, there are many things we can't make ourselves, like drain stoppers and laptops and nails. (I don't have a forge. Do you?) So if we can't make it ourselves, we:

3. *Buy used.* If you're patient enough, you can find almost anything used. Furniture, appliances, electronics, sports gear, building materials, and vehicles can be found in your local online classifieds like Craigslist. We also shop eBay and thrift stores and yard sales and the curbside.

If we can't find it used, we:

4. *Buy local.* This isn't just a nice sentiment to make hipsters feel better about buying five-hundred-dollar laptop bags. It's a practical way to start turning the economy around.

When it comes to sweatshop labor, the argument is often made that it offers employment to people who would otherwise have none. This is true; it's the unscrupulous corporations that set the slave wage, not us. It would be misguided—and impossible—to boycott all sweatshop labor. But we also have the opportunity to

build up an alternative: the local market. Many people lament the deplorable state of our farmers. Let's do something about it. Let's give them our money. For us, that means sourcing as much of our food as we can from local farms instead of grocery superstores.

If it can't be found in our local area, we:

5. *Buy domestic* (Canadian made, in our case). Domestically manufactured goods cost more money, but we can afford it now that we're not impulsively lavishing money on cheap goods. And we can be sure of just wages for the worker.

If it's not made in Canada, we:

6. *Buy it on our own continent.*

If it's not made in North America, we:

7. *Buy offshore, but fair-trade.*

As a last resort, we:

8. *Buy conventionally.* Good morning, Walmart! Where's the Scotch tape?

I cringe a little even as I write this, partly because I know how it all sounds—so smug. How does one promote social justice without smacking of lifestyle elitism? Without wearing a label on the outside of my 100 percent organic, fair-trade, free-range, hand-dyed clothes?

Believe me, I can smell the hypocrisy oozing from my pores. I'm like one of those people who says, "It's really easy to be skinny and fit. All you have to do is exercise all the time and eat all these health foods." (Argh. Go away.) But really, this isn't about a smug organic label. It's about being better stewards of what God has entrusted to us. Truth be told, this lifestyle change took sacrifice and self-denial, something I'm not good at. I'm not the martyr type. I'm more the consumer type. Once I start wanting something, it's hard work saying no. This lifestyle change means I have to say no a lot more often. It means that some purchases simply aren't made. We've had to make do without certain beautiful, useful things that would have enriched our lives.

In a tiny, humble way, it's an embrace of poverty. I don't romanticize poverty, but it's not necessarily a bad thing to feel solidarity with the poor of the world by denying ourselves some luxuries of the first world.

It's a good life lesson for our children too. Who knows what the world will be like when they're adults? Maybe they'll need to know how to do without.

I'm not suggesting we should give away our furniture, turn off our heat, switch to outhouses, or become vegetarians—although saints and religious have set a good example of voluntary poverty, and our Lord himself had "nowhere to lay his head" (Lk 9:58). I'm only asking, What can we do?

Your family manifesto might not look like ours; your priorities and options will be slightly different. But it's good to start talking to your husband and children about these things. Make one or two changes—perhaps switch one product to fair-trade. (Maybe an industry with well-documented human rights abuses like coffee or chocolate? Or diamonds! Yes, stop buying all those diamonds!) Yes, fair-trade is three times the price, but perhaps we need to relegate food luxuries to the occasional treat.

And finally, "Those who seek the LORD lack no good thing" (Ps 34:10). How true this has been for our family. When we put our finances in God's hands, trying to live frugally, to put our money where it won't harm our brothers and sisters, and to share it with the poor, God has blessed and provided for us in unexpected ways. Being frugal doesn't mean being shabby. With our society's surplus of material things, we've always found really nice used items that suit our taste. Bills have been paid, somehow or another. Truly, we have lacked nothing good.

— Mary

SWABBING THE DECKS

Ten years into this parenting gig, I'm still a middling to poor housekeeper. I've learned to savor the simple pleasures of housekeeping—the heavenly smell of laundry fresh from the line, a sparkly cleaned window, the quiet moment with a cup of tea while I survey my house or write a shopping list. I've learned there will always be a quiet hour, at some point, to put the house back in order, finish planting a row, paint a wall, or wash up from last night. And if it doesn't happen—oh well. I've seen my children grow, in the blink of an eye, from hurricane-force toddlers to intelligent, responsible young adults. I've realized that our time with our children is precious and short, that the real joy is watching their personal development, and that the real miracle is the slow metamorphosis of my husband and me from selfish and idealistic young people into more forgiving, patient adults. Everything else is gravy.

Still, meals need to be made, laundry needs to be washed, and the chaos needs to be held at bay. As I bumble along, trying to find that balance between meeting all the needs around me, I've learned a thing or two about *not working*, about laying aside unrealistic expectations and just observing each child to see what he needs to thrive.

When I had my first baby at the advanced age of twenty-five, I decided I wasn't going to be like all those sloppy mothers out there and let my child get away with murder. I was going to train him. He was going to be delightful and well-behaved and a productive member of the household. I morphed from a sweet mama of a nursing baby to Tyrant of Unrealistic Expectations. I am ashamed of how often I locked horns with my small child over meeting my expectations, all in the name of training (i.e., micromanaging). As years went by and one, two, and three more children joined our family, I slowly came to grips with reality: no amount of training can make a child older or more capable than he is.

Oh, ladies, all that wasted stress!

With time, our family life has changed. Our oldest hit his stride around age eight. Although he had plenty of skills before that point, he still needed help with follow-through. But his eighth year was a maturity landmark for independence. Eventually all the other kids hit their stride too; even I did. We started small:

simple household tasks, a five- or ten-minute time limit, a bit of adult guidance "just to show you how it's done". And repetition. Lots of repetition.

How Much

I always ask experienced mothers about chores. How much do you expect your kids to pitch in? The answer is always "It depends." Temperament, age, ability, your personality, your spouse's personality, and the needs of your home must all be considered. At our house, we spend our time wildly swinging between creative projects, work overload, social events, and mild personality crises. Since none of us came to this family and marriage with good personal habits, it suits us to do chores by schedule. That way at least *something* gets done.

I would like to say that our day, like J. Alfred Prufrock's coffee spoons, is measured out by family prayers. But it isn't. It's measured by our bellies. Three times a day a meal has to be made, eaten, and cleaned up. We never waver from this basic structure, even if we think we'd like to spend twelve hours kayaking or painting pictures in a field. Hunger reins us in. Mealtime is the natural scaffold on which we build our chores, and thank goodness! Without it, our house would look like something between a barn and a war-torn landscape in France circa 1917.

It's no exaggeration to say that involving my children in the cleanup of meals has single-handedly saved my sanity. For most of my parenting life, I've been outnumbered by messer-uppers. Now the messer-uppers and the cleaner-uppers are nearly equal in number, and everyone benefits. The visual pleasure of a clean table and floor is restful for the mind and eyes. And as my highly organized engineer brother says, "It facilitates

clarity of thought." It does indeed! More important, we have more time to have fun with the children. When we "clear the decks", we have more space, mental and physical, for projects we like, such as wood carving and fort building.

After each meal, and before they scamper away (believe me, they try!), our kids have to clear the table, wash the dishes, wipe down the table and chairs, and sweep the dining room floor. Lastly, the two-year-old pushes in the chairs amid admiration and applause. Because consistency has always been my challenge, I see it as a major achievement to stick to these specific meal chores. Sometimes my children ask to swap chores or do something different. I say, "No way, man! Don't mess with the plan!" At this stage, you see, I'm not trying to turn my children into well-rounded experts on domestic cleanliness. I'm just trying to keep this ship afloat.

The Realm

In addition to meal chores, each child also has a realm, which we call his "kingdom". The realms are the high-traffic areas that need daily tidying up: mudroom, bathroom, living room. The king of each kingdom (excuse our gender-exclusive monarchy; we're an all-boy family!) has to check on his realm throughout the day and make sure it's tidy. Each king has a little brother to be his "squire", or helper. The squire's job is to take orders, such as "take these books upstairs" or "bring me the broom" or "you do boots". The king has the decided pleasure of ordering around the squire, and the squire has the fun of being important, I suppose. There might be some feudal perks; I overheard something about "I'll give you candy if you sweep for me." I see this as a lesson in leadership. "Be patient … Show your

> There is not in the world a kind of life more sweet and delightful than that of a continual conversation with God.
>
> — Brother Lawrence
> *The Practice of the Presence of God*

little brother how to …" is my ongoing drone. Our children work more quickly and don't get overwhelmed if they focus on one little job at a time.

In theory, having a responsible child moderate the high-traffic areas keeps the house clean. In reality, we're not very good at it. Everyone is still a little forgetful; much depends on me reminding the king that his kingdom needs sprucing up. Since I'm often as forgetful as the children, it's a work in progress. But with time and persistence, we're settling into a more orderly life.

Realizing we could put a child in charge of part of the house was revolutionary for us and appeals hugely to our children. We keep a chart on the fridge, which, like a nation's constitution or legal document, saves us from bickering too much about who's on what. Also, each child can finish his chore in his own time, giving him a feeling of independence, rather than being perpetually on call for Mom and Dad. In theory, this gives him more free time. Also, he earns the pride of responsibility. This keeps him from feeling like an overworked, unpaid laborer.

If you, dear reader, are a parent of a young family—let's say ages seven and under—take courage! It gets easier; you will get the hang of it, and soon you will have a troop of little helpers. I barely believed this was possible when my children were littler. Now I can honestly say that we're working like a team. We're a noisy, yelling, squabbling team sometimes, but I see the seedlings of the adults-to-be in my children. The kind word of encouragement to a little brother, the unnoticed act of service, the automatic hanging up of coats and clearing of plates, the mastery of a new skill. I see the joy and peace of, well, not a perfectly clean house or perfectly well-behaved children, but a family pulling together. After all, as I tell the children, a family is like a ship: if we don't pull together, the whole ship goes down.

— Mary

STAY

I like change. I am famous among my family for rearranging the furniture every few months, and not just trying the armchair over *there* instead of *here*, where it's always been. I once moved the master bedroom furniture into the living room. It made for awkward entertaining. And I discovered that having a view of the kitchen at night made for restless sleep. I could practically hear the dirty dishes calling me to come clean them.

For a variety of reasons, none of them having to do with employment, the military, or witness protection, my family moved five times before I turned eight and my parents divorced. I went on to attend nine schools before graduation, not because I was a troublemaker, but just due to a variety of quirky circumstances. I went to university (five years, seven addresses, one school), got married, and rented a few places. We moved around from city to city, rental to rental, trying to find the right fit between affordability and a reasonable commute.

At last, we had the great fortune to buy a house in a nice small town that was a good place to raise our growing family and a somewhat long but doable commute from work. We thought we'd trade up to something bigger and closer to work someday, but as it turns out, I am still here, ten years and counting, the longest I've ever lived anywhere.

I've now had twenty addresses in forty-two years, which has given me great adaptability but little experience staying in place and maintaining friendships. My normal experience was to move to a new town or school, quickly make a best friend, be close buddies for a year or two, move on to a new school or town, and find a new best friend. In the age before Facebook, old friends faded into the woodwork of life. I kept the good memories, but that was it.

There was a day once, about eleven years ago, when my late husband wanted me to look at some houses an hour north of where we were renting. I dug my heels in, resisting, wanting to make the place we currently were our permanent home. I'd always wanted to give my family stability, a hometown, and life-long friends. Benedictine monastics make a promise unique among the religious: the vow of stability. How hard can it be to stay in one place the rest of your life?

Sunday came, and the Gospel reading was the story of the Transfiguration. Though I was a lifelong Christian, I never quite understood what this story was about. Jesus showing off his heavenly glory? Our priest that day told the story of Peter, James, and John following Jesus up Mount Tabor, being dazzled by white glowing light, and falling on their faces in worship when they saw Moses and Elijah standing next to Jesus. The disciples begged the prophets to stay and offered to build tents for them to rest in. But Jesus said no. It wasn't the plan, just a foretaste of what was to come. It wasn't time to stay yet; there was more to do and much to suffer for the building of the kingdom. Our priest said, "You can't hold on to your idea of what is the right plan; you have to listen to Jesus and do what he wants." I felt like the Holy Spirit had spoken to me as clear as could be, and I went home and told my husband I would look at houses with him in the small town where I still live today, though he and I are now parted by his untimely death.

Some days I still feel the itch to pack up and move somewhere different … more interesting, more … I don't know … something. Starting over again is invigorating. I settle instead for a three-day weekend road trip or a visit to see my far-flung family (not surprisingly, we all put down roots in different cities). Usually, a few days on the road reminds me that as fascinating as other places are to visit, there is truly nothing like the comforts of home. It's fun to zoom around Google Earth and imagine living in the Outer Hebrides or the middle of a metropolis, but when it comes down to it, for all its shortcomings, my own little piece of suburbia is just fine.

After ten years, some of the people I met in my first year here are still here. It's a strange thing for me, having longtime friends. I'm learning that the intense friendships we start with mellow out into a long-standing feeling of trust and the pleasure of knowing a person for such a long time, through many different seasons of life. The best friend my daughter had in kindergarten is no longer her best friend in high school, but they are still friends, familiar with what makes the other laugh, what kinds of books they like to read, and their longtime squabbles with their older brothers. They share dozens of stories just by virtue of

---

We vow to remain all our life with our local community. We live together, pray together, work together, relax together. We give up the temptation to move from place to place in search of an ideal situation. Ultimately there is no escape from oneself, and the idea that things would be better someplace else is usually an illusion. And when interpersonal conflicts arise, we have a great incentive to work things out and restore peace. This means learning the practices of love: acknowledging one's own offensive behavior, giving up one's preferences, forgiving.

— Sister Kathleen O'Neill, O.C.S.O.,
on the vow of stability held by the Trappist Nuns
of Our Lady of the Mississippi, Dubuque, Iowa

having attended the same schools for a decade. They'll be friends when they're grown and raising families of their own, even if they're never kindergarten-best-friends close again. It's a very different childhood from the one I had.

I'm not a monk and I've made no vow of stability, but God the Father has always known the desires of my heart. As a child of divorce, I feared abandonment, but for sixteen years I was blessed to have the most loyal and loving husband I could wish for. As a girl who moved and changed schools a lot, I've been blessed with this stability and the opportunity to grow and learn the value of staying in place in the midst of change.

— LeeAnn Balbirona, Washington

BEGINNING A THEOLOGY OF LOCALITY

For the past year, I have been jotting down thoughts on how to build a culture of life, practically speaking, from the viewpoint of a Catholic housewife and mother. Changing the world begins with changing our own hearts, so surely it follows that changing our culture might begin with changing our own homes? And change in hearts and homes must be organic, gradual, plantlike in its apparent insignificance, noticeable only when we look at our past. So I have been examining various aspects of life in the home and how they intersect with the culture. I have been trying to preserve within our family what is good in our culture so as to pass it on to the families of the future.

One struggle in modern life that is clearly our generation's battle is the advent of social media, in so many ways a joy and in other ways a distraction that leaves television and video games in the dust as a time drain, at least for me. With fierce conviction, I kept television and screens to a minimum in our house, but my own iPhone appears superglued to my palm, and I find, to my horror, that like Bilbo Baggins and the Ring of Power, I can't seem to leave it behind; I keep putting it in my pocket.

Insidiously, my problem began as most do, with the corruption of an innocent love. One of the treasures of my life has been my dozens of far-flung friends, connections from school and previous homes that are precious pearls. To find them all on social media was thrilling. The chance to share lives with them again, to feel less lonely, to encourage them, to interact again was a delight. But the newness has worn down to a troubling addiction to news feeds and notifications, and I find myself a poor model for my children. Now that the global world is demanding my time, attention, and prayers, how do I prioritize? This is where I began with the need to understand better and formulate what I call a "theology of locality".

Once you begin to look at the matter, you see that Holy Mother Church has been unrelenting in her insistence on geography and proximity. The sacraments must be offered and received face-to-face. One cannot hear confession by avatar. Parishes are geographical; one must live in a certain area to call a certain church home. Christ said "Love your neighbor", meaning love the one who is geographically close to you. He could have said "Love humanity", but instead he chose a word that indicates (in the singular) the person proximate to you. I don't think this was an accident, any more than it was an accident that the sacraments are set up in such a way that none of them could ever be received online. The sacraments, like the love in the greatest commandment, require proximity to be operative. In an online age, Christ and his Church emphasize real, face-to-face interaction over the virtual or the avatar.

Neighbors are odd in today's society, a stubborn reminder that geography exists. In a world where it has suddenly become easy to choose friends, we rarely get to choose neighbors, and often we resent them. But our test of love is how much we love those whose dogs chase our children, whose teenagers leave tire marks on our lawns, whose music and clothing we critique from behind our blinds. My parents taught me to be proactively cheerful and conciliatory with neighbors, to initiate positive interactions with them to offset the negative interactions that are bound to occur.

There is grace in befriending those you would not normally choose as friends simply because they are proximate to you—just as there is grace in befriending your brother or sister who was chosen for you by birth. I am reminded of Chesterton's image of a man climbing down a random chimney and trying to get along as best he can with the people he finds there because "that is essentially what each one of us did on the day that he was born."[4]

And certainly, living gracefully with family members is the surest test of true charity I know: if you can courageously and consistently love those relatives who live with you or near you, you are undoubtedly on the path to virtue.

One can go as a missionary to a far-off land, or one can be a missionary at home, in the terrible chasms that separate one family member from another and in the gorges deepened by experiences with neighbors. This is how Saint Thérèse of Lisieux could be a missionary in one convent with random relatives and strangers clustered around her; the human heart is as much a labyrinth as are the jungles of South America and Asia.

Today, my community is my tribe of ten born children; one in heaven; my husband; our homestead; our road of amiable and grumpy neighbors, with our good friends the Hatkes at the end; our parish of St. John the Baptist; and our town of Front Royal, Virginia. When I set out to write about a theology of locality, I thought to myself, *Perhaps I am a hypocrite. I have many online friends and soulmates, but have I truly built community with those around me?* Circumstance complied with the question of my heart and pruned away my online work, giving me new work in our fledgling parish hybrid school and putting me in the heart of a thorny, blossoming nest of relationships old and new. And I began to realize what locality means. The more I understand it, the more I am convinced it is the key to the way forward for our culture.

How much time do I give to my children, my neighbors, my fellow parishioners, and the people whose lives intersect with mine, compared to time given to email, Instagram posts, messaging, and the like? If time is a measure of my love, where is my love spent? Again, Holy Mother Church offers us another chance to redeem the time: an hour spent in proximate distance to the Lord of the Universe, her Bridegroom, under the appearance of lowly bread. Spending time with the Bread of Life is being his neighbor for an hour. As we set out to use our time rightly, to gain wisdom of heart in living our lives, we may as well begin there.

— Regina Doman, Virginia

MAKESHIFT MERRIMENT

We tried a risky experiment these past couple of weeks. As we transition into our new home, we've been packing boxes here and there. I decided to pack the majority of the children's toys a full three weeks prior to the move. Whatever were they to do? Once upon a time, children didn't have very many toys. The items in a home were almost all functional, economical items. A girl might have a homemade doll and a boy a whistle or slingshot, but by and large the pastimes of most pioneer children were largely improvised with found items, created items, or imagined items. It was in honor of this spirit that I wanted to see what would happen if the toys were gone from the home. (Disclaimer: The building blocks stayed. They are such a fundamental part

[4]G. K. Chesterton, *Heretics* (Garden City, N.Y.: Garden City Publishing Company, 1905), 190.

of everyday play around here that I couldn't bear to have three weeks without them.) I think it's rather obvious that most American children have an excess of toys, so this article isn't to preach on that. It is to explore the idea of play from an improvised, thrifty perspective. Just like food, "fun" isn't something that must necessarily be purchased from a store. The joy in created, simple toys is immense. The savings and relief from feeling pressured to buy kids shiny, expensive toys are immense too. The fact that most created toys have a limited lifespan is also great for novelty and sanity's sake. And while you are blessed if you can sew or do woodworking, such craftiness isn't necessary to help create fun.

There is no need to extol the virtues of the cardboard box; it's been inducted into the National Toy Hall of Fame, after all.[5] But here are some ideas on acquisition: Ask an employee at an appliance store for a refrigerator or washing machine box. Super-sized fun abounds. Produce boxes from the grocery store tend to be hardier and can withstand rougher play. Cereal boxes and other food packages from your recycle bin can be used for impromptu grocery store play or painted to create cityscapes or villages. Egg cartons can hold all sorts of treasures and are great for displaying little collections.

Here are some more easy ideas on how to reclaim that spirit of improvisation that was once a staple of childhood experiences:

- Rocks. Rocks ought to be inducted into the National Toy Hall of Fame too. Large, smooth river rocks are excellent for painting. Rocks can also create borders, towns, or mini structures (read or reread the story *Roxaboxen* by Alice McLerran). Especially pretty rocks or agates have been used as a form of currency around our house.
- Papa's sock drawer—the home of old, unloved single socks. Such disconsolate creatures are born

> Ah! there is nothing like staying at home, for real comfort.
>
> —Jane Austen
> Mrs. Elton, *Emma*

again into hand puppets. They can be used just as they are or embellished with paints, markers, sequins, or pipe cleaners.
- Dad's stuff. PVC pipe pieces and connectors offer hours of building fun, as do a few small nails, a hammer, and remnants of wood from Papa's workshop.
- Garbage glory. I went through the house one day with the kids and gathered up all the scraps of seemingly useless items (half the fun is in the treasure hunt). This involved raiding the junk drawer, salvaging playing pieces from games that have been used and abused, and looking in the couch cushions and under the oven (who knew there were such treasures if you only take out that drawer on the bottom?). We came up with all sorts of interesting items: dominos, paper clips, beads, marbles, bottle caps, peanut shells, safety pins, fabric bits, nuts and bolts, errant LEGO® pieces, drinking straws, bouncy balls, bobby pins, cotton balls, and so on. We keep these items in a huge glass jar and add to it when we come upon odds and ends. This jar has provided tremendous fun! Sometimes I choose a theme and ask the kids to build something that might be found in space or under the sea, which inspires all kinds of kooky inventions. I use the jar for sorting activities for my young one. We get out a muffin tin and I have him sort items by color, size, material, or shape. We raid the jar on occasion for craft activities or artwork. Combined with some strong glue, these odds and ends can turn into excellent sculptures. If you buy those large cans of coffee, find some twine, make a hole, and turn those cans into walking stilts for kids.

[5] National Toy Hall of Fame, The Strong National Museum of Play, accessed May 14, 2024, www.museumofplay.org/toys/cardboard-box.

- Water or sand babies. Fill up plastic soda or juice bottles with sand or water for children to lug around. You can put faces on them with a Sharpie or try dressing them in doll clothes, but that is not necessary. They are nice and heavy like a real baby; I think that might be the magic of it.
- Fabric. Blankets, sheets, and fabric pieces have been fort makers and costume providers for centuries now. The hard part is simply allowing the mess.
- Paper. Even if you aren't an origami maven, you can still learn how to make fun toys from paper. Choose cardstock for customizable paper dolls, houses, and even cars!
- Toys from food items. The original Mr. Potato Head did not come with a body; it was only the facial features and appendages that were sold. You can make something similar with actual potatoes, but don't limit yourself to potatoes. All sorts of fruits and veggies and even their pits and seeds can be used for fun. Of course, we ought not waste food, but I'm sure there's not too much trauma involved if Bobby must eventually eat his pet coconut monster or corncob car.
- Outside. The possibilities are only as finite as a child's imagination. But an intentional mother will encourage the imagination to lead to a healthier lifestyle with lots of exercise and a strict diet of limited toys.

— Ellie

MY HOME IS MY MONASTERY

Removed from temporal concerns. That is how life goes for monks and nuns of religious houses. I've always been attracted to that, perhaps romanticizing their lives at times. As a mom, I sometimes lament that this quiet calling is not mine. Even before I became a Catholic, I admired monks and nuns in their picturesque cloisters praying and working gently with a devotion to last a lifetime. There is something compelling in their ascetic life of reading, gardening, praying, working, and enjoying other pastimes that deeply resonates with human nature and makes it appear (and actually be) so fulfilling.

Now, of course, I'm sure the reality is much more fraught with difficulty than the pastoral picture of monasticism in my head. Still, when I visited Ireland and the stone beehive-shaped huts of the monks on the Skellig Islands, their radical commitment to holiness and simplicity struck me and continues to inspire me.

Sometimes I wonder about the possibility of truly attaining holiness in my relatively comfortable, middle-class, American life. Somewhere inside, I harbor the fallacy that the religious life is better or holier than the life of a layperson. I've even written about wanting my house to be like a monastery: a place of peace where people grow in love of the Lord and his goodness. I envy the reprieve that religious men and women have from worldly concerns.

Here's a revelation that struck me today: my home is not *like* a monastery. It *is* a monastery. And just like the messy reality in the lives of actual monks, my life is pretty messy. But my home is the place where I pray and work (*ora et labora*, the central tenets of the Benedictine Rule). It is the place where I serve my family and where I aim to raise up children of God.

And while I envy the reprieve from worldly concerns, it turns out I have that too—in an unexpected way. You see, one day I was complaining to my darling husband about how annoyed I was at my little sister for telling me, "You're such a mom." The implication was that moms are "messy, pudgy, and uncool", a trifecta I invented myself. (How flattering, right?) Of course, many moms are beautiful, fit, put together, and chic, but I am not. In my uncharitable self-analysis,

I reasoned that I am messy because I have a toddler and a baby sloshing food and pulling my hair out of my ponytail all day; I am pudgy because I've carried two humans in my abdomen (on separate occasions) and have not quite recovered yet; I am uncool because I have little free time to spend consuming pop culture. Grilling my kindhearted husband, I asked him, "How do you see moms? Messy, pudgy, and uncool?" He thoughtfully responded with a phrase that held more meaning than I first understood: "No," he said. "In moms, I see women who are removed from temporal concerns."

Wow. "Removed from temporal concerns". He did not mean that I don't have to worry about food preparation, dirty diapers, or crumb-covered floors. Those are very temporal (at least I hope they won't be in heaven). What he meant was that moms are removed from that deadly, worldly striving of constantly trying to get ahead, be noticed, and "make it" in secular terms of success.

Instead, moms embrace sacrifice. We give of ourselves for the sake of those in our charge. And in my case, I spend so much time chasing my little boy, cuddling my infant girl, and cleaning up in between it all that when I have free time, it is a precious tiny moment that I typically do not use to browse YouTube or catch up on the latest movie releases, TV shows, or hit songs.

And this, I think, is the biggest reason that my home is my monastery. As I care for my children, husband, friends, and my home itself, all the noise from the outside world slowly filters out. Like the monks, I remain in my abbey. I perform works of service and small works of love. I am reprieved from worldly concerns. I am in the world but not of it (for this season, at least, of having young children). I can't say I know as much about religious life as I ought to, but I'm starting to think that my family's little suburban home is not so different from the serene convent.

— Stephanie Pacheco, Virginia

THE DIRTY LIFE

I read a book a few months ago called *The Dirty Life*. I immediately felt that were I to write a book about the current state of my life, it would be called the same. Only *The Dirty Life* is the story of a couple of farmers, while my husband and I fall more into the category of wannabe farmers. We live on a couple of acres. We garden; we keep bees. But we aren't really farmers. My husband has a day job, and I'm preoccupied with raising our family. With seven kids, though, six of them old enough to go in and out of the house on their own, we do indeed live the dirty life.

As much as we embrace our lifestyle, I find myself sometimes wishing for both worlds: childhood days literally immersed in God's beautiful earth, the evenings spent in a perfectly clean and cozy house. I think we pretty well have the immersed in earth part down.

Spring has just arrived in our neck of the woods. My older boys spend hours on excursions with their

metal detectors. They come home with dirty knees and hands and then proceed to empty pouches and pockets full of dirt-encrusted bits of this and that on the kitchen table. It's true that they find some real treasures, but if it comes out of the ground, you know it's dirty. Meanwhile, the little ones are engaged in their favorite activity, what they simply call mud-pie kitchen. Just as I think everyone is settled, I hear banging on the back door. My two-year-old, hands and arms covered in mud, is shouting for me to let him in. His hands are so muddy he can't turn the handle. This isn't the first time today, either. I haul him to the bathroom, wash him up, and change his clothes. He will stay inside for a few minutes, but he will end up outdoors again, and eventually this scene will replay. As much as I've been looking forward to warm weather, I confess that I begin to question just how this spring and summer are going to play out. Maybe I'm tired of being the country mouse. But then I find myself with a rare hour to plunge my own hands into the dirt. I plant lettuce and beets, kale and radishes. I don't wear gloves. I stand up to admire my work, wiping my dirty palms on my jeans, clearly nothing more than a big kid myself. By this time, several little ones surround me, begging for "just a few seeds". I dole them out into grubby hands, all the while thinking, *I've got to remember to scrub their fingernails before Mass on Sunday.*

At the close of the day, we all end up inside our little old house for dinner, dishes, books, and bed, or something along those lines. And I think my kids would tell you our house is cozy. But I can't promise it's always clean, especially in the springtime. We're living the dirty life here. I tell my little ones, "God made the beautiful flowers. God made the trees."

Let's not forget that he made the dirt too.

—Ginny Sheller, Virginia

A HOME IN HIS HEART

I desire a home: a permanent place where I can nest, creating a good resting place for my family; a place where I can make and grow babies; a place where I can host dinners and spread my finest tablecloth, a place where I can rest in my own bed or have a cup of tea whenever I desire; a place where I can raise children, make beds, and mend clothing; a place to call my own, to settle in and put down roots, painting my walls whatever color I fancy and hanging up my favorite pictures; a place where I can be whoever I want to be, in shelter and comfort under my very own roof. I desire that little slice of goodness and beauty—a foretaste of heavenly joy and heavenly peace.

But physical homes are not always permanent. I no longer have a permanent home. As a renter, I move a lot. So I find consolation in reflecting on how we are pilgrims journeying toward heaven, and no matter what earthly home we have, each home is only temporary. We will never truly be at home or completely at peace until we reach this heavenly home where our true treasures will be. Here on earth, some mothers never find that place to call home. They move dozens of times, or they are lonely and never feel that they've found a community or circle of friends or the right house. Or they are in a temporary home, waiting for the next, more permanent, place to dwell. This can be the case for military families, those experiencing job transfers, those whose communities are changing—the situations and scenarios are endless.

Even Mary, about to give birth, was passing through, stopping at the inn on the very night she was to give birth to her child. She was a pilgrim, a traveler. But she traveled with God himself, and he was her home. He was her sustaining Love.

Many of us also know pain and suffering on our personal journeys; I do. But what is the life of a Christian without suffering and pain? Nowhere in the Gospels does it say that our paths will be easy. However, we do indeed read that Jesus himself is the Way; that in him there is peace; that in him we can find rest; and that his yoke is easy and his burden light.

All of us, no matter our circumstance, can take comfort in remembering that this is just a passing life, a passing place. We have a home in Jesus' heart, where Love dwells. We all can rest in him, in his love, knowing that wherever he is, that is our home. He is in the tabernacle; he is in our hearts; he is in our neighbor. We have a home in Love himself.

—Sia

READ

KRISTIN LAVRANSDATTER: A NOVEL FOR EVERY WOMAN

BY SIGRID UNDSET

Sigrid Undset was born into a family of Norwegian bohemians. Her parents and their circle were part of the intellectual, "forward-thinking" elite of the late-nineteenth century, freethinkers and agnostics who didn't believe in marriage or religion. Her home was full of books and conversation, and she and her sisters were encouraged to read, to think, to question. As a young woman, Sigrid worked as a typist to help support the family. She worked long hours during the day and spent her nights writing. She corresponded with famous writers of the decade, got noticed, and was published. Her youth passed while she worked and wrote. It was a lonely time with few friends.

At the age of thirty, she moved to Rome and experienced a springtime in her life. Living among the artistic and literary society of her homeland, she met artist Anders Svarstad, who was nine years her senior, married, and with three children. Sigrid and Anders fell in love, and Anders obtained a divorce so he could marry Sigrid. They moved back to Norway, where she bore two children and became stepmother to the three children from Anders' previous marriage. Two were mentally disabled and required continuous care. Sigrid strove valiantly to hold this large and busy family together, but seven years later, while she was expecting her third child, Anders divorced her and she was left alone to support herself and her children. Once again, Sigrid began writing to keep the wolf from the door.

It was during this dark time that she produced her masterpiece, *Kristin Lavransdatter*, the epic fictional story of a woman in medieval Norway, starting with her early childhood in the idyllic and beautiful dales and ending with her dramatic death.

Kristin Lavransdatter is a trilogy of three separate novels that, like Greek tragedies, can stand alone but are best read together. Part 1 is the story of Kristin's girlhood, betrothal, and marriage. Although she has all worldly security, Kristin betrays her parents' honor by falling in love and running off with a handsome, aristocratic adventurer, Erlend, risking everything to marry him. Part 2 tells the story of her life as a wife, mother, and mistress of a vast estate. In part 3, Kristin and Erlend's stories become ever more complicated, and finally, with her children grown, Kristin joins a monastery. It concludes with the coming of the bubonic plague, also known as the Black Death—a dark but spiritually triumphant end.

Like all great novels, the plot alone can't convey the power and scope of the story. (It does, in fact, sound a bit like a Harlequin romance, medieval style.) But the plot is just the skeleton of the real drama, the moral choices and human passions that drive history. It's not a gentle story. Undset doesn't gloss over the harshness of preindustrial society: brutal childbirth, infant mortality, patriarchy, disease, starvation, survival. There's also the moral tragedy of Kristin's inner life. She loves fiercely and powerfully, but much of the story revolves around fierce loves that undo the characters. Kristin's love for Erlend, for example, leads her to choices that cause her to forfeit her integrity, and for this she can never forgive him.

But Undset never paints in simple black and white. Erlend is not just a scoundrel, an Austen-style profligate running off with an innocent girl. As readers, we see what Kristin sees: a talented, intelligent man whose high ideals and noble enterprises are thwarted by his moral shallowness. It is a sometimes-painful read. Likewise, we watch as Kristin, who is beautiful and kind and good, brings suffering upon herself through recklessness. And yet we can understand it and can't help but feel that we'd probably do the same. As one friend put it, reading *Kristin Lavransdatter* for the first time as an impressionable teenager, "So this is what sin looks like *from the inside.*"

Sigrid Undset is a modern novelist, so while *Kristin Lavransdatter* is meticulously researched and full of historical detail, it is first and foremost a psychological novel. Given the world it came out of (early modern Norway), it might have been bleak indeed. But Sigrid Undset is not a typical modern writer. Her own personal suffering was transformative and led her through personal purgation, philosophical pursuit, and sheer grit to conversion to God and eventually the Catholic faith. She leaves small signposts of God's hand working in the lives of all her characters. On her deathbed, Kristin takes off her wedding ring and sees the mark of a cross imprinted on her finger from some flaw in the ring. Kristin sees it as a mark of Christ's loving protection throughout a lifetime consumed by what Evelyn Waugh would call a "fierce little human tragedy".[1] The reader sees, even when Kristin cannot, a pattern and purpose to her life's events: her bad choices, her refusal to forgive, her tumultuous and passionate relationships, and even her misspent love made possible her heroic death. "In despite of her self-will, in despite of her heavy, earthbound spirit, somewhat of this love had become *part* of her, had wrought in her like sunlight in the earth, had brought forth increase which not even the hottest flames of fleshly love nor its wildest bursts of wrath could lay waste wholly."[2]

There is so much to unpack in *Kristin Lavransdatter* that you could return to the novel yearly for the rest of your life and not exhaust its richness. From the historical point of view, it's fascinating. We glimpse medieval Christian society, where even the worst sinner knew he could be saved (or at least knew

It's no use going back to yesterday, because I was a different person then.

— Lewis Carroll
Alice, *Alice's Adventures in Wonderland*

he was damned). I loved the details of the medieval household where Kristin, a highborn lady, is also a farmer, businesswoman, employer, and master of the household arts of brewing and food preservation, herbs and medicine, and crafts such as spinning, weaving, and needlework. We read stunning descriptions of landscape and weather. We meet the barely sleeping pagan Scandinavia, and Kristin has a mysterious and never-explained encounter with an elf maiden standing on the edge of the wilderness like a warning of what lies beyond the borders of Christendom. We feel the constant tension between conventional society with its security and rules and self-determination with its sometimes-terrible consequences. We witness painful wrestling with sin and salvation, passion and freedom. We are given a small but wonderful portrait of one of the holiest characters in literature, Brother Edmund, who like Father Zosima in Dostoevsky's *Brothers Karamazov* plays the part of prophet and chorus, quietly telling another narrative, alongside Kristin's, the narrative of God's love working to save and heal a broken and often bitter existence. (Did I mention it's kind of a heavy novel?) Yet the story is simple enough to be read by a tired mom, in little bits and pieces, between starting supper and finishing the laundry.

Kristin Lavransdatter has been read and enjoyed by many men, especially those who love the Russian authors. But I think of it as a woman's novel because Kristin experiences throughout her life a full range of female experiences. As a young woman, Kristin is sexually assaulted while walking home in the woods. Though

---

[1] Evelyn Waugh, *Brideshead Revisited: The Sacred and Profane Memories of Captain Charles Ryder* (Boston: Little, Brown and Company, 1945), 351.
[2] Sigrid Undset, *Kristin Lavransdatter*, trans. Charles Archer and J.S. Scott (London: Alfred A Knopf, 1923), 1040.

no bodily damage is done, Undset portrays the psychology of trauma and shame with stark brushstrokes. She also powerfully conveys the experiences of infatuation and naive love, traumatic childbirth, the loneliness and ecstasy of first motherhood, marital strife, jealousy and divorce, single motherhood, and the painful letting go of her grown children.

I suspect, from the vividness of her storytelling, that Sigrid Undset experienced it all. But whatever she suffered during her own dark years of struggle and conversion to faith, nothing was wasted. A seed was taking root inside her, and, as for Kristin, it yielded a crop of insight that gives the reader perspective about even the harsh tragedies of life because they can, and often do, create depth of character and impart that all-important perspective, the long view, which carries a person through. It's not without reason that Sigrid Undset won the Nobel Prize in 1928 and accepted her laurels as one of the world's great novelists. She proclaims that life, even a life characterized by suffering and personal tragedy, is worthwhile.

— Mary

WILLFULLY WANDERING WORDLESS: A TOP-TEN LIST

Some of my very favorite picture books are completely devoid of words. I used to write (no pun intended) these kinds of books off as novelties without any real sort of lasting merit. But as my bookshelf space shrunk and my exposure to children's literature grew, I was proven wrong—very, very wrong.

Wordless picture books can be an excellent vehicle for prereaders who want to "read" books like big brother or sister. They can serve beautifully for creative narration prompts too. Instead of playing the memory game and being asked, "Okay, what was the story about?" (to which they promptly regurgitate a couple of quoted sections word for word to show they've been listening), children are required to tell a story entirely in their own words. In the wordless world, it's all about attention to the details, to sequencing, to the art of what's happening. Many are written in comic-book fashion, which helps little ones learn the concept of left-to-right-to-down directional reading. Teachers have often used wordless books for prompts to creative thinking: "What do you think he's looking for?" "Why might she be feeling sad?" and so on. Since none of the answers are "given away" with text, even shy children might open up with some interesting interpretations.

In regard to wordless books in this family, my children take a few different approaches that are refreshingly different from their reactions to traditional picture books. My five-year-old boy likes to take a wordless book off to a corner by himself and study it through. Then he asks me to "read a story with him", which entails us sitting on the couch together while he tells me everything that's going to happen on the next page. He gets a giddy delight out of finally being the one in the know with a book, while I am simply the willing audience to his interpretation. My seven-year-old boy engages in a great deal of personification in his life. If he sees an image he likes with just enough figures for our family, he promptly gives one of our names to each one. I am honored to have been labeled an ant, a banana, a Chinese spinster, and a flying frog, among other things. With wordless books, he's in hog heaven describing who's who and bringing all the people from his real world into the story with unnamed characters. My nine-year-old boy is a bit more like me with the wordless books. He just curls up somewhere with a blanket and reads it quietly to himself, slowly turning the pages and letting his eyes feast on the artwork. The canvas is totally blank when it comes to this kind of story, and his imagination can run wild.

Here is a top-ten list of my very favorite wordless books, though it really is cruel to limit myself in this wonderful genre:

1. *The Arrival* by Shaun Tan. This book is stunning, and the artwork will weave you right into its spell. I spent the better part of an hour reading this book by myself; it is living proof that picture books aren't just for kids. I would happily keep this surrealistic story of an immigrant on my coffee table. While it was fun to go through with my children, the message really can be quite profound for adults too.

2. *Rain* by Peter Spier. A perfect springtime book full of lovely, imaginative imagery. Peter Spier is one of those wonderful authors whom the world seems content to forget. So many of his gems (some others are wordless also) are out of print, and I wrinkle my nose in disgust sometimes when I think of the fodder that's replacing his books at stores everywhere.

3. *Anno's Counting Book* by Mitsumasa Anno. Get all of Anno's books; you won't regret it! This book doubles as a superb and innovative counting book with folksy artwork that I adore. *Anno's Journey* is another title in this category that is a lot of fun to follow with children.

4. *Tuesday* by David Wiesner. Wiesner is the master of the wordless genre. While we love his *Flotsam*, *Free Fall*, and *Sector 7* too, this book about flying frogs (yep, that's me!) on an adventure in the middle of the night wins my boys over every time. These pictures are feast worthy indeed.

5. *The Lion & the Mouse* by Jerry Pinkney. Now, Pinkney lucked out in that the story was already provided for him—remember that fable from Aesop about the mouse who helps out the lion? Pinkney just happens to be an incredible artist who took this story for a beautiful spin in 2009 with the release of this book.

6. *Rainstorm* by Barbara Lehman. Lehman is more well known for her Caldecott-honored *The Red Book*, but this one tickles me just a bit more. A young, well-to-do boy feels the restlessness and boredom of a rainy day before finding a magic key that offers him a portal into his imagination. There's something clean about Lehman's illustrations that make her a refreshing read.

7. *A Boy, a Dog, and a Frog* by Mercer Mayer. My first introduction to wordless books was this one. I love the size; I love the limited color scheme. I love all the sequels to this book. I have to admit that I came into it biased because Mercer Mayer illustrated my all-time favorite series of childhood chapter books, *The Great Brain* by John Fitzgerald. I was delighted to see this kind of art again. (One way to sneak out of the limiting top ten is to throw in other titles by the same author. In this case, I'd point you to a very recent fun title by Mayer called *Octopus Soup*.)

8. *The Silver Pony* by Lynd Ward. This is a strange, magical book. I don't guarantee it will win everyone's hearts, but its peculiarity won mine. I love the old-fashioned black-and-white sketches.

9. *The Boy, the Bear, the Baron, the Bard* by Gregory Rogers. How refreshing! Are you studying Shakespeare? Add this to your unit to round out all the romantic, poetic imagery of the man. Here a contemporary boy gets lost on a stage hosting the Bard himself, who becomes enraged at the interruption and chases the boy through old London. The great thing about graphic novels is that you get lots of bonus perspectives to complete the comic-book boxes, so an extreme close-up of Shakespeare's face or a panoramic bird's-eye view of the city fill out the pages quite nicely.

10. *Mirror* by Jeannie Baker. Baker is a collage artist, and she uses an assortment of materials, fabric, and natural foliage to construct this very novel book. It shows once again that wordless stories aren't just for preschoolers; in fact, you'd need to be at least eight years old to really appreciate what's going on here. The volume is uniquely constructed to provide two narratives simultaneously, side by side—one relating the details of the everyday life of a Moroccan child and the other depicting life for a child in Australia. It's a beautiful social studies lesson illustrating the uniqueness of two very different cultures while at the same time showing that the same threads of family, meals, and home life bind us all together.

— Ellie

LAUREL'S KITCHEN CARING: RECIPES FOR EVERYDAY HOME CAREGIVING

BY LAUREL ROBERTSON, CAROL LEE FLINDERS, AND BRIAN RUPPENTHAL, R.D.

Laurel's Kitchen Caring is both a cookbook and a goldmine of practical wisdom for the care of sick people. A tiny volume, it's packed with ideas for making the home recovery room healthier, calmer, and more beautiful and the food more tempting and nutritious. Although it was written for caregivers of sick people, the advice applies to caring for small children, the elderly, and anyone who depends on you for feeding and affirmation.

Laurel's voice is humorous and down-to-earth, and her information is always illustrated with personal stories. Reading *Laurel's Kitchen Caring* is like having a friend standing in my kitchen giving good, sensible advice. Her friend and coauthor, Carol Flinders, opens the book with the story of a car collision that landed her in the hospital with a broken back. The homespun care she received during the ensuing months testifies to the healing power of nutritious food lovingly prepared and thoughtful attention to simple comforts, such as bedding and light.

The recipes include comfort foods such as (healthy!) crepes, puddings, pancakes, and mac and cheese. The authors share advice on how to pack in extra calories. A chapter on fluids provides ideas for making savory broths and drinks and gives excellent advice on selecting and preparing herbs for herbal teas. The book contains dairy-free and egg-free options, and nifty ideas such as using prune puree (yes, you read that correctly) in chocolate brownies to replace the fat. (Prune puree, Laurel tells us, contains sorbitol, which holds moisture, and pectin, which makes the batter hold air bubbles. Oh yes, it is a very interesting read!)

The philosophy behind it all is that the love and attention to detail in food prepared by hand contributes as much to the patient's recovery as the nutrition. We all know this from experience. No one knows but me, for example, exactly how much ginger my husband needs in his tea to feel like he's beating his cold (a lot more than you might imagine). Or the special kind of toast our child needs after stomach woes. But sometimes, when I am exhausted, distracted by the numerous demands of mothering, or faced with baffling fussiness in a cranky child, my creativity feels taxed and depleted.

That's where a book like *Laurel's Kitchen Caring* is so wonderful. It gives simple, short recipes and plenty of peppy advice, including a whole chapter on care for the caregiver.

Here's a quote from the book:

Hold tight to your sense of humor. Resist courageously when your mind tries to convince you you are wasting your time, not doing a good job, worth more than this, going to have a nervous breakdown, etc., and all the other weasely scenarios our lower self uses to bring us down. Learning to recognize them is an education in itself. Patiently to overcome them, and to keep on helping even when it's hard, is better than college. Afterward, life opens to a different perspective, and very likely you have grown closer to your real self—a happier, kinder, wiser, and more peaceful person than before.[3]

Sound familiar? Does that sound like the stretching and growing we mothers do on a regular basis? Laurel Robertson affirms the dignity of the patient (and by extension the child, husband, or whomever is in your care) as worthy of being loved. It encourages the caregiver (mother, wife, helpful friend in the postpartum house) to give it her whole heart and discover something in the process—something wonderful, something we Christians might know as *the fruits of the Spirit*.

Best of all, I can attest that the recipes are truly fantastic. I haven't tested every one, but I've been cracking the book regularly for ten years, when I have sickies in the house or am in need of culinary inspiration for something quick and nutritious, especially during pregnancy when normal food offends.

These are recovery foods, little dishes that tempt the appetite and nourish the body: gentle vegetable broths, cup custard, "special" applesauce. Not one has failed me yet. Some, like oatmeal pancakes, have become household staples. And no wonder! Laurel has been feeding people—young and old, sick and healthy—in her community kitchen for thirty years.

A note of warning: the nutrition advice is based on the whole food, vegetarian model, and has the usual prejudice against fat. Those of us, like me, who like to slather everything in duck fat can surreptitiously substitute butter for her "nonstick lecithin spray" and sneak in a few extra egg yolks here and there.

— Mary

PAY ATTENTION, CARTER JONES

BY GARY D. SCHMIDT

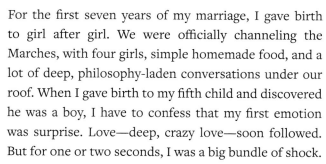

For the first seven years of my marriage, I gave birth to girl after girl. We were officially channeling the Marches, with four girls, simple homemade food, and a lot of deep, philosophy-laden conversations under our roof. When I gave birth to my fifth child and discovered he was a boy, I have to confess that my first emotion was surprise. Love—deep, crazy love—soon followed. But for one or two seconds, I was a big bundle of shock.

My little man is three years old now, and neither the love nor the shock has worn off. Along with those emotions, however, has come another: the sense of tremendous responsibility. I want Gabriel to grow up to be a true gentleman. I want him to love God above all things, to use his strength to serve, to be devoted to the helpless and passionate in his pursuit of truth and justice. I want him to hold doors and read books and be unashamed of running a vacuum or shedding a tear.

I thank God every day that Gabriel can grow up with an example of a man like this in his father. Not every boy is so lucky. In our culture, examples of godly gentlemen

[3] Laurel Robertson, Carol Lee Flinders, and Brian Ruppenthal, R.D., *Laurel's Kitchen Caring* (Berkeley, Calif.: Ten Speed Press, 1997), 19.

are few and far between. Even my Gabriel will see, someday, the sad imbalance between the few true men and the millions of imposters—the ones who use their strength to hurt and belittle, their hands to consume instead of create, their time to serve themselves.

As much as I try to surround my children with extended family and friends who will act as layer upon layer of good role models, I know this won't be enough. So I turn to the gift that helped my husband grow into the man he is today: the gift of books.

Do I overestimate the importance of reading? I don't think so. My husband told me that *The Sword in the Stone* taught him to love peace and treat men justly, *The Lord of the Rings* taught him that greatness is found in little things, and *My Side of the Mountain* taught him how to forage for wild mushrooms and train a falcon to hunt for him—er, also, something about God giving us all that we need to survive. As author Sarah Mackenzie wrote in *The Read-Aloud Family*, by exposing them to stories, "we give our kids practice living as heroes. Practice dealing with life-and-death situations, practice living with virtue, practice failing at virtue…. We consider whether we would be as brave, as bold, as fully human as our favorite heroes. And then we grasp—on a deeper, more meaningful level—the story we are living ourselves as well as the kind of character we will become as that story unfolds."[4]

We all know where to find stories of King Arthur and Hobbits and children who were swept into another world through a wardrobe. But it's quite a bit harder to find stories of normal children, in today's world, that can inspire heroic virtue. The culture's ebbing sense of morality and relativistic attitude toward truth is seeping into children's literature in books aimed at younger and younger children. So when I find a newly published book that fits the bill, I snatch it off the shelf, read it in a gulp, and talk about it to everyone who will listen.

Gary D. Schmidt's book *Pay Attention, Carter Jones* is one of those gems, perfect for nine- to fourteen-year-olds. As the story opens, we see Carter Jones, the oldest child in his family, caught up in the chaos of getting ready for his first day of middle school. His sister can't find her socks, another sister is crying, the milk is gone, the dog has vomited on the floor. His dad is deployed in Germany, and his mom is barely holding it together. Suddenly, the doorbell rings, and Carter's life changes. His English grandfather, whom Carter has never met, has essentially "left" them his butler. Mr. Bowles-Fitzpatrick, a "gentleman's gentleman" who could have stepped straight out of *Downton Abbey* or *Jeeves and Wooster*, has arrived to help.

As you've doubtless experienced, change for the better often isn't easy. Carter and his sisters are less than thrilled with the type of help "the Butler" offers. The girls are brought to the bookstore so they can replace television time with E. Nesbit stories. Piano practice is enforced. Healthy meals are eaten. Homework is completed on time, complete with essays on why perhaps the American Revolution wasn't such a good idea after all. Carter is roped into stepping into the role of the man of the house—even when that means cleaning up dog vomit instead of waiting for his mom to do it.

The hardest change of all, however, is that of looking past the chaos of everyday life and facing the real messiness in Carter's life: the deep, dark tragedies that he blames himself for; the pain that his own father ran away from rather than faced; the hurt that left his mom so uncertain of God that she slowly drifted away from attending Mass.

But Carter realizes—as we all must—that there is grace in the pain. Happiness and peace aren't achieved by turning away from life's messes but rather by turning toward them with acceptance, courage, and even laughter. It takes a real gentleman to attempt such a task, but luckily Carter has the Butler by his side to teach him to become one—or, rather, to remind him that he is one already.

If this sounds dark, well, in moments it is. I won't pretend that I didn't bawl my eyes out for the better part of the day while I read *Carter Jones*. But life can be dark too. The key is finding ways to smash our way out

---

[4]Sarah Mackenzie, *The Read-Aloud Family: Making Meaningful and Lasting Connections with Your Kids* (Grand Rapids, Mich.: Zondervan, 2018), 48.

of the cave and into the light. That is precisely what Gary D. Schmidt does, with tremendous grace and subtlety, in this book. On one page, he makes you cry in pain. On the next, you'll cry laughing. The darkness never wins. There is always laughter, love, and light.

And as I consider what will help my son grow into the best man he can be, what better aid can I ask for than that? Confidence in God will let him laugh in the face of danger. God's love will empower him to mirror that love to the world. And God's light, his ever-present though sometimes obscured light, will help my son charge out into the darkness and shine.

— Faith Elizabeth Hough, Connecticut

THE BOOK OF CONFIDENCE

BY FATHER THOMAS DE SAINT-LAURENT

Attention weary mamas with little time to read! To all who need your prayer life rejuvenated but cannot escape for a retreat to connect with our Lord, I have happily chanced upon the most incredible little gem of a book that seems written particularly for those of us in the mucky trenches of life.

Your prayer life will be transformed in a mere afternoon spent with this volume of about eighty easy-to-read pages. If I was able to finish this book in the midst of homeschooling, hospital visits, newborn baby-ness, toddler teething, Christmas, New Year's, and a partridge in a pear tree, then I assure you this is a book you can finish.

The Book of Confidence is by far the most helpful book I've read on spirituality. It came to me while I was in the midst of great anxiety and stress, at a time when seemingly endless work was sapping my energy. It immediately breathed life and vigor into my prayer life.

Father Thomas de Saint-Laurent is not only a holy, wise priest but also an expert on psychological themes. His simple writing is emotionally soothing and cuts to the chase about how to pray effectively. If you think praying with confidence is the same thing as being presumptuous, as I did, think again. As the author puts it, "This virtue, indeed, brings such great glory to God that it necessarily attracts exceptional favors to souls."[5] I don't know about you, but sign me up for attracting exceptional favors! Lord knows I need them!

If you are weary and spinning your wheels, as I was, do not hesitate to beg God confidently for help. It is necessary, the author urges, to petition God ceaselessly, for this pleases God. "Far from bothering the nurse who suckles him, the baby brings her relief."[6] How much this statement resonated with me as I read this book while breastfeeding! Surely, when our babies sleep too long and don't cry out for a feeding, all the more we feel the need to nurse them. And finally, when they wake and are screaming to eat, how we rush to them, ready to relieve ourselves of all the nourishment we have stored up for them. So too, with confidence, we should always call on our Father, for his merciful heart is bursting all the more with Divine Mercy, waiting to nourish our spirits.

I ended up highlighting, dog-earing, and underlining the majority of *The Book of Confidence*. This is a Catholic nightstand staple. Put it right next to your Bible, for it will continually encourage you to press on through all that life throws at you. This book is a treasure, and I think it will change your prayer life forever, resulting in quite possibly the most effective praying you've done yet.

— Annemarie Thimons, Florida

---

[5] Father Thomas de Saint-Laurent, *The Book of Confidence* (Hanover, Pa.: America Needs Fatima, 2015), 56.
[6] Louis of Granada, First Sermon for the Second Sunday after the Epiphany, quoted in ibid., 12.

READING HARD BOOKS

Early into motherhood, I turned to books for diversion and interest. Any bibliophile reading this knows what I'm talking about: laundry piles and temper tantrums can be handled with grace as long as you have the salve of *Pride and Prejudice* or an inspirational Brené Brown book waiting for you offstage. In those initial isolating years of limited adult contact, books become a woman's best friend. This is good.

Over the past few years though, I have reconsidered my reading habits. When I began keeping a reading journal (and this is as fancy as a two-dollar spiral notebook where I write down the title of what I read and two or three sentences of my impressions of the book), I noticed the uneven distribution of *types* of books I read. So often, I was a consumer for the sake of consuming and binged on mind candy. And while I fully support the idea that motherhood is an important, sacrificial, all-consuming gift of self, I rather resented the fact that I had little mental energy left over for anything weightier than memes and HuffPo articles. I had diapers to change, homeschooling lessons to write, and food sensitivities to research; who in the world has time for metaphysics? But my reading journal has now developed into a personal challenge for myself in that it inspires (taunts?) me to be more proactive in using my brain, developing my whole self. Because if any one of us thinks we've mastered the art of being educated—or even fully human—once we earn a college degree or successfully raise a child to age eighteen, we are sorely mistaken.

I seek now to graze from a more diverse literary palate, and hard books are part of this. To me, there are three kinds of hard. My personal goal is to read one of each kind each year, along with liberal quantities of fun or purely interest-driven books.

1. A hard book is a long book. Our lives are so centered around technology that our brains are rewiring themselves to skim and sort and turn away after only nineteen seconds of interest.[7] We are Generation Click Bait. I once read somewhere about a study that predicted that the next generation of college graduates will be unable to read or comprehend something like Tolstoy's *War and Peace*. Their brains just won't have the processing power. I hope this is a false prophecy, of course, but it does give me pause. This year I finally began and completed Dostoevsky's *The Brothers Karamazov*, which has been on my list for over a decade. I faltered in and out of interest, as I was knee-deep in mandatory textbook reading at the time, but I finally finished it as an audiobook on a long road trip—hearing the Russian pronunciations was quite helpful.

---

[7]Joseph Firth et al., "The 'Online Brain': How the Internet May Be Changing Our Cognition", *World Psychiatry* 18, no. 2 (June 2019): 119–29, https://www.ncbi.nlm.nih.gov/pmc/articles/PMC6502424/.

> Why must people kneel down to pray? If I really wanted to pray I'll tell you what I'd do. I'd go out into a great big field all alone or into the deep, deep woods, and I'd look up into the sky—up—up—up—into that lovely blue sky that looks as if there was no end to its blueness. And then I'd just feel a prayer.
>
> — L. M. Montgomery
> Anne, *Anne of Green Gables*

2. A hard book is an unwelcome book. Sometimes, I think it is a good practice to read things we *don't want to read*. Yes, we risk living in a closed-off world of self if we read only things that confirm our own religious biases or lifestyle choices. Not interested in changing up your diet? No problem. But consider reading food expert Michael Pollan's books anyway. This year I read *Primal Loss: The Now-Adult Children of Divorce Speak*, edited by Leila Miller, even though I already have firm convictions about the devastation of divorce. It's a book I didn't want to read but did anyway, just to become familiar with the experiences of this demographic (I recommend it for all people, by the way, whether they are in troubled marriages or not). I think my next unwelcome book will be in a totally different vein: *Harry Potter and the Sorcerer's Stone*, by J.K. Rowling. I have zero interest in this series, but Potter-isms have become such a part of our cultural fabric (what with rides at Disneyland, references to Hogwarts ... even my college professor quotes somebody named Dumbledore!) that I honestly feel a resigned sort of obligation to acquire a basic understanding of what the heck people are talking about.

3. A hard book is an intellectual book. This is the type of book where you have to read the same paragraph three times to understand what's being said, and you suddenly realize you have spent the last page composing your next grocery list or Facebook update. Not everyone needs to read the *Summa Theologica*, but everyone should challenge his own intellect at whatever stage of development by reading something that requires discipline and focus. It can be theology, philosophy, history, foreign affairs, whatever. The point is to push yourself to learn something from someone smarter than you and create new pathways in your brain to *think*. The intellectual book I wrestled with and conquered this year was *A Conflict of Visions: Ideological Origins of Political Struggles*. I think it may have been the most difficult book I've ever read. Thomas Sowell's language is extremely academic. However, this book may also have been one of the most rewarding I've ever read because it made me understand *why* there is such a gaping chasm between people's political values. I now feel far more understanding toward people whose views differ from mine, for which I am grateful.

I love excellent fiction as much as any booklover. And I have read some works of *enjoyable* fiction that have taught me more about my faith than the *Catechism* did (thank you, Elizabeth Goudge!). I also love reading little bits from Malcolm Gladwell and regularly dip into the self-help genre. So don't get the idea that I'm trying to take away all the most entertaining aspects of reading. I'm just suggesting that hard books are important. They challenge us. They inspire us. They sharpen our intellects. And they remind us that God gave each of us a beautiful brain to nourish and stimulate insofar as we're able. So after you read Plato's *Republic*, you can curl up to watch *The Office* reruns without any guilt.

— Ellie

BRIDESHEAD REVISITED, REVISITED

BY EVELYN WAUGH

Many years ago now, when I was a liberal arts undergraduate, I sat around a student-dive living room with my roommates at ungodly hours, smoking cigarillos, drinking cheap wine, and discussing the complexities of Evelyn Waugh's *Brideshead Revisited*.

Because we were Catholics—and aspiring intellectuals—one of the plot points we kept coming back to was the terrible climax where Charles (the main character and narrator) is told by his lover, Julia, that she has to leave him. A cradle Catholic with an awakening conscience, Julia has come to the realization that she can no longer continue "living in sin", but she cannot marry Charles either because he is divorced and, according to the teaching of the Catholic Church, those who are divorced cannot remarry.

Julia says, "I've always been bad. Probably I shall be bad again, punished again. But the worse I am, the more I need God. I can't shut myself out from His mercy…. It may be a private bargain between me and God, that if I give up this one thing I want so much, however bad I am, He won't quite despair of me in the end. Now we shall both be alone, and I shall have no way of making you understand."

Charles responds, "I don't want to make it easier for you. I hope your heart may break; but I do understand."[8]

Even as undergraduates with barely a fistful of experience of life and love, it hit us right in the gut. We both feared and believed this idea that giving up "this one thing I want so much" was God's coinage, the currency he couldn't resist. Charles appears to understand Julia's reasoning, even perhaps to accept Julia's faith, or at least he acknowledges that something transcends the "fierce little human tragedy"[9] of his life.

As a Catholic novel, it was surprisingly unsettling. Where was the triumphant ending that made this fierce little tragedy worthwhile? Where was the blatant good versus evil? Why did religion appear to destroy the happiness of the main characters? These were the questions we debated and argued, and I'm still arguing to this day (mostly with myself). No doubt about it, *Brideshead Revisited* has stood the test of time.

If you haven't read it, do. First, because then you can understand *Brideshead* geekology and use terms like *chivvy* and *plover's eggs*. Second, because you don't have to be an English student to find it completely mesmerizing. It's a short but exquisite piece of literature, written in rich, dense language; reading it is like sinking your teeth through layers of chocolate ganache. And third, because it deals with that messy place where faith and experience collide.

Brideshead falls into two parts. Part 1 takes place in Oxford, where Charles finds himself in the orbit of a group of young bohemians, the flamboyant "aesthetes" of Oxford. Charles forms an intimate friendship with Lord Sebastian Flyte, the beautiful and charming son of an old aristocratic Catholic family.

> I was in search of love in those days, and I went full of curiosity and the faint, unrecognized apprehension that here, at last, I should find that low door in the wall, which others, I knew, had found before me, which opened on an enclosed and enchanted garden, which was somewhere, not overlooked by any window, in the heart of that grey city.[10]

He finds what he calls the "low door in the wall", the lifestyle less traveled, which leads to the enchanted garden, the carefree life of his student days, with all their exploration and liberality. It also leads to his deepest loves: friendship and art. But the garden of youth is an enclosed garden—sooner or later everyone has to leave and make his way in the world.

---

[8] Waugh, *Brideshead Revisited*, 340–41.
[9] Ibid., 351.
[10] Ibid., 31.

Part 2 is about life after Oxford. Charles marries, has a successful art career, and rises in the world, but he feels empty and shallow. His marriage fails. Sebastian cannot find happiness anywhere and descends painfully into alcoholism.

Eventually Charles falls in love with Sebastian's sister, Julia. Waugh portrays Charles and Julia's relationship as seamlessly perfect, mature, and peaceful, which makes their dilemma (Julia's Catholicism) seem particularly cruel. In the real world, as one friend aptly put it, a rich family could have solved their problem with a convenient annulment. But Waugh chose to write this scenario without a *deus ex machina*, and Julia leaves Charles heartbroken and bereft.

At twenty, I found this crushingly tragic. To me, the story had more the character of a Greek tragedy than a Catholic novel. "God" was the unseen power—fate. You can trick it, outrun it, and ignore it, but like the cursed Oedipus or the loyal Antigone, you cannot escape it without destroying yourself. In order to gain God, you have to sacrifice your heart's desire, and in the end you have … well, it doesn't really say. Just "God", whatever that was. This seemed a very poor deal indeed.

What seems to be unclear is why? Why did Waugh craft a story where his characters are forced to choose between God and love? Was it for art—excruciating, painful, beautiful, "good" art? Or was his worldview, like the worldview of the *Brideshead* Catholics, that God always wins no matter what, that even if you run to the ends of the earth, God has you by an unseen hook and invisible line and can bring you back with "a twitch upon the thread"?[11]

The hook and line are terrifying things if you don't know the hand that's reeling, if you believe, like Lady Marchmain (Sebastian's mother), that God is simply *truth*, but do not know him personally as *love*. This was the Catholic piety of Julia's nursery and Sebastian's childhood catechism. It was the world of British boarding schools and austere English Catholicism clinging to a foreign, ostracized religion. But the adult Julia finally admits what she has always known: there is another love out there, stronger and better even than human love.

"To know and love one other human being is the root of all wisdom",[12] the young student Charles said. This is the wisest line in the book, and, I believe, the key to the story, for it turns out to be true—through loving Sebastian and Julia, Charles becomes wise. He knows his love cannot save Sebastian, but he loves him anyway, with a completely loyal love, and remains his friend to the end. He doesn't try to "possess" or cure or influence Sebastian. His love has room for freedom. And even though Julia breaks his heart and he disagrees with her reasoning, he loves her enough to know that she's going to leave him—even before she knows—and he lets her go. Loving her gives him the wisdom to set her free.

Julia is called away—from the story, from Charles. Her real story begins outside the pages of *Brideshead Revisited*. Sebastian just sort of fades away from the story. His life ends in the care of monks in a Tunisian monastery, where he dies broken and soul weary but loved. Charles hears about it secondhand.

I don't believe I could have grasped the full power of *Brideshead Revisited* in my twenties. It's a novel for middle age. It's about a man who has fallen out of love with life—his marriage has failed, his lover has left him, his art is exhausted, and he is wearily soldiering with the British Army of the Second World War, a war which will usher in an age of utilitarian ugliness and emptiness. He returns to the scene of his youth, his first loves, and recalls all he has lost. But the funny thing about *Brideshead Revisited* is that it's not a cynical book.

11 Ibid., 220.
12 Ibid., 45.

And yet that is not the last word....

Something quite remote from anything the builders intended, has come out of their work, and out of the fierce little human tragedy in which I played ...: a small red flame— a beaten-copper lamp of deplorable design, relit before the beaten-copper doors of a tabernacle; the flame which the old knights saw from their tombs, which they saw put out; that flame burns again for other soldiers, far from home, farther, in heart, than Acre or Jerusalem. It could not have been lit but for the builders and the tragedians, and there I found it this morning, burning anew among the old stones.[13]

The book ends with a small flame of hope. At twenty, I thought it cold comfort compared to the garden of delights in Oxford. But life has a way of changing you, doesn't it? You grow older, you find love, lose love, and find love again. You experience tragedy, but it doesn't crush you. Your perspective lengthens. Charles, too, seems to begin his life only after realizing that all his old loves, and his youth, were dead. Like King Lear, he had to lose everything before his new life could begin. That's the flickering hope of middle age, something to carry into our Acre or Jerusalem, or whatever crusade we're fighting: our story doesn't end with our failures. There *is life* among the ruins.

— Mary

MYTHOLOGY: LITERATURE'S HANDMAID

Some people, whom I respect greatly, belong to the camp of "Mythology is purely pagan nonsense that has no business in the formation of children." The aim of this article is not to refute that point. While I personally think it can be done, I don't want to fritter away my energy in a mythology apologia. I will, however, for the sake of warming you skeptics or fence-sitters out there, say a few words that may cause you to give a longing look at the green grass on my side of the fence, the side where fantastical, mythological, and nonsensical stories are told in abundance (provided the concepts of Good and Evil are presented in clear, proper positions—a whole other topic).

First, we look at the pure logic in it. Mythology, like it or not, has a rich history in our culture, and references to it abound. I pity the day that will come, and perhaps already is here in some cases, where people will make a reference to Pandora's box or Achilles' heel and receive nothing but quizzical looks or blank stares in return. William F. Russell makes this point in the introduction to his excellent and highly recommended book *Classic Myths to Read Aloud*, where he goes on to say, "Children are constantly trying to make some sense of their world, and when they are allowed to acquire a store of traditional information, when they are given meaningful reading materials that draw upon that store of shared knowledge, children (and adults, too) are able to create mental 'hooks' on which they gather and attach new pieces of information."[14]

He goes on to relate how two college students (headed to the education department) were overheard trying to make sense of "the wooden horse of Troy", asking, "And who in the world is this guy Troy, anyway?"[15] Oh, how the literacy advocate in me wants to weep! More than just allowing us to stay on top of important references, the tales of gods, goddesses, heroes, wars, love, and tragedy in mythology have delighted people for generations. They teach many good lessons, stir up emotions, inspire meaningful discussions, and expand

[13] Ibid., 351.
[14] William F. Russell, *Classic Myths to Read Aloud: The Great Stories of Greek and Roman Mythology* (New York: Three Rivers Press, 1989), 2.
[15] Ibid., 3.

> Mythology is the handmaid of literature; and literature is one of the best allies of virtue and promoters of happiness.
>
> — Thomas Bulfinch
> *Bulfinch's Mythology*

vocabulary. You will find that the added bonus of understanding stories behind many of the sky's constellations is quite satisfying for children too.

Onward now. I can share a bit about a gorgeous children's book that may whet your appetite for more mythology. Apart from a couple of compilations (like the superb *D'Aulaire's Book of Greek Myths*), only a few titles in the picture book world directly tell traditional mythology tales. But the story of Pegasus told by Mariana Mayer and illustrated by K.Y. Craft is at the top of this list. The first thing you'll notice about this book is its incredible artwork. Each page deserves its own frame and a moment to linger over it. I love it when a story devotes the occasional wordless spread to illustrate a piece of the story. Craft is a sublime artist who has won more than a hundred graphic-arts awards. She chooses her commissions well, because all of her children's books are worthy of looking over; they are fairy tales or mythological tales (e.g., *The Twelve Dancing Princesses*, *King Midas and the Golden Touch*, *The Adventures of Tom Thumb*, etc.). The work she puts into the story of Pegasus draws you right in, makes you feel the

fear of the chimera, the indifference of the villagers, and the nobility of Bellerophon. Mariana Mayer does an excellent job of staging the story and staying true to its meaning. There are many little tangents available for further research if you are so inclined. The names are difficult to pronounce, and some of the relationships are taken for granted, but with a perceptive reader (someone who speaks in a slow whisper when Bellerophon first sees Pegasus or who raises her voice in excitement while the battle blows are told), children fall deep under the spell of the story and are left a little bit thoughtful by its ending.

My children may not go through life knowing all of pop culture's references (that's fo shizzle), but they'll definitely not go to college wondering who in the world this guy Troy is. I'm determined to stoke the fires of their imagination with the great stories of Greek and Roman mythology. And I feel great satisfaction when they try to make Orion out of the glow-in-the-dark star stickers in their bedroom.

— Ellie

CONQUERING THE CHAOS OF EVERYDAY LIFE

Last summer, a friend handed me Holly Pierlot's well-known book *A Mother's Rule of Life*. Pierlot, a mother of five, moved from mismatched socks on the living room floor, bored and unruly children, and chronic lack of prayer time to a peaceful and orderly household. The

serene picture of an organized home she paints in her book has always been my ideal. Organization is in my bones, you see. I thrive on routines. Discovering the best ways to lay out clothes closets, grade student papers, or host dinner parties gives me tremendous satisfaction. My logical mind always seeks the most efficient approach to every aspect of life. When I became a mother, however, my beautifully methodical world fell apart. So I was curious about Pierlot's story, but also skeptical. I had heard the chorus of criticism about the book: "She is too rigid", one person said. Another opined, "She lives in the middle of nowhere. Her life would never work in the suburbs." I harbored my own reservations. *My children would never comply*, I thought, recalling the helplessness I experienced after the birth of my first daughter, the aspiring anarchist who resisted all schedules, made child-rearing books seem useless, defied tricks suggested by veteran mothers, and at six years of age *finally* began to sleep through most nights. Pierlot's book appeared unrealistic.

Fast-forward a few weeks. We were visiting a new family in town. Their house was surprisingly uncluttered, comfortable, and tidy without being oppressive. Five young children, soon joined by my daughters, spent the afternoon playing. Dinner simmered in the Crock-Pot, while the grown-ups sipped wine and enjoyed uninterrupted conversation. As we talked, I discovered that our hostess followed practices similar to Pierlot's methods of organization. The results were impressive. I was envious. I decided to give it a try.

I started by designating a moment each morning for the daily readings and prayer. This entailed teaching my children to respect my silence. Laundry was from now on limited to specific days. Bathrooms and floors fell into their own slots, as did other chores. I'm still experimenting with the optimal time to bake our bread and gauge the volume of groceries so that I will need to go shopping only once a week. Several benefits have emerged as a result. First, my weekly schedule is lucid and predictable. Second, I am happier because I

know how and when toys, books, clothes, and random objects will go back to their places. Third, I actually have more energy, for instead of plodding ceaselessly all day, I complete tasks and move on. Fourth, my children are learning responsibility by following their own procedures. For example, they have learned to get themselves and their books ready for the biweekly homeschoolers' co-op we attend. Even the would-be-anarchist daughter has joined the bandwagon. Having responsibilities means being in charge, and she likes that very much.

Taking steps to banish confusion from our rooms and activities has given our family a small new start. Our life has gained flexibility, allowing us to accommodate small crises as well as spontaneous holidays. The underlying routine keeps us steady, rested, and prepared for the next day. It is an excellent thing, it seems, if our house can reflect some measure of the supernatural order that pervades all things.

—Justyna Braun, New York

FOR MY SON

This is how you hold a book. This is how you turn the page. This is how you rub your thumb on the moth-eaten corner to release the scent of last century's sunshine. This is how you press a peacock feather between the forty-sixth and forty-seventh pages. Stories bear talismans, even when you haven't put them there. This is how you read one sentence over and over and over, until it is flesh, and stone, and bread. This is how you avoid spotting the margins with coffee. This is how you write in the margins—*but you said you shouldn't write in a book*. You shouldn't, but if you have to, you should write with small hands. This is the way you read poetry. This is the way you read Shakespeare. This is the way you read a fairy tale: out loud, with an eye cast over your shoulder, a pocket full of breadcrumbs, and a litany of saints behind your lips. This is how you digest a book you don't like: leave it in the trunk of the car for three years and read it again. Then you will be better able to feed on the cherries and spit out the pits.

— Christie Ricardo, Conwy, Wales

THE TEMPERAMENT GOD GAVE YOU

BY ART AND LARAINE BENNETT

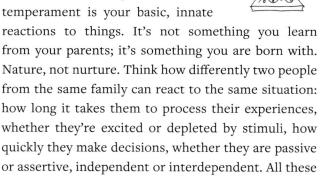

No mother needs to be told that her children are born with different personalities. Do you sometimes look at your little mini-me or mini-him and think, *What planet do you come from? How can someone be the spitting image of his father and yet so … (fill in the blank)?* Do you sometimes wish children came with a set of instructions? What about your spouse? Sometimes it's all peace and harmony, and sometimes you think, *Are we even speaking the same language?*

As mothers, we are equipped with special intuitive powers to help understand our children. We're fueled by that powerful, passionate motherly love that is God's great gift to the young of the species. (Thank goodness we're not crocodiles—not usually anyway.) But, and here's the catch, we come to the table with our own distinct temperament too, and so we react to our children, husband, neighbors, coworkers, and God in a unique way.

The Temperament God Gave You was written to be a practical guide for understanding the traditional four temperaments: choleric, melancholic, phlegmatic, and sanguine, as understood throughout the centuries. It describes the strengths and weaknesses of each temperament and gives concrete advice for parents, couples, and coworkers so they can bring out the best in one another and grow their relationships.

So what is a temperament? Your temperament is your basic, innate reactions to things. It's not something you learn from your parents; it's something you are born with. Nature, not nurture. Think how differently two people from the same family can react to the same situation: how long it takes them to process their experiences, whether they're excited or depleted by stimuli, how quickly they make decisions, whether they are passive or assertive, independent or interdependent. All these characteristics are factors of temperament.

The words "choleric", "melancholic", "phlegmatic", and "sanguine" come from the ancient Greeks, who first named them. Other cultures have similar categories, like the *Vata, Pitta, Kapha* temperaments in ancient Ayurvedic practice or traditional Chinese medicine's earth elements—fire, water, earth, metal, and wood—that correlate to temperament. In more recent times, the famous Myers-Briggs personality test recognizes sixteen types, roughly grouped into four main categories. (The Myers-Briggs test, by the way, makes a great parlor game for family gatherings on a long winter's evening. How well do you know one another? Debate, but be kind.)

It's probably safe to say that each of us fits somewhere, with some overlap, into one of the traditional four temperaments:

- Choleric: The go-getter. Cholerics react quickly and take charge, and their decisions usually translate into immediate action. Leadership, intelligence, and high productivity are some of the cholerics' strengths, but they can also be dictatorial, ambitious, and resentful of criticism.
- Melancholic: The deep thinker. Melancholics react slowly, take a long time to process experiences, and are not usually quick to make decisions. They have high ideals and work methodically. They tend to perfectionism and have a great capacity for contemplation and love of ideals, such as beauty and truth. Social interactions are often exhausting for them, but they're good at teamwork.
- Phlegmatic: The diplomatic. Phlegmatics are generally even-tempered, helpful, and self-effacing. They usually take a long time to process their experiences. Because they are not quick to react, they sometimes need help standing up for themselves or taking initiative, but they are usually very good in relationships and service to others.
- Sanguine: The fun lover. Sanguines react quickly and love stimuli, but the reactions don't usually last long. They are adaptable and people oriented. They tend to be joyful and love to please people, but they can also be impulsive, disorganized, and live on the surface of things.

These are broad generalizations, but maybe you recognize some of these characteristics in the people you live with and love. Each temperament has its strengths and weaknesses. Gentleness, for instance, is a lovely quality, but a gentle person might be so passive that he really struggles to confront injustice. A choleric person might make a good leader but might also be bossy and despotic. As a textbook sanguine, I see clearly how my love of fun and beauty leads to great friendships, parties, and beautiful surroundings, but I'm disastrously lacking in the budgeting and long-term planning department.

Understanding our temperaments can help us grow in self-knowledge and pinpoint the areas where more work is needed. This is a great gift to those we live with. It can lead to more empathy, understanding, and conflict resolution, because so many conflicts in the home and workplace come down to a difference of temperament. It can really help a marriage as we learn to root out bad habits and build a better team.

There was a time when I became a bit anxious about my eldest son, a dyed-in-the-wool melancholic. He is a shy, "dreamy" type, an observer who doesn't jump into a crowd. When I saw him hanging around on the edge of a group of kids, my heart would ache for him. He also seemed to bottle up his feelings, which dismayed me even more. What were we doing wrong? Aren't we all such good communicators around here? I felt I had to push him into social situations, make endless play-dates for him, and force him to be friendly. This only seemed to isolate him more.

Reading *The Temperament God Gave You* really helped me relax about the poor kid and accept his differences. It was like a mirror that showed me that my own reactions were typically "sanguine". Having friends and being in the center of things are very important to me. They're not important to my son. And that's okay. My job is to help strengthen his social skills by gently teaching and encouraging communication and friendship, but also to make sure he has his solitude and space to think, dream, and create. Above all, I must not try to turn him into a sanguine. His gifts as a melancholic are what fuel his art and phenomenal creativity.

Since I started following the advice from *The Temperament God Gave You*, I've noticed some subtle but important changes. My son has become more relaxed because his temperamental needs are being met. He also now knows what to do in a social setting: shake hands, say hi, look Mrs. So-and-so in the eye—which he does by rote. This takes the pressure off having to figure it out himself. This, in turn, has helped his inner light to shine.

This book has also given me more understanding of my husband, the classic choleric, and how his instant decision-making isn't meant to be rude and overbearing. I've been able to help him learn to let me in on decision-making, to be patient, and to make space for others. And it's helped me be merciful to myself, realizing that my temperamental weaknesses aren't necessarily moral failings, just character traits in need of direction and discipline.

While I'm slightly allergic to self-help material, *The Temperament God Gave You* has been enormously beneficial for my family relationships. It provides advice for every combination of temperaments. The section for husbands and wives is pretty great—and very practical. The section for parents could also apply to teachers. Workplace relationships are discussed in the section for the coworker, boss, and employee. And, finally, a section addresses the temperament and spirituality—how to grow in holiness. It is not lofty or philosophical but full of common sense.

There may be mothers and fathers out there who intuitively understand how to parent every temperament. There may be husbands and wives with flawless communication. There may be blissful workplaces where everyone gets along like cogs in a well-oiled machine. But many of us are still in the process of learning. I keep this book on my shelf of reference materials. (And, being a sanguine, I don't read it cover to cover.)

— Mary

THE ONE-STRAW REVOLUTION

BY MASANOBU FUKUOKA

Those who are fond of Wendell Berry, the American farmer-philosopher, will be fascinated by his Japanese kindred spirit, Masanobu Fukuoka. Like Berry, Fukuoka lived a quiet life on his little farm in an old-fashioned agricultural village. Like Berry, he was a writer and philosopher who knew that how we farm, how we live, what we eat, and what our culture values are woven together in the same cloth.

Before it was cool to use words like "organic" and "sustainable", before farmers' markets and Community Supported Agriculture (CSA), before hippies, before countercultural agriculturists started developing ideas of biodynamic farming, one man in postwar, industrialized Japan was questioning the latest agricultural practice of his nation. How could it sustain itself, he wondered, when it virtually raped the earth, taking everything and giving nothing back? At the same time, was traditional Japanese agriculture, with its backbreaking labor and dependence on a large peasantry, a viable answer?

Fukuoka pursued a quiet and almost invisible life on the same land his family had been farming for hundreds of years. But rather than following the majority of Japanese farmers into modern agriculture—American postwar "development", with its use of pesticides, machines, and chemical fertilizers—he chose to let nature teach him how to farm. Nature, he observed, thrives; species living in community with each other, in mutually beneficial competition, grow healthy and keep each other healthy. And with great results!

Frances Moore Lappé, author of *Diet for a Small Planet*, writes in her introduction to Fukuoka's book, "The myth remains that organically raised produce is inevitably more expensive than food produced with the benefit of chemicals and must therefore be a luxury, impractical for the masses. Even many who are deeply engaged in sustainability movements revert to the idea of 'lack' or of doing without in order to save the environment. Fukuoka, by contrast, encourages us to trust nature's bounty."[16] In *The One-Straw Revolution*, Fukuoka describes how his yields rivaled and exceeded those of his machine- and chemical-dependent neighbors.

For centuries, Japanese families had grown the same crops on the same small plots of land without robbing the soil of nutrients. By careful cultivation, strategic flooding, composting, manure spreading, and the painstaking transplanting of crops one plant at a time, they had managed to keep fertile their small parcels of land for thousands of years. When Fukuoka took over his father's farm, he thought, *Surely there's an easier way*. And so he sought a third model. Rejecting the unnecessary labor of traditional Japanese agriculture, he developed a new method with no tilling, but instead mulching, or throwing the remains of each crop (stalks, straw, plant waste) back onto the fields, building up the soil and protecting it the same way a forest floor builds up the soil. In this way, the soil was continually enriched, the frail seedlings of the next crop were protected from weather, weeding was eliminated—and all this from one thoughtful innovation learned at the knees of Mother Nature.

Masanobu Fukuoka spent most of his life pursuing a slow way of living. He woke at dawn and worked until sundown every day. But he worked with joy, keen observation, and something you might call love for his crops, orchards, gardens, and land. He worked at a sustainable pace that left him time for reading, writing poetry, and taking leisurely meals with the students, vagrants, and pilgrims who traveled, sometimes in crowds, to live with him and learn his approach.

As farmer-philosophers ourselves, my husband and I were intrigued by his way of life. He writes jokingly about "'do-nothing' farming"[17] and his characteristic laziness, which led him to question traditional practices, on the one hand, and exploitive modern practices, on

the other. But Fukuoka actually loved work—work, that is, with a purpose. For Fukuoka, work was another part of leisure, a necessary part of an integrated human life.

Lappé, with the passionate voice of the long-term activist, calls the paradox of today's lifestyle "life-stunting overwork and deprivation for the majority" on the one hand and "life-stunting overwork and surfeit for the minority" on the other.[18] What if, like Fukuoka, we sought a third model? What if we took a good hard look at our lives and asked ourselves, *What am I working* for? *Should I do less but do it more passionately? Should I take less pay but live a more enriched life?*

Unlike most of his Western readers, Masanobu Fukuoka approached life from a Buddhist perspective. As a young man, he had an epiphany, an "aha moment", while gazing at a crane descending on a lake. It was a time of intense physical suffering for him, as he was in the midst of a health breakdown, alone and isolated in an underequipped hospital. Experiencing his own frailty, he came to believe that all human endeavor was futile, life was short, and everything we really care about is no more than a passing moment. Only nature endures, he thought, and so nature must show us how to live. This may sound bleak to our Western ears, especially to us Christians who try to see eternal significance in the smallest things—the kingdom of heaven in a mustard seed. But rather than withdraw into nihilistic apathy, Fukuoka became a pilgrim. This, in my opinion, is the greatest gift Buddhism can give to the world: a profound humility in the face of life, reverence for the earth as a kind of teacher, and the idea that we, too, are pilgrims on this earth, with no right to waste and exploit what has been given to us as a gift.

As Wendell Berry writes in his preface, "Mr. Fukuoka's is a science that begins and ends in reverence—in awareness that the human grasp necessarily diminishes whatever it holds. It is not knowledge, he seems to say, that gives us the sense of the whole, but joy, which we may have only by *not* grasping."[19]

---

[16] Frances Moore Lappé, introduction to *The One-Straw Revolution*, by Masanobu Fukuoka, ed. Larry Korn, trans. Larry Korn, Chris Pearce, and Tsune Kurosawa (New York: New York Review Books, 1978), viii.

[17] Ibid., xiii.

[18] Ibid., ix.

[19] Wendell Berry, preface to *The One-Straw Revolution*, xiv.

The One-Straw Revolution has lots of practical information about crop rotation, deep mulching, barley planting, and so on, but it's not just a farm manual. It's a story, an essay, and a delightful ramble that any mother, father, gardener—in short, anyone with a love for the earth and for life—can enjoy. The words and stories are simple and beautifully written. This is not surprising, considering it was Wendell Berry who midwifed the English translation into existence. Perhaps it will be part of *your* own tiny, one-straw, or one-window-plant revolution. Or maybe it will just be good bathtub reading to dream on.

— Mary

THE WAY OF A PILGRIM

BY AN ANONYMOUS NINETEENTH-CENTURY RUSSIAN PILGRIM

TRANSLATED BY R.M. FRENCH

This is a humble book. A simple Russian man wanders into his local church on Sunday to attend the Divine Liturgy. It is the nineteenth century, pre-Communist Russia; the vast, mysterious Russia of the past. The monasteries are full; the people have faith. The man hears the words of the apostle being read: "Pray constantly" (1 Thess 5:17). He wonders, *What can it mean? How can one pray constantly when you have to turn your mind to other things all day long, to earn a living, and to eat your daily bread?*

Intrigued and deeply moved, he travels to different churches to hear sermons on prayer, but they fail to enlighten him. So he sets out to find someone wiser and holier who could teach him the way of prayer. "I walked at least 125 miles, and then I came to a large town, a provincial capital, where I saw a monastery."[20]

The Way of a Pilgrim is the story of this unnamed man's wandering through the cities and countryside of Russia in search of holiness. Some of the men and women he meets are extraordinary people, full of wisdom. He writes down their conversations, pondering them in his heart, then travels on. He carries nothing but the coat on his back and a knapsack with a little dry bread and a Bible. He is utterly poor. He feels his soul is empty because he knows nothing, feels nothing, except a yearning for God that isn't satisfied. In the tradition of the Russian pilgrim, he relies on the charity of others to feed and shelter him. He prays, listens to the *starets* (spiritual elders), and reads from *The Philokalia* (the spiritual classic on interior prayer). He reads it over and over again.

From *The Philokalia* he learns the prayer of the heart "Lord Jesus Christ, have mercy on me."[21] This prayer is called the "summary of the Gospels".[22] At first, for the pilgrim, it's just an exercise, drawing in the breath, feeling his heartbeat, and matching each word to a beat of the heart: Lord. Jesus. Christ. Have. Mercy. On. Me. Over and over. But the people he meets through his journey tell wondrous stories of the changes this prayer effects in their hearts and in the circumstances of their lives.

As Lent approaches, it's time for spiritual house-cleaning once again. Few of us can go on a real pilgrimage. Usually the best we can do is say our prayers, maybe squeeze in a little reading here and there. The best my husband and I can do, with four very young children, is light a candle (if we can find matches) and sing some sacred songs at the end of the evening. (Not all of us are emotionally pulled together; some

---

[20] R.M. French, trans., *The Way of a Pilgrim and the Pilgrim Continues His Way* (New York: HarperCollins, 1965), 5.
[21] Ibid., 11.
[22] Ibid., 28.

of us have lost consciousness; some of us are wishing we could be at the botanical gardens, six miles away, instead of singing with wailing toddlers. But it's a start.) It's also a good time for spiritual reading.

I don't know about you, but the words "spiritual reading" always sound a little daunting to me. They're in the same category as "weight training" or "raw vegetable diet", a necessary evil. But when I picked up *The Way of a Pilgrim*, I found it was simple enough for even my

sleep-deprived brain or that five-minute lull in activity when a mother needs to (but usually doesn't) put her feet up. It's not the usual kind of spiritual reading. It doesn't describe spiritual "technique" or require great intellectual concentration. It's actually a simple and charming story, and it has a very simple effect: it makes you want to be a pilgrim, not in reality but in your heart, not leaving your duties behind but lifting them into the mysteries of God. It could be seen as the story of the Jesus Prayer and the transforming power of calling on the name of Jesus as often as we remember, even with every breath.

As you go about your day, nursing your baby, going to the office, teaching fractions, or whatever fills your waking hours, you can turn the inner eye of your heart to the manger and just sit quietly gazing at the little Prince of Peace, or at the feet of the Risen Christ, who is in our midst.

— Mary

FAMILY SUMMER READING CHALLENGE

"Summertime and the livin' is easy ..."

Welcome to the modern age, where easy living ain't what it used to be. How many lazy hours of a day at home can go by before your children plead with you to let them watch a television show or participate in some form of digital communication or recreation? We open the door to the technological world for the sake of its pleasures and conveniences, but how quickly it feels like an unwelcome guest in the home and we wish it would leave us alone for a little while.

Each family needs to figure out their own ways of corralling the tech beast, but may I suggest as a supplement to your efforts this sweet little challenge?
Needed:

- A good bulletin board or empty wall space
- A quality book list
- A sampling of books on the list or regularly scheduled library outings

- A log chart
- Cash prizes

The first thing to do is post a big colorful sign:

FAMILY SUMMER READING CHALLENGE: FIRST PRIZE $100.00, SECOND PRIZE $50.00, THIRD PRIZE $25.00. All other participants who read 250 pages or more will win a participation prize of $10.00.

Obviously, one can adjust these prizes according to budget and needed motivation, but this seemed about right for my kids.

Next, hunt down a good book list. There are nice lists in the appendices of *Honey for a Child's Heart* by Gladys Hunt, *A Landscape with Dragons* by Michael D. O'Brien, and *The Well-Trained Mind* by Susan Wise Bauer. There are some great online book lists out there too, including the "Thousand Good Books" list by John Senior.

Photocopy or print the list (or age-appropriate sections) and post it in a spot that can be seen and referenced throughout the summer. Next to the book list hang a log chart with each family member's name and columns for book titles and number of pages. On a separate paper, post the rules:

- At the end of the summer, the reader with the greatest number of pages wins.
- Books selected must be on the approved book list and match the individual's grade or age according to the chart. Special permission for books not on the list may be granted by a discriminating parent.
- If someone wishes to read a reasonable book from below his grade level, he may with a 25 percent reduction of pages credited to him.
- When a book is completed, the individual must record it in the log with title, number of pages, and parental signature.
- Mothers and fathers can and ideally should participate.

It's nice to have some good reading options on one shelf or basket for easy perusing and access, or you can commit to weekly library outings. I've had bad luck with library fees, so I tend to buy used books and try to stock up our home library. I purchase used copies of a few titles to add interest to our collection and tell our kids if they know of a book we don't own that sounds interesting to them, I'll obtain a copy.

To keep my testimony real, I admit we started strong but by the end of the summer were definitely less into it. Our oldest son had a job, so he had less free time and less financial motivation, and he barely made the participatory requirements. But a couple of our kids really took to it, worked hard, and expanded their minds more than they would have otherwise.

And it motivated me to finish *Anna Karenina*, which had been sitting by my bed waiting to fill my soul with color.

— Hope

ON INCORRUPTIBLES

The most shocking discovery I made as I began to learn about the Catholic faith was the miracle of incorruptibles, those saints and blesseds who so united themselves to Christ in life that even their very flesh defies the laws of nature and does not decay in death. In college, I had learned the teaching of the utter depravity of man. I learned Martin Luther's illustration that Christ's grace was to us as "snow on a dunghill"; our sins were covered, but our fallen nature was so tainted by sin that it could not be perfected in this life. I really think dwelling too much on this teaching had caused me to become cynical and despair of my own sanctification. When I found Joan Carroll Cruz's book *The Incorruptibles* in a tiny Catholic bookstore in Irving, Texas, another possibility opened up for me. Now,

armed with Cruz's amazing chronicle, I have evidence that it is possible to become so sanctified in this life that Christ has entered even the decomposable flesh and transfigured it for immortality. This miraculous sign of sanctity gives me joy and hope that I can follow their example, if imperfectly.

How had I missed this great miracle my entire Christian life? As so often happens, once I saw it, I began to see it everywhere. Incorruptibles are in Augustine's *Confessions*. In Book 9, Saint Augustine talks about a vision Saint Ambrose had that led to the discovery of the incorrupt bodies of two martyred saints, Protasius and Gervasius, whose relics then cured a blind man. They are also in Dostoevsky's *The Brothers Karamazov*. In the chapter "The Odor of Corruption", Alyosha is profoundly disappointed to discover that his beloved teacher, the holy priest Father Zosima, is not incorrupt after his death. So present was the reality of incorruptibles in the Russian Orthodoxy of the nineteenth century that decay was more surprising than preservation in the body of a holy person.

Reading account after amazing account of these holy souls, one thing becomes clear: incorruptibility is a mystery. Why do the bodies of some who have led exemplary lives decay while others do not? Why are some preserved entirely, while others are preserved only in part or only for a time? As with other mysteries, one is left confounded, asking who can know the mind of God or limit the imaginative ways he manifests himself. In the case of Saint Anthony of Padua, only the tongue of this great teacher and preacher was found incorrupt. Other incorruptibles are found entirely preserved. Many of these are saints who had important public missions in this life. Their preservation after death is a glorious end for an excellent life. Saint Catherine Labouré, to whom the Blessed Mother revealed the Miraculous Medal, was found perfectly preserved. Cruz writes that upon her exhumation, two elderly ladies "who had known Sister Catherine easily recognized the features of their Saintly friend".[23] Saint Bernadette Soubirous, to whom Our Lady appeared as the Immaculate Conception, was found thirty years after her death entirely incorrupt: "They discerned no odor, and the virginal body lay exposed, completely victorious over the laws of nature."[24]

Sometimes it is the seemingly insignificant whom God elevates to this honor. One of the most surprising and moving incorruptibles Cruz describes is Blessed Margaret of Metola (1287–1320). Her story begins, "Because she was dwarfed, blind, hunchbacked and lame, Bl. Margaret was kept hidden by her parents throughout her childhood."[25] When they took her to a healer and she was not cured, her parents abandoned her to the streets. Rather than growing bitter about her lot, she was known for her cheerfulness and earned her keep by caring for small children, the sick and dying, and prisoners. After a holy death at age thirty-three, two hundred miracles were attributed to her. She reminds us that anyone, in any circumstance, can choose to love heroically.

It is also a delight to discover all the little miracles that occur through the great miracle of incorruptibility. On occasion, a mysterious and lovely smelling healing oil exudes from the body of the incorruptible, as in the case of Saint Hugh of Lincoln (1135–1200).

More recently, the incorrupt body of a great Eastern saint of the late-nineteenth century, Saint Charbel Makhlouf of Lebanon, continues to this day to exude a mixture of sweat and blood that has healed over 1,200 people. Cruz notes that his body was buried, as was the custom, in a shallow, muddy grave without a coffin. Only after a mysterious light shone on the grave for forty-five nights was his body exhumed and discovered perfectly preserved.

I cannot recommend Cruz's book highly enough for its thrilling and surprising accounts of how people, from all times and all walks of life, found their paths to holiness. It reminds us that incorruptibles, though seldom discussed, permeate the Christian history of East and West. If we look around, they are still a very real part of our time. In 2015, Pope Francis sent the incorrupt body of Saint Maria Goretti, the Little Saint of Great Mercy, on a Pilgrimage of Mercy to the United States. I had the privilege to be in her presence in Houston, and the lines to see her were long and lasted all day. Imagine the many miracles, seen and unseen, that happened all over the country because of the presence of this incorruptible. In Rome, the incorrupt remains of Saint Pio were exposed during the Ash Wednesday Mass at St. Peter's Basilica in 2016.

[23] Joan Carroll Cruz, *The Incorruptibles: A Study of the Incorruption of the Bodies of Various Catholic Saints and Beati* (Charlotte, N.C.: TAN Books, 1977), 269.

[24] Ibid., 276.

[25] Ibid., 81.

His remains then traveled throughout the world for the rest of the year with the Missionaries of Mercy, who preached and heard confessions "as a living sign of how the Father welcomes all those who seek his forgiveness", Archbishop Michele Castoro said. The archbishop added that Padre Pio's incorruptible body would be "a precious sign for all missionaries and priests, who will find strength for their own mission in the wondrous example of this untiring, welcoming and patient confessor".[26]

That same year, Saint Charbel's remains traveled to thirty-six Maronite parishes in the United States. At St. Joseph Maronite Catholic Church in Phoenix, a thirty-three-year-old blind mother of three was restored to perfect vision after venerating his relics. As a priest on her left side laid hands on her, she distinctly felt the presence of someone on her right side as well. She had been approved for a nursing facility because she could not care for her children prior to her healing.

Most recently, it was announced in March 2016 that the body of Orthodox Archbishop Dmitri of Dallas, who died in the summer of 2011 and was buried unembalmed, was discovered unchanged when his body was moved to his new tomb in St. Seraphim Orthodox Cathedral in Dallas. No one who knew him was surprised that this joyful and holy man's body is incorrupt.

In a cynical and increasingly corrupt time, incorruptibles inspire and lead us as lights in the darkness. Incorruptibles are signs to us of what we might become, with God's grace operative in us. They are also direct conduits of his mercy, mysteriously healing many who come into their presence. Above all, they point us to our final destiny of immortality in Christ. With them and in the words of the prayer after Communion for the third Sunday after Easter, we can pray with hope and joy, "Look with kindness upon your people, O Lord, and grant, we pray, that those you were pleased to renew by eternal mysteries may attain in their flesh the incorruptible glory of the resurrection. Through Christ our Lord."[27]

— Celia Neumayr, Texas

THE FIVE LOVE LANGUAGES OF CHILDREN

BY GARY CHAPMAN AND ROSS CAMPBELL

This past summer, I had a conversation with my husband about how to reach out to our children with their individual personalities and needs. I was feeling discouraged by my terrible qualifications for motherhood—namely, feeling burnt-out all the time. I said, "I love them with every fiber of my being. I would die for them. But all this love is a useless sentiment if I don't find a way to show it."

Not long after, my friend Jen, bighearted and attuned to people's needs, decided that what we mamas needed to kick-start the school year was a mini book club devoted to one book: *The Five Love Languages of Children*. As Jen predicted, most of us felt starved for fresh ideas and tools to help us in this sometimes-mountainous journey of parenting.

The book is written for people like us: parents with good intentions and good hearts who want to do a better job. It aims to give parents positive tools to fill our children's emotional needs, the "emotional love tank" as the authors call it, something we mothers are

---

[26] Ann Schneible, "Missionaries of Mercy to Be Sent Out under the Gaze of Padre Pio", Catholic News Agency, January 6, 2016, www.catholicnewsagency.com/news/33201/missionaries-of-mercy-to-be-sent-out-under-the-gaze-of-padre-pio.

[27] *Ignatius Pew Missal*, Third Sunday of Easter (Year A), www.pewmissal.com/brand_new/index.php/planning-guide/easter-2/third-sunday-of-easter-year-a.

required to do on a minute-by-minute basis. There is nothing more important in the world we can do, and yet we're often frustratingly limited. We might be tired,  rushed, ill, postpartum, prepartum, or just too busy filling basic needs and going through the motions of feeding and clothing our children to hear the needs of their hearts.

You might remember the dinosaur days when *The Five Love Languages*, published in 1992, was making the rounds on coffee tables and night tables. Author Gary Chapman identified five major ways that human beings express and seek love in relationship: physical touch, giving gifts, acts of service, quality time, and words of affirmation. These five "languages" have entered the jargon of everyday life. Although I never read the book, I'm familiar with the expression, and I try to speak my husband's love languages and make him aware of mine. We see wonderful results when we really try.

The Five Love Languages of Children applies the same ideas to the fragile and urgent emotional needs of children. First, it walks us through the five love languages and how they might look in a child's life. Then it helps us identify our own child's love language through observation of our child. How does your child express love to you? Is he verbal? Physical? Does he give you gifts? Does he love to do little services for you? You are probably seeing your child's own love language and a key to his emotional health. Our son Hugh, for example, is a great gift giver. He spends most evenings before bed stitching little bags or drawing pictures for people. Sometimes his gift is simply a cool rock or leaf he found outdoors. Material possessions mean a lot to Hugh. So it's no surprise that he gets great emotional satisfaction from a gift from his mom and dad. This doesn't mean we spend a lot of money. A "gift" could mean a special pancake shaped like an *H* or an old calendar to cut up. But when I say "I thought you'd love this," he knows it comes from my heart.

Another diagnostic tool is considering what your child requests most often. For example, if your child often comes to you to show off his achievements—art,

homework, something he built, and so on—he is probably looking for words of affirmation. Another tool of observation is noticing what your child complains about. For example, his complaining that "you never have time to play with me!" might mean your child is hankering for quality time.

The author also provides a script for conversation with your child to help you find his love language. Give your child a choice between two options, each representing a different love language. For example, you might say to your son or daughter, "I have some free time Saturday. Would you rather …" Personally, I found this diagnostic tool useless because my children just gave me strange, misgiving looks, as if to say, *Why are we having this weird, artificial conversation?* But for some families it might be a fun game.

The Five Love Languages of Children is not just about positive emotions. The book has several chapters on what to do with negative emotions, especially anger. In my opinion, this is the most important, even crucial, chapter for families, even families who don't have an "anger problem". Anger is a natural human emotion, like sadness, joy, grief, and embarrassment. It's a normal response to frustration or hostility, and it's found in every household, no matter how gentle and intentional our parenting. Yet more than any other emotion, anger can tear down relationships. Teaching our children to divert anger (without becoming passive-aggressive) is a life skill that will bless their adult years as they become roommates, coworkers, spouses, friends, administrators, and fellow sojourners in the Christian life. Coming from a family where anger was usually buried, I understand how important it is to acknowledge anger, confront people peacefully, and resolve problems.

When I was reading *The Five Love Languages of Children*, I can honestly say I found the keys to three of my children's emotional health in as many days. After trying a few changes, I saw positive results almost immediately in their mood, confidence, and overall happiness. For example, I have a touchy-feely, squirmy-wormy, rowdy six-year-old. As a nursing mother, I often approached story time with this squirmer with a modicum of dread. I felt a little "touched out". I wanted space. I could feel myself getting cross with him. After reading the chapter on physical touch, I decided to make one small change. The next story time, I finished nursing the baby, put her down on the floor, took my six-year-old on my knee, and gave him a big squeeze. Then I read him a story while holding him on my lap. This small change made a huge difference. After the story, he jumped off my lap, said "Thanks, Mum", and ran off to play with his brother. Over the next several days, I tried to preempt his needs by starting the day with a story and cuddle. Almost immediately he stopped "pestering me". He no longer hurled himself at my body when he wanted to say something or climbed all over me when I sat down. Now when he begins throwing himself at people, climbing on them, tickling them, or running his fingers along their arms, that's a sign to me that I've neglected his "love tank" and that he needs my intentional, gentle physical touch. Sure enough, a few cuddles with a story are all he needs.

That was just one example. Some love languages are harder to implement, and of course some ages are more difficult, like the teenage years. Also, the book does *not* address the languages of children with special needs like ADHD or autism spectrum disorder. So if you have a child with social or mental health challenges, you would need to look elsewhere for resources. Also, it's primarily written for parents of one or two children. The amount of suggestions and dos and don'ts it offers could be overwhelming if you tried to implement them in a big family. For example, the suggestion to "Go for a special shopping trip together" to meet the need for "quality time" makes no sense when your calendar looks like ours and there's barely time to shower! I take "quality time" to mean "Let's do chores together!" Working side by side, I give my "quality time child" my full attention when he talks, listening to his bad puns or his long explanations of LEGO® engineering or just being silly together. I would rather get the job done quickly, but this together time is worth more to him than my saying "I love you" a million times. Or I might let him ride shotgun in the car on our way to soccer or the grocery store. Some of our best conversations have happened while driving. This is especially true for the child who craves quality time but doesn't like it to be all about him: sometimes it's easier to discuss personal problems and heavy issues when you're staring out the window.

What I took away from *The Five Love Languages of Children* was not a fail-proof plan but a new way of looking at my children, really observing them and trying to understand what their behavior could tell me. It's almost laughably simple. I consider myself a fairly intuitive mother, but I wasn't picking up my children's emotional cues until I learned what to look for. I love that *The Five Love Languages of Children* offers such simple solutions too. I'm looking forward to a new chapter in our home with happier, more peaceful children.

— Mary

BIMBA MAKES ART

I have seen some pretty expensive and elaborate products out there designed to turn children into art-literate geniuses. I bought into a couple of them myself only to lose interest quickly as the art postcards sat on my shelf dusty and unused. As the school lessons requiring my attention and effort have only compounded with each child, I shamefully relegated Art Appreciation into the "nice idea but who has time for that?" category while focusing on the seemingly more urgent subjects of math, language arts, and history. Pity.

I won't spend my word count here on an apologia for Art Appreciation. I'll assume you already know it's important but, like me, just don't find the time to devote to any sort of program. Enter picture books to save the day. Most of the big-name artists have at least one, if not a half dozen, picture books written about them (check out Mike

Venezia's multiple *Getting to Know ...* series for starters), and most of these are pretty decent all around. But there is one illustrator out there who doesn't get nearly the press she deserves for excellent books on artists, probably because she's based in Italy: Bimba Landmann.

I first discovered Landmann when I found her illustrations in the book *A Boy Named Giotto*. Giotto is probably one of the earliest period artists you'll ever want to study, and there are precious few children's books on him. This one is signature Bimba: strange, Byzantine-style paintings with plenty of gold leaf throughout. Included in the story, like all her others, are excellent mini reproductions of the featured artists' paintings.

Next, we read *The Genius of Leonardo* to add to our studies on da Vinci. Unlike Giotto, there are lots of picture books on this artist in addition to Landmann's title, and we slogged our way through one and a half of them before agreeing that Landmann's was the best. The others had too much text. Landmann's was an actual story and artfully skirted around some of the controversies surrounding Leonardo and his boy servant.

Finally, we read Landmann's award-winning diamond *I Am Marc Chagall*, which is based on Chagall's actual autobiography. To be fair, I haven't read any

> Do you want an adventure now, or would you like to have your tea first?
>
> —J. M. Barrie
> Peter, *Peter Pan*

other picture books on this artist, but I can't imagine any of them doing the man justice the way this book does. It is the perfect type of book to leave lying on a table for a seven- to twelve-year-old child to find and drink up unwittingly. Each page is mixed-media, diorama-style strangeness and is absolutely enchanting. The text pairs with the art excellently, and I felt like I understood Chagall better after reading this book than I did reading an entry on him in an art encyclopedia. One picture book, and you have an education—it's unbelievable.

Now, you can accessorize this education all you want according to your time and energy. I occasionally print out photos of artists' works, and my children place them in their own special photo albums designated just for this purpose. The *Discovering Great Artists* book by MaryAnn Kohl is superb for projects in the styles of specific artists. It's one of the books I plan to add to our curriculum every August. But then reality hits fast and hard around October or so, and it's all I can do to shove some broken crayons in front of the children and say "Here! Color something!" Such is life. So I am thankful there are beautiful books to fill in the gaps. Bimba Landmann's are the best of the best in this regard. (See also her book *Francis and Clare*, which is one of the most beautiful picture books on the market.) I only wish she had more titles in English for us to enjoy.

— Ellie

AND THE AWARD GOES TO ...

In the first decade of *Soul Gardening Journal*, we decided to categorize some of our favorite books by creating artificial award categories. While we don't pretend this list is comprehensive, we thought it would be fun to share our "Best of ..." titles for your amusement. Without further ado:

History

A Little History of the World, E.H. Gombrich
How the Reformation Happened, Hilaire Belloc
The Guillotine and the Cross, Warren H. Carroll
The Restoration of Christian Culture, John Senior

Comedy

My Family and Other Animals, Gerald Durrell
Summer Moonshine, P.G. Wodehouse
The Winter's Tale, William Shakespeare
Something Other than God: How I Passively Sought Happiness and Accidentally Found It, Jennifer Fulwiler

Romance

Ramona, Helen Hunt Jackson
Middlemarch, George Eliot
My Antonia, Willa Cather
"Enoch Arden", Alfred Lord Tennyson

Biography/Memoir

He Leadeth Me: An Extraordinary Testament of Faith, Walter J. Ciszek, S.J., with Daniel L. Flaherty, S.J.
Enduring Grace: Living Portraits of Seven Women Mystics, Carol Lee Flinders
Tumbleweed: A Biography, Eddie Doherty
An American Childhood, Annie Dillard
St. Gemma Galgani, Leo Proserpio, S.J.
The Long Loneliness: The Autobiography of the Legendary Catholic Social Activist, Dorothy Day

Liturgical Year

Around the Year with the Von Trapp Family, Maria Augusta von Trapp

A Continual Feast: A Cookbook to Celebrate the Joys of Family and Faith throughout the Christian Year, Evelyn Birge Vitz
The Year and Our Children: Catholic Family Celebrations for Every Season, Mary Reed Newland
All Year Round: A Calendar of Celebrations, Ann Druitt, Christine Fynes-Clinton, and Marije Rowling

Classics

A Tree Grows in Brooklyn, Betty Smith
The Brothers Karamazov, Fyodor Dostoevsky
Heart of Darkness, Joseph Conrad
Pride and Prejudice, Jane Austen

Underappreciated

The Death and Life of Great American Cities, Jane Jacobs
Island of the World, Michael D. O'Brien
The Trees, *The Fields*, and *The Town* (The Awakening Land trilogy), Conrad Richter
Kristin Lavransdatter, Sigrid Undset

Contemporary Fiction

Peace Like a River, Leif Enger
Dinner at the Homesick Restaurant, Anne Tyler
Life of Pi, Yann Martel
Green Dolphin Street by Elizabeth Goudge

Arts/Crafts/Hobbies

Making Handmade Books: 100+ Bindings, Structures and Forms, Alisa Golden
The Encyclopedia of Country Living: The Original Manual for Living off the Land and Doing It Yourself, Carla Emery
The Book of Tea, Okakura Kakuzo
Creating the Not So Big House: Insights and Ideas for the New American Home, Sarah Susanka

Health/Nutrition/Cookbooks

Food Rules: An Eater's Manual, Michael Pollan
Nourishing Traditions: The Cookbook that Challenges Politically Correct Nutrition and the Diet Dictocrats, Sally Fallon, with Mary G. Enig, Ph.D.

Festivals, Family and Food: Guide to Seasonal Celebration, Diana Carey and Judy Large

The New Laurel's Kitchen, Laurel Robertson, Carol Flinders, and Brian Ruppenthal

Contemporary Issues

Alone Together: Why We Expect More from Technology and Less from Each Other, Sherry Turkle

Last Child in the Woods: Saving Our Children from Nature-Deficit Disorder, Richard Louv

The Shallows: What the Internet Is Doing to Our Brains, Nicholas Carr

The Gift of Good Land, Wendell Berry

Spiritual Guidance

Abandonment to Divine Providence: How to Fulfill Your Daily Duties with God-Given Purpose, Jean-Pierre de Caussade

Divine Intimacy: Meditations on the Interior Life for Every Day of the Liturgical Year, Father Gabriel of St. Mary Magdalen, O.C.D.

Let Us Pray to the Lord: A Book of Daily Prayer according to the Byzantine Tradition

The Reed of God, Caryll Houselander

The Beauties of Motherhood, Placidus Glogger, O.S.B.

Written by a Saint

An Introduction to the Devout Life, Saint Francis de Sales

Diary of Saint Maria Faustina Kowalska: Divine Mercy in My Soul, Saint Maria Faustina Kowalska

The Collected Works of Saint Teresa of Avila, translated by Kieran Kavanaugh, O.C.D., and Otilio Rodriguez, O.C.D.

Story of a Soul: The Autobiography of Saint Thérèse of Lisieux, Saint Thérèse of Lisieux

Mothering

Real Learning: Education in the Heart of the Home, Elizabeth Foss

Ina May's Guide to Childbirth, Ina May Gaskin

Secrets of the Baby Whisperer: How to Calm, Connect, and Communicate with Your Baby, Tracy Hogg, with Melinda Blau

Hold On to Your Kids: Why Parents Need to Matter More Than Peers, Gordon Neufeld and Gabor Maté

Unconditional Parenting: Moving from Rewards and Punishments to Love and Reason, Alfie Kohn

Beautiful to the Eye

The Country Diary of an Edwardian Lady, Edith Holden

In the Midst of Chaos, Peace, Sister Wendy Beckett

Tasha Tudor's Heirloom Crafts, Tovah Martin

Mary Cassatt: Reflections of Women's Lives, Debra N. Mancoff

Current Favorite

33 Days to Morning Glory: A Do-It-Yourself Retreat in Preparation for Marian Consecration, Michael E. Gaitley, M.I.C.

Quo Vadis, Henryk Sienkiewicz

Redeemed: Stumbling toward God, Sanity, and the Peace That Passes All Understanding, Heather King

Healing for Damaged Emotions, David A. Seamands

Life-Changing

Happy Are You Poor: The Simple Life and Spiritual Freedom, Thomas Dubay

Preparation for Total Consecration according to Saint Louis Marie de Montfort

War and Peace, Leo Tolstoy

The Evidential Power of Beauty: Science and Theology Meet, Thomas Dubay

I Believe in Love: A Personal Retreat Based on the Teaching of St. Thérèse of Lisieux, Father Jean C.J. d'Elbée

Too Good to Miss

The Read-Aloud Handbook, Jim Trelease

Mrs. Dunwoody's Excellent Instructions for Homekeeping: Timeless Wisdom and Practical Advice, Miriam Lukken

Miss Manners' Guide to Excruciatingly Correct Behavior, Judith Martin

Into the Wild, Jon Krakauer

O Pioneers!, Willa Cather

WOMAN

MILK AND HONEY

Food that flows. Sustenance that comes to you in response to your hungry cry. Nurture that touches, that cradles, that fills you with a spreading warmth, inside and out. Surely a mother's milk is the gentlest form of nourishment. The Promised Land was called "the Land Flowing with Milk and Honey", and I have felt myself to be a part of that promise. First, consider the matter from the point of view of the land. I'm speaking of biblical Canaan, Eretz Israel itself. What would you expect to find? I should think a flowery, meadowy expanse, well watered, a lush spot for flocks and herds, with sweet-blossomed orchards as well, supporting myriads of fat bees. Second, look at it from the point of view of a woman. I remember thinking when I was pregnant that whereas my hus-  band was *only* a person, I was a person *and* a place, a place where yet another person dwelt. And my sense of being a place did not dimin- ish after childbirth; in fact, it intensified. If, gravid, I was burgeoning within, afterward I was like a headland after rain, flowing with springs.

Milk and honey, together with fruits, are the only foods that are actually *given* by nature as food. Meat has to be killed. Fattening a piglet for slaughter seems treacherous when we explain it to our little children; the little girl Fern in *Charlotte's Web* isn't the only one who thinks so. Eggs: Were these intended to be food for our young? They are the young, snatched from the mother birds, eaten by thieves. Even vegetables are torn from their stalks or uprooted from the earth. I don't count this as moral violence, of course, yet force and struggle are involved, a wresting of food. But milk and honey come down graciously. Bees make so much of their sweet syrup in a good season that the surplus seems a fair bounty to the harvester. A cow actually appreciates being milked; dairying is a reciprocal work, a fair and friendly thing. Milk and honey:

they were made to be food, the best of food, and nothing else. They are given gladly.

Is a nursing mother, then, just a milk animal after all? No. Emphatically not. Mother Nature may be a matter of soil and water, of vegetative and insect and animal life; the nursing mother is much more: a person. Everything she does has the multidimensions of the God-icon, the thoughtful and deliberate, the enfleshed and inspirited being. That's why I recoil inwardly even from an innocent term like "breastfeeding". It sounds crude to my ears, like the repellent term "having sex", which is used—in some circles—in speaking about the self-donating acts proper to marriage. As if married intimacy were some "thing" you could "have" or "get", or as if nurturing a baby were just a physical "input" between a mammary gland and an alimentary canal. But what's called "breastfeeding" is actually more like making love: it's a relationship between a whole person and a whole person. And what a revelation this was to a person like me.

This admission would surprise some of my friends, but for years I thought I had no mothering in me. Okay, I was a certified pro-lifer: a full-time writer-lecturer-organizer-agitator, with eleven arrests on my rescue rap sheet. But as for personal maternal passion, well, it wasn't there. Looking back, I suppose it was mostly a matter of inexperience. I had no younger brothers, sisters, or cousins. I didn't play with baby dolls. I never babysat. I had never even touched a newborn. I didn't know how to hold an infant. I felt as I suppose many men feel: out of place in the presence of the little wiggly space aliens. Out of place. But when God blessed me with a dear husband and we conceived, I became a place. And when I gave milk, I became the headland after rain. And that was the spring of mothering for me.

Hormones play a role, if you want to know. The effects of prolactin and oxytocin in supporting tender, mellow feelings are well known. A suckling infant brings on more milk (a classic case of demand creating supply)—but he brings on more than milk: he brings

> She would wake up hungry in the night where she slept in her basket by my bed. I would turn on the light, change her diaper, and then turn the light off. The rest I did in the dark, by feeling. I took her into bed with me and propped myself up with pillows against the headboard to let her nurse. As she nursed and the milk came, she began a little low contented sort of singing. I would feel milk and love flowing from me to her as once it had flowed to me. It emptied me. As the baby fed, I seemed slowly to grow empty of myself, as if in the presence of that long flow of love even grief could not stand. And the next thing I knew I would be waking up to daylight in the room and Little Margaret still sleeping in my arms.
>
> — Wendell Berry
> Hannah, *Hannah Coulter*

on changes within the woman that unfurl every tightly closed bud of mother-instinct, mother-passion, and mother-empathy. Yes, you can give your little ones rubber nipples to suck on and bottles of synthetic formula to ingest and still be a good mother. Neither my husband nor I were breastfed babies, and we're not *too* weird. (Huh. Well, on the other hand, maybe that explains a lot.) But anyway, we were both cherished and bottle-fed by good mothers who were not notably short on instinct, passion, and empathy. But both they, and we, feel that something was missing.

Our mothers, we've since found out, had both wanted to give us mama-milk, but they were of the generation of women that was actively discouraged from doing so by ignorant gynecologists, clueless pediatricians, and aggressive manufacturers of milk substitutes who touted the formula, the sterilizer, and the schedule and who made natural mothering seem hillbilly, backward, and bovine. And what a tragedy that was. Calculating the deficits, the heart losses, you don't know where to start.

I suppose it was the near abandonment of breast-feeding that paved the way, at least in part, for that sick and depressing phenomenon known as the sexual revolution. First of all, women's breasts lost their sweet connection to children and family and were reduced to the status of sexy ornamentation. Seductive, somewhat smutty (think of the 1950s!): something tight, lifted, separated, padded, and pointed for the attraction and satisfaction of men. Bottle-feeding may have paved the way for contraception by suppressing the natural child spacing that tends to happen as a result of mothering hormones, thus making all those perverted drugs and devices seem necessary and reasonable.

And what could be more pleasing than the sweet fragrance of a nursling! I was astonished by it myself. I used to associate babies with a stink of strong urine and sour milk. That's what the baby-full households of the populous poor smelled like when I was a young girl. But little ones raised on mama-milk have a light, meadowy fragrance. Even their poop doesn't stink. I kid you not. This counts for something, for a parent. You're content, breathing in this honeyed atmosphere with your little one. I would imagine it counts for much more from the baby's point of view. An infant's whole body is a sense organ. How dreadful it would be for an infant to perceive himself as a foul and stinking little thing. But if he sees that his mother and father smile to breathe him in, he knows he is precious and worthy. Worthy he is to be pressed to his mother's breast and held there long and long. This sensitive silky-skinned nursling who is all sense organ, who hungers for touch as well as for taste—doesn't he need, want, deserve this intimacy?

I met a woman once who said she would never want her child to have that kind of contact, that total access to her body. I'm afraid I stared at her bug-eyed. I was thinking, *How in the heck did you conceive that kid, lady? Would you say to your husband, "I love you, dearie, but please, nothing skin to skin"?*

The great Swiss theologian Hans Urs von Balthasar marvels at the nursing mother and child as a miracle of unity, a sacred unitive embrace, as much for sacrament as for sustenance.[1] My goodness, the kissing of hands and feet that goes on! The gazing at faces! The rituals of devotion! And the baby gazes long and long. He contemplates the icon of his mother's face. He sees his universe in a face. He feels the cosmos is a face. Your face.

You sing. There's nothing else to do. (Suckling takes a long time—longer, by the way, than feeding with a bottle.) Old campfire tunes. The Beatles. Bob Dylan. Doc Watson. Best of Broadway. I found that, after twenty-five years, I still remembered a fairly elaborate *Kyrie* and *Gloria*, two verses of *Veni Creator Spiritus*, and half the *Credo*. Then I conscientiously looked up and memorized the other half—and all the verses of "I'm Being Eaten by a Boa Constrictor". (Yes, always upgrading those parenting skills.) And what does the baby hear? What does he see? What does he feel, even humming through flesh on flesh and vibrating the bones of his sensitive little head? He hears the universe singing. It was a nice time to rummage around in my memory for Eucharistic hymns. I had only one year of Latin in school, but phrases now seemed to breathe a new poignancy. *Qui vitam sine termino/Nobis donet in patria.* "Bring us to our true homeland, Lord! Give us life without end!"

"The mother can give her child to suck of her milk, but our precious Mother Jesus can feed us with himself, and does, most courteously and most tenderly, with the blessed sacrament, which is the precious food of true life."[2] So says my namesake, Julian of Norwich. Christ permitted himself to be slaughtered in order to feed us with himself; feeding a baby at the breast, too, can entail great sacrifice.

I remember when my friend Elizabeth had just given birth via a rather horrific emergency cesarean section. There had been problems with the placenta and a terrible loss of blood; she had nearly died. And there she lay, white as the hospital linens, propped up on pillows as she had insisted so she could nurse her tiny newborn. "Take and eat: this is my body, broken for you." Or another hero-friend, Cheryl, whose premature infant was born sick and far too frail to suck milk from her breast. Cheryl, though exhausted herself from the birth ordeal, stayed close to her baby in the Neonatal Intensive Care Unit (NICU) almost around the clock. With fortitude and determination she pumped and pumped to produce an ounce or two at a time of her own precious milk, feeding it to her baby through the isolette from a tiny bottle. Ignoring and sometimes defying standard NICU procedures, she touched and stroked her wee fragile daughter as much as she was able despite the ghastly monitors and tubes and wires. The baby thrived. The doctors were astounded. It was a miracle, sure enough—a miracle of intelligent, splendid, dedicated mothering.

What kind of society will not love, will not honor, will not sustain the unity of a mother with a baby at the breast? A bad one, I say. A sad one. The denial, the drying up, the forced separation, the refusal, the chilling and killing of mothering is all around us.

One day recently when I was on the bus, my giggly four-year-old son decided to stand up and lean over the back of the seat in front of us. Without thinking about it much, I reached up and stroked his cheek. He turned and looked at me. I said, "Snuggle up here beside me, Ben," and he sat down happily with his arms around me. We started babbling some nonsense ("Yup-a-doop-a-deedle-oop", his word for the general affirmative) until we were interrupted by the lady sitting in front of us.

"How did you do that?"

"Do what?"

"How did you get him to listen to you?"

"I just—I don't know. I touched his cheek."

---

[1] See Hans Urs von Balthasar, "Movement toward God", in *Explorations in Theology*, vol. 3, *Creator Spirit*, trans. Brian McNeil, C.R.V. (San Francisco: Ignatius Press, 1993), 15.

[2] Julian of Norwich, *Showings*, trans. Edmund Colledge, O.S.A., and James Walsh, S.J. (New York: Paulist Press, 1978), 298.

"I've got a boy about that big, and he hasn't looked me in the eyes like that since—I don't know when."

I felt embarrassed for her. Ben hasn't sucked mama-milk for a year now, but he still looks into my eyes a hundred times a day. Yes, he gets rambunctious, and we have anger and (I'm sorry to say) yelling too—*but he looks into my eyes.* And he fits easily and willingly under my arms, and always has.

We're just a mother and a little boy. What we have is as common or as uncommon as good bread or a good cabbage or a good glass of home brew. Fashion us a world, great God, and send your angels to defend and preserve us. I think this is the way it's supposed to be.

— Juli Loesch Wiley, Tennessee[3]

WOMEN'S WORK

My mother "didn't work". At least, that is what some people said. Instead, she stayed home with nine children, feeding them and clothing them and keeping the house from burning down—a very real possibility when the two-year-old set the pile of papers on the top of the piano on fire and then locked himself in the bathroom. She line-dried all our laundry, grew a huge garden full of vegetables and flowers, and supported my father in his many entrepreneurial adventures. These were various in scope—hog raising, bee keeping, and, when the southern spring had settled into full-on glory and the eager pilgrims could escape the icy death grip of the never-ending late Wisconsin winter, guiding tours of devout elderly people down to Alabama to visit Mother Angelica. Between the farm and the nine kids and my father's dreams, it was clear that my mother had a full-time job on her hands. These days, she is a substitute schoolteacher in the tiny, rural Catholic and public schools that my siblings who are still at home attend. She often uses the time at work to catch up on the reading and correspondence she fell behind on during the past thirty years. I often receive letters that begin "Dear Kate, I'm at school, and it's so lovely and quiet I thought I would finally write!"

Though she is teaching much of the school year, my mother is passionate about the importance of the wife and mother as the heart and hearth of the home. She feels that it is vital for a family to have the mother creating a home, in the home. We often have heated discussions on this matter as I attempt to speak for the working women of my generation. So many women I know are working alternate shifts with their husbands to avoid the need for daycare, working all night so they can be with their kids when they wake up. These are not selfish women; they are far tougher than I am, and they are fiercely dedicated to their families. They work to pay the mortgage, to gain access to insanely expensive health insurance programs, and to pay off crushing debt. They forego sleep and they pump milk on every break, fighting to keep their milk supply so that they can continue nursing and receiving a level of raised eyebrows that no smoker I know has experienced.

In my early twenties I thought a lot about the kind of mother I wanted to be someday. I wanted to be able to be at home with my kids, but it was important to me that I be able to contribute to the financial well-being of my family. As my father would tell you, with a great and gusty sigh and a shake of his head, it is tough to raise a big family on one income in this day and age, and it is getting tougher on a regular basis. It was tough for him. Still is. I spent a lot of time in the past ten years working to acquire skills that I could use to earn income for my family without working in a conventional forty-hour-a-week job. I am grateful

---

[3] The complete version of this article first appeared in the *Caelum et Terra Journal*, a former publication on agrarian, Catholic living.

that I am able to play the harp in fancy ballrooms and gritty nursing homes. The bulk of the marketing and practicing occurs within my home, and the baby is often a bonus at the job instead of a detraction. This is also true when I'm teaching or performing dance. As the eldest child of homeschooling, back-to-the-land parents, I acquired a great deal of experience in living thriftily, hanging out my laundry, baking my bread, and growing my own food. All these things help pay our bills. They also help me define myself. I am a wife. I am a mother. I am a harpist. I am a dancer. And I am sure that I will someday again be a person who works with farmers.

While I felt it was important that I stay home with my children, I have always struggled with the idea that when you stay at home, your entire identity becomes that of Mother and Wife. It seems to me this position often stems from a defensive response to the dismissive attitudes of "working women". Conversely, I think women in the workplace sense tight-lipped disapproval from "full-time mothers" at home. It is often when we are feeling the most vulnerable that we begin to toss spears. This seems to be the cause of so many of the sharp words hurled back and forth between the encampments of working women and stay-at-home mothers. Our culture does not support women in a way that allows them to grow gracefully into the role of woman and mother. Instead, so many of the women I know struggle to create a precarious balance in their lives.

I recently read a book that helped me broaden my concept of what it means to be a wife, mother, and worker. *Women's Work: The First 20,000 Years* by Elizabeth Wayland Barber provides a fascinating view of the early years of history through the roles of women in making cloth. This book revolutionized my view of women and working by pointing out the obvious fact that women have always worked. Not only did they care for children and do a great deal of work in creating and maintaining hearths and homes, but they also spent a vast amount of time creating practical and surprisingly complex and beautiful cloth and garments.

Women were able to create cloth from rotting weeds, which contributed not only to the home but also to society at large because it was something they could safely do while caring for their children. In the many thousands of years before baby formula, women's work was integrated into their motherhood. Reading this book led me to think about the concept of work and the fact that in our present society there is a great divide between work and home. This segregation of work as something that almost always happens away from home may be part of the reason that work is tearing women apart. I believe it is crucial to expand the idea of what work means in the life of a woman and mother and to expand opportunities for women to contribute to their families through their work.

It is embarrassing to admit, but before reading this book I always wrinkled my nose at the idea of the virtuous woman of Proverbs—she whose worth is above rubies. *What a boring woman!* I thought, imagining her sitting in a corner somewhere while her mean, patriarchal husband gloated over possessing such a prize. How wrong I was. It would probably be a good idea to read the Bible more often, but in the meantime, it was amazing to stumble over this passage in a scholarly work, illuminating my concept of this Proverbial Woman:

It is a part of woman's life to be preoccupied with food. She nurses her child; she has nourished him for nine long months in her womb; it is her grief if her breasts fail her; she weeps if her child refuses to eat. Her work as food provider is her pleasure and her pain.

— Dorothy Day
On Pilgrimage

Who can find a good wife?
    She is far more precious than jewels.
The heart of her husband trusts in her....
She seeks wool and flax,
    and works with willing hands.
She is like the ships of the merchant,
    she brings her food from afar.
She rises while it is yet night
    and provides food for her household
    and tasks for her maidens.
She considers a field and buys it;
    with the fruit of her hands she plants a
        vineyard....
She perceives that her merchandise is profitable.
    Her lamp does not go out at night.
She puts her hands to the distaff,
    and her hands hold the spindle.
She opens her hand to the poor,
    and reaches out her hands to the needy.
She is not afraid of snow for her household,
    for all her household are clothed in scarlet.

She makes herself coverings;
    her clothing is fine linen and purple....
She makes linen garments and sells them;
    she delivers sashes to the merchant.
Strength and dignity are her clothing,
    and she laughs at the time to come. (Prov 31:10–
        11, 13–16, 18–22, 24–25)

This woman is amazing. She "considers a field and buys it"! I love the strength of this portrayal. She is a businesswoman, an artist, a farmer, and a wife. She gives generously to the poor. She provides for her household in so many ways. She is confident and strong. For me, spending time with this passage was exhilarating. I felt free to continue working to use the gifts God has given me in my life as a woman, wife, and mother. I have realized, of course, that my mother is also a Proverbial Woman—and that is what I want to be as well.

— Kate Stapleton, Pennsylvania

THE ANNUNCIATION

I empathize with my dog panting on the porch.
In here, the clicking fan swirls the same air around
    the room
as the sun heats the house
like the solar oven you make in third grade.

I wipe sweat from my upper lip
and consider the dust on the coffee table.
My glass of water has left its mark
and is no longer cold.
There's more ice in the kitchen
but then I'll see last night's crumbs and today's
    flies.
Even yesterday's laundry bleaches in the late
    afternoon sun,
no breeze to make it dance.

I too am motionless, here on
    the couch
witnessing a miracle.
For this stillness is not for me,
but rather for you, my small one,
tucked away in my fragile womb.

The dust and dishes and laundry and flies
are mere signals of our mortality.

Gabriel told me of your coming by a different
    sign,
but he told me all the same.
I said, "May it be done unto me as you have
    said,"
and the doctor insisted, "You must rest."

So I shall be still and know that he is God
who placed you in my body
I so soon made wife and mother.

As the glaring sun sinks
and pink and blue clouds fill the sky
the dog and I will enjoy the colors
and the first cooling breeze.
I'll describe to you its beauty and sensation
until your eyes and hands open to see
this wild and beautiful world.

And now that dried laundry awaits me
more patiently than I await your sweet father.
I go to it obediently,
careful not to trip over the zealous dog.

Cautious on the stairs I slowly bring it up
to start folding as if it were my favorite leisure
   activity.

Your father unlocks the gate
as he whistles our usual greeting.
Then our family embrace—the three of us—
while the jealous dog whines to be let in.
Your father kisses you so softly on my skin,
you, our little creation, born of love and God's
   grace.
We live with forgotten laundry and gathered
   dust
and hearts full of wonder and hope.

— Julianne Ulrickson, Ecuador

THIS IS MY BODY

Once upon a time, what feels like long ago, I used to wear a two-piece bathing suit. It was super cute, and with boy shorts it wasn't terribly immodest, although yes, friends, I could have done better. I have a picture of me wearing it while swimming in a Vermont river. I had strong, flat abs, tanned and toned arms and legs, and a smile like I had no idea what was coming.

I didn't. Both the good (so much good) and the bad (just a little bad). But human as we are, we can sometimes dwell on the bad and think that the bad is bigger than it is. The bad that I'm confronting lately is something that all women must face, and women who have lots of babies have to face it faster. It's the giving up of our bodies. Slowly it happens, and despite our best efforts or lame efforts, we see the signs of age and the signs of wear on these beautiful baby-making machines that we walk around in. I remember after baby number five I was trying on some clothes in a dressing room, and in the multiple full-length mirrors I saw … my bum. I didn't recognize it. It looked more like the rear end of one of the lunch ladies I had stood behind as a kid in public school than something that belonged to me. *This is my body?* I thought.

It kept happening. Some of us know firsthand what becomes of breasts that have been nursed many times. In use they look great; out of use they can be a sad little sight, resembling deflated balloons. *This is my body?*

I've inherited problematic varicose veins that are especially bad with pregnancy. I generally cover them up, but recently on a warm day I walked around the house without any leggings under my above-the-knee skirt. My twelve-year-old son noticed them for the first time and without thinking blurted out, "Ugh! What's wrong with your legs?" My husband immediately reprimanded him, and good boy that he is, he felt awful about it. I fought back tears from sensitivity, and we had a nice talk about how it's a small price for me to pay to bring a new life into the world and how we must watch what we say when we see things that repulse us.

This is my body.

You might guess where I am going with this. Jesus is teaching me a lesson, and he is teaching you a lesson, and he reminds us of it at every Mass. He was in the prime of his life when he offered his sacred flesh for us, and he did not spare himself. His figure on the Cross repulsed many; even some who loved him didn't want to witness the grotesque sight of the Crucifixion. Yet it is that bloody, messy, fleshy, gruesome drama that wins our birth into heaven and proves him to be the best kind of King, not one who coldheartedly rules over his people but one who loves them to the point of death.

Besides nausea and vomiting, fatigue, stretch marks, swelling, skin irritations, and possibly a temporary diabetic state, pregnancy is an invitation to almost any weird and unfavorable condition. (Drew Barrymore grew a goatee!) It's sometimes laughable, but mostly uncomfortable, and we must remember that we are fortunate to be able to imitate our Redeemer so closely in our self-donation and physical sufferings. Our lives as mothers can be living witnesses to the Last Supper and the Crucifixion.

I recently read about a woman in Massachusetts who jumped out the window of a burning second-story apartment building with her eighteen-month-old son to escape death. She landed in such a way that he was not harmed, yet her own spine and legs were so damaged that she may never walk again. When she woke up in the hospital and heard the news, her only thought was of the safety of her son. I think of this woman, sacrificing her ability to walk for her child, and I try to be grateful that my crosses are so small in comparison.

There will always be a temptation for us to use our bodies for personal gain, glory, and vanity—just look at any modern magazine. Lucifer was the most beautiful of angels, and he's the one who got into trouble—eternal trouble. I'm not saying we shouldn't try to do the best with what we've got. (I think we have a duty to do just that!) Yet we are all on our way down, and we might as well enjoy the ride while gaining spiritual profit from our decline. Give it up with a smile, let things go when it's time for them to go, and see heaven as the prize.

"You are very tired, my child," the lady went on....

Then she carried her to the side of the room ... she was going to lay her in the large silver bath;... as she looked into it, again she saw no bottom, but the stars shining miles away, as it seemed, in a great blue gulf. Her hands closed involuntarily on the beautiful arms that held her, and that was all....

When she opened her eyes, she saw nothing but a strange lovely blue over and beneath and all about her. The lady, and the beautiful room, had vanished from her sight.... From somewhere came the voice of the lady, singing a strange sweet song, of which she could distinguish every word; but of the sense she had only a feeling—no understanding. Nor could she remember a single line after it was gone. It vanished, like the poetry in a dream, as fast as it came....

At last she felt the beautiful hands lay hold of her, and through the gurgling water she was lifted out into the lovely room. The lady carried her to the fire, and sat down with her in her lap, and dried her tenderly with the softest towel.... When the lady had done, she stooped to the fire, and drew from it her nightgown, as white as snow.

"How delicious!" exclaimed the princess. "It smells of all the roses in the world, I think."

— George MacDonald
The Princess and the Goblin

There is a movement in the Church pushing for the priesthood of women; however, we as women already participate in our own spiritual priesthood even more closely than laymen. Not only can we spiritually offer to the Father the Body, Blood, Soul, and Divinity of Jesus through our prayers (such as the Divine Mercy Chaplet), but as part of our vocation we can also physically offer up our own bodies and blood like our Good Shepherd, as we join in the lifelong process of laying down our lives for our sheep.

Throughout Church history, the pelican has been a sacred symbol of the Eucharist. According to legend, during a time of famine pelicans will peck at their own flesh, drawing blood, which they feed to their young.

What a beautiful image this is of Christ, and it speaks of our call as mothers too. Saint John the Baptist proclaimed, "He must increase, but I must decrease" (Jn 3:30). Can we say the same of ourselves regarding our children? It is the nature of things, and it is God's way, that they may increase in stature and beauty and that we may decrease in the eyes of the world.

During this time of spiritual famine in our country, may we not lose sight of the privilege it is to be as pelicans to our children and echo the sacred words of Christ: *This is my body, which will be given up for you.*

— Hope

SHE

In the gardens someone said to me,
"Your hands are lovely."
And I thought of you,
Miles away,
In the five-acre wood,
Imagined you pasting old photos,
Laughing and weeping over
Days gone.
I thought of you
Lying beside me in sickness,

Singing old hymns from the
    thick of your throat
And brushing back the hair I
    never let you cut.
I thought of you,
A black Swede, still
And stubborn as a Saxon,
Eyes as clear as the Eastern seas.
I thought of you,
Your laughter
So thick and feminine,
Warm like your breasts and belly
That gave life to me.

— Lindsay Younce Tsohantaridis,
Oregon

WHAT MAKES ME CRY

Really good ballet makes me cry. There is something wholly pure about the emotion, the drama, and the reality of human existence expressed through graceful movement. I used to be a dancer. Many little girls harbor dreams of becoming ballerinas, but my dream was persistent as a child and all-consuming as a teen. I spent my time practicing, perfecting, and studying my art. My dreams were violently broken when I was

sixteen by a tragic assault that left me with a serious spinal injury and a fractured soul.

It took me a long time to find my passion and my vocation. Before I stopped dancing, my faith was strong and true, if a bit naive. I did not lose my faith when I lost dance, but I lost the ability to pray with the same abandon, the same totality of focus. I did not blame God for what had happened to me. Instead, I knew that it was Evil that had attacked me, and God who had saved me. I trusted in God, but I had difficulty trusting in his creations.

In college, I turned my attention away from the arts and toward logic, philosophy, and law. I dated good Catholics, but the relationships were not good. I had not yet healed, and my faith was too separate from my heart. I graduated without any idea what I would do. Perhaps because my hopes had been thwarted, God granted me an easy and generous path to a career in canon law. Canon law combined logic, order, and reason with faith and the desire to aid in the salvation of souls and minister to the broken. During my graduate studies, I met my husband, a non-Catholic musician. Though my friends were surprised that I would choose someone outside my faith, I found that my husband brought me closer to the center of my faith. He caused me to reflect and ponder what I believed in a way I never had when I was with someone who shared my faith. His creativity helped soothe the deep longing I had for art, which I could no longer pursue myself.

Through my work in canon law, I began working in a diocesan marriage tribunal. I am able to help heal the wounded, who often feel lost or abandoned by their faith in their darkest times. Though I am not divorced, I identify with the divorced. They, too, have had a dream violently taken from them. Often, I see that divorced Catholics entered marriage with the earnest hope that this would be a lifelong partnership that would fulfill their soul's longing. When they divorced, they suddenly found themselves forced to forge a new identity apart from what they had spent years planning and working for.

I had my first daughter three years after I began tribunal work. I was in complete awe of the happiness I felt. The day of her birth was the happiest day of my life. Giving birth to her trumped even the exquisite happiness I felt at the height of my days of ballet. It eclipsed my wedding day, which was marred by my own nerves and discomfort with public displays of emotion and sentimentality. When I became a mother, for the first time I felt truly complete, healed, and satisfied with my earthly vocation.

I became pregnant again nine months after my daughter's birth. I learned of the pregnancy a day after I learned that my father had suffered a massive stroke—a stroke that would eventually claim his life. My second pregnancy was difficult. I suffered the kind of morning sickness that is healed only with childbirth, and the birth of my second daughter was a true reckoning with the price of original sin. It was as if my body was dealing with the physical pain since my soul was inadequate to handle the emotional pain.

My daughters, however, are a delight. I find myself hoping and praying for more and more children. Recently, I suffered an early miscarriage. This miscarriage was difficult, but it reminded me that in life, I have only so much control. When I focus on my wants and needs, I forget that there is a divine plan. My dreams and wishes are often thwarted and changed unexpectedly, but God continually rewards me with far more than I deserve and far more than I would gain if life proceeded as I planned.

I attended my father's funeral while I was six months pregnant. I did not cry. Death does not make me cry. I took great comfort and consolation at the unexpected beauty of the funeral liturgy. Several of the priests I work with graciously attended the funeral Mass, and I took solace in their faith and company. Crying does not come easily now to me. I do not cry while watching Pampers commercials, during fights with my spouse, or in the face of frustration.

Really good ballet makes me cry. It reminds me of what I once felt and was able to express with my body. Now I struggle and usually fail to express those emotions through my work and through my vocation as a wife and mother. But, just as I persevered as a child to learn how to manipulate my body into the proper movements of ballet, now I must train myself to express my faith and my being through my daily actions. My body was broken so that I could no longer rely on it to express my love. I still do not know how to express my emotions in other ways, but as I gaze on my daughters and dream of the future, I know I must learn.

— Shannon Fosset, Maine

AN INVITATION TO SAVE THE WORLD

All of us have suffered a deep sort of sorrow in light of all the recent scandals in the Church. We are one body, and the failures and sins of one affect us all. That such atrocities could be committed and covered up among the highest prelates in our Church likely fills us with anger and anguish.

The response from the laity has been heartening. Social media has been used effectively to spread the *#sackclothandashes* movement, which called upon us to unite in prayer and acts of penitence in reparation for the evils committed by our shepherds. There has been a renewed interest in Ember Days: "Fasting gives wings to prayer", they say. And it is true. The efforts people are making are good and right. Truly our Mother of Sorrows has never had so many like-minded children.

But there is also another way to approach this. This fall, I hosted a "Save the World Party". I considered calling it a "Beauty Synod" but just learned I'd been mispronouncing that word my entire life and decided I better not fake-intelligentsia my way through this. The concept is simple: evil cannot be beat simply by a negation of evil. Darkness is overcome not by an absence of darkness but by a flooding of light. Here is the exact wording on the invitation I sent out:

Fighting against all the darkness and bitterness in the world and in our Church, what can we do? Yes, there's the #sackclothandashes approach of prayer and penitence. And that is good, but there is something else too. The wisdom of our saints often teaches that the way to eliminate Evil isn't just to fight it but to replace it with Good.

Please join me for an evening of friendship, laughter, and wine in my home. Let's celebrate Good and go into the crisper, darker rhythms of autumn, sharing a glass of red and a slice of beauty with the company of lovely women.

Please bring something tasty or a bottle of wine. And please bring *something beautiful, something real to share that inspires you lately*: a poem, a beautiful picture, a quote or passage from a book, or even a piece of music I can queue up on Spotify.

Let's reclaim a small part of goodness and *beauty* in our own hearts. And may it then spill over into our smiles and be transmitted to others. *That's* what we can do to save the world.

Someone brings a beautifully illustrated prayer book by which her family has been blessed. Another reads a T. S. Eliot poem. One woman shares a YouTube channel she found that shows a live twenty-four-hour image of our exposed Eucharistic Lord. Another simply shares her four-week-old newborn daughter— beauty incarnate. We are offered a newly discovered artist from Wales, an incredibly large dahlia, a recording of Bach's Mass in B Minor, and on and on.

The options are endless. The point is to stand up against darkness and infuse a bit of light and beauty into our world. As a character in one of Dostoevsky's novels said, "Beauty will save the world." The depth of that statement is something we should attempt to plumb all the days of our lives. What better way to do so than in the company of good friends?

— Ellie

Thank you, *women who are mothers*! You have sheltered human beings within yourselves in a unique experience of joy and travail. This experience makes you become God's own smile upon the newborn child, the one who guides your child's first steps, who helps it to grow, and who is the anchor as the child makes its way along the journey of life.

Thank you, *women who are wives*! You irrevocably join your future to that of your husbands, in a relationship of mutual giving, at the service of love and life.

Thank you, *women who are daughters* and *women who are sisters*! Into the heart of the family, and then of all society, you bring the richness of your sensitivity, your intuitiveness, your generosity and fidelity.

Thank you, *women who work*! You are present and active in every area of life—social, economic, cultural, artistic and political. In this way you make an indispensable contribution to the growth of a culture which unites reason and feeling, to a model of life ever open to the sense of "mystery", to the establishment of economic and political structures ever more worthy of humanity.

Thank you, *consecrated women*! Following the example of the greatest of women, the Mother of Jesus Christ, the Incarnate Word, you open yourselves with obedience and fidelity to the gift of God's love. You help the Church and all mankind to experience a "spousal" relationship to God, one which magnificently expresses the fellowship which God wishes to establish with his creatures.

Thank you, *every woman*, for the simple fact of being *a woman*! Through the insight which is so much a part of your womanhood you enrich the world's understanding and help to make human relations more honest and authentic....

Necessary emphasis should be placed on the "*genius of women*", not only by considering great and famous women of the past or present, but also those *ordinary* women who reveal the gift of their womanhood by placing themselves at the service of others in their everyday lives. For in giving themselves to others each day women fulfil their deepest vocation. Perhaps more than men, women *acknowledge the person*, because they see persons with their hearts. They see them independently of various ideological or political systems. They see others in their greatness and limitations; they try to go out to them and *help them*.

— Pope Saint John Paul II
Letter to Women

HILDEGARD AND HEALTH

I want Hildegard back. Do you know who she is? In 2012, Pope Benedict XVI declared Saint Hildegard of Bingen to be a Doctor of the Church (that's shorthand for a really smart, really important person who had really good things to say about the faith). I want her back because she's been hijacked by all the wrong kind of people. Angry uber-feminists claim she defied all patriarchal Church authority. They call her a prophetess and hold her up as the emblem for women's ordination. But feminists aren't the only ones. New age, natural medicine proponents consider Hildegard *their* mascot and claim she was the original "heal your inner chakras" leader.[4] Well, it would help if people read their history a little better, but there is no doubt that Hildegard was one of the most important women in medieval times, and her canonization is perfectly timed to what our world needs today. She is the picture of what Pope Benedict means when he talks about the "ecology of man".

To the angry feminists, the pope would say this of the ecology of man: "If the Church speaks of the nature of the human being as man and woman, and demands that this order of creation be respected, this is not some antiquated metaphysics." The pope acknowledged that rainforests and water and air must be protected, but even more than that, mankind must be protected from itself.[5] What does all this have to do with Hildegard? What could some nun from the Middle Ages possibly have to do with preventing the implosion of mankind? And exactly how does feminism threaten the destruction of the human person? This: Hildegard lived out the feminine genius. Today's women's liberation in the Church cries about the injustice of a male-only priesthood, the teaching against contraception, and on and on. It has a distorted view of woman, in a sense wanting to destroy the very essence of who woman is with an "equality" that amounts to androgyny. On the other hand, Hildegard was a *true* feminist. She wanted equality that amounted to complementary gender specific paths to reflect the perfect facets of who God is. Hildegard knew you couldn't put God in a box labeled "Alpha Male: works as a CEO". Neither could he fit in a box labeled "Mother Earth: nurturer type". Nor could you put him in a box labeled "Genderless Being: physiological, mental, spiritual, and emotional differences end here". He won't fit in the feminist box. But unlike what some on the other extreme think, God didn't design every woman to be a submissive doormat, pregnant and barefoot in her kitchen, silently serving an abusive husband while never exploring her own gifts. There is a feminine genius to every woman. Women have a mysterious power in the universe, and Hildegard was revolutionary in living that. She was a preacher, a theologian, an herbalist, a musician, a composer, a visionary, an abbess, a spiritual director, a scientist, and a writer.

To the New Agers who want to associate her with pagan spirituality, saying she used magic and medicine both, I say this: back off. She was Catholic. She once wrote this to a community of women religious: "The spiritual life must be tended with great dedication. At first the effort is burdensome because it demands the renunciation of caprices of the pleasures of the flesh and of other such things. But if she lets herself be enthralled by holiness a holy soul will find even contempt for the world sweet and lovable. All that is needed is to take care that the soul does not shrivel."[6]

The ecology of man refers to the wholeness of what it means to be human. Traditional, Western medicine has deepened the chasm between man and spirit. While there is absolutely a place for general practitioners and conventional medicine (and especially surgery), there is also unfortunately a scorn for its

---

[4]Melissa K. Treharn, "Hildegard of Bingen: Visionary Woman Who Encouraged the Role of Feminism", Otterbein University Undergraduate Distinction Paper, April 8, 2015, https://digitalcommons.otterbein.edu/cgi/viewcontent.cgi?article=1009&context=stu_dist.

[5]Benedict XVI, Christmas address (December 22, 2008), no. 1.

[6]Quoted in Benedict XVI, General Audience (September 8, 2010).

> Let us rejoice then and give Him thanks that we have so good an architect, so excellent a stone, and a workman who gives His own blood for the cement of our edifice, and makes it so firm and strong that neither hail, nor wind, nor tempest can overthrow it unless we give our consent.
>
> — Saint Catherine of Siena

organic, God-given brother: natural and homeopathic medicine. The problem, like the problem with feminists distorting what it means to be a woman, is that many (not all) naturopaths distort what it means to be connected to Mother Earth. Hildegard's medicinal texts are still consulted today by those seeking natural cures for human ailments. But the perversion happens when these naturopaths stray down paganistic paths. Hildegard knew that the order of God's creation has to be respected at all times, in all places. There can be none of this channeling of spiritual energies or meditating to achieve a sort of enlightenment by way of self-emptying. (Catholics can and *should* meditate, by the way, but instead of practicing Zen methods or other aspects of Buddhism, which seek emptiness, we should consult our own powerhouses like Saint John of the Cross and Saint Teresa of Avila, whose methods seek the fullness of Christ.)

Hildegard was brilliant with plants and herbs. She understood that illness was a sign of man not being in balance with nature. She sought to restore this balance using God's gifts. Tylenol and Pepto Bismol aren't bad, but like most of modern medicine, they treat the symptoms, not the problem. I think some Catholics are suspicious of "getting into" natural medicine for two reasons: First, it's demonized by pop culture and the big business of health care (which is interested in protecting the pharmaceutical industry) as being either useless or dangerous. Second, many fear alternative types of healing because of their often pagan roots. Unfortunately, here in the United States at least, we have this perception that to utilize homeopathy, essential oils, and herbs means we have to turn up our noses at things like SUVs, pasteurized milk, and capitalism. It's okay, everyone. Breathe deeply. You can live an orthodox Catholic life and have something in common with the coffee-shop squatting, earthy hipsters. Even if they exhibit a certain elitism about their "green" lifestyle, we have just as much right to drop by the holistic remedy shop and reap the benefits of natural medicine. It's ours too!

Getting back to the ecology of man means restoring our bodies and souls to the harmony present in the natural universe. Don't be intimidated by "green" people who push a secular agenda. And don't be intimidated by proud feminists. The beauty of Catholicism is that, like all its teachings (which are too often misunderstood), it offers a balance and encourages the faithful to live life to the fullest. Women should discern their vocation and live it to the utmost; they should utilize their unique gifts in the ways God has called them to. And natural medicine should live side by side with traditional medicine. Hildegard understood this. And we should listen to her; she's *our* Doctor, after all.

— Meredith Aster, Oregon

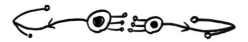

MARY AND FEMINISM

A couple of summers ago, my family took a trip to the sea. My eldest daughter loves the ocean and immediately dove into the surf. The first day the waves were gentle, and she swam across the beautiful cove all on her own. Emboldened by this experience, she decided to try it again the following day. But this time, the waves were livelier, and she found herself carried away by the surf. A cry went up on the beach as we saw a wave throw her body against a rock. In a rush of fear and adrenaline, she pulled herself up and swam for shore before it could happen again. Later I sat with her on the towel with my arm around her as we discussed the fickle nature of the ocean and the need to be wary of waves.

The imagery of waves has been used to describe many movements. Feminism has been described as having three waves: first wave (1848–1920), second wave (1963–1980s), third wave (1990s–present). Waves can carry us to beautiful new places, but they can also, as my daughter discovered, throw us against the rocks. It can be difficult to navigate feminism in its unpredictability. This phenomenon has given rise to the Christian woman who feels uncomfortable allying herself to feminism and to the Christian feminist who feels isolated among feminists in the secular world. The resolution for both these groups in understanding feminism is an *authentic model of feminism*. This model must reconcile the duality of a woman's nature in her calling to maternity and her need to be an integrating force in the world, while respecting the dignity of persons of all ages and in all walks of life. Mary, in her mysterious union of Virgin and Mother, offers such a model. Indeed, Mary is the perfect icon of feminism.

Merriam-Webster defines "feminism" as the advocacy of women's rights on the grounds of political, social, and economic equality to men. These goals are a positive good. As Christians, we believe both that women are created equal in dignity with men and

that there is an imbalance in the dealings between men and women because of our fallen human natures. Industrialized society offered *even more* opportunities for women's dignity to be threatened due to the breaking apart of village life and structural supports that assisted the woman outside that of her husband. The loss of these supports, coupled with the shift of men toward work that was away from the home, left women isolated, vulnerable, and without access to education or employment. No longer was their work in the home part of a cottage industry or connected with civic life. This initiated a response in men to protect women. Because of the ability to carry and nurture life, women can and do become the target of the fallen male tendency to dominate and control. Feminism sought to protect women's rights and restore their right to employment and education. However, feminism has not always accomplished what it set out to do, and sometimes, like the wave that injured my daughter, it has even crashed down upon the very women's issues it is trying to address: single motherhood, divorce, abortion, poverty, and pornography, to name a few. Indeed, sometimes it seems that the list of injustices has lengthened, not shortened, in spite of accomplishments such as greater availability of education for women and the right to vote and hold jobs (in the United States).

But where does Mary fit into this? What does an obscure Jewish girl from the first century have to do with a political movement that gained steam almost two thousand years after she lived? Mary is the pivotal person for all of humanity because through her *fiat*, the Incarnate God entered the world. But for women in particular, she established a shift in their function both in society and in the redeemed order. When we remember that Mary was raised and lived as a pious Jew, the radical nature of her role as a woman is thrown into relief. Although there are notable exceptions (Judith,

Esther, Deborah, the woman of Proverbs 31) before Mary, the primary means of expression of the feminine genius in the Old Covenant was the bringing forth and rearing of the next generation. Holiness was to be found in the duties of being a wife and mother, since through the generation of children, the Jews were brought closer to the fulfillment of the coming Messiah. Motherhood is lifted up even more in the New Covenant. Through Mary's *fiat*, saying Yes to God, a woman became the Mother of God. Let me reiterate: the Mother of God! No other human being, man *or* woman, has ever attained such an elevated status.

But, in mysteriously retaining her virginity, Mary also offers another mode of holiness to women. As exemplified by the Virgin Mary, women now, in union with God, can be fruitful in the world, apart from a man or physical marriage. Mary models this by not remarrying following the death of her husband, Joseph, and thereby continuing her consecrated life and following her Son to participate in his work in this world. The mysterious union of Virgin and Mother is held up as the model for *all* women no matter what their particular vocation. In some mysterious way, those called to the life of consecrated virginity or singlehood can be spiritual mothers, and in turn, those called to marriage and family life must retain, in a spiritual sense, some notion of the role of virginity. This is both a great mystery and a great comfort and offers each woman a way in which to live out her individual calling as a woman that is in full harmony with her nature.

Outside this union, it is easy to arrive at an imbalance: either an inward-focused and self-satisfied virginity devoid of spiritual motherhood, or a motherhood in which one's self is so lost to the demands of motherhood that the woman has no identity apart from her children. Worse yet is the possibility of a selfish motherhood in which the mother's emotional needs are met by the children and she values comfort over gift of self.

Mary, in her dual role as Virgin and Mother, is then the prototype of feminism, in which neither part of the woman's nature is eliminated or compromised. There are numerous examples of this in the Scriptures and according to tradition. Mary follows Christ in his public life to assist him as his Mother, but also, in turn, is the initiator of his first miracle. She leaves her home in Nazareth following the death of Joseph to live on the road with Christ and then, following her Son's death, comforts the apostles in the Upper Room. She is there with the disciples in the outpouring of the Holy Spirit on Pentecost. According to tradition, she uprooted herself in order to follow and to be cared for by the apostle John, whom Christ made her adopted son, just as he made her John's adopted mother. In Ephesus, she lived out her days among pagans, far from her native home. Mary's life defies both extremes: that of the childless career woman and that of the socially withdrawn housewife.

It is easy to see how those who live a life of consecrated virginity can participate in spiritual motherhood, but perhaps what is less obvious is how women in married life can be emblematic of Mary in her virginity. When virginity is viewed only as something negative—the absence of sex—this can indeed be difficult to envision or comprehend. But if, rather, we define virginity as the aligning of sexuality and its energies and its channeling into nonsexual activities and accomplishments, suddenly virginity becomes a powerful force at the disposal of, on occasion, even the married woman. There are married women in a variety of situations for whom this can be realized. For a Catholic woman who makes the choice to postpone having more children, there are periods of abstinence that she must experience. But what if these times become a chance for her to align her natural energy and creativity toward a spiritual virginity of sorts? While still being present to her husband in nonsexual intimacy, she can prayerfully discern how she can also mysteriously imitate Mary in her virginity. For married women who suffer the great burden of infertility, this can be another such opportunity. Lastly, for the married woman who has discerned that God is calling her to be always nurturing life, it can mean remembering to take small times away from her role as mother so that she may nurture her own identity apart from her children. This will enhance her familial relationships, give her a life outside her home duties, and provide the opportunity for the Holy Spirit to make her fruitful in society.

Mary lost none of her identity when she said Yes to virginity and motherhood. Rather, in putting herself at the service of the Holy Spirit, she harmoniously brought these two feminine archetypes into a beautiful union within her nature. Mary invites us to a full life as women, in union with the divine life of God. In reconciling Virgin and Mother within her nature, any woman, no matter what her vocation, can work toward a fully integrated life. Feminism does not mean denying any one part of the woman's nature or artificially forcing a side of her nature at the expense of the other or, worse yet, at the expense of human life. But we do not have to lose feminism to secular ideologies that have attached themselves to it. We can embrace feminism as Christians and in doing so offer the world an uncompromising, radically new alternative model of feminism, a feminism that brings us into the fullness of our natures and a feminism that benefits all members of society, male and female, born and unborn, current and future. And at the center of this model is Mary.

— Anna Hatke, Virginia

RETHINKING SKIRTS

New Light on an Old Topic

Ready your tomatoes for firing! I'm tackling a beast of an issue here: Should women wear skirts and dresses more frequently? *Boo! Hiss! Go back to writing about the beauty of motherhood and the sanctification of hard work!* Indeed, it's tempting just to forget the whole topic, as it has suffered brutally from both sides and left chips on many shoulders. But life's no fun walking forever on tiptoe, so I will lay out ten reasons why I personally have decided to wear skirts more frequently than I used to. Do note that my thoughts are intended as a *proposition*, not as an *imposition*. No one need be concerned that I'm condemning my pants-wearing friends or judging the lady in shorts at Mass. Church teaching does not mandate dresses, and it's important to not confuse opinions with doctrines.

Furthermore, I am not ignorant of the fact that we've much larger battles to wage on the faith and morals front, and asking women to shop the dress aisle more frequently can seem trivial or even insulting in comparison. But I am of the opinion that in forming the minds of ourselves and our children, the small things matter and influence the larger issues of our day. For that reason, I challenge you to reflect on your own convictions and see if any of these points are compelling at all. Perhaps you see things differently or God is working on your heart in another way right now.

We are all his masterpieces, and he never chisels at his creations in the *exact* same way. That's fine. But simply allow me to explain the beauty of feminine attire as I have come to see it. Without further ado:

Ten Reasons to Wear Skirts and Dresses More Often

1. *The External Converts the Internal.* Before I began wearing skirts more regularly, I noticed that whenever I did dress up, I acted differently. On those occasions I was a little less rough-and-tumble with the boys or sloppy in my posture. Because I wore skirts or dresses only on Sunday, it was a novelty to me to be very conscious of my comportment. I then wondered that if it made me act more graceful and composed and ladylike on Sundays, wouldn't those be good attributes to cultivate on other days of the week as well? So, wearing skirts more often can help me become the kind of woman I envision as embodying the vocation of wife and mother.

2. *Gender Identity.* I have several boys, and I want them to grow up noticing that there is something very different about the woman of the family. I'm not simply one of their wrestling buddies. Women are distinctively different from men in that they

> *The Church sees in Mary the highest expression of the "feminine genius" and she finds in her a source of constant inspiration. Mary called herself the "handmaid of the Lord" (Lk 1:38). Through obedience to the Word of God she accepted her lofty yet not easy vocation as wife and mother in the family of Nazareth. Putting herself at God's service, she also put herself at the service of others: a* service of love. *Precisely through this service Mary was able to experience in her life a mysterious, but authentic "reign". It is not by chance that she is invoked as "Queen of heaven and earth". The entire community of believers thus invokes her; many nations and peoples call upon her as their "Queen".* For her, "to reign" is to serve! Her service is "to reign"!
>
> —Pope Saint John Paul II
> *Letter to Women*

bear children, and what a sacred role this is! Throughout centuries women have worn beautiful dresses that distinctively set them apart from men. Priests and religious wear robes, habits, and other skirt-like garments because there is something distinctively sacred about their role. It does, in a way, signify "sacred", "special", "unique". I think about how that pertains to my role in the family. My subtle cues are manifested in an outward and obvious way by what I wear. Not all pants are immodest and not all skirts are modest, but a modest skirt is usually more feminine than pants. (Note: Whenever I refer to skirts, I'm speaking of the modest types and excluding the tight leather mini.) Even when we wear pants, we are called to be feminine; it helps us in our vocations, whatever they may be. But my wearing skirts regularly helps my children and others have a consistent reminder of my role in the family and helps foster a sense of the uniqueness of what it means to be a woman—and, accordingly, what it means to be a man.

3. *Restoring Chivalry.* When I wear skirts, I receive better treatment—offers to help with my groceries, doors held open, seats offered to me, and so forth. Right or wrong, this has always been the case. Men will rise to the occasion of chivalry (a tragically lost concept in our culture) much more quickly and consistently when a lady looks (and, don't forget, acts!) so obviously and unmistakably like a lady. I think this is good for society at large. I'm the true kind of feminist who thinks that there ought not to be pay gaps and that women should have the right to pursue careers. But we are so trained to value equality in the wrong way, a way that ignores the inherent differences and gifts of each sex. An androgynous race is not good for human beings. When women wear skirts, it helps demarcate the sexes in a society that wants to blur the lines. It stirs up that buried, beaten part of a man that wants to take care of a woman. Women have shot themselves in the foot with a rampant distorted feminism, and we wonder—amid our screams for equal rights and treatment—why men don't treat women the way they ought to!

4. *Temperature Control.* Believe it or not, skirts allow for optimal conditions in which to fine-tune your temperature levels. They are cooler in the summer and warmer in the winter. On hot days, you can take advantage of a lightweight fabric that allows a cool breeze to circulate around you. And in winter, you can layer in a way that actually allows you to be warmer in a skirt than in pants. My cold weather attire often involves leggings

underneath a skirt, even triple layered with fleece pants if needed. Toasty as can be! Also, a whole new world recently opened up to me when, as a joke, I googled "snow skirt". They do exist! And some are much cuter than I ever would have guessed.

5. *A Class Act.* I am never underdressed! Regardless of the situations that pop up spontaneously, I am always prepared. I am one of those rare souls who don't consider it progress that people go to the grocery store in sweatpants and T-shirts. Fifty years ago, people dressed up just to run errands. Even in nice pants, when we dress as if we respect ourselves and the people we interact with, we treat one another better all around. It may be a stretch to say this, but I would argue that dressing up helps maintain the dignity of the human race. Seriously. When you consider the attacks on the human person and the desensitization of society, any little bit of dignity helps.

6. *The Trompe-l'œil.* Ever wish you had a real-life airbrush? The right skirt does *a lot* to hide your less-flattering parts. As pants shopping is a bear when you are in your childbearing years, it's wonderful to be a bit less self-conscious than you inevitably are when you try on thigh-hugging, love-handle-accentuating pants. The female posterior generally loses a lot of its charm over the years, and skirts cover a multitude of evils.

7. *Modesty.* Whenever the outline of your rear end is on display, modesty comes into question. Some pants are loose enough to avoid this, but baggy clothing doesn't usually flatter anyone. According to the multiple-Oscar winning costume designer Edith Head, "A dress should be tight enough to show you're a woman and loose enough to prove you're a lady." Wearing a skirt can be a sign of modesty, a sign our world desperately needs.

8. *Rage in Elegance.* Do not be angry. But if you should get angry, make sure you are wearing a full, flouncy skirt! Seething in pants is so prosaic. Should you ever need to slap a man in the face and turn on your heel in a huff, the effect is much more dramatic if a skirt twirls indignantly with you.

9. *Charity.* In the way we dress, we should strive to be attractive, not attracting. For better or worse, men are visual creatures and have a hard time not focusing on the shape of a woman's body. I was naive on this point for twenty-five years before my husband enlightened me and research backed it up. Usually, pants are more likely to mark out the lines of a woman and engage the imagination of a man more quickly than a skirt would. It's not charitable to think, *Well, if he's a pervert, that's his problem.* Wearing a skirt can help "lighten the load" of our Christian (and non-Christian) brothers on purity issues, as one friend of mine put it. Attention to modesty can help men look up and meet the eyes and thus the soul of the woman rather than focus on her body. Pope Saint John Paul II said, "Men must be taught to love, and to love in a noble way; they must be educated in depth in this truth, that is, in the fact that a woman is a person and not simply an object."[7] We women are the gatekeepers of morality, and we have the power—by the way we dress—either to educate men concerning the dignity of womanhood or to perpetuate their struggles with lust and objectification.

10. *Evangelizing All Types.* This is one of the lesser discussed benefits of wearing a skirt. I have been blessed to engage in at least two conversations with fundamentalist Protestants who likely would not have taken seriously what I had to say if I hadn't been dressed modestly. This shouldn't be the case because a religion's teachings should always stand independent of its fallen messengers, but it helps

---

[7] Quoted in Jason Evert, *Purity 365: Daily Reflections on True Love* (Cincinnati: Servant Books, 2009), 86.

to be able to look Roman when in Rome. A woman wearing a skirt almost never offends anyone, but sometimes a woman wearing pants or tight clothing loses credibility (unfortunately) with fundamentalists, Jehovah's Witnesses, Mormons, and Muslims. That's a lot of souls that could potentially be converted by a woman wearing something they respect.

One reason people feel turned off by skirts and dresses is that many of the examples they've seen are, quite simply, unattractive: tired denim jumpers or sad florals from Aunt Maude's attic. Making an effort to wear skirts more regularly does not mean you have to jump on a piously frumpy bandwagon. Alternately, this is not a call to try to become some sort of fashion-hungry imposter or trend chaser. It is a call to be current and attractive in our fashions, while simultaneously being everything to everyone. Winning people over to the idea that women can look classy and modest at the same time is a very delicate art, but it can be done, on any budget, with patience and creativity, and it's a noble goal worth pursuing.

We must, of course, keep in mind that any exterior emphasis is always secondary to the "inside of the cup", and our first goal is to maintain our own humility and guard against pharisaism. A quest for improvements in feminine dress and dignity should be balanced with a healthy sense of meekness and self-mortification so we aren't tempted to judge others based on their appearances or their convictions on matters unrelated to faith itself. Thankfully, God has allowed innumerable embarrassments in my life and shortcomings in my spirituality to help me regard myself as just a ragged mutt on the pathway to grace.

— Ellie

LULLABY

I can only describe motherhood
in elemental ways—
breast milk leaking through my shirt
warm as blood
the ache of fullness and
relief of letdown;
the odd paradox of its sweet
taste turned sour smell when dry.
The damp delicacy
of rosewater on my skin,
a perfumed rain:
fragrant invoking
of Mary's mantle
to enfold my maternity
within hers.
Perfect repose
of a child at the breast
eyes of each resting
in the other's gaze,
a pure and silent regard.
Like the call to Vigils
the baby's cry in the night
an office I cannot neglect,
my feet on the floor
in the dark
I move toward him
by the tender velvet
of maternal instinct.

— Amber Cummings,
British Columbia

I understood that every flower created by Him is beautiful, that the brilliance of the rose and the whiteness of the lily do not lessen the perfume of the violet or the sweet simplicity of the daisy. I understood that if all the lowly flowers wished to be roses, nature would no longer be enameled with lovely hues. And so it is in the world of souls, our Lord's living garden.

— Saint Thérèse of Lisieux
Story of a Soul

ECCE FEMINA

"I don't believe in 'mom hair'," my hairdresser calmly said with a smile as she began to clip away at my overgrown, dull locks. I'd told her to give me anything but a "suburban mom cut". What she meant was that every woman deserves to have a great haircut, and moms are no exception.

Her words have stuck with me, and while I'm sure she didn't attach any profound meaning to them, I think they represent something fundamentally wrong with our culture. All too often women today seem to adopt the idea that their *beauty* ends once their *motherhood* begins. It's as if once we have children, the identity of "female" melts away into nothing more than a frumpy appearance featuring mini vans, yoga pants, and shuttling kids to and from art, karate, or Little League.

Part of the problem is what we women do to ourselves. We throw ourselves so deeply into our job as mother that often we lose ourselves. I'm not leading a charge to increase "Me Time" here, in the sense that women run off to the spa or gym to escape from their domestic demands. I'm concerned about women not fully developing the gifts and talents they have been given and also not fully developing into the women of God—daughters of God—that we were called to be from all time. Our spiritual growth is stunted because we tell ourselves that our children and the laundry and the diapers are our prayer. But that's true only to an extent.

Our growth as women is stunted because we don't *make* time to nurture our own selves and gifts. "Love thy neighbor as thyself" presumes that one has a healthy self-respect and self-love to begin with. Some of us have an aversion to the idea of self-love because it has pop-culture, New Age connotations rife with selfishness or self-deification. How can we be humble while still loving ourselves? The answer is simple if we would only realize that our goodness and worth do not derive from anything great that *we* have done. But we *can* love ourselves because of something great that *God* is (the all-powerful, all creative God) and something great that *he* has done (creating us, loving us, redeeming us).

Even the "survival season" of motherhood, when we are simply trying to keep our head above the waters of challenging toddlers, food allergies, and endless bills, does not need to be bleak and joyless. We can still make our beds when we wake up, wash our faces, and put on clean, well-fitting clothes and maybe even a streak of red lipstick if we're feeling saucy. But every day we should try to carve out a certain space for our gifts, even if expressed in small ways. I want to add an important disclaimer here: it seems whenever people talk about "using one's gifts", the assumption is that "gifts" refers to the arts. Not all women can sing, paint, or craft. But all women have been given *something*. It might be the gift of leadership, organization, writing, empathy, cooking, right judgment, and so on. How beautiful the world would be if we each tapped into the potential that he has given us!

So many of us have bought into the lie that for a gift to be valuable, it must be monetized. This is far from the truth. Our greatest contribution to the world is making our homes warm, loving, and joy-filled places, not running lucrative businesses or successful marketing plans. Gifts certainly can be turned into a source of income for a woman's family, but the measure of what we do, of who we are, has no price tag.

There's no happiness anywhere for a person who doesn't look forward to coming home; let's put our efforts into making our homes rich with our own creative and unique imprint. Writers can send out thoughtful letters to family and friends (who does that anymore?) or journal for their children. Artists can draw little pictures to slip into their children's lunch boxes or paint a mural on their wall. My own mother has a gift for making homemade comics, and today, when her nine children receive in the mail (not email!) a custom comic strip about their families, we swoon with a sense of honor that no price tag could measure. Some women have a knack with fashion or makeup; making others look and feel their best is a gift. Some women have the energy and warmth and social artistry to host fantastic parties; hospitality is a gift. I have a friend who is a clear, calm, and confident thinker in crisis situations; I have appealed to her gift many times. Another friend has an infectious laugh and subtle way of directing conversation to make new or awkward people feel comfortable; this is a gift. One is a genius at engaging toddlers with storytelling and meaningful play; this, too, is a gift.

We won't all be able to master everything. I know I am disorganized at home and a distracted house cleaner. I can't sing lullabies to my children without embarrassment. I can cook, but it's nothing to write home about. But my family looks forward to my birthday cakes months out from their creation. And my husband makes space for the pride I take in providing a rich literary environment for our family. I am not blessed with creative hospitality, but my friends know my door is always open for a slice of real life—just step over the toys and forts please—and a cup of tea.

We are each enough. We are complete as *woman*. Motherhood alone is not what defines us; it is our daughterhood that gives life to our spirit. Let's rejoice in the gifts our Father has given each of us and use them for his glory!

— Ellie

WHAT IS A WOMAN?

A woman is a fountain. She is a source of mystery and wonder, even to herself.
Come, and drink.

She is a fertile valley. It is in her nature to make, produce, nurture, tend, relieve, receive, and give life. In her person is a passing on of life to life.
Come, be fed.

Though she thinks brightly, she feels acutely. She notices the sensitive and subtle movements of the living world, both within her and without.
Come, and be understood.

Color belongs to her. They penetrate her deeply, compete to catch her, and whisper playfully to please her keen taste.
Come, and be captivated.

The salt air finds a welcome home in her throat.
The mountain air evokes her song

And the desert her silence.
Come, and breathe.

What binds her to the moon and the waves?
Curves that belong to the circle and cycle form her breasts and hips.
Come, and come again.

Her glory is proportional to her "being vessel",
Receiving, carrying within, pouring out, emptying.
A woman's heart is made to bleed, bringing forth life only through its piercing.
Come, just come.

Lay your head on her shoulder, or fall into her arms. Be received. She cherishes that which she loves, and she loves that which comes to her in need. Mercy is her velvet garment, and wisdom her gracious crown.

— Hope

LOVING MY POSTPARTUM BODY

I sit here with a sleeping baby lying on my lap and my other little darlings sleeping upstairs. As I look down at my youngest, I find myself thinking about what a blessing it is to embrace womanhood. Recently I've come to understand more fully how fertility is such a big part of womanhood. So many women have been taught that their fertility is something to suppress, stop, and sometimes do away with altogether. But I am in awe at how fertility, in all its natural goodness, is so rich, beautiful, and powerful.

There is so much, long forgotten by many, that comes with a woman's fertility. One thing I've discovered recently is the appreciation for the changes in a woman's body in all the different stages of childbearing: before, during, and after pregnancy. So many times I've heard the compliment "Wow, I can't believe you have children; you look great!" or something along those lines, as if the goal for women is to look as though they've never had a child. But embracing the changes like weight gain, stretch marks, a soft little baby pouch—all this, when a woman accepts and comes to love the changes, can bring a peaceful comfort. I fought these changes for five years. I didn't want anyone to take my picture because I thought I was just so fat. I would look at myself in the mirror in disgust because I had extra layers of fat after having a baby. Then I would work hard to lose the weight, and only after losing the weight would I allow myself to enjoy life.

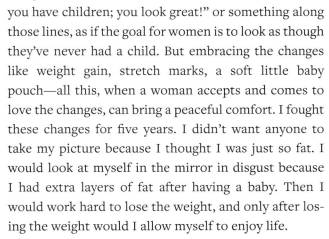

After our third baby was born, I prayed a lot about my weight and my issues with weight, and I then found myself in a place of acceptance. I was given lots of clothes that actually fit my soft, curvy postpartum figure—and you know what? I started to love my body. Now, I didn't get all into being curvy and showing off my new figure. Instead, I started to learn to love modesty—and not because I thought I should cover up ugliness but rather to keep hidden what was sacred and lovely, preserving my true beauty.

Think about it: my womb grew and carried *life*. If that's not sacred I don't know what is. Covering my midsection became a beautiful practice instead of a shameful hiding of stretch marks. This change in mindset and understanding of the human person and human body has brought me a freedom that I know God wills for so many mothers—a wonderful love and appreciation for the beautiful gift of a woman's body. This is a beautiful thing for mothers as well as women who have not carried a child in their womb. Our female bodies resemble the Blessed Mother; her womb carried God himself. From her Yes to God, she lifted up *all women*. Now all women share in this great honor of having a womb. The womb is sacred even for women who may be infertile. The womb still holds the beautiful capacity for life, and this great honor can be veiled with lovely humility and modesty.

I share this experience along with the joy that Christ has given me through this process, and I pray for your hearts to be pulled toward Christ in every moment and in every way, from changing a diaper to falling on your knees in prayer.

— Rhianon Chavarria, Florida

HAPPY BIRTHDAY

How old are you again? Twentysomething? Thirty-something? Fortysomething?

I just wanted to let you know that you look great. Whatever you have been doing, keep it up. Sure, you've had a couple of weird haircuts, but they always grow out. Pregnancy and child-rearing take their toll on your body, but they come with perks too. Your arms got pretty buff carrying that last one around, and although there is always room for improvement, you eat healthy, girl, and it shows.

You know what I can't stand? Seeing those women in their forties dressed like teenagers and dancing in night clubs looking to pick someone up. It's so gross. But you know what I love? Seeing women who look their age, act their age, embrace their age, and make it look good. And that's you. You are a mother; you have given yourself wholeheartedly to your vocation as a mother, and you still have that special something that makes you even more than that. You are an individual with various talents and gifts that make you a wonder.

I watch you in action and I marvel at what you do: the food on your table, the smiles on your children, all that you are able to accomplish in twenty-four hours … It leaves me amazed. Just look at how the Lord has blessed the work of your hands!

What keeps you looking good is no secret—it is your smile and how you love. Some women look stunning on the outside, unconsciously boasting of the time they have to keep up such an appearance, and yes, it turns heads. But you have a heart that has learned to love with such a habit of self-forgetfulness that I am forever inspired, and I just wanted you to know. It shines through you and I can see it. So celebrate this year, this turning of the age, with a gratefulness for and a confidence in your beauty, because

This is your year,… and … It always starts here,… And oh … You're aging well.[8]

— Hope

[8] Dar Williams, "You're Aging Well", *I'll Meet You Here* (album), released October 1, 2021.

JOURNEY

MAKING ME

The Christian songwriter Rich Mullins wisely said of the Apostles' Creed, "I did not make it, no, it is making me." Mullins found the root of this idea when reading G.K. Chesterton's book *Orthodoxy*. Chesterton describes coming to Christian faith in this way: "I will not call it my philosophy; for I did not make it. God and humanity made it; and it made me".[1] I have found no better way to describe the continued conversion of being Catholic. Though I was raised to think that a faith should be my own, something I form from a reading and study of Scripture guided by the Holy Spirit and the "inner light" of my conscience, the great humiliation of my life (first of many) was when Jesus wooed me into the Catholic Church. A Church that I had once believed was filled with arbitrary and restrictive rules has, surprisingly, set me free. It is not something I created or formed from my own interpretation of Holy Scripture. Rather, the Church is creating and forming me.

I mistakenly thought that on the night I was baptized and confirmed Catholic, my crucible was over and the jubilation could begin. I was ecstatic, to say the least, and so relieved. It had been three humiliating, terrifying, and exhilarating years of studying, wrestling with Scripture and theology, and prayer. I had alienated nearly everyone I was close to—friends, family, church community. And it had finally come to an end.

I couldn't have been more wrong. It was only just beginning. I had forgotten that one's baptism is the *beginning* of new life. And new life does not begin entirely with peace and sweetness, as we mothers know. Bringing new life into the world is painful, laborious, and gritty. Yes, it's also glorious and beautiful, but it leaves scars and marks; the umbilical cord has to be severed. The baby wails from the shock of his new world. And there I was, the day after my baptism, a wailing babe in shock of my new world, mourning the severing of that umbilical cord of comfort I had felt throughout my conversion. I had seen his glory and power when he brought me through the saving waters of the Red Sea, but like the Israelites, I started to grumble in the desert, afraid his holy bread would not be enough to sustain me.

I knew so little of what it meant to live as a Catholic. I knew to immerse myself in the sacraments, but I didn't imagine life would be much different. I had received a great gift in being exposed to an entirely different culture—the orthodox Catholic culture of Holy Rosary parish in Portland, Oregon—where families had multiple children, homeschooled, and loved and adored Holy Mother Church. So I knew life *could* be different. Potentially. But I was nineteen years old; I had just completed my freshman year of college and was looking forward to completing my degree in English and Performing Arts. I had big plans for my life, none of which included marriage and children or the religious life.

As I was becoming Catholic and started reading Catholic works, especially the writings of Saint Thérèse of Lisieux, I noticed a different meaning for the word "vocation". My understanding of the word "vocation" was limited to one's occupation, one's job. And I knew what I wanted my vocations to be—actress, teacher, writer, travel journalist, and so on. Saint Thérèse used the term in the context of her calling to the religious life and then later as her call simply to love. I was interested in this but had no context to put it in. Marriage was, in my opinion at the time, the opiate of the masses, something people did when they ran out of life to live. I knew someday I wanted to have children, and marriage was just an unfortunate and frightening mile marker somewhere in the distance.

Just as God surprised me with the Catholic Church, he had another surprise in store for me, another gift of humiliation, a reminder that his will is far better than

---

[1] G.K. Chesterton, *The Collected Works of G.K. Chesterton*, vol. 1, *Heretics, Orthodoxy, The Blatchford Controversies* (San Francisco: Ignatius Press, 1986), 211.

any plans I might dream up. I met someone in college and tried my best to keep him just a close friend, but quite against my will I fell in love with him. I knew I was a better human being around him. He challenged me tenderly and lovingly; he honored and respected me. And during a particularly difficult trial of my life, he faithfully offered support. We were both in *A Midsummer Night's Dream* at our university—I as Hermia, he as Demetrius—and I nearly burst backstage with the dreaded "I think I love you." Then we went onstage and even though I had to spit in his face, I really just wanted to run away with him.

Poor, patient man! I still kept pulling away from him, especially as I began to wonder what my vocation was, in the Catholic sense. After studying Saint Thérèse, I felt somewhere deep inside me that if Jesus really loved me, he would call me to the religious life. If he really desired me, he would want me for his spouse. I actually felt offended, like a spurned lover, that I didn't have a call to the religious life. By learning from the example of some older married friends of mine and thinking more carefully about the lives of saints like Gianna Molla and Thérèse's parents, I realized marriage is not a lesser vocation but a very holy calling that raised up saints. My wise friends reminded me that marriage is a partnership that is supposed to help souls get to heaven. Soon I found myself engaged and in no doubt of my vocation to the married life.

We married in July of 2004. The film *Thérèse* by Leonardo Defilippis was set to be released the following fall, and I, who had played the title role, was traveling a lot on public relations tours. This was my dream come true, or at least the dream I had before getting married. Now I felt tired; I missed my husband. I liked being at home with him. I felt safe and loved with him, not afraid of how I looked or what I said, as I often felt while on tour. Everyone kept telling me what I needed to do next to wholeheartedly pursue an acting career. It sounded exhausting and forced. I couldn't believe it, but what I wanted more than anything was to have a baby. Who was this person?

Our life began to surprise us both as we willingly had one, two, three children. Our parents' minds were whirling as they imagined us ten years down the road with a good two dozen. But by the time we conceived our fourth child, I was barely treading water. The previous five years suddenly caught up with me. I had to admit a scary truth: I didn't like my life. I had three beautiful, interesting, and well-behaved children, but I was so exhausted I couldn't see straight, and I didn't appreciate them. I felt like I had disappeared. I didn't think I was a good mother. I didn't know how to stay at home. I didn't have any at-home hobbies; I had been trained for the so-called "working world".

But as difficult times can be, my fourth pregnancy was a time of great blessing and growth. After four children and six years of marriage, I needed to make my peace with my vocation. Everything had happened so quickly that I had never thought about what I was doing. I had gone from interviews and cameras to a quiet apartment where few really cared about what I did all day. I had gone from feeling beautiful to feeling like a misshapen stranger. I had gone from believing I had a grand purpose to feeling as though I had none.

After the nausea and dizziness of the first trimester had set in, I remember sitting in the tub sobbing. I was terrified of labor. I was terrified of the postpartum blues. I was worried about our finances; we were struggling already and now we were adding another person to the bill. We didn't have insurance, so I was worried about that. I was on the precipice of despair. It could have gone badly. But it didn't.

As a convert, it didn't often occur to me to ask Mary for help. I understood Marian devotion, her role in the Church, her importance, but I didn't often think of her intercession in my own life. I started praying, and the Holy Spirit reminded me of a homily I had heard once in which the priest encouraged the entire congregation to ask for more love. It was a prayer God would always answer. So I did; I asked God to give me more love to love my family with. And the Holy Spirit whispered in my ear, *Ask Mary*. So I did. I asked for Mary's help. I asked her to pray for me that I might be a better mother. I asked her to love the life inside me until I could. It wasn't instantaneous. But about seven months into my pregnancy, when I had grown so excited about this new baby that I'd forgotten my previous worries, I realized one day how much admiration I had for my kids. I was starting to appreciate them and take notice of their unique personalities. I was starting to enjoy the days instead of watching the clock. Mary had helped me love and appreciate not only my new baby but also the three lovely ones already in my care.

She must have known how desperate a state my soul was in because she clearly turned my request over to her own parents. Our fourth baby, a little girl, was born on the feast of Saint Anne and Saint Joachim. God provided miraculously—I had a healthy and quick recovery, breastfeeding came more easily than it had before, and my husband mysteriously received a slight raise in pay. Not only did God provide, but he left little presents everywhere. Life didn't get easier; four kids was definitely more work. (God bless all you mothers with more!) But the lens through which I perceived life had altered, thanks to the mercy and power of God and the intercession of our Blessed Mother. As the Memorare says, "Never was it known that anyone who fled to thy protection or sought thy intercession was left unaided."

Saint Thérèse says of her Christmas conversion that God made her "grow up in an instant".[2] In short, I think that's what happened to me over those nine

months. I grew up. I had been acting like a child on her birthday, surrounded by loads of beautiful presents but crying for something she didn't have. Taking on the vocation of marriage wasn't something I fully understood or grasped—who does? But it is *making* me. I can see now how the married life is a purgatorial cottage of sorts that can prepare me for heaven, if my eyes and heart are open and willing. No one takes pictures of me doing dishes with lovely captions in *Catholic Digest*. No one keeps a tally of laundry loads with smiley-face stickers noting my achievements. No one applauds my dramatic reading of *The Giant Jam Sandwich*. But no one understands the beauty of a hidden life more than the Holy Family, which is why I know Jesus, Mary, and Joseph are at my side daily to help me appreciate its treasures.

I don't know how I would have told the story of this chapter of my life without having first become Catholic. But being Catholic is *making me*. It has changed the way I think of God, love him, approach him, and worship him. At baptism, the dam breaks and that grace flows into every facet of life. I had no idea it would change the woman, wife, and mother I am too. But I'm so grateful it has.

— Lindsay Younce Tsohantaridis, Oregon

SLOW SKILLS

We had just moved into our house and the property was, to say the least, neglected. All the fence lines were a solid mass of vines and shrubs: poison ivy, poison oak, poison sumac. I had heard about the wonders of vine-eating, brush-clearing goats, so after contracting horrifically itchy rashes from numerous encounters with this overgrowth, I took the plunge and got a triplet of milk goats because it was economical. I thought at the time how nice it would be, perhaps one

day, to have the option of milking them. This was two years ago.

The buck escaped his bachelor quarters several times. Shortly thereafter, I thought the does were probably pregnant, but I had no idea when they might be due. But kid they did, in the middle of an icy pasture in single-digit weather. I was very postpartum at the time, so this was traumatic for me. Slowly but surely, we fine-tuned our skills and got better and better at

---

[2] Thérèse of Lisieux, *Story of a Soul: The Autobiography of St. Thérèse of Lisieux*, trans. John Clarke, O.C.D. (Washington, D.C.: ICS Publications, 1976), 97.

this goat thing. We built a stall and I learned to calculate when the does were due to kid. I was correct almost to the day. We lost some babies. We laughed at the kids. My neighbor decided to take two bucklings, as bottle babies, to wether and clear her brush. Then lo and behold, I started milking! Someone brought over a milking stanchion and set it up, and there was my daughter, Aibhilin, on my back and Murielle, the goat, with her head in those bars and my friend's son and I milking that goat. I was doing it! But in looking up the average output for a milk goat, I learned that I was getting less than half of what even a "freshener" should give. Never mind that we were the worst combination: an inexperienced milker trying to milk an inexperienced doe. Clearly, I was no good at this! Milk was streaming down my arms and squirting on my pants, and Murielle was protesting away, her hooves in the milk pot.

We lost the kids last year and had to wait another year to try again. It's not like getting a car fixed or even like being able to pull out some rows of knitting to start again. I've made a mess of my garden too, in numerous ways; each year I have to wait, rethink, and plan better for the next year. I hope these hard lessons from the land travel with me the rest of my life: to be patient with the slow growth of my children, my marriage, my soul. But it's so worth it, because our God is not a God of haste. He moves slowly, and though it is hard to wait on him, this waiting builds strength so we can later mount with the wings of a bird.

Oh, these slow, hard skills of the land. I try to take it one day at a time, solving problems, looking forward, waking up to each new day. In a world of notorious instant gratification and the even more recent explosion of "Everyone can be a virtuoso", these slow skills may be difficult and elusive, but they are worth every grueling, tedious stage. It is beautiful to see that these little lessons in his creation—the waiting, patience, and perseverance, practiced a little bit every day—do lead to concrete results.

—Jaime Gorman, Virginia

KADDISH FOR ROSIE

You weren't just a no-one
You were a special someone
Whom we'd never know

Arriving with the New Year
We thought you were a curse
Then accepted you as blessing
And then you went away

In our amniotic shadow
Where it seems a boy is smiling
Fetal being forms his mouth

So I hold your faded picture
Dates of entrance
And of exit now are
Scribbled on the back

For I'd saved it like a postcard
Or a talismanic promise
From a love I longed to know

Still a rush of blood and water
Took your shadow and its smile
For you were but a tourist
Never destined to come home

Now these twenty-eight years later
Feel you hover at my shoulder
In the home of ghosts and angels

Behind my purposed present
You are waiting for forever
In time's errant shifting mirror
As I hold your only picture

Is it you for whom I mourn
Or just the death of summer
And
All I've lost unborn?

—Madeleine Sklar, Oregon

THE SOUND OF SILENCE

The house is eerily silent. I am standing on a stepladder, leaning over upside down to paint inside a closet—our home goes on the market this week. The baby is sleeping, and the older children have scattered, intuiting with that sixth sense that chores will be required of them soon. (How do they know? They're here in numbers when my husband and I try to sit down for a quiet glass of wine.)

I'm unused to silence and the troops of foreign thoughts that march in when all the noise disappears. I don't like silence. I never have. I am an extrovert by nature, craving human connection above all things, and I crank my music. "Waste no time!" That is my motto.

I wipe my paintbrush, balance it on the tray, and step down the ladder to find a podcast so I can make the most of my time while I paint. My Superwoman cape flutters behind me. As I scroll through my podcasts, a thought just kind of floats up inside my heart, a single word: "Silence". *No thanks.* "Sit with the silence." *No way.*

"Lean into the silence."

What?

It is not words but a gentle insistence swelling up inside. I have been listening to Brené Brown all week (those of you who are unfamiliar with her work, google her now!) and reflecting on what it means to "lean into discomfort" and "lean into joy" without shielding ourselves from heartbreak. It all sounds wonderful. I'm all in when it comes to intentional living.

But "lean into the silence"—why? What does silence offer? There's nothing there. It's a negation, an echoing emptiness.

And then it hits me like a thump on the head: I've been filling up every minute of every day with noise, stimulation, talk, emails, relationships, children; I'm frantically fulfilling responsibilities or escaping from responsibilities. Even while walking around the house at night finishing up little tasks and folding laundry, I have a show on or listen to talks "to keep my mind occupied". Even when I pray, I'm usually reading something.

But what is in silence? Could there be an "other", a presence, God himself? Or would I find me, my own self that gets shelved while I gallop through life filling needs, reacting to this and that, cramming experiences? Or would I find nothing, a yawning chasm?

We are so afraid to let go of good things in case we find nothing. We are afraid to fast from food, afraid of the nihilation that comes with hunger, afraid of emptiness. We are afraid to take risks, even for the sake of great adventure; afraid to let go of the comfortable and familiar. What if I leap and there's no one to catch me?

So I reason while I stand gazing at my computer. But something makes me close it. I walk back to my ladder. I embrace the silence. (We have five children. I have exactly four minutes of silence to enjoy.) And suddenly the silence becomes *loud*.

What is in those four minutes of silence? Well, me—memories, resentment and anger, gratitude and joy, my heart with all its baggage and its gifts.

I become aware that there is also "Other", God himself, the divine Spirit that infuses our lives, fills all space, charges the world with flaming grandeur (à la Hopkins), and continuously renews the world even while we're stopping our ears with podcasts. As my mind and heart quiet down and I humble myself before the Lord in silence, I feel his presence. For the few precious minutes before my kids come thundering in, I am filled with awe.

> Only the silent hear and those who do not remain silent do not hear.
>
> —Josef Pieper
> *Leisure: The Basis of Culture*

In my little house, on a stepladder, upside down in the semi-dark (if you want the comical visual), the Lord is present. He has been here all along. He was here fifteen minutes earlier when I was yelling at someone, when I was rocking the six-year-old with the stubbed toe, when I was chatting with my husband, when I was tearing down and building up, when I was succeeding and failing, when I was busy about the "cares of the world" (Mk 4:19).

In silence, I see my heart like a neglected garden, and I bring it to the Lord: "Oh, Lord, I am not worthy that you should come under my roof—in fact, it's pretty dark in here—but only say the word and my soul shall be healed."

Silence isn't just golden. It's necessary. If we want to know the truth about ourselves so we can heal what's broken and bring our best selves to our marriage, children, friends, and work, we need to sit quietly with ourselves. We need to be present to God, who is everywhere present and makes all things new. We need space and time to look into the eyes of the Lord and one another. We need to turn off our devices, shut our laptops, and switch off the music.

As I write this, I'm already blushing with hypocrisy-shame. I'm a sinner who will likely forget my resolves by this time tomorrow and screw up all over again. But there's hope in this: his mercies are new each day, and I can always find him again in the silence.

— Mary

BLUNDERING TOWARD HEAVEN

There is a misconception among secular culture that saints are superhuman people: angels, superheroes. That they are the elevated mystics, the untouchables, the ones "over there" in their own light-filled aura, sort of like God on earth. Not so! They were born, and they encountered trials and sufferings and sorrows and joys and blessings. They laughed, cried, ate, slept, went to the bathroom, picked out an outfit for the day, fought colds, and struggled with sin. In many ways, they were just like you and me. That's precisely what I love about the saints: they are relatable. Phyllis McGinley says in her book *Saint-Watching*, "They lost their tempers, got hungry, scolded God, were egotistical or testy or impatient in their turns, made mistakes and regretted them. Still they went on doggedly blundering toward heaven."[3]

Saints were just ordinary people living ordinary lives (for instance, Pope Saint John Paul II, Saint Teresa of Calcutta, and perhaps others you and I have known in our lifetimes who will indeed someday be saints). But what made them special? What gave them that light we all have read about and seen? What, in the end, made them saints? I think it's that they put their hearts and eyes on heaven. They totally surrendered their lives to God, knowing that this life was but a passing one and that they were to do God's work, not their own; they knew they were vessels. They put first in their lives the commandment to know, love, and serve God. They tried always to say yes to God.

I struggle with feeling downhearted about my failings. Once in a while I fervently pray novenas for particular intentions, but most of the time I fall asleep while praying them or I forget. Though I am so far from becoming a saint, I know it is achievable; I know I can, with bucketfuls of God's love and grace and an

[3] Phyllis McGinley, *Saint-Watching* (New York: The Viking Press, 1969), 6.

how to direct my gifts and tone down the more negative aspects of my nature. For instance, I love Saint Teresa of Calcutta. Like me, she was an active and passionate woman, doing hands-on work. Saint Francis de Sales and Saint Louis de Montfort had hot tempers but *overcame* them. I love Saint Hildegard of Bingen for her musicality, healing wisdom, and love of plants. The saints, through their examples, inspire me to take the temperament that God gave me and turn it into something blessedly balanced. Art and Laraine Bennett, in *The Temperament God Gave You*, mention that it is very hard to figure out which temperament the saints were because they did such a heroic job striving for virtue.

So, as I deepen my prayer life and hopefully grow in discipline, humility, and self-knowledge, I trust that God will mold me. The Holy Spirit can help me channel my weak and strong personality traits, my gifts and talents, even my handicaps toward the Good, toward God. Using my strengths to glorify God, I can whittle away at the weaker points and build on the stronger points, read the lives of the saints, turn to other God-loving folks in my own life for counsel, and stay close to the sacraments. Even I, a great sinner, can become a saint. And oh my, *bless* him if I can, because that would be a true testament to God's abundance of mercy and love.

— Sia

outpouring of his mercy, get there. I know I can take every single bitter, wounded, broken part of my being and give it to God. I know that in doing so, I am storing up treasure in heaven, as Jesus taught in the Sermon on the Mount. For me, an often-weary pilgrim, and for everyone else stumbling along our respective rocky paths, this knowledge holds so much hope.

Another very comforting and joyous thing about the saints is that they're my fellow brothers and sisters who lived in this same broken world as I do. They can relate to my struggles. Therefore, I can turn to them for companionship, example, and, best of all, intercession, asking them to pray for me to God the Father in heaven, in whose presence they dwell.

On an entertaining note, Phyllis McGinley described how there are saints she can't identify with: "Charles Borromeo is too steely for my taste, Rose of Lima too extravagant in her mortifications, and Theresa [*sic*] of Lisieux too incorrigibly girlish to give me comfort. But the rewarding thing about watching saints is that there are so many of them, far more than enough to go around. And for every fanatic or bore among them there are a thousand delightful ones to adopt as friends."[4]

I must admit, too, that there are saints to whom I simply can't relate. So I find myself turning to those saints who are a bit more like me: opinionated, passionate, strong, fiery. I love it when I find saints with a temperament like mine because then I can see in them

> It's all in God's hands. You may die in your bed or God may spare you in a battle.
>
> — Leo Tolstoy
>
> Márya Dmítrievna, *War and Peace*

[4] McGinley, *Saint-Watching*, 11.

NO NEED FOR DESPAIR
JUMP UP, KEEP PLAYING, KEEP LIVING, KEEP LOVING

Every mother knows this trick: your child takes a spill, and since it is clearly not a major injury, you cheerfully coax, "Jump up! It's okay! Come here and I'll give it a kiss." The "it" is the "owie", which you may need the child to point out since it's probably invisible. Sensing your lack of concern, the child is suddenly quite able to jump up and run to you for that kiss or maybe even to trot off and continue playing without taking advantage of your motherly "first aid". If every mother knows this trick, why bother to recount this familiar scene? Because we tend to forget that just as our kiss can make our child's owie all better, so, too, our heavenly Father's kiss can make our owies all better. He wants *us* to jump up, heal, get stronger, and keep going when we stumble.

The analogy works well because at times our stumble may be such that it leaves a visible wound, which will take a bit of time to heal. But at other times, our owie is so minor as to be essentially invisible. Yet we do not say to *our*selves, "Jump up. Keep going. It's okay." Too often, we become discouraged and overly downhearted. We pick at the scab of this minor owie and hinder its healing. We can't believe our stumble into perhaps an all-too-familiar sin. One thing to ask yourself is, Why am I so distraught? Is it because I have offended God, whom I should love with my whole heart, or because "the ideal image that we have of ourselves has been brutally shaken"?[5] That's an important distinction.

Before entering the Catholic Church at the age of thirty-one, I had a First Confession. Me—a child of the '60s and '70s, hitchhiking for years all over the country, living a vagabond, wanderer, bohemian life—making a First Confession! Suffice it to say, it was not short and I'm sure the priest was not bored. But many years after that First Confession, some of those same sins for which I had already been forgiven began to nag at me. So I sought out a priest and asked again for forgiveness for some of these same sins. Alas, a year or so later, I began beating myself up again. So again, I sought out a priest. Fortunately, this wise priest explained the situation: the devil was trying to take away the sense of peace I should have felt from absolution. He instructed that the next time I was assaulted by guilt or remorse, indeed the next time I even sensed myself glancing back at those sins, I was to say emphatically, "Get thee behind me, Satan!" I did as he told me, it worked, and I have not been plagued since.

Ah, but what of those (seemingly) smaller sins? Do we forgive ourselves and confidently move forward, dispersing gloomy thoughts of failure and disappointment? I am not for a moment saying that these sins aren't worthy of confessing or that we should accept them as just part of who we are. We must own our faults, admit them, and try to do better. But then we need to move on.

Father Jacques Philippe has written a wonderful, easily read book entitled *Searching for and Maintaining Peace: A Small Treatise on Peace of Heart*. In it, he points out that as we struggle to eliminate those faults and imperfections that seem to plague us all too regularly, we must never lose heart or become agitated or mad at ourselves. That is counterproductive. That is exactly how the devil whittles his way into our very being. Father Philippe says, "If our soul is agitated and troubled, the grace of God is able to act only with much greater difficulty" because "God abides in peace and it is in peace that He accomplishes great things."[6] While this is not meant to be a book review, please be patient as I offer a few quotations from this 110-page treasure:

---

[5] Jacques Philippe, *Searching for and Maintaining Peace: A Small Treatise on Peace of Heart*, trans. George and Jannie Driscoll (New York: Society of St. Paul, 2002), 58.
[6] Ibid., 5, 11.

The sign of spiritual progress is not so much never falling as it is being able to lift oneself up quickly after one falls.[7]

And why is this?

For the person of goodwill, that which is serious in sin is not so much the fault in itself as the despondency into which it places him. He who falls but immediately gets up has not lost much. He has rather gained in humility and in the experience of mercy. He who remains sad and defeated loses much more.[8]

And,

After committing a fault of whatever kind, rather than withdrawing into ourselves indefinitely in discouragement and dwelling on the memory, we must immediately return to God with confidence and even thank Him for the good that His mercy will be able to draw out of this fault![9]

As I mentioned earlier, a priest helped me recognize how unhealthy it was to dwell on my past (already confessed and absolved) sins. But it is, of course, important to feel at least some pangs of guilt when we fall. So how to tell the healthy guilt from the unhealthy guilt? Once again Father Philippe:

We must know that one of the weapons that the devil uses most commonly to prevent souls from advancing toward God is precisely to try to make them lose their peace and discourage them by sight of their faults....

Not all of the reproaches that come to our conscience are inspired by the Holy Spirit! Some of them come from our pride or the devil and we must learn to discern them. Peace is an essential criterion in the discernment of spirits.[10]

At age sixty-two, I am still at war against my "smaller" faults. I know all too well many of the battles that younger mothers are facing every day. I may no longer have those same challenges, but we are all tasked with the challenge to grow in holiness each and every day of our lives. To do that, we need to be at peace and let God do his work in us. Remember, we are people of "goodwill", what Father Phillipe calls a "necessary condition for interior peace".[11] What, exactly, is goodwill? It's just one word, yet it is packed with so much import and meaning as it relates to the health of the soul. Father Philippe says goodwill "is the stable and constant disposition of a person who is determined more than anything to love God, who desires sincerely to prefer in all circumstances the will of God to his own, who does not wish to consciously refuse anything to God".[12]

I'll wager that if you are taking the time to read this journal, you, too, are a person of goodwill. This word has helped me immensely to believe in myself. Yes, I may fall again and again, but God sees that I have goodwill. He knows that I long to love him more fully, that I yearn to give myself to him more completely. So I sense his Fatherly care and allow him to kiss my owie, knowing that I need not despair because God knows I have goodwill. With his kiss of forgiveness, I can pick myself up and keep playing at this game of life.

I will let Father Philippe have the last word: "[Goodwill] is not perfection, nor sainthood achieved.... But it is the way ... which permits the grace of God to carry us, little by little, toward perfection."[13]

— Dru Hoyt, Ohio

[7] Ibid., 64.
[8] Ibid.
[9] Ibid., 62.
[10] Ibid., 63.
[11] Ibid., 16.
[12] Ibid.
[13] Ibid., 17.

MY NUMBER'S NOT UP

At the earliest of ages, I can remember wanting to be a mom. I still have a book from my childhood called *My Book about Me*. In the middle of the book are two pages on which appear many kinds of animals dressed up in all sorts of vocational garb. Across the center of the page is a sentence beginning, "When I grow up I want to be a _____." In my most darling, little-kid handwriting is the word "mother".

Mother. That word, that reality, that vocation was just *it*. The most beautiful, sacrificial, glorious *it*. Of the plethora of options, I had no desire to be or do anything else. At some point in my premarriage years, I decided I wanted to have twelve children. I don't remember exactly when I first had that thought or how I came up with that number, but it was definitely twelve. I do remember, though, in my mid to late teens thinking that I would hands down be married by the time I turned twenty-five. Why twenty-five? Again, I don't know. It was arbitrary, I guess, but middle of the road, and at the time it sounded eons away. Well, twenty-five rolled around and I was still single. Twenty-six, twenty-seven, twenty-eight … Alas!

I found the love—*love*—of my life at age twenty-eight. We were married eight months later, shortly after my twenty-ninth birthday. Our first baby, Fran, was a miscarriage, born on my own mom's birthday. But now I was a mother! And even then it was every bit as beautiful, sacrificial, and glorious as I had dreamt it would be. Actually, exponentially more so. Our first live birth was to arrive one year later on Thanksgiving morning. Leonie was perfect! I went on to have another three miscarriages and another four live births (in varying orders). After the fifth live birth, I had three more miscarriages in a row. I started getting somewhat anxious and began to wonder whether my fertility might be coming to an early end. I was pondering and praying about what it was that God wanted me to do next with my life. With our biggest gap between children, he answered; he wanted me to be a mom again.

I was pregnant and for the first time ever went on progesterone at five weeks to help my body sustain the pregnancy. One night, at the very beginning of this pregnancy, around five weeks, my husband, David, said to me as we were standing in the kitchen, "This baby is going to be a girl. Her name will be Mary. And she will be our last." He was four for five correctly guessing gender, so I could pretty easily go with him there. I had always known he wanted a baby girl to be named after Our Lady—but this time it was as if the skies had opened and the Lord God himself had spoken—so I was with him there as well. But as for this baby being our last? *Pshaw!* No way! But I let it go. I didn't think about those things again, not for seven more months.

After the twenty-week ultrasound, my midwife informed me that I had a condition called placenta previa. I had heard of it, sure, but I really had no idea what it was. In short, instead of my placenta attaching to the upper part of my uterus, it had attached at the bottom, covering my cervix. It meant I would have to have a C-section. The last four of my five deliveries had been C-sections, so we were already planning on another one. Annie, my beloved midwife, referred me to a trusted surgeon who would perform the surgery. Upon first meeting with Dr. Broms, I was immediately put at ease. He was kind, interested, thorough, intelligent, and unhurried. We discussed what a previa was and how the surgery should go. Then Dr. Broms brought out a form for me to look over. He explained that it was a waiver I needed to sign saying that in the event that the previa was also an accreta and I would need a hysterectomy, I needed to give my consent for them to take my uterus out. Say, *what*? But in reality, I played it cool and asked what exactly all that meant. He explained that a placenta accreta is when the placenta actually *grows through the uterus*. It can even begin to grow around other organs. *Um, okay* … After momentarily losing my cool, I quickly regained my composure and asked, "What are the chances that will happen to me?" To which dear Dr. Broms reassuringly responded, "I have been in practice for the last thirty years and I have done one." With that, I was somewhat relieved, though still shaken up. "Oh! Aha! My number's not up."

Annie, Dr. Broms, and the team that was selected to perform my surgery decided to schedule the C-section three weeks prior to my baby's actual due date. On July 10, 2013, my husband and I got up early in the morning for an early surgery. In all my previous C-sections, the mood in the operating room was generally light, jovial, anticipatory. But not that day. That day there was very little sound, the team of personnel was large, and the mood was quiet, concentrated, all business. Two surgeons, my midwife, the anesthesiologist, and what seemed like a dozen nurses were all busily prepping. None of us knew what we would find once I was opened up, but we all knew that we had to hope for the best and prepare for the worst.

I don't remember much about the first part of the surgery. I do remember that once the baby was out, I looked to my left and saw Annie holding her up. I weakly said, "Oh, she's beautiful" and cried a few tears of joy. Then the baby was whisked away to a nearby room. David went with her but returned soon after to check on me.

My focus turned to what I could hear. The two surgeons on either side of me were speaking medical language that I did not understand. It seemed by their tone, however, that they were working fast and that the situation was serious. I don't know how long that went on, but it must've been just minutes. Then I clearly heard Dr. Broms say, "Okay, guys, it's coming down to decision time." And I knew. Immediately I started to pray faster and in a more concentrated manner, begging all the saints, angels, Our Blessed Mother, and God Almighty to please save my womb. "Ursula." I opened my eyes and saw Dr. Broms looking at me from the top of the blue protective sheet. "I'm sorry, there's nothing we can do." I nodded and said, "Okay." I remember seeing my husband slowly walk around from behind the sheet. He had tears in his eyes. I whispered, "I'm sorry." He took my hand, put in it the beautiful rosary my mom had made for me, and said, "Don't be sorry. I love you."

I've had nearly two years now to look back and reflect on that experience. The obvious reality is that I have six exquisite children. I am infinitely blessed and am truly living the life of my dreams. I have a husband whose love for God, for me, and for his family far surpasses my dreams. So really, that's it. Once upon a time I heard someone say, "Want what you have." That is my goal. To live and love here in this reality in each moment. It's the only guarantee. (And you know what? God gave me even more … I have *thirteen* children. And I am a *mother*.)

— Ursula Crowell, Oregon

CELEBRATING OUR WAY THROUGH CANCER

Secretly, I had this hope that Ben would be some kind of anomaly and would not lose his hair at all, but just about the time I thought I might get my wish, my little boy lost all his hair in a Tupperware bowl. We took turns looking into the giant bowl full of hair. It seemed so outrageous to see bunches of blond in the round plastic, which moments earlier had been an over-the-top dancing hat, and there was nothing left to do at that moment but giggle. In the face of a diagnosis of leukemia and intense chemotherapy, I had prepared to mourn the loss of that hair but instead found myself belly laughing.

Cancer has held many surprises. After four years of tracking my baby's every milestone, evaluating healthy food options, mulling over organic brands of everything, even contemplating the use of antibacterial soap, I had to admit that as much as I tried to control things, I could not control this. And that slowly became okay.

We commended our little boy to the care of brilliant doctors and nurses, but we knew immediately that we needed to trust God completely in this situation. From that point on, what choice did we have other than positivity? We decided that as long as treatment was going well, we were not going to consume ourselves with information overload and scary statistics. We were going to lean on our faith, love our little guy to pieces, and have as much fun through it as possible. Let's face it: four-year-olds are naturally pretty fun people, so we just had to follow his lead.

During the most intense chemo, Ben was exhausted and gained so much weight he could hardly climb our stairs. Neighbors, looking through our window each night at bedtime, would view a human family transformed into silly turtles migrating to bed. During spinal taps, doctors and nurses would join us in singing rounds of "Old McDonald", and Ben, still semiawake from twilight anesthesia, would lie in stillness and sing along through his procedures. The clinic became a playground. We met friends going through the same thing, and Ben used the clinic staff as a captive audience for his favorite jokes.

Cancer was never center stage. Faith, healing, and family were. Just weeks after Ben's diagnosis, a new baby girl arrived in our family. A few years later, but still during treatment, we welcomed a fourth child. Together, this little duo emitted a lightheartedness and joy that distracted us all from most of the consuming worries about cancer.

And while we were busy with our young family, we were taken care of. Prayers for strength and health enveloped us. They came from our closest friends and from people we never met, in countries we never visited. Mass intentions were offered. Meals and random gifts arrived. During one round of treatment, Ben was delighted to receive a Canadian themed package in the mail. We found ourselves flying maple leaf banners and planting little red-and-white flags in the front yard. Although we did not know our sweet Canadian prayer warriors, their thoughtfulness made a family forget cancer for a bit and celebrate.

A dear friend from our church brought healing water to us from the Lourdes Grotto in France. Once, during Mass, a parishioner we had never met noticed that Ben was sick and gave us a special bottle of oil, making us promise to use it. I still do not know exactly what was in that bottle, but we did use it frequently and found it bone-dry the week Ben's chemo ended.

Our home never felt like a place with a sick little boy in it; it was a house filled with laughter, dancing, healing, and joy on a grander scale than we had ever known. Since Ben is the oldest, our other three children have grown up experiencing frequent trips to the doctor. Words like "cancer" and "chemo" roll easily off their tongues, but so do words like "blessing", "thankfulness", and "joy". From cancer we learned we had an amazing support system rooting for our family. We learned the power of celebrating even the littlest graces, and we learned that our trust in God is perfectly placed.

— Dawn Kujawa, Illinois

Dear friends, may no adversity paralyze you. Be afraid neither of the world, nor of the future, nor of your weakness. The Lord has allowed you to live in this moment of history so that, by your faith, his name will continue to resound throughout the world.

— Pope Benedict XVI
Homily, Twenty-Sixth World Youth Day, August 21, 2011

WHEN HE CAME

I used to be a runner,
  putting long-winded miles behind me.
    The river halfway would remind me
      of how strong I am
        how fit I am.

I used to be a poet,
  my pen was never able to keep up
    with spilling-over ideas and too small a cup.

I used to be an actress,
  a different face a different day
    shows, lights—always at play.
      But at a price to pay
        and never a thought to pray.

I used to be a dreamer,
  planning on world travel and the fever of fame,
    building for a life anything but tame.

Then he came. And next, He came.

And now my knees are broken,
  aching from genetics and age.
    And now my ink runs dry,
      and real life is my stage
        And now my dreams are quiet,
          but there's a freedom
            in my cage.

Who I was kneels down to who I am
  —creaky knees and all.
    My pen still plunges into my soul
      —if only at a baby crawl.

And I've more hats to wear upon my misshapen head,
  than the curtain could ever call.
    And it's tempting to fall,
      crippled by the weight of them all.

But every day is now. The tangible is here.
  My folly is in my fear.
    The truth of then is even truer now;
      Grace is always near.

And that is enough.

— Ellie

PROOF OF (A) LIFE
THE PHOTOGRAPHY CONUNDRUM

I bought my first Pentax single-lens reflex (SLR) camera when I was sixteen years old. I was thrilled to hold that little piece of magic in my hands and promptly enrolled in a photography class at the local community college to learn everything I could. I didn't start out with much skill, to be honest; I had the eye but kept getting tripped up on the technical components of developing and processing prints in the dark room. But with simultaneous enrollment in Video Production, I quickly picked up what I needed to know about "capturing" a moment. Looking at the world through that lens was a certain kind of intoxicating, and I longed for the day when I could get a digital SLR camera and explore fully what I could do.

In 2007, my husband bought me that camera in a single, sacrificial, expensive gift of love. His hands were shaking as he presented the camera to me—we both sensed the significance of taking my photography to the next level and how momentous it was finally to own a camera of such high quality. And I dove right in. I read that manual back and forth and quickly put ads on Craigslist, offering cheap portrait shooting in order to build up a portfolio and gain some people experience. I loved that camera. I took it everywhere. I subjected my children to spontaneous photo shoots all the time. I absolutely *hated* when we'd be somewhere picturesque or witness something beautiful and frame worthy and I didn't have my camera with me. I have thousands and thousands of photography files on my computers.

Never before have we seen such a proliferation of photographers and wannabe photographers in our world. It used to be a fairly expensive hobby, but when film turned digital and costs were driven down—and the novelty of an in-phone camera burgeoned—everyone got shutter-happy. (Great news for eager amateurs, terrible news for professionals.) I read a very astute observation on the modern phenomenon of taking pictures of *everything* (be it your dinner, outfit for the day, or workout sweat): *Proof of a life is now more important than having a life.* And I see this every day at the park across from my house where moms chase their kids around with their phone in hand, trying to catch the happy smile or perfect angle on the slide antics.

I realized that what had changed for me was how I experienced life—not necessarily always savoring it and living in it, but capturing it, trying to keep "the moments" from running away from me. The wake-up call came on a hike through the island hills of Washington a few years ago. The boys had run up ahead and found a really cool stump. When I caught up to

them, my oldest was bossing his brothers, who were trying to poke at banana slugs: "Stop it! Guys, get up on the stump so Mom can take a picture!" I felt startled and sheepish that the camera-happy mom had influenced her children to such a degree that they now stopped their playing and enjoyment of nature to pose for pictures. *Sheesh. Let it be, Ellie.*

I feel something of a disconnect from "the moment" when I have my camera with me. Maybe it's my production training, always looking at the angles and lighting and trying to foresee great shots so I can be ready when they happen. This changes the way I experience something. To me, it seemed that the very act of shooting something became just as important as living it. Pumpkin patch visits? A day at the beach? Baseball games? Corpus Christi processions? Christmastime? All these found me with the camera in my hand, frantic to capture them on film (er … hard drive).

Now I say, "Enough." I want a balance. I want to employ my memory again. It's great to look through bursting photo albums (or online files that never get printed) with the children. But more valuable to me is just soaking it in. I get so distracted when I lug my camera around with me—or, worse, when I have the handy iPhone to snap some quick shots—that I often forget to savor these all-too-short moments. It takes a lot of discipline to allow myself to do nothing but experience the present.

Yet, I'm a realist. I recently upgraded to a newer, quicker, sharper DSLR and some accessory items. I'm not going to *stop* taking pictures. I just struggle mightily to balance it out. Despite having a fuller, busier life and more children now (read: *excellent photo ops!*), our camera gets taken out less and less often. I do deliberate portrait shooting with the kids, of course. But I'm not concerned about dragging out the gear (or whipping out the phone) every time a child does something cute or my dessert looks especially appealing. I love the line Sean Penn's character delivered in the movie *The Secret Life of Walter Mitty*. As a professional photographer, he is hunting the elusive snow leopard, and once he finally finds it and has the perfect shot framed up, he doesn't take the picture. Ben Stiller's character is confused and asks him, "When are you going to take it?" The photographer responds, "Sometimes I don't. If I like a moment, for me, personally, I don't like to have the distraction of the camera. I just want to stay in it."

And that's what I want. I want to stay in the moment. I want to be *here*. I want to live a rich and full life, not prove I have a rich and full life. Part of that means sometimes leaving the camera at home and being okay with missing a killer shot or sweet moment.

I think in the end, it'll be worth knowing that just because something would make a great photo doesn't mean it should.

— Ellie

AD PLURIMOS ANNOS

Mary Odell was born in Wisconsin in the year 1923. She arrived somewhere in the latter half of a family of eleven children, offspring of a devout Protestant minister whose efforts to provide for his family had to go halves with his divine call to learn ever more about his Lord and Creator; his farming career was punctuated with sabbaticals to seminaries in California and Oklahoma. Hence it was that in the early 1940s, as the nation fought Germans in Europe and the Great Depression at home, Mary found herself in Weatherford, Oklahoma, where she noted gratefully that under the trying national circumstances she no longer stood out due to her made-over dresses and patched shoes, and where she met and married my father-in-law, Francis Kelly Dougherty, thus beginning the family that was to give me a husband, a home, and a faith.

Mom, mother to me in soul and in love and in wisdom, dear to me as my own mother, took me in without knowing enough about me to steer her better. Indeed later, when she heard something of my background, she shaded her eyes and thanked God that she learned these things only after she knew and loved me and my sister; for, she said, she could never have believed the good she knew of us if she had first known what our childhood had held. That was the nearest she ever came to regret or criticism, and it was neither.

Rich in listening silence, and in the patience that is sister to mercy, she seldom gave me advice. For this reason, the little she did give I remember and apply to my life daily. Watching my entirely untutored, childish, and often selfish attempts to make myself into a wife and mother, she helped me with the encouragement of gentle service. I do not remember the occasion, or what burden, real or imagined, I was complaining about, but I remember her words often: "Whatever it is, this, too, shall pass."

This sentiment is applicable to an hour of colicky baby or a season of surly, intransigent adolescence; to extended marital misunderstanding or prolonged therapy for depression; to that periodic hour of unreasoning fear undermining, if possible, even our most devoutly held assertions and resolute decisions; and to the piles of dirty laundry on the mudroom floor. Her voice is never further from me than the inclination to despair and is its unfailing answer: this, too, shall pass.

It is my guarantee that with whatever the universe addresses me at the moment—pain, insecurity, tedium, or, perhaps most fearsome, meaninglessness—its eternal aspect, hovering just below the surface in divine comedy and solemnity, is divinely beneficent, divinely comprehensible; that in a short while—a year, a decade, a death and resurrection—I will look again upon this present moment and laugh with joy. For this, too, shall pass.

I wish I could say it as well as Mom did.

— Beth Dougherty, Ohio

THE LAND OF THE LIVING

I called on the name of the LORD:
  "O LORD, I beg you, save my life!" …
For you have delivered my soul from death,
  my eyes from tears,
  my feet from stumbling;
I walk before the LORD
  in the land of the living. (Ps 116:4, 8–9)

I will not pick up the phone in this passing, ordinary moment. Instead, I will listen to the tea kettle boil. I will stand up straight and tall, stretch, think, pray. Instagram and Pinterest, you are for my leisure time, not for my work time. I will sing to my five-year-old daughter; I will read her a poem. I will let this sacred moment before me, in the peace of my mind and heart, expand and bloom and flourish into the transformative moment it has the potential to be.

I will not turn on the radio right now. I will slip on these sunglasses, buckle up, and pray en route. It is the hour of three, the sacred hour of our Brother's Passion. I will chant the Chaplet. I will invoke the prayers of the Communion of Saints. I will talk to my grandmothers above. I will set my eyes on the road and bask in the love of the Father. I will honor my journey, honor this moment, honor the life inside me.

I will not have that extra drink tonight. I will not wallow in my misery, my pain, my heartache. I will have *just* enough, letting the lightness come over me, grateful for the gift of this drink. I will not let the beautiful, life-filled soul of mine despair, become discouraged, or sink into the deep. I will live. I will take care of myself. I will love myself.

I will not have that second cup of coffee that I *want*; I do not *need* it. I will pour water into a wine glass, squeeze some lemon juice into it, and drink it reverently. I will take my vitamins, comb my hair, and wash my body with oil from olive trees. I will stand in front of the mirror and carefully trace, with coconut and frankincense oil, each new wrinkle on my face. I will take care of this body God gave me. I will love myself so that I can do the work that my Father has sent me to do. I will put into this body what is good. I can bloom and I can thrive.

I will not fall asleep watching the BBC's latest series. I will close the computer before sleep comes. I will drink some water, meet my challenges, face my anxieties and fears, and breathe. I will lie on my back and close my eyes and say a prayer. I will pray, I will pray, I will pray. I choose to rest in Christ's love, to let Mary enfold me in her mantle of love, to dwell on the stars and the sun and the moon, the song of the crickets, the call of the night owl, or the afternoon mourning dove. I will let the light shine into my whole being; I will say yes to life in my soul.

I will say yes to grace, say yes to life running through, say yes to walking in the light. I choose to live in the land of the living.

— Sia

PRAY

POP-UP CHAPEL

Do you realize the greatness of your vocation? The enormous responsibility? Perhaps you do. And if you do, that is good. But perhaps, like me, in the humble tasks of daily living you can lose sight of the cathedral you are building, and, covered with the mortar of the day, you can find yourself feeling worn out and insignificant.

Echoing the Curé of Ars, Pope Benedict XVI proclaimed, "The priest must above all be a man of prayer."[1] I, in turn, proclaim, "A mother must above all be a woman of prayer." Since the dawn of religion, women have been the custodians of the faith, and it is the quiet way that the faith is lived out and passed down by women that keeps it alive and flourishing. I am not at all trying to underestimate the gravity of the role men play, but this is a mother's collective and we'll let the men discuss their importance among themselves through their own platforms. *You, as a mother, are a portal of grace for your family.* It is through your heart that many graces can enter the lives of those in your care. In order to be effective, you must above all be a woman of prayer.

"But how", you may ask, "am I to be a woman of prayer, without the time, space, and freedom to pursue a contemplative life?" I am here to tell you it's not as hard as you think. As the poor widow from the Gospel pleased God by giving just a small amount of money, we can please him by giving him a small amount of our time, ordered in the right way. Our Lord lovingly said, "Remain in me" (Jn 15:4).[2] We cannot remain in a place we have not first visited, and by spending a few moments with him (preferably first thing in the morning), we will set up the tent of our day beside the Living Waters, where we can later refresh ourselves amid our labors and live out the psalmist's words, "He will drink from the brook by the way; therefore he will lift up his head" (110:7).

Busy mothers, we must be like hummingbirds, darting to and fro and stopping for small sips of divine life throughout the day to keep us going. But first, we must drink deeply, to condition our taste, so that in the heat of the day our hearts will thirst for those waters that alone can satisfy.

Okay, so here comes 6:00 A.M. and your alarm. Enter the pop-up chapel. Most of us aren't so fortunate as to have a home chapel, a special place in the house set aside for prayer and reflection. I had one, but my husband needed a home office more, so away it went.

I've since found I can set up shop just about anywhere in my home, with the following items:

- A candle
- A holy icon, crucifix, or statue
- A Bible or spiritual reading
- Ten blessed minutes
- (Obviously very optional: a cup of coffee)

I often set up my pop-up chapel in my entryway, but sometimes in the living room or kitchen. The bathrooms and closets are also options. If my little kids saunter in, I let them hang around if they can keep quiet, or I send them back to their rooms until 7:00 A.M. I think it's good for them to see me praying and good for them to learn to leave me alone. All a mom needs to get started is to rise from bed at least a quarter of an hour before the rest of her people. Your ten blessed minutes might turn into fifteen, and then twenty, and then thirty. You might find yourself wanting to wake up earlier, because it's a delicious thing for a busy person: time

[1] Benedict XVI, Chrism Mass Homily (April 13, 2006).
[2] NABRE.

> Man is the creature with a mystery in his heart that is bigger than himself. He is built like a tabernacle around a most sacred mystery.... Certainly, in the sinner, this sanctuary is neglected and forgotten, like an overgrown tomb or an attic choked with rubbish, and it needs an effort—the effort of contemplative prayer—to clean it up and make it habitable for the divine Guest. But the room itself does not need to be built: it is already there and always has been, at the very center of man.
>
> — Hans Urs von Balthasar
>
> *Prayer*

alone, time to read, be quiet, rest in the Lord, and speak openly and honestly with him. Your personal tête-à-tête with our Lord will flow into the rest of your day, and your entire spiritual life will flourish, veering you away from a formulaic faith and toward a more personal and authentic one.

Maybe you are not a morning person. Maybe it takes many cries from your children and many grumpy snooze-button hits before you are able to drag yourself out of bed. We can work with that! Once the dust of the morning settles, set up your pop-up chapel and find fifteen minutes of moderate calm to turn your attention to the One who loves you the most. *Do not* underestimate the importance of a candle in this morning recipe. The flicker of a candle has a life of its own: it serves as a visual reminder that God is present, alive, risky, and dangerous (in the best of ways); it brings a subtle yet meditative warmth and marks clearly the beginning and end of your solitary prayer time. Either way, be sure to get your prayer time in before 10:00 A.M.; it will arm you with the grace you need to handle the unknown trials of the day. You would not attempt to climb a mountain on an empty stomach, so do not attempt to bear your day patiently without first letting your Shepherd feed you the spiritual food he desires to give. Only then will it be easy to remain in him. And be aware of the temptation to let your to-do list creep into the forefront of your morning hour!

Saint Teresa of Calcutta knew well that time set apart for prayer is an investment in the effectiveness and productivity of one's day. She advised a nun who was frustrated at her lack of time that the antidote was an extra half hour of prayer.

Don't wait for the perfect house with a spare room that can be converted into a home chapel, or for the perfect season of life with extra time. I've long heard the saying "Your home is your chapel, and your children are your prayer." I love it, but I think our homes are more likely to be chapels if we treat them as such, at least once a day. Give the Lord even a few minutes and see for yourself what beautiful fruits it will bear. "Whoever remains in me and I in him will bear much fruit, because without me you can do nothing" (Jn 15:5).[3]

— Hope

[3]NABRE.

THE HEROIC MOMENT

One of my favorite things about being Catholic is just how diverse our roads of spirituality can be. If the spiritual exercises of Saint Ignatius are too tough for you, try Saint Thérèse and her "Little Way". If you can't relate to the youthful holiness of Saint Catherine of Siena, dive into Saint Augustine. Are you Marian focused like Saint Louis de Montfort? Perhaps you are  Eucharist-focused like Saint Peter Julian Eymard. The Benedictines pray and work. The Carmelites pray and detach. The Dominicans pray and teach. The Franciscans pray and serve. All these charisms are so beautifully expressive of the different faces of Christ. I can't think of any other religion in the world that unites so much spiritual variety under the same theological umbrella. Truly, ours is a universal Church.

There are a couple of saints' writings that speak to me in a very particular and personal way. It's as if they are my own spiritual directors, especially needed since real-life ones are scarce. I love all our saints! But I'm too wimpy for Saint Ignatius and too cynical for Saint Thérèse. I need someone who can slap me upside the head and hold my hand at the same time. That's where the likes of Saint Francis de Sales, Saint Teresa of Calcutta, and Saint Josemaría Escrivá come in.

When I read *The Way* from Escrivá, I found myself slowly digesting each little point as if it were an entire sermon. Certain nuggets have stuck with me for the long term:

Don't say, "That person bothers me." Think: "That person sanctifies me."[4]

"The Mass is long," you say, and I reply: "Because your love is short."[5]

If things go well, let's rejoice, blessing God, who makes them prosper. And if they go wrong? Let's rejoice, blessing God, who allows us to share the sweetness of his cross.[6]

But there is a little gem from Saint Josemaría for which I am especially grateful. It is his teaching on the Heroic Moment. This is the act of mortification that is tremendously hard and beautiful: waking up like a saint. The good padre expressed it like this:

Conquer yourself each day from the very first moment, getting up on the dot, at a set time, without granting a single minute to laziness.

If, with the help of God, you conquer yourself in that moment, you'll have accomplished a great deal for the rest of the day.

It's so discouraging to find yourself beaten in the first skirmish![7]

Get up immediately. Don't hit the snooze button. Cross yourself. Kiss the floor. And say the opposite of what Lucifer said: "*Serviam!*"—Latin for "I will serve!" To think of all the ways in which we fail throughout the day, this is at least one way in which we can set the tone for the day, one way in which we can cry out to God in mind and body that whatever else may come, we at least *want* to offer our day to him and to serve him. It's a way to mortify the flesh for those of us who are terrible at fasting and aren't inclined to wear sackcloth. It's the Heroic Moment. I still don't have it mastered, but this year is going to mark my latest attempt at making it happen consistently. I want to be awake and ready for the little Christ child, eager to greet him at first dawn like the shepherds and say, "*Serviam!*"

— Ellie

---

[4] Josemaría Escrivá, *The Way: The Essential Classic of Opus Dei's Founder* (New York: Image, 1982), no. 174, p. 29.
[5] Ibid., no. 529, p. 91.
[6] Ibid., no. 658, p. 115.
[7] Ibid., no. 191, p. 31.

A PREGNANT WOMAN'S PRAYER

Lord, help me stay focused and calm as my due date approaches. Cast out all fear and anxiety from my soul and restore peace and confidence. Protect my baby from unnecessary stress and assist me during labor.

Grant me the courage to welcome the pains of birthing, to embrace them with generosity, and to recognize them as the life-giving gifts they truly are.

Instill in me a complete acceptance of the pain and keep the desire to escape it far away from my mind. The moment of transition will leave me exhausted and desperate, feeling as if I cannot go on any longer. Only trust in your love and mercy can sustain me then; please do not abandon me! I ask for your strength during the final phase, when I am pushing my baby out, and I thank you beforehand for the ring of fire that will bring me to the other side—motherhood.

Throughout it all, keep my spirits high and receive the prayers of my heart. With immense gratitude, I ask you to bless my faithful husband and wonderful midwives and doctors.

I abandon myself into your hands, trusting that you designed my body to be capable of giving birth and that it is very good. Bless my labor and delivery, and may it empower me for the tasks of mothering that await me.

As my beautiful baby enters this world, let him find all the safety and reassurance he needs in the loving embrace of his mother. May the shock of birth not harm him, and let him feel in his flesh that he is worthy, welcome, and unconditionally loved.

I praise you, life-giving God, for the gift of family and of motherhood. Queen of all laboring women, Mother of Christ, pray for me! Amen.

— Mariola O'Brien, British Columbia

UNDERSTANDING ICONS

In the Byzantine Christian tradition (both Catholic and Orthodox), we strive to use all five senses in our encounter and engagement with God. You will find our temples covered in colorful icons (sight), saturated with incense (smell), and reverberating with bells and chant (sound). You will find our faithful kissing crosses, icons, and one another (touch). And in addition to the Body and Blood of our Lord received in Communion, you will find koliva (boiled wheat dish to commemorate Saint Theodore or the deceased), blessed grapes and apples (blessed on the feast of the Transfiguration), and multiple forms of blessed bread and wine consumed reverently during the dismissal rites of festal liturgies (taste). A worshipper is immersed in the beautiful paradox of sensory rest and stimulation.

"Seeing" an icon is a very inadequate term for iconography's role in Christian worship. Icons, if created properly or blessed, become windows into heaven. They are grace-filled mediums for every human but also transcendent engagements with Christ, the saints, and events in salvation history that are mystically transported to the present time and space. Centuries of adoring and devoted prayer have produced a trove of informative and inspiring symbolic traditions within iconography that engage the person praying as he stands before an icon.

The figures in an icon are not meant to look realistic. Inserting lifelike images into a prayer tradition that treasures awe and mystery can actually be distracting. The captivating beauty of an icon comes not from an ordered face or healthy complexion but rather from the revelation of the person and qualities of the saint depicted. Take an icon of Jesus Christ. His forehead is abnormally large to symbolize wisdom. His mouth is small to symbolize humility. His nose is pronounced to reveal his receptivity to our prayer (which is symbolized by the incense that naturally rises to the heavens). Oftentimes, one of Christ's eyes looks at us (judgment) while the other looks over us (mercy). He is wearing a deacon's vestment over his shoulder to symbolize both authority and service. In one arm he holds the good news (the Gospels), and the other offers a blessing. His inner garment is red to symbolize his original divinity, and over this he wears blue to symbolize the humanity he was "clothed in" (an icon of the Mother of God will have the opposite order).

A church may have an image of a "saintly" man, but only after he is declared a saint or blessed does he receive a halo. This is because a halo symbolizes a hole in the fabric of heaven, where the saint looks down to intercede for us. For this reason, the inside of a halo is usually real gold leaf, revealing the glory and preciousness of the kingdom where the saint dwells. In Christ's halo is the Greek phrase "O ΩN" (He Who Is). This proclaims that Jesus Christ is the same God as that of the burning bush in the Old Testament (Ex 3:14). The unapproachable God of the Old Covenant is now the completely approachable God who invites us to share his very life. The "IC XC" above Christ's head is a Greek abbreviation for "Jesus Christ".

A few years ago, one of my nieces was having a rough night and she climbed into bed with my brother and sister-in-law. Her mother told her that she needed to go back to her own bed, but she lamented that she was lonely and really wanted to stay. She was told that she always has access to Christ, who dwells in her heart and always wants to hear from her. She considered this for a moment and then said, "But I need a Jesus with skin." Our Lord knows, and doesn't begrudge us the fact, that even as adults we need him to reveal himself through symbolism that we can perceive through our senses. He created us with eyes, ears, a nose, taste buds, and skin. Our faith is empowered when we use these gifted senses to engage him as the humans that we are.

—Father Michael O'Loughlin,
Proto-Cathedral of St. Mary,
Los Angeles, priestly contributor to
Soul Gardening Journal

THE QUIET MAN

Can I tell you a story? It's about fire, friendship, and undeserved gifts. The silent, unsuspecting hero is a person you may already know, though perhaps you wish you knew him better. Our best stories are those unforgettable moments that bookmark the larger drama of life, when the mysterious lines of the everyday converge for a second, or an afternoon, to allow us to catch a glimpse of the masterful plan that is actually happening all around us at each moment. These stories, though few, are the ones truly worth telling.

My story begins with a book of old Catholic prayers called *Pieta*, familiar to some as "the little blue prayer book", with the cover image of Our Lady holding Christ after his Crucifixion. My mother had many copies and would place them in the carry-on bags of her friends, daughters, neighbors, and husband before a flight. "There's a prayer in here that promises you will not die by fire if you keep it with you."

"Yes, Mom," said I, or my sister, as we too often let the prayer book drift unopened into the bottom of our backpacks.

I started praying for my husband in high school, when most of my peers were getting physical and I was trying to hold out for more. It didn't take long; I met him when I was eighteen. Justin was twenty-two, mature, and very good. I'll never forget him lovingly scolding me, saying it was *not okay* to use a fake ID at a bar (a welcome-to-college-gift from some awesome friends), and between him and my own conscience, that fake ID made its way into my dorm trash can. He was the best boyfriend. He made me a dress (!) and my own book of prayers out of brown paper bags, holy cards, and hemp rope. It held handwritten Marian consecration prayers, night prayers, and a certain very old prayer to Saint Joseph. We prayed those prayers every day the whole time we were dating and in the early years of our marriage.

When I was nineteen, I went to Austria for a semester, and during those three months Justin and I wrote to each other every single day. The letters were precious, filled with hopeful expectation and longing for God

and each other, and we saved them all. At some point during this European expedition, I found myself in Vienna, inside St. Stephen's Cathedral, on my knees in front of the friendliest image of the Sacred Heart I had ever seen. His eyes were so *evocative*. His smile was so *secretive*. His commanding softness made me feel that all the tenderness of a woman and all the strength of a man were bound up in his very person. His burning heart seemed to pass through the painting and into my own, and I couldn't move. A friend noticed me noticing him and bought me an eight-by-ten-inch cardboard print from the gift shop, which she gave to me on the steps outside.

Of course I hung it in my dorm room, and then in my room at home, and before long, the unframed piece of cardboard became a tattered relic, with tack holes and bent corners, and it drifted into the background of life so that I almost forgot about it. Life, as she does, demands forwardness. I married Justin, we had baby after baby, and we moved about every two years for a decade, shuffling along our ever-changing possessions.

In 2010, with five kids in tow, we scrounged up the money to buy the house we hoped would be the landing place for our family. (It was, and the house is a treasure!) The house was a 1960s rambling ranch with enough room for our family to grow, and the property had trees to climb and space to garden. And it was an easy commute for Justin. The house came with a soulful, very large old red wood barn in the back. For those of us who grew up with barns dotting our childhood landscapes, old barns can somehow have a claim on us. We notice them; we hear them whisper inaudible stories of early mornings, quiet evenings, and dedicated farmers slipping out of their cozy quilts and into their boots to care for the animals that provided their livelihood. To find a barn like this in southern California, land of sunshine and strip malls, on a property we could afford (barely) felt like a dream come true.

Months after we closed on the house, I awoke in the night to a terrible crackling sound outside my bedroom window. It was the sound of a raging fire. I choked as I looked out to see the old barn swallowed up in flames, top to bottom, far too close to the house, my sleeping children, and the flammable eucalyptus trees that could easily carry the fire through the entire neighborhood. My husband called for help and stayed behind to help the firefighters. I loaded up the kids and drove away, getting lost in my own neighborhood, my mind overrun with anxiety.

Some real treasures burned in that fire. Near the top of the list was my husband's fully restored baby blue 1972 Volkswagen bus, but the one thing that was truly irreplaceable was the box of daily love letters from our time apart, those many years ago. I sat down one day in my living room, cried, and wrote a song about it called "Fire Came Down".

To complete the insurance claim, we had to do our best to remember *everything* that was in the barn, and we finally put on gloves and started sorting through the rubble, looking for evidence to remind us. It wasn't easy; the fire had been so hot that entire bicycle frames had completely

disintegrated, and pictures, furniture, and camping equipment were gone without much of a trace. When we finally reached the very back of the barn, we found something (the only thing) not completely burned. It was a blue plastic storage tote with a lid, melted from the heat, black from the smoke, and wet from the fire hoses. We pulled it out into the sun and pried it open, and the first thing we saw was my cardboard image of the Sacred Heart of Jesus from Vienna. The smoke had burned the left side of his hair and face, covering one eye, leaving him looking like he was peeking out coyly from behind a black curtain.

Under this image, we found, to our great surprise, all our love letters, wet but perfectly intact. We both cried as we sorted through this miracle—that of everything, these *pieces of paper* had survived such an intense and all-consuming fire. And, at the bottom of the tote, under all the letters, was a damp little blue *Pieta* prayer book. Immediately I remembered my mother's words

about protection from fire and a certain prayer, and I frantically searched through the book to find out who was responsible for this mini-miracle and whom I needed to thank: I soon found my answer.

The prayer to which these promises are attached is none other than the very old prayer to Saint Joseph that my husband and I prayed daily through our courtship and early years of marriage. All along, Saint Joseph was a silent friend and hero who guided our marriage and family, though I hardly paid him any attention. This story is my story, but it could have been yours.

In the spring, we celebrate two feasts to Saint Joseph: one in March, the second in May. Perhaps through these feasts we can renew our fidelity to him, who is so quietly faithful to us. Despite his power, however, I admit I've found that this enigmatic man can be hard to get to know. He has no recorded words in any of the four Gospels, and we are left with little to go by except knowledge of his righteousness and obedience. Last year I happened upon the book *The Life of the Blessed Virgin Mary* by Blessed Anne Catherine Emmerich and found within its pages some tender details about the early life of Saint Joseph.

If you've seen Mel Gibson's *The Passion of the Christ*, you have already had some exposure to Blessed Anne Catherine Emmerich, as Gibson based his film upon her visions. A German nun and mystic born in 1774, she was gifted with such astounding and detailed visions of the life of Christ and the Blessed Virgin that I can't help but put stock in them. Of course, like any approved private revelation, the faithful are permitted to enjoy its edification or turn it aside if it would not be of help to one's spiritual journey. For many of us, however, these writings add tremendous color to the familiar stories that we strive not to take for granted.

According to Emmerich, Saint Joseph was the third of six brothers. His family lived outside Bethlehem in a large old house, once an ancestral home of David. The six brothers all shared the upper story and slept in a circle in one room. She could see them playing with wooden animals, and they were taught by an aged Jew who lived in the topmost tower. She relates, "Joseph, whom I saw in this vision at about the age of eight, was very different in character from his brothers. He was very gifted and was a very good scholar, but he was simple, quiet, devout, and not at all ambitious. His brothers knocked him about and played all kinds of tricks on him."[8]

The boys each had a separate little garden, and "I saw how Joseph's brothers often went in secret to his garden and trampled or uprooted something in it. They made him very unhappy. I often saw him under the colonnade in the outer court kneeling down with his face to the wall, praying with outstretched arms, and I saw his brothers creep up and kick him.... He did not lose his temper or take revenge, but found a hidden corner where he continued his prayer."[9]

According to Emmerich, to escape the torments of his brothers, Joseph would retreat to the hillside, in particular the shepherds' caves, to pray quietly alone or make "all kinds of little things out of wood".[10] Years later, it was to these very caves, as a last resort, that he would lead the pregnant Virgin Mary, when he was overcome with shame that he could find no friend or relation to house them in Bethlehem. (This part kills me. Just imagine going back to your hometown with your new bride and being faced with the shameful reality that you have no friends there, when you needed them the most.) Emmerich continues, regarding his youth, "Joseph's parents were not very well satisfied with him; they wanted him to use his talents in some worldly profession, but he had no inclination for that. He was too simple and unpretentious for them; his only inclination was towards prayer and quiet work at some handicraft."[11]

Emmerich relates that Joseph eventually made his way into the hands of a well-to-do master, who taught him a high form of carpentry; meanwhile, the rest of the family dispersed, passed on, and came "down in the world very rapidly".[12] Years passed, and Joseph remained devout in prayer, above all praying fervently for the coming of the Messiah. An angel appeared to him and said, "As once the patriarch Joseph at about this [age] had, by God's Will, been made overseer of all the corn of Egypt, so he, the second Joseph, should now be entrusted with the care of the granary of salvation."[13]

These words are, to me, the strongest reason we have for confidently entrusting our lives to the patronage of Saint Joseph. In his humility, Saint Joseph has great power, and in God's kingdom he possesses all the privileges that the first Joseph possessed in Pharaoh's ancient Egypt, the distribution of goods in particular. To get to know Saint Joseph is to get to know a quiet man; he doesn't make a flashy first impression but is faithful to his children and likes to do them good without needing glory or attention. Reading Emmerich's character sketch, I would categorize Saint Joseph as the best sort of melancholic. Steady, loyal, intelligent, artistic, deep, obedient, unassuming, fair, simple, and just the sort of person you'd want in charge of your granary, if you had one. I feel privileged to know someone like this—maybe you do too—and it's made me appreciate this temperament all the more.

The next time you're traveling in New England, see if you can journey a little farther north to Montreal, where Saint Joseph's Oratory, the largest shrine to Saint Joseph in the world, looms atop Mount Royal. It's an incredible place, with an equally incredible story of the humble, infirm, and barely literate Brother (now Saint) André Bessette, whose devotion to Saint Joseph was contagious and his desire for a shrine resolute, as he attributed the many healings and miracles associated with him to the power of Saint Joseph. Today, a pilgrim to the shrine can see both his smaller primary church and the final iconic oratory, but the

[8] *The Life of the Blessed Virgin Mary: From the Visions of Anne Catherine Emmerich*, trans. Sir Michael Palairet (Charlotte, N.C.: TAN Books, 2011), 120.

[9] Ibid., 121.

[10] Ibid., 122.

[11] Ibid.

[12] Ibid., 124.

[13] Ibid.

best part of this place is the candlelight crypt. Thousands of candles illuminate the seven titles of Saint Joseph inscribed along the wide hall: "Protector of the Universal Church", "Guardian of Virgins", "Support of Families", "Help of the Sick", "Patron of Departing Souls", "Terror of Demons", and "Model of Workers".

To walk this hall, any person, despite his age, gender, race, or place in life, can find a reason to kneel and beg the faithful assistance of Saint Joseph. We are his Church. We are his young, his families, his sick and suffering souls. We are his wounded addicts, his dying pilgrims, his living laborers. We are his people, whether we know it or not.

— Hope

Ancient Prayer to Saint Joseph

Oh, St. Joseph, whose protection is so great, so strong, so prompt before the throne of God, I place in you all my interest and desires. (Mention your requests.)

Oh, St. Joseph, do assist me by your powerful intercession, and obtain for me from your Divine Son all spiritual blessings, through Jesus Christ, our Lord. So that, having engaged here below your heavenly power, I may offer my thanksgiving and homage to the most loving of Fathers.

Oh, St. Joseph, I never weary contemplating you, and Jesus asleep in your arms; I dare not approach while He reposes near your heart. Press Him close in my name and kiss His fine head for me and ask Him to return the kiss when I draw my dying breath. St. Joseph, patron of departing souls, pray for me. Amen.

This postscript is commonly included:

This prayer was found in the 50th year of our Lord and Savior Jesus Christ. In 1505, it was sent from the pope to Emperor Charles when he was going into battle. Whoever shall read this prayer or hear it or keep it about themselves, shall never die a sudden death or be drowned, nor shall poison take effect on them; neither shall they fall into the hands of the enemy or be burned in any fire or be overpowered in battle. Say for nine mornings for anything you desire. It has never been known to fail.

WORKS OF MERCY

The Lord says, "If any one thirst, let him come to me and drink. He who believes in me, as the Scripture has said, 'Out of his heart shall flow rivers of living water'" (Jn 7:37–38). Jesus places himself before us many times each day. Husband and children are often waiting to be fed, comforted, clothed, and sheltered by the labor of our hands and hearts. Works of mercy fill our lives; these are sweet opportunities to stand face-to-face with, and to serve, our Lord. As Saint Teresa of Calcutta taught, we love him in the distressing disguise of the poor (for us, usually the endearing disguise of our children).

But I am certain that Jesus is standing before us in search of another work of mercy, and his intention may take us unawares. He is waiting not for *our* works of mercy but for the work of mercy that *he* wants to perform for us. He invites us to come to him for a refreshing drink, and one of the most creative moments in our day is when we manage to climb over those heaps of laundry and past the dirty dishes to his heart, which aches to welcome us.

One method I have discovered for meeting Jesus in my home comes from a diocesan priest I knew twenty-five years ago. Father Richard Gilsdorf explained that the Catholic Church does read the Bible, and frequently. He taught that the Church reads the Bible as liturgy. She offers us appetizers, main courses, and desserts of Sacred Scripture throughout each day in the liturgy of the Holy Mass and the Divine Office, or Liturgy of the Hours. An easy way to satisfy Jesus' thirst and hunger, and to let him satisfy ours, is to meet him in his Word through the liturgy.

Shall I be honest? I am a grazer. Whether in my own kitchen or at the divine feast the Church sets before me, I tend to want some of everything all day long. In order not to overdo it, small bites are best for me. In the pantry, this might mean a little bread and cheese between meals or a cup of tea and a graham cracker. At God's table, it means antiphons.

An antiphon is a short verse or two from the Bible. In the liturgy, we find antiphons at the beginning and toward the end of Mass (the entrance and Communion antiphons), and in the hours of the Divine Office, they frame the psalms. You may have heard of the O Antiphons, which come in Advent. During the eight days leading up to Christmas, the O Antiphons introduce Mary's Canticle, the Magnificat, which is always part of Evening Prayer. These antiphons are most familiar to us as the verses of "O Come, O Come, Emmanuel", where they express our longing for Jesus to hurry back to us.

Starting in Advent last year, I began to put my *Magnificat* magazine next to my breakfast at the table. This monthly missal contains each day's Propers, Mass and Scripture readings, and much more. As I satisfied my morning hunger with eggs and pita bread, I satisfied my—and Jesus'—hunger for love. I would start with the entrance antiphon for the day's Mass, and sometimes that would be enough to chew on. Other days, it would be all I had time for before my early solitude was interrupted by Jesus in his endearing disguise. The Advent antiphons and readings were so delectable that my appetite for them grew, and I found myself as eager for God's Word as for my breakfast.

What began as a seasonal devotion continued as the liturgical year progressed. But still you might ask, "What do antiphons have to do with us on every ordinary day?" The way I see it, we are all starving for God. When you find a starving man, woman, or child, you can't begin by serving all that's needed at once. You might begin with sips of water, then progress to crackers, helping the malnourished work his way up to a whole healthy meal. Consider, too, Saint Augustine's beautiful interpretation of the parable of the good Samaritan. As I suggested at the outset, the work of mercy dearest to Jesus' heart is the one he performs for us. Saint Augustine identifies Jesus as the Good Samaritan who has found us lying in the road, robbed, beaten, and left for dead by original sin and the Fall. He lovingly binds up our wounds and takes us to the nearest inn, the Church, where he leaves us for a time, but only after giving the innkeeper enough money to pay for our care. He promises to return.

So here we are at the inn of the Church, and the innkeeper is determined to nurture us back to health on Jesus' behalf. If you want to know the truth, I suspect Jesus himself can't stay away. He is pretending to be the innkeeper without letting us know him, just as he kept his identity hidden from Mary Magdalene at the Resurrection, allowing her to mistake him for the gardener. But whether it is Jesus our Head, or his Body, the Church, the innkeeper starts by giving us sips of cool refreshing water, the very same living water that Jesus promised to the Samaritan woman at the well. Maybe we will soon be ready for large tankards of divine ale and platters of the delicious heavenly food they serve at this inn, but initially, water and morsels of bread—the antiphons—are more proportioned to our starving condition.

Jesus often provides but never requires special equipment for our meetings with him. If you don't get *Magnificat* in the mail and don't have a daily missal on your bookshelf, a scrap of paper and a pen tucked into your purse or diaper bag before Sunday Mass will suffice to prepare you for the week ahead. Sometime before, during, or after Mass, copy the entrance and Communion antiphons for the day; these are used all week long in daily Mass, unless they are superseded by the antiphon in honor of a particular saint, feast, or seasonal day. (For instance, all the days of Advent have their own antiphons.) Or maybe you will prefer a line from the Sunday Gospel, or the Alleluia verse that precedes it. Whatever touches your heart, surprises you with God's tenderness, and awakens you to his love is a great verse for you. These antiphons are precious because they shine with the gleam of authentic treasure and take only a moment to pluck up and grasp to your soul.

When you move into the week, perhaps breakfast in your home will not be the most peaceful time of the day. Is there another moment before or after it that is better? When you are waking up or brushing your teeth? You can put your week's (or day's) antiphon near your bed, on the bathroom mirror, or by your coffeepot.

For me, on the days when I remember to find an antiphon, gratefully receiving it from the Church's liturgical feast, I find refreshment and peace, which go very well with eggs and tea. Whatever awaits me in the day ahead—and each day does seem like a mystery waiting to unfold—I've held Jesus' hand at the outset and felt him hold mine. I feel more capable of being merciful after having first been touched by Mercy himself.

— Suzie Andres, California

YOU ARE SO VERY LOVED

It's 2:00 A.M. I am alone in a hospital room with my hours-old firstborn son, trying to figure out how to feed him. I have never held a baby so small before. I don't really know what I'm doing. The shock of having my own child in my arms hasn't worn off yet and won't for another couple of weeks.

He's crying. I'm lost for what to do or say, so I tell him the only thing I know for sure: "You are so loved. God loves you. Jesus loves you. Mother Mary loves you. I love you. Your daddy loves you. Your grandparents, aunts, uncles, and friends you haven't met yet—they all love you so very much."

In speaking these words to my little one, I find strength. I don't know what I personally have to offer this brand-new person yet, but I know that the love that already exists for him is true and pure. He has done nothing to deserve it; he is loved simply because he exists. Motherhood has done a great deal to deepen my faith. In particular, watching the tremendous love that has been poured out over this child from every direction, even when I was still pregnant with him, has offered me a new perspective on the way God loves me. I was once a baby too, and then, as now, I was loved simply because I existed. It was not because of anything I did or didn't do, not because of who I was or who I was not. Just as I know my love for this little boy

will never fade, neither will the love that my parents, my family, and God have for me ever wane.

Although his first name, Jacob, can be found multiple times on both my husband's and my side of our family, our baby boy is the first of a new generation, a new limb on our family tree. He is our first child, the first grandchild on either side, even the first child among our cousins and among most of our circles of friends. Because he is the first in a lot of ways, he is also, thus far, the only: our only child, our parents' only grandchild, our aunts' and uncles' only great-nephew. When more come along, that love will certainly not decrease, but now it is made even more special because it is exclusive. It is the same way God loves me—as if I were his only child. I think of all the amazing things that have happened since Jacob came into our lives: He made my parents grandparents. He made my brother an uncle. He made me a mother. But most importantly, for my husband and me, he transformed our marriage into a family. Simply by being, simply by existing, he has initiated the most incredible change in our lives. For this I will always be grateful. For this, he will always be loved.

— Lindsay Schlegel, New Jersey

LOVING AND BEING LOVED

THE ULTIMATE CONVERSION

When I became Catholic three years ago, after a childhood spent within the spiritual vacuum of atheism, my assent to belief in Christ and Christian theology was mainly intellectual. I saw my conversion as a step in the search for truth—a pathway to God, to be sure, but a pathway of the mind. My upbringing within the mental rigors of atheism had taught me that it was wrong to use religion as a crutch, and for that reason, there was no room for the heart, and especially for uncontrolled emotionalism, when it came to our thinking about God and the wider questions of existence.

And yet, the first discovery my intellect made was that God is Love. This was where I arrived in my search for truth, and it was also the beginning of the journey. New spiritual vistas opened before me as I realized that Divinity itself is a unity of love and life—a sublime fusion after which the mind yearns but only the heart can begin to penetrate.

Opening my heart to God's love also led me to open myself—and my life—to God's life. Being open to life and all that openness might mean: *that* was the challenge set before me as a new convert. However, when I became a mother—when I really had opened myself to life—I was frightened, almost dismayed. I no longer had time for God. Drained of mental energy, physically exhausted, and always pressed for time, how could I cope? I could no longer connect with God as I had in the ecstasy of my first conversion. There was no place for contemplation or serious theological study left in my life. To say a few prayers on the rosary beads, to remember briefly, or rather hope, that God was there, in my life and in my day—was this all that was left for me? Had God pulled the intellectual plug on my faith life?

While still pregnant, I spoke to my priest about my concerns. He was the same loving father who had baptized me and received me, with open arms, into the Church. His simple wisdom never failed me at my need, and this instance was no exception. He mentioned other parents he had known who also complained that they no longer had time to meditate, or that there was no silence left in their lives. But, he assured me, this didn't mean their spiritual lives were at an end. Rather, our form of spirituality—how we live for and connect with God—has to change. "Go to the Lord through Baby," he advised me. Reminding me that prayer is not exclusively contained within meditation, he added,

> It is not always easy to see just how much progress we are making toward our goal.... We are very much like the tapestry workers, who work not from the front of the tapestry, but always from the rear, keeping ever before their eyes the model of the work to be achieved. They go on drawing thread after thread in a monotonous but thrilling way, never destined to see their completed work until the last thread has been drawn, and the tapestry is turned about to show them how well and how truly they have labored.
>
> —Venerable Fulton Sheen
> *Go to Heaven*

"Remember: 'I am loving, and I am being loved.' *This is the prayer*."

During my daughter's infancy, I was able to realize the full truth of his simple words. Yes, as a new mother, I felt like a simpleton. I realized I hadn't had a clue what life was all about—or the full beauty of its mystery—until then. I began to see people in a new light because I was learning the preciousness of life itself. In my mundane "pots and pans" existence, I discovered that I was not simply thinking abstractly about the things of God anymore. I was *doing* them, or at least trying to do them, failing sometimes, yes, but really beginning to live in the light of faith. God's mystery was enlarged a thousand times over. I had to have faith simply to get through the day; I didn't have time to ask vast theological questions, and my hidden existence allowed me to do only very small things for those around me. I began to realize that religion was not just made of high thoughts and sublime silences but could also consist in being where we are needed, in taking care of those we love. In fact, my assent to the truth that "God is Love" was no longer merely intellectual. It had to be tangible if I was going to be the mother I hoped to be; I had to live it out.

Our whole life is a journey toward knowing God. A search for truth, yes, but, as Saint John of the Cross said, "At the evening of life, we shall be judged on our love."[14] He who is Love is Being Itself—*Love* is the One in whom we "live and move and have our being" (Acts 17:28). If motherhood has taught me anything, it's that living with God is certainly not a state of knowing all but of doing what we can, of being open and available, and of loving to the fullest capacity of both mind and heart. This is what God has made us for, and it is enough.

— Erin Brierley, Georgia

PRACTICE MAKES PERFECT

Want to know a secret? Sometimes I feel sorry for Judas. It's like someone wrote a beautiful play and needed an antagonist. Scanning the candidates lined up, mostly bearded men competing for twelve lead roles, he makes the cut and gets a part—not the one he wanted, but hey, it's got a lot of lines, and he even gets to throw some pieces of silver at people.

In all seriousness, I am grateful the Church does not declare him or anyone to be certainly in hell. I am head over heels in love with the image of Divine Mercy. Juxtaposing it to Our Lady of Fatima's message regarding the number of souls falling into hell makes my heart ache and my head spin—so much that I have almost become humble enough to stop trying to figure it out. Almost.

A priest recently mentioned to me C.S. Lewis' *The Great Divorce*, where Lewis makes the point that people actually *choose* hell because they are so absorbed in themselves that they are not ready to spend eternity thinking about someone else (God, for instance). Because in reality, heaven is probably less about one million flavors of ice cream and swimming with dolphins and more about joining the choir of voices that will be singing the praises of the Lamb. So as much as we want the peace, the joy, the painlessness of heaven, the glaring reality is that heaven is not all about us. Are we ready to spend eternity *not* thinking about ourselves? Honestly, I am not so sure I am. I am still too self-absorbed. But God is a genius—really, he is. And he has come up with a genius way to get us there, and it starts with two pink lines on a test strip. It ends with learning to put someone else's needs before our own, and to do it so often that we don't even realize we are doing it. This plan comes fully equipped with

---

[14] John of the Cross, *Dichos* 64, quoted in *Catechism of the Catholic Church* (*CCC*) 1022.

a number of humiliating experiences, like tantrums in the grocery store or not having baby wipes at a critical moment, so as to protect the whole beautiful thing from crumbling down because of our pride.

All women are called to be *Mother*, either in a physical or spiritual way, and it is God's plan to bring us to heaven by turning us into the kind of people we need to be in order to want heaven.

It's traditional for Franciscan religious to wear knotted ropes around their waists, with three knots representing their vows of poverty, chastity, and obedience. I recently befriended some Franciscan nuns who had four knots, the fourth representing availability. *Ah!* I thought. *You know what it's like to be a mother.* Each interruption—each putting down of the phone, project, you name it—to attend to someone else helps us live a life in which we become secondary and another becomes primary. A busy mother rarely has the time to think of herself, and before she knows it, a habit of selflessness is formed. And you know what a good habit is called, don't you? It's called virtue.

When I was in Paris, I saw the incorrupt body of Saint Catherine Labouré enclosed in a glass coffin. She was a short little lady with a real French nose like my own, but what struck me most about her were her shoes. They were leather, with heavy creases across the front under the toe line, where the shoe had been flexed over and over again from spending so much time on her knees. Now those creases are encased in memory, and she is spending eternity with someone familiar. Christian life is sacrifice. And just as the bad we have done in this life cannot be undone, the good we have done cannot be undone either. May our bodies lie in the grave wrinkled and tired and worn, like our dear Saint Catherine's shoes, and may our own creases, be they stretch marks, cesarean scars, varicose veins, or wrinkled smile lines, be our signs of virtue, signs that our good Lord loves us enough to save us from ourselves.

— Hope

SAINT ANNE

What do you picture when you think of your ancestors? Is your family big boned or petite? Quiet or loud? Hardworking? Dreamy? Large nosed? It's fun to think about meeting our ancestors someday. Who was the first Viking convert? Who were the persecuted Catholics who kept the faith? And who was the jerk who started the famous family temper?

Every family has a unique history. In my family, we inherited a patrimony of poetry, alcoholism, itinerance, wheat intolerance, curly hair, and storytelling from the Irish; love of home, hard work, and children from the Russians; and a stiff upper lip and the sovereign importance of tea from the English. The family traits and the family wounds incorporate the good, the bad, and the ugly.

When the all-holy, immortal God became a man, he was born into a human family and inherited

genes from his mother, his grandma and grandpa, and all his ancestors. He had family traits, family features, family culture. Do you ever wonder what these might have been? I like to picture Jesus with the beauty of King David, who was called "ruddy and handsome", with a special authority and nobility from his kingly ancestry. Jesus was also born into a home of carpenters. He was a craftsman, with hands and shoulders accustomed to lifting and building. Above all, he was a Jewish man. He inherited a culture of legal observance, devotion to Scripture, and holiness. "Shema, Israel …" "Hear, O Israel: The Lord our God is one Lord

> Make it a habit to raise your heart to God, in acts of thanksgiving, many times a day. Because he gives you this and that … Because someone has despised you … Because you don't have what you need, or because you do have it.
>
> And because he made his Mother, who is also your Mother, so beautiful. Because he created the sun and the moon and this animal or that plant. Because he made that man eloquent and you he left slow of speech …
>
> Thank him for everything, because everything is good.
>
> —Josemaría Escrivá
> *The Way*

(Dt 6:4). These words were embedded in the doorway of every Jewish family and inscribed on their hearts, according to the Law.

Jesus' grandparents have a special place of honor in the Christian tradition. Saint Anne and Saint Joachim were Mary's first teachers. What was their role? How did they form their little girl to be disposed to listen so attentively, beautifully, constantly to the Holy Spirit, to "charm" God, as the early Church Fathers said? I like to think of Saint Anne and Saint Joachim as a typical Jewish family. They were Mary's first teachers in the practice of prayer and in the habit of obedience. From them, Mary would have inherited a culture of worship, the tradition of holiness that Yahweh had been cultivating in his people.

She would have learned about the all-important "disposition of heart", which enabled Abraham and Joseph and her other forefathers to hear God's voice as he protected them, led them to the Promised Land, and entered more deeply into intimacy with them. Wouldn't that be something to pass on to our children, a culture of worship? A love of Scripture, a heart of fire, a listening ear, and an intimate relationship with the Holy Spirit?

I've entrusted the education of my children to Saint Anne's prayers, because while she's not officially the patroness of homeschoolers, she is, to me, the archetypical educator. After all, she had an enormous responsibility, much bigger than yours and mine. Although Mary was conceived without sin, all her perfection was just potential, a little seed. Somehow, it had to be watered, nurtured, pruned, and taught.

In my imagination, I envision Saint Anne as a wise, Jewish matriarch—a little bit earthy, a little bit fierce, and full of common sense. I imagine her as a young grandmother, with salt-and-pepper hair, making food for her family, counseling them, bossing them around, and loving them.

Holy Mother Church gives great honor to Saint Anne, and Saint Anne honors her adopted grandchildren by showering them with miracles, blessings, and graces. I grew up next to a town that was nearly a ghost town for most of the year but perked up each summer around July 26, when hundreds of pilgrims would visit the shrine of Saint Anne for her feast day. In secular, Protestant Canada, this was quite phenomenal. More phenomenal still was the plethora of conversions and healings, especially inner healings, from the kindly Saint Anne. I've felt her presence strongly in this latest pregnancy. And why not? By baptism, we're adopted into Jesus' family. Saint Anne is our adopted grandmother.

— Mary

MICHELANGELO MOMENTS

Like many women, I look back on my wedding day as one of the best days of my life. Yes, the magic of it all, the excitement, our family and friends surrounding us with their love, but one thing in particular made it most extraordinary for my husband and me: a double rainbow. I know, what are the chances, right? It misted in the morning, and by afternoon there were gorgeous billowing clouds broken by streams of heavenly sunlight. As the party was coming to an end and my husband and I were saying our goodbyes to everyone, it appeared in the sky over the gentle green mountains and remained there as we drove away; friends told us later that it looked as if we drove right under it.

Who doesn't love a rainbow? And yet they are especially meaningful to my husband and me. Justin is a Jewish convert, passionate about the fulfillment of the Old Testament in the New, and the rainbow is an Old Testament sign of God's promise and faithfulness to his children. A rainbow is also a sign of hope (my name). As a little girl I loved to draw rainbows. I'd fill notebooks with them until I was embarrassingly too old to be doing so. And on the day we had waited for so long and would forever remember, there it was—actually, there *they* were—filling our sky and our hearts with promise, tears, and light. On that day, the veil that separates us from heaven seemed so thin, and I felt like Adam in Michelangelo's *Creation of Adam*, so close to God that I could almost touch him.

Fast-forward nine years, and I am calling 911 because I am alone, scared, and ill. Justin has taken the children out of the house so I can rest. The room is spinning, and I am on the verge of passing out. My heart is pounding out of my chest, and all I have been doing all day is lying on the couch. Soon the ambulance comes to take me to the hospital. My children return just in time to see their mommy being driven away with all the sirens and flashing lights. It turns out I have pneumonia, which I eventually recover from, but it sends me into a tailspin of health problems from which I have yet to recover fully. And now, for the first time in my life, I feel like I have been given a genuine cross. Call it growing up, or "the dream is over", but all of a sudden life's gotten harder for me. I realize that this happened to me later than it happens to most people; for many, life is difficult from the very onset, but for whatever reason, I was spared genuine hardship until my adulthood.

God gives me an abundance of gifts to get through the hard times: consolations, the resources needed to deal with my condition, loving friends and family members. But he also allows me to flirt with despair, to want to give up, to get frustrated to the point that my own suffering consumes me (and I feel hesitant even to call it suffering, for it is not the intensity that has been difficult but the duration). But the gift of the cross does not come without lessons. Everyone has a cross, and for many it is a visible cross, like that of our Savior. Think of your friends who love God and then think of their crosses. Most of the time they are not hidden. Be it the death of a loved one, a physical suffering, financial burdens, a difficult marriage, an addiction—you get the picture. I can practically envision a first-grade two-columned worksheet titled "Match Your Friend with His Correct Hardship", and I mentally draw the crisscrossing lines between them.

There are times when we are blessed to receive consolation in our sorrows, but then there are the times when we feel that our cup of hope is running out, and we want to run and hide. It is at these times that I think we are meant to call upon our "Michelangelo Moments". As in the case of my wedding memory, we all have these moments we can look back on, when the veil was thin. Likely we can count them on one hand. Yet I think they are lifelong gifts to us, meant not only for the moment in which they were given but also for later when the veil would thicken and our faith would be tested.

Can you imagine what it must have been like for Peter, James, and John to have witnessed the Transfiguration? I'm sure they were beyond floored to witness His Sovereign Majesty while still on this earth. That moment was given to them to be their strength

later, when on a separate mountain they would witness the scandal of the Cross. Doubtless, that glory moment continued to be more than a touchstone for them as they endured immeasurable hardships and eventually martyrdom for the sake of the early Church.

I am reminded of a hike I would often take up Mount Elmore, a mountain near my old home in Vermont. It is a lovely hike, mostly wooded, with a fire tower at the top and a spectacular 360-degree view. A little over halfway up, and before the hike becomes difficult and rocky, there is a clearing with a view of the lake below. It is very pretty, and although it pales in comparison to what's coming, it gives the hiker a foretaste and a renewed sense of purpose for the rest of the journey.

What are your "Michelangelo moments", when you knew without a doubt God's purpose and love for you? Our glimpses of heaven in this life are not accidents, and neither are our times of aridity. Let us remember those times of hope as the gifts that they are and cling to them when our paths become difficult.

— Hope

I WILL TAKE THE CROWN

I will take the crown, oh Mary, that you offer me
The crown of thorns worn by your Son, your hand
   extends
Yes, I will take the crown, but withdraw not your hand
If it comes with you, I will love it, because you will
   hold me through it

I will take the cross, though I am not strong enough
   to carry it

Greater souls would seek it out, it is my hope just to
   bear it
I do not desire to suffer, though I do desire to love
   you
And so I take what is offered, and put not comfort
   above you

— Hope

WHY I LOVE THE SEDER

It is Easter Monday. We have just been through the Sacred Triduum, and each year I am all the more enriched and blessed by the prayers, liturgies, traditions, and inheritance of our faith. We have forty days of fasting and then forty days of feasting. And through it all we have a shocking, stirring, moving reality to ponder in our hearts: that God became man (a flesh-and-blood man, with a beating heart), sanctifying our mortal lives and earthly work. This is why we call our faith incarnational. Jesus, growing up in a Jewish home, washed his hands from a bowl of water and worked with wood alongside Joseph. He cooked his fish over a beach fire with his disciples. He was like us. He was human. Yet being the radical, against-the-grain man of his time, he taught his elders in his local synagogue, walked on water, commanded the storm and the sea, and talked intimately with a Samaritan woman at Jacob's well. He lived as one of us, obediently went to his death—a brutal, bloody crucifixion—and then triumphed, coming back from the dead and into new life all the stronger, working miracles among the people he so loved. Then he breathed his breath into us by leaving us with his Holy Spirit. This we ponder in our hearts: he became our brother; he taught us to love.

The Jewish heritage and the beginning of Catholicism in the first Breaking of the Bread come together in the Catholic seder meal, which we celebrate on Holy Thursday of the Triduum. It connects the past to the present, the Old Testament to the New, Jewish roots to Catholic realities, God of the Old Covenant to God of the New. It is a celebration of our heritage, involving biblical history and education, all revolving around the table, the meal—the Passover feast that Jesus celebrated as a child and then made new when he celebrated the last Passover before he died.

Holy Thursday is the holy feast of the Eucharist; *seder* is the name for the Jewish Passover meal. *Seder* means "order", which, applied to the seder meal, means the order of prayers. Its central focus is redemption from slavery, recalling the exodus from Egypt and renewal and rebirth in Christ. Again, old and new, united in the sacred sharing of a meal—the breaking of bread.

The Catholic seder meal, involving hard-boiled eggs, bitter herbs, salt, apples, chopped nuts, vinegar, lamb, flatbread, wine, candles, pouring and dipping vessels, scripts for all, songs, music, and alteration of schedules, takes a hefty amount of preparation: careful grocery shopping sometimes the week before, several hours of kitchen work, and at least an hour of planning.

There are several guides on blogs and Catholic websites for the basics of planning the meal and finding a script; find one that works best for you, depending on length or brevity. The second year I hosted the seder, I went to my local secondhand shop to buy special dishes for the feast. I found tiny fifty-cent wine glasses for all the children and vessels for pouring. I bought some large and small Bavarian pottery plates that did not match but looked lovely sitting next to one another on the table. We have integrated into the meal a Holy Thursday Catholic hymn for the beginning of the feast and a festive Jewish song for the end. I

have created a playlist including Yiddish folk tunes, Passover prayer songs, and Jewish roots music to play at the end of the readings, prayers, and slower parts of the meal, just as I turn on the lights and serve the main course. One can serve any Middle Eastern food for the main course, but I usually serve lamb and spices, flavorful curried rice, flatbread, and a vegetable side. We eat the remaining haroset and hard-boiled eggs and "bitter herbs" (parsley). There's a great album to turn to as you start to compile your own music. It's *Songs of Our Fathers*, traditional Jewish melodies by Andy Statman and David Grisman. "Shalom Aleichem" (tracks 1 and 12), "Shomer Yisrael" (track 3), and "For the Sake of My Brothers and Friends" (track 8) are so beautiful they will probably give you goose bumps. The mandolin and the clarinet played by these fine musicians are riveting in this genre. And "Shabbos Waltz" (track 7) will get the feast going with joy; if you've got dancers in the house, it may be hard for them not to jump up from their chairs, erupting in dance.

It's a pieced-together, creative, beautiful, homespun tradition, and each year my seder meal is a little nicer, a little more organized, a little more delicious, a little more planned. Someday I want to ask my mother to make me a set of scarlet napkins. (I don't sew, but those of you who do, you could do this!)

Each year I begin my work in the morning, after our breakfast and the morning rush off to schools. With my coffee or tea, and with my little ones home and eager to help alongside me, I prepare the meal and the table while listening to and singing along with the traditional hymns from the Holy Thursday Mass. I use my finest silverware, table linens, candleholders, platters, and dishes. I use the only all-white tablecloth I own, and for place cards I cut out white cardstock squares and fold them in half; my daughter or I write in careful script each person's name; the children decorate them and draw borders. I pray for the nourishment of the hearts and bodies gathered around my table.

I prepare all morning, setting the table, going over the scripts and music, and cooking. Then I pick up the kids from school early. I send them off to their rooms to find something nice to wear. The boys throw on button-down shirts with the jeans they're already in, and my daughters put on nice tops or dresses. They both show great love for this special meal by placing blossoms or single tulips into a waiting vase of water. Once, to my surprise, my oldest daughter honored the formality of the meal by putting on one of my own necklaces; I loved this! The little ones come to the table with a sparkle in their eyes, eager to see what this commotion is all about. Yes, there is bickering and noise, and no, it's not perfect, but that is to be expected. Half the challenge is adjusting my expectations of them and having compassion and tenderness for myself in all this.

To start the feast, I lean on the sung prayer we all already know. And as I light the candles of the feast with my children gathered around me in the natural light of the room, I recite this prayer as mother, as woman of the home: "In praising God we say that all life is sacred. In kindling these festive lights, we are reminded of life's sanctity. With every holy candle we light, the world is brightened to a higher harmony. We praise you, O Lord our God, King of the Universe, who hallow our lives with commandments and bid us to light these festive holy lights." In this sacred moment, I feel deeply rooted as a woman of God. I am overwhelmed with gratitude for tradition and beauty and my faith. I have reverence for my dignity and role as woman of the home.

A couple of hours later when we go to the Holy Thursday Mass (my favorite liturgy of the entire year), I feel connected, again, as I did when lighting the candles at the beginning of the seder, to Christ's mother, Mary; to Anne, her mother; to her cousin Elizabeth, to Mary Magdalene, who were all Jewish but also knew Christ. And then I think of all the women of the Old Testament and all the women of the New and beyond, and I feel like one star among millions, in a galaxy of life. By our very existence as women, we are vessels of meaning, tradition, beauty, and nourishment.

— Sia

MISERICORDIA

In reflecting on my own pitifulness the other day, I was frustrated to think of the squalor I had to offer God: broken promises, halfhearted prayers, and a controlling greed in trying to manage my own life. People like to point out how Saint Thérèse was so humble and sweet and just wanted to be a tiny, insignificant flower in the garden of our Lord. In a jaded huff, I wondered whether God loves the weeds in his garden too.

What do I have? Nothing.

And then my three-year-old crashed my pity party by tramping in, pants torn, nose running, face and body covered in various shades of filth from robust play in the muddy section of our yard, and tears on his cheeks over some infraction by a rowdy sibling. He looked remarkably like an orphan from a Dickens novel. My heart melted. My thoughts went from my egotistical musings to my child. I scooped him up and held him on my lap, rocking him and smoothing back his hair and letting him wipe the runny nose on my shirt. It was gross. But it was precisely this grossness that tugged at what mercy I have in my selfish heart. Had he been clean as a whistle, carefully groomed and composed in coming to me, my love would not have overflowed in such a powerful way.

"Mercy" in Latin is *misericordia*, which means having a pain in your heart. In so many revelations to saints, especially to Saint Faustina, Christ discusses how his divine heart is actually *attracted to misery*. I was perplexed when I first heard that, but I think we mothers can understand it. When are we most merciful and nurturing? When a child is hurt or sad. All the great spiritual masters warn us not to dwell on our failings lest the evil one start to manipulate our minds. We are to shake ourselves off and try again with new resolve, even if we have to do this dozens of times every day. If God comes running when we are in our most pathetic state, I can't think of anything more consoling. We can be his ugly, broken children, but we are not orphans. Just as my son in his pathetic moment was not just a disheveled, distasteful boy, we are not the sum of our ugliness and sin. Our disorders do not define us. And just as I managed

to look past his grime to see his innocent little heart—wanting nothing more than to restore him to peace and make him feel loved, our Father desires to do the same with us. He is not repulsed by our miserable natures; his greatest desire is to heal us and show us his love. He is not the angry schoolmarm in the sky tsk-ing our every bad move. God is love, and mercy is "love's second name".[15]

— Ellie

THE SACRED HEART OF JESUS

When Saint Gertrude and Saint Margaret Mary (several centuries apart) encountered Jesus in visions, they both did something curious. Ears pressed close to his breast, they listened to the heartbeat of Jesus.

This is the act of a lover. A lover wants to know the beloved entirely, to be one with him. In some sense, a lover wants to exist within the beloved and desires the beloved to exist within him. To listen to the heartbeat of a beloved is to try to reach out and put one's finger on the other's self, to cherish the sound, so to speak, of his existence.

Because of their love, Saint Gertrude and Saint Margaret Mary were spellbound listening to Jesus' heart. But when you observe a human heart, you notice something else in addition to the heartbeat. You notice a wound. This is the case with every human heart, and Jesus' heart is no exception. It is beating; it is alive. But it is also pierced, and it bleeds.

Mysteriously though, because it bleeds, the desire of the lover of Christ can be answered yet more deeply. For the blood that flows from that Sacred Heart is caught

in a chalice at each celebration of the Mass. Encountering the "I" of Christ in his sacramental lifeblood, the lover can now do more than just listen to a heartbeat. He can actually touch that which flows from that heart and can take it into his own self.

And when this happens, our hearts can become a kind of source of Jesus' blood. Joined to his mystical body, the blood that flows from our wounded hearts can spread his precious blood. And when that flow touches other people in some way, they can also become joined to the stream that comes from Christ and can likewise enter the movement of his lifeblood as it gradually covers the world.

And when the whole world is filled with Christ's blood, we will no longer need to strain our ears, listening for his heartbeat. For we will be within him, within his Most Sacred Heart.

— Father Luke Hoyt, O.P.,
Holy Innocents Parish, New York,
priestly contributor to
Soul Gardening Journal

[15] John Paul II, encyclical letter *Dives in misericordia* (November 30, 1980), no. 7.

OXYGEN

Now that both my parents and my in-laws have passed away, even my prayer life has been affected. I can no longer claim to be in the "sandwich generation"—that is, caring for both the older and the younger generation, parents and dependent children. No denying it! I *am* the older generation. In the case of parents, whether we are their primary caretakers, one of several caretakers, or long-distance caretakers, they nevertheless are a very real part of our lives. This means they are a very real part of our prayer lives as well.

All this changes when they are gone from this earth. I still pray for my parents' and in-laws' souls, of course, but those are rather succinct prayers, quickly dispatched. With all my children out of the house, folks feel compelled to ask what I do with all my spare time. Lest we forget, little children have little needs, but big, especially adult, children have big needs. So I still have plenty, if not more, to pray about! But here is the question we should all be asking: Do we remember to pray for ourselves? I'm not referring to our morning offering or asking for help in overcoming bad habits or divine assistance to treat a spouse with more love and patience. What I mean is, Have you ever offered a decade of the Rosary or (scandalous!) maybe even a *whole* Rosary just for yourself?

On an airplane, we learn that in an emergency we should first put on our oxygen masks ourselves before we help others (like our children) put on theirs. This simple, obvious, but certainly not instinctive instruction came to mind the other day while I was on my Rosary walk. It struck me that we as mothers naturally find ourselves praying for our children (constantly, it seems), friends, the pope, bishops, priests, our neighbors, and the world, but where is *our* direct line of oxygen?

I didn't grow up Catholic, and after coming into the Church at age thirty-one, I didn't pray the Rosary for years (ten, to be exact). Why not? Because it never even occurred to me! I was acclimatizing to the Catholic

Church. It was foreign, "other", an unfamiliar land to explore little by little. The sheer act of entering the Church meant that I had exchanged my "Berserkeley" (as a long-term resident of the great city of Berkeley, I use this title fondly) passport for a passport from this new country, the Catholic Church. But I was slow in learning the language and the culture of this new land. And if the Catholic Church was "other", then the Rosary and other devotions I hadn't even *heard* of yet were "uber-other". Since I moved then and still move at glacial speed in my spiritual growth (albeit, in God's perfect time, no doubt), it was many years before I recognized the comfort praying the Rosary offers and the depth of the mysteries. The Rosary is imbued with a richness that can never be exhausted. Then one year, I discovered that there are *fruits* of the mysteries! Here was another layer to ponder: how these mysteries from the life of Jesus and Mary are connected to the fruits.

So, back to my Rosary walk and oxygen revelation. It came to me as I recited the Holy Spirit prayer. You may be wondering what that prayer was doing in my Rosary. Years ago, it became a tradition to pray it every day for fifty days during that wonderfully rich time between Easter and Pentecost. We also tack it on after each Hail Mary while pondering the third Glorious Mystery, The Descent of the Holy Spirit. The prayer (which we all know) is "Come, Holy Spirit, fill the hearts of your faithful and kindle in them the fire of your love."

As I spoke those words ("spoke" because I try to be in a place where I am able to say the Rosary aloud), I heard the plural in "heart*s*" and "kindle in *them*" and thought, *I know I can pray that* all *the faithful have the fire of your love kindled in them, but today I am going to say it differently. I'm going to say, "Kindle in* me *the fire of your love."* And, feeling like a revolutionary, I proceeded to eliminate the *s* from "hearts" and to replace "me" for "them" all ten times. Gladness flooded into me. It was as if I had been oxygen starved and the Holy Spirit was giving me permission to pray for myself and even instructing me, *Give* yourself *a hit of oxygen!*

So now, as well as praying for everyone and everything, I remember to give myself a hit of oxygen once in a while, and I'm convinced it helps me pray better for others. Since I have five children and since there are five mysteries, at some point I naturally found myself assigning a child to each mystery. I don't always start with the oldest and go down the line to the youngest, though, because that would mean my oldest child would always get the Annunciation, the Baptism, the Agony in the Garden, and the Resurrection. I randomly mix them up and, along with meditating on Jesus and Mary, I place that child right into that mystery. I can't count how often the mystery is absolutely *the* perfect one to meditate on for *that* person at *that* specific moment. Even the fruit of the mystery is just the virtue needed for whatever that child is going through.

In case you aren't familiar with them, here are the fruits of the mysteries:

The Joyful Mysteries

The Annunciation—Humility
The Visitation—Love of Neighbor
The Nativity—Poverty of Spirit
The Presentation—Obedience
The Finding of Jesus in the Temple—Joy in Finding Jesus

The Luminous Mysteries

The Baptism of Our Lord—Openness to the Holy Spirit
The Wedding Feast at Cana—To Jesus through Mary
The Proclamation of the Kingdom—Trust in God
The Transfiguration—Desire for Holiness
The Institution of the Eucharist—Love of the Mass and Eucharistic Adoration

The Sorrowful Mysteries

The Agony in the Garden—Sorrow for Sin, Conformity to Will of God
The Scourging at the Pillar—Purity, Mortification of the Senses
The Crowning with Thorns—Courage, Detachment from the World (I always add Humility)
The Carrying of the Cross—Patience
The Crucifixion—Forgiveness for our Enemies, Holiness

The Glorious Mysteries

The Resurrection—Faith
The Ascension—Hope, Desire for Heaven
The Descent of the Holy Spirit—Love of God, Wisdom
The Assumption—A Holy Death, Love of Mary
The Coronation—Perseverance, Eternal Happiness

Happy and fruitful breathing and praying!

— Dru Hoyt, Ohio

RISE UP, O FLAME

Bedtime at our house is a wild time. While other families seem to have a nightly ritual, ours is a big free-for-all of running away from Mama, jumping on the bed, crying, and, I'm sorry to admit, shouting. What we need, we finally decided, is a winding-down time, a time that combines our goal of family prayer, our need for a calmer bedtime, and our desire for more beauty and simplicity in daily life. So, a couple of months ago, with the approaching Dark and Cold (up here in Canada, October is the month to turn on the heat and bring out the winter woolens), we plunged into a new family tradition: the candlelit Rosary. I'm writing this to share with you the goodness that has come into our home since starting this tradition.

Aside from the grace of praying together, we have experienced such blessedness from this quiet twenty minutes before bed. I can't say it's exactly zen. We are

still a noisy family, and we occasionally have jumping Rosaries, dancing Rosaries, story-reading Rosaries, and conking-out-on-the-pillow Rosaries. But bedtime is now a little more peaceful. Above all, we have a little oasis in the day when we can all sit together in candlelight.

In a corner of the children's room, we established a prayer space. It reminds me romantically of the Russian "beautiful wall", where all the religious images in the house are hung like tiny windows into heaven and a lamp burns perpetually. In our home it is just one icon, Our Lady and Child painted by my father, and one candle below. We turn off all the lights, light the candle, and pile onto the bed. My children sleep together on a big cotton futon on the floor, so there is room for everyone, and it is quite cozy. Then a designated child has the special honor of handing out the rosaries.

If we have time, we sing the Rosary. It takes a bit longer, but oh, the beauty! We use mode VIII (for those who like technicalities), the tone used for singing the Magnificat at the end of the day. I love this continuity with the universal Church, knowing that around the world, men and women are returning to the chapel from field and workbench and cloister to sing the very same thing.

We light our candle and start to sing. Then our two sweet contemplatives snuggle under their covers and gaze quietly at the icon, listening to the beautiful tones of mode VIII. They follow along on their beads and drift into sleep.

Just kidding. This is what really happens: the baby, showing no signs of having spent the day peacefully in my sling, wakes up for his evening fuss. Hugh attempts his nightly challenge of fitting his entire body, feet first,

through his rosary. Willie, more the meticulous type, wraps his rosary carefully around each toe to produce a basket-weave effect (very pleasing to the eye). Rosary spinning, of course, is very popular, as is rosary losing, along with wails of "I can't find my roooossarrry!"

Us: "Hush, dear. It's quiet time."

Child A: "I neeeeeeed my rosary!"

(Who knew he was such a pious child?)

Us: "Okay, let's look through the blankets."

Child B: "His rosary is in his pants."

Us: "What?"

Child B: "I put it there."

Us: "Everybody calm down! It's Rosary time! Hey—you. Lie down on the pillow. You! Get your rosary out of your pants!"

No, it's not exactly a monastic experience. We're terribly distracted. Like so many choices we make (eating our vegetables, keeping our home free of bleeping toys), it can feel dull and ordinary in the present moment. But when I see my children daydreaming in the glow of soft light, their eyes shining, it gives me such joy. Candlelight, Mama's and Papa's arms, singing and just sitting together—that's good, good stuff. And my greatest hope is that it's all being knitted into their imaginations and memories—that this tradition, if we cling to it, will take root and bear fruit in the years to come.

In the meantime, the candlelit Rosary has become part of the rhythm of life, as natural as eating and sleeping, the time between bedtime stories and final lullabies. Long after they have left their little beds, our sides, and our home, our children will have the memory of the family as a domestic church. We are praying, singing, holding one another, and, yes, at times fighting in the sweet candlelight that flickers on the face of the Mother of God, who watches over us all. It reminds me of a round we sang when we were kids:

Rise up, O Flame,
By thy light glowing
Show to us beauty,
Vision, and joy.

— Mary

FIAT

From the beginning, we dedicated *Soul Gardening Journal* to Our Lady. It wasn't that we wanted to or that it was a sweet idea (though both are true); it was more that we needed to, and we all felt it.

Motherhood makes us desperate. It brings us to our knees. The care of even one single soul is such a grave responsibility that we can tremble or cower or distract ourselves because it's just too much for a sinful soul to handle. Yet we have a friend in this, nay more than a friend, a mother, and the tenderest one at that.

There is a motherly eye keener than our own that can see all the hidden movements in the hearts of our children: their hidden temptations, struggles, impulses, resentments, and virtues. This eye desires to, and is able to, attend to each and every one. Mary goes beyond our blindness; she goes beyond our failings, our fatigue. Spouse of the Spirit, she works with her Spouse to inspire us in all the decisions of parenting—which faults to address and which to let go, which household tasks to attend to first and which next, which schooling option is best for the kids, and whether or not to pursue a professional career and in what capacity. A life lived in union with Mary is indeed the secret to our vocation. A day lived with her is a day holding her hand. She both leads us and follows us, making up for our shortcomings.

Throughout time, but especially in this day and age, living a humble, hidden life of service to one's family is perhaps the most unglamorous thing a woman could do. Yet for many of us, when we try to listen to that still, small voice in our hearts, it is exactly what our Lord is asking. On a good day, I can cheerfully make muffins and attend to the never-ending laundry symphony with a spring in my step. On other days, my rebellious nature kicks in, and the tedium of the same tasks and the lack of glory involved begin to feel distasteful. Yet Mary is the secret to victory in this battle. If living a quiet, humble life in the home was good enough for the Queen of Heaven, then I should be able to find the courage to change out of my sweatpants and tackle the day with a smile.

Mind you, Mary's patronage is not stale or stodgy. It is wildly colorful, and that's one of the things we have delighted in while composing and compiling these reflections. She has entered into each culture (always to the humble) and into each commonplace task, from sweeping the kitchen (Our Lady of the Broom) to driving a car pool (Our Lady of the Highway). She meets us in the ordinary and makes it beautiful. May we strive to make our domestic churches places of color, joy, and charity under Mary's protective care. Queen of Heaven and our mother, help us follow you so closely that our Lord may see us and say, "Like mother, like daughter". That would be our greatest desire and your greatest gift to us.

THE VISITATION

In those days Mary arose and went with haste into the hill country, to a city of Judah, and she entered the house of Zechariah and greeted Elizabeth. (Lk 1:39–40)

Let us contemplate the Visitation, the second Joyful Mystery of the Rosary: Mary travels through the hill country to see her cousin Elizabeth. Both are expecting babies. Mary bears Christ in her womb, and Elizabeth carries Saint John the Baptist, who leaps in his mother's womb when Mary comes close, for he knows that Christ is in his midst.

How joyful Mary must have been to see her cousin at this time, when they were both with child! I feel a special thrill when I have a friend who is pregnant at the same time as I am. Often it's "Hi, baby!" with smiles. We ask how the other is feeling. We exchange notes on our babies' movements, their growth, and their position. We sometimes talk about what we're craving or what our struggles have been: our sensitivities, our physical difficulties. It excites me to think of Mary at such a young age leaving her own home to visit her elder cousin—looking up to her and wanting to help her in her older age, but sharing in the same joy, that of life within the womb.

Why is this granted me, that the mother of my Lord should come to me? For behold, when the voice of your greeting came to my ears, the child in my womb leaped for joy. (Lk 1:43–44)

We, too, have had foretastes of that joy! Whether our conversations with our fellow mother-friends are full of profound thoughts or simple surface stuff, there is always a connection from woman to woman. We women have a special bond when we're both participating in this miracle of bearing a new life.

Ever since I was a young woman, I have had a passion for motherhood, womanhood, and the Visitation. I don't know whether the mystery of the Visitation brings me so much joy because I have always loved greeting my mama-friends, bringing baskets of bread or pots of soup after a baby is born, and being on the receiving end of such generosity or whether it's the other way around. Perhaps the fact that I have long loved this mystery of the Rosary is *why* I so love the companionship and intimacy with my mother-friends. Perhaps this tremendously joyful mystery became part of the formation of my woman-heart. This mystery features the wonderful Saint Elizabeth, Mary's cousin and the mother of Saint John the Baptist, whom we can think about and pray to. (Catholics have a beautiful long-standing tradition of praying to our patron saints.) Or perhaps it was my name that paved the way for this love; my middle name is Eliza, and around age fifteen I started to pray to Saint Elizabeth of the Visitation because I loved the connection between our names. I savored the mystery of Christ coming into her presence and the joy that stemmed from that meeting. It wasn't until I became a mother that I found out that Saint Elizabeth is one of the patron saints of expectant mothers. And then my connection to her in meditation was even more joyful. She got to meet the mother of our Lord! She watched her son and Christ grow up together as cousins. Imagine that! Saint John the Baptist himself, that infant in Elizabeth's womb, was the greatest of the prophets, the one who would proclaim Jesus at the beginning of his public life. At the words of Our Lady's greeting—under the inspiration of the Holy Spirit—Saint John the Baptist was cleansed from original sin in the womb of his mother.

The Visitation is one of the three mysteries of the *Holy Spirit's work*, a stage along the way of the Holy Spirit's creative passage through human history, the first being the Annunciation, the second the Visitation, and the third, the Nativity. In the Visitation, Mary is moved by the Holy Spirit to travel to her cousin.

Perhaps the most important aspect of the mystery of the Visitation—that of bringing Christ into the world, just as Mary brought Christ to her cousin—Pope Saint John Paul II could say in no better words:

Like Mary, you must not be afraid to allow the Holy Spirit to help you become intimate friends of Christ. Like Mary, you must put aside any fear, in order to *take Christ to the world* in whatever you do—in marriage, as single people in the world, as students, as workers, as professional people. Christ wants to go to many places in the world, and to enter many hearts, *through you*. Just as Mary visited Elizabeth, so you too are called to "visit" the needs of the poor, the hungry, the homeless, those who are alone or ill.... *You are called to stand up for life!*[1]

This passage is food for all mothers and nonmothers alike. No matter what our vocation, we can all bring Christ into the world.

In this mystery, Mary utters the words of the beautiful hymn of gratitude and praise, the Magnificat: "My soul magnifies the Lord, and my spirit rejoices in God my Savior, for he has regarded the low estate of his handmaiden. For behold, henceforth all generations will call me blessed; for he who is mighty has done great things for me, and holy is his name" (Lk 1:46–49). This calls us on to a spirit of joy, fear of God, and the heart-tingling image of Mary as the Christ-bearer.

Mary went to serve while she was pregnant. This is a reminder not to be self-consumed when we are ourselves with child. Although we may need more rest, we can still maintain a spirit of courage, generosity, and sacrifice.

In dwelling on this mystery, we can also contemplate how it affects our relationships with our fellow mother-friends. Christ was the joyful center of Mary and Elizabeth's meeting; so, too, is he the center of our meetings with one another. Sisters, he is the root of our joy. Bringing his love to all we meet, let us rejoice in him who is in our midst! We try to keep him at the center of our hearts, intentions, and actions. Everything we do is for him. We greet one another not for our own glory or pride but for him! We bring a meal to Mother and new baby not just because she's our friend or community member but because she is our fellow *pilgrim-friend* who needs Christ at her side right now. And we can be Christ to her. We women have a special intimate bond because we are partaking in his gift of creation; we are bearing God's children. We are bearing pieces of his love. And his love is triumphantly on view when we greet one another with our maternal smiles of radiance, put together care packages, give advice, assist at births, rejoice in a new life, pour out our women-hearts to one another, and pray for one another in sickness, suffering, and grief. "To Jesus, through Mary!" is a motto in our faith as Catholics. He came to us through a woman, and she always points to him. So let's carry him everywhere we go, being bearers of his light, his joy, his life.

— Sia

SAINT CATHERINE LABOURÉ, THE MIRACULOUS MEDAL, AND ME

She worked at a bar. Men made inappropriate comments and gestures toward her. In 1830s Paris, Catherine wanted to be a nun, but her father disapproved. She was sent off to work in her brother's pub as a distraction. In her spare time, Catherine visited the Sisters of Charity, housed in a side-street convent, to volunteer and to serve the poor. On her first visit, while waiting in the parlor of that convent, she saw him. A large portrait of an old priest hung on the wall; she immediately recognized the face as one she had seen in a dream

---

[1] John Paul II, Eucharistic Celebration for the Young People (New York, October 7, 1995), no. 6.

years before. In her dream, she was assisting him at Mass; he kept holding her gaze, making her feel uncomfortable. She eventually ran from the church and stopped at the home of an infirm person. The old priest was there also, and he said to her, "You flee from me now, but one day you will be glad to come to me." Back in the convent parlor, she calmly asked a sister servant the name of the priest in the portrait. The sister replied, "Why, my child, that is our Holy Founder, Saint Vincent de Paul!"

Catherine eventually joined this order, a strong and thriving community of sisters dedicated to serving the many poor people in Paris. (Picture *Les Misérables* as the setting.) She took their costume-like habit, which to modern eyes features a funny white winged-newspaper hat. The Sisters of Charity had such a visually and effectually strong presence in Europe at that time that even the Muslims had a tenderness toward them, calling them "the swallows of heaven".

Then the visions started: first, of Saint Vincent's heart in varying colors (it is no small matter that a saint loved her, chose her, and gave her his heart); second, a mysterious and seemingly political vision of Christ the King; and finally, the great visions of Our Lady.

At the age of nine, Catherine had lost her earthly mother. When she thought no one was looking, she pulled a chair up to where she could reach the family statue of Mary. She threw her arms around the statue and exclaimed, "Now you will be my mother!"

As a sister in the convent, Catherine told her patron Saint Vincent of her strong desire to see the Blessed Virgin with her own eyes. One night, she was awakened by a small child, who led her to the chapel. "It was lit up like Midnight Mass", Catherine recalled, and the child stopped in front of a folding chair used for conferences. Instinctively, Catherine knelt. She waited until she heard the sound of swishing silk as a lady approached and sat in the chair. The child instructed, "This is the Blessed Virgin."

Of all those privileged to see Our Lady, from Juan Diego to Bernadette, Catherine is the only one known to have touched her. She knelt beside her chair, put her hands and head in her lap, and poured her heart out with the tears of a little girl. Our Lady listened and offered words of wisdom and strength for all that Catherine would have to undergo and warnings of the future of the world, France in particular.

Our Lady said, "Come to the foot of the altar. There, graces will be shed upon all, great and little, who ask for them. Graces will be especially shed upon those who ask for them."

The next time Catherine saw Our Lady, it was during her daytime prayers. Mary stood in the sanctuary, shining like the morning rising, and Catherine stayed on her knees, noting every detail in bliss. Mary's robe was silk and white like the dawn. She wore a long white veil with a lovely lace head wrap beneath it. She held in her hands a golden ball, which she offered to God; suddenly, her hands were resplendent with rings set with precious stones that shone brilliantly, and the lights coming from them fell upon a white globe at her feet.

She said, "The ball which you see represents the whole world … and each person in particular." As she spoke, the rays became blinding. "These rays symbolize the graces I shed upon those who ask for them. The gems from which rays do not fall are the graces for which souls forget to ask."

Around her, Catherine saw the words "O Mary, conceived without sin, pray for us who have recourse to thee." Mary instructed her to have a medal formed, showing her what the reverse was to look like, with twelve stars bordering the hearts of Jesus and Mary, and an *M* with a bar and a cross. She said, "All who wear it will receive great graces; they should wear it around the neck. Graces will abound for persons who wear it with confidence."

Do you wear a Miraculous Medal? You should.

Even while Catherine maintained anonymity for most of her life, the medal gained tremendous popularity throughout Europe and around the world. Originally called "the Medal of the Immaculate Conception", it soon came to be known as "the Miraculous Medal" due to the astounding number of miracles reported from its devotees.

The story of Catherine Labouré is such a great one, and it reveals to us a few very important things. First, it shows that our relationships with the saints are real. I've heard it said that saints have a habit of choosing us. In recent years, I have felt that a certain saint was revealing to me his desire to be my patron, and after reading the story of Saint Catherine Labouré, I've come to believe it's not all in my head. Whether it's finding a holy card in a random place, having a dream, or seeing his name on a street sign, these heavenly patrons are longing to tell us they want our friendship and communion. Like our earthly friends, certain people just click with each other.

Second, Saint Catherine's story teaches us that we need to *ask* for grace. Catherine was known to say to her sisters, "Ask, ask, ask! In all things you must ask!" Mary has extraordinary graces ready to distribute to us, for every necessity, but if we don't ask for them, many will remain in those gems on her fingers from which the rays do not fall. Just as you want your children to come to you, she wants us to come to her.

Third, and I say this half-jokingly, because I know it may be superficial of me to care, but this apparition is just another example of how Mary has great style. As women, we love pretty clothes, jewelry, makeup, and hairstyles. And despite her profound humility, Mary is a woman who isn't afraid to overwhelm us with her beauty in each apparition. I just love that in this one she is wearing rings of dazzling gems (three on each finger!). She is always modest but always stunning, and this time even slightly funky. Mary has a rockin' style.

Many saints have promoted the Miraculous Medal, but there is one story I've read that my children always ask me to retell. Saint John Vianney, the beloved French country priest and famous confessor, was hearing a young woman's confession. At some point during the confession, Saint John Vianney, who had the gift of reading souls, said to her, "You were at a dance last night. There was a handsome man present with lots of young women around him; you wanted to dance with him so badly, but he never asked you to dance, and you were disappointed."

Surprised, she answered, "Yes!"

"That man was the devil. And he couldn't come anywhere close to you because you were wearing the Miraculous Medal."

Does this story mean that by wearing the Miraculous Medal we will be automatically immune to the devil, temptations, and sin? No. But it does mean that it will offer us far more protection from these things than we will ever be aware of.[2]

* * *

My own mother always wore a Miraculous Medal. When I was six, she dropped me off at summer camp and lovingly placed her medal around my neck for me to wear during my two weeks away from home. At some point during my adventures, I left it on a rock by the lake, and when I went back to look for it, it was gone. Nevertheless, it was my first taste of Our Lady's protection, which at the time felt like an extension of my own mother's love.

I grew up in rural Vermont before cable TV and the Internet. Dirt roads, honey houses, lakeside fires, hanging out on railroad tracks, and lots of long, quiet days, most of which I shared with my absolute best friend, Triona Wilder Marno-Ferree, also known as Tree. She had flaming red hair, a temper to match, more freckles than we could count (we tried!), and a passionate love for two things: horses and me. I remember my parents coming to pick me up from her house after a sleepover. As we pulled away, I watched Tree standing on her front porch with a face as flaming red as her hair, screaming in protest at my departure. She was ferociously loyal, and I can't remember *not* being her friend.

Tree's family was interesting, artistic, earthy, and not Catholic. Not even Christian. Her dad laughed at "ignorant" Catholic superstitions but let her come to Mass with us if she was around on a Sunday, and he let her wear my Miraculous Medal, which she never took off. In sixth grade, her parents divorced. Her mom moved to Colorado and Tree went with her, while her dad and sister stayed behind.

In Colorado, she found a third passion, snowboarding. One day she had a terrible snowboarding

---

[2] For further reading on Saint Catherine Labouré, I recommend *Saint Catherine Labouré of the Miraculous Medal* by Joseph I. Dirvin, C.M.

accident, and in the chaos of the emergency room, the Miraculous Medal went missing. Somehow, either by the generosity of her parents or by her own rummaging through family belongings, she found a replacement. Handmade by her Catholic great-aunt, it was large, artisan, silver, and stunning. It was the prettiest medal, religious or not, that I had ever seen, and she wore it with pride all through high school and into college. In every picture, it was around her neck, as lovely as she was.

Years passed and our paths diverged more and more. Our visits were less frequent, but she was one of those people with whom time never seemed to go by, despite the different journeys we were on. In college, I met Justin, my future husband, and I couldn't wait to bring him home to meet my family. He was flying into the inconvenient airport of Boston, and no one in my family could lend me a car to pick him up. I called my old friend Tree, who was back in our home state, and without hesitating, she jumped in her gas-guzzling pickup and came to the rescue, driving a total of twelve hours with me to meet him at the airport. She was so good. And she would still do anything for me.

Justin and I married young, and Tree was a bridesmaid in the wedding. I wonder now how uncomfortable she may have felt in the mix of all my bubbly college friends who were high on Jesus; perhaps she felt like an outsider, but more likely she was just happy for me, because she was good like that.

When we opened the gifts after the wedding, hers was in a small box. I cried when I saw her great-aunt's shining Miraculous Medal on a silver chain, accompanied by the children's book *Best Friends* by Steven Kellogg.

I immediately called her, crying in disbelief that she would give me what I knew was her greatest treasure. She laughed and said, "You know, it's funny. My mom found the medal you gave me when we were kids in the pocket of an old corduroy coat, and that one means even more to me. This way, I'll always wear the one you gave me, and you can always wear the one I gave you."

Two weeks later, she was in a horrible car accident. She was hit by a semitruck and died on the spot. My parents came over to my house, and my father calmly delivered the news, while my mother, red faced with streaming tears, couldn't look at me. Tree's body was cremated, and the funeral service was in a Unitarian church. Through that whole grueling time, I had in my heart the secret that perhaps only I knew: she was wearing a Miraculous Medal when she died.

I can't remember when the first dream happened. But I saw her. I saw her canoeing, away from me and through a swampy forest. And that was all. In the second dream, she came to me. I hugged her so tightly, and I stammered, "Tree! How are you? *Where* are you?" She let me hug her, and she answered, "I haven't seen *him* yet, but *she* doesn't leave my side. She doesn't say anything. She just looks at me and smiles." I awoke to a pillow wet with tears. I understood that she was in purgatory and that Mary was taking care of her.

You can imagine that her Miraculous Medal became my most treasured possession. It was my turn to wear it always, in every photograph, every day and every night. Six babies played with it while they nursed, and I never took it off. I intended to give it to my eldest daughter, Triona Mary Wilder (Tree) when she got married, if I could hold on to it that long. (Triona is short for Caitriona, the Irish form of Catherine, and she was born on July 27, which I recently discovered was Catherine Labouré's canonization day.)

My last dream of Tree came when I was visiting my parents. That day I had driven by Triona's old house. It was much smaller than I remembered, the paint was chipping badly, and the gardens were unkempt. In the backyard, I saw the old tree fort her dad had made, but instead of sturdy wood and a shiny slide, I saw a dilapidated, rotting, hazardous resemblance of our childhood hideaway. It was hard to believe it had been over twenty years since we had whiled away the days in its privacy. In my dream that night, I saw her as a child, swinging, swinging, head back, laughing, and swinging on that rotted, dilapidated structure. She didn't know, or seem to care, that it should have been condemned long ago and that a child would not attempt playing on it. Another pillow wet with tears.

I lost the medal last summer. I was at a winery with some friends and realized that it, along with some other pendants, had fallen on the ground when the chain broke from around my neck. We scoured the property and found all the missing pendants except the Miraculous Medal. It was Justin's birthday, and he was the one who had the hardest time giving up, but eventually we got in the van and pulled away, my heart strangely at peace with the loss of my precious treasure. After all, fourteen years is a long time for someone as scatterbrained as I am to keep anything.

I always tell my children to pay attention to dates, that God loves to use dates to show us heavenly connections. I always thought Tree died on an unremarkable day in the Church calendar, and I was slightly disappointed. This year I realized (I don't know why it took me so long!) that the date of her death, August 14, is the eve of the feast of the Assumption and the feast of Saint Maximilian Kolbe, who had an intense devotion to the Immaculate Conception and the Miraculous Medal. Pretty dang perfect.

I dare to hope that the loss of the medal and the dream of Tree swinging, although strange and slightly dark, mean she has made it to heaven. In that last dream, I tasted her, tasted the immortal world and the sense of childhood joy that is regained in the next life. Regardless of where she is right now, I feel confident that she is in the care of Our Lady. Looking back, I think of Tree as one of the few people I've known who really knew how to love selflessly. How lucky for me

that I got to be the object of that love; her devotion and fidelity to me were nothing short of a witness of Jesus Christ.

How did I deal with the loss of Tree's medal? I bought a nice vintage replacement on eBay and had it blessed; I felt zero attachment to it, of course. My daughter woke up in the night with a bad dream, and in the spirit of my own mother, I placed it around her neck. My second replacement was a large golden medal I found secondhand. A friend was having a difficult pregnancy, and I passed it on to her. My best friend from college told me she didn't own one, so my third replacement was sent airmail to Indiana. Now I have fun with it. I buy the best quality and best-looking Miraculous Medal I can find (because everything Catholic should be beautiful) and wear it until someone comments on it. That person, I've decided, is meant to be the owner, and I have jokingly and generously titled myself "Hope Schneir: Ambassador of the Miraculous Medal." Hopefully Saint Catherine Labouré approves; good thing for me she is probably desperate enough to let me have the job.

So, if I ever get the chance to meet you, dear reader, and you are not wearing a Miraculous Medal, I hope you will be so bold as to compliment the one I am wearing. And it will be my privilege to place it around your neck.

— Hope

MYSTICAL ROSE, A PRAYER

Mystical Rose, pray for us!

Catholics have a beautiful hymn to the Mother of God called the "Litany of Loreto" in which Mary is hailed by her many titles, such as Mother of the Redeemer, House of Gold, and Morning Star. This prayer has been in use since the sixteenth century and has been translated into most languages from the original Latin.

Some titles are self-explanatory, like Mother Inviolate (although as a child I always wondered why she would be in violet, when pictures show her wearing blue!). Some titles are more mysterious, like Gate of Heaven and Tower of Ivory. These come from lesser-known biblical symbols, and each has an interesting history.

One of her titles is Rosa Mystica, the Mystical Rose. Why rose? Why mystical? The idea is that Mary remained hidden from the world during her earthly life, like a rose in bud, while inside she was a little "paradise" for God to come and live in, a garden of breathtaking beauty, scent, and color.

Mary is mystical because she can never fade, being nourished by the eternal waters that are Christ himself. Water works almost invisibly. It comes from underground, unseen, sucked up silently by thirsty roots, yet the result is miraculous: the glories of greenery and the rich, breathing, luxuriance of leaves.

"A garden locked is my sister, my bride, a garden locked, a fountain sealed" (Song 4:12). The exquisite love poetry of Solomon is interpreted by some of the Church Fathers as depicting God's relationship with Mary. It is also seen as portraying the spiritual union between God and each soul, or the mystical life, of which Mary is the model. Like a walled garden, the mystical life is something you can see only if you open the gate and enter. And the further in you go, the richer, more beautiful, and more teeming with life it is. Like petals unfurling, Mary's beauty is most fully revealed as we approach the center.

What does this mean for us? From the outside, Mary's life was humble, quiet, insignificant. She was one among millions of peasant women. She lived quietly as a temple virgin, married a tradesman, lived as a refugee in a foreign country, and returned to her home village to live a life of service to her family. She is the opposite of human expectations: little, insignificant,

and invisible, yet inside her was such spiritual richness and purity that the Lord made his home in her, taking her flesh for his own. The Word became flesh and dwelt among us.

— Anonymous

* * *

There is no rose of such virtue
As is the rose that bear Jesu.
Alleluia.

For in this rose contained was
Heaven and earth in little space:
Res Miranda.

By that rose we may well see
There be one God in Persons Three:
Pares forma.

The angels sang, the shepherds too:
Gloria in Excelsis Deo:
Gaudeamus.

Leave we all this worldly mirth
And follow we this joyful birth:
Transeamus.[3]

—Unknown medieval author

OUR LADY, THREE-HANDED VIRGIN

In our home, the Three-Handed Virgin hangs between altar and kitchen, ever ready to lend a hand as we live out the mysteries of each day. I like to invite her into my least favorite tasks like washing dishes or diapers; behind her are jottings of our most demanding intentions. In the Orthodox church, the icon is commemorated on June 28, just after midsummer has shifted

us to a darkening of days. She is a mother for the dark times, a mother for long nights and cold mornings, for persecution, for uncertainty. One whose arms never tire of holding her loved ones closer to Christ.

She is a patron of desperate situations, of extreme need—healing what is severed completely and binding up wounds. She came to be when Saint John of Damascus

[3] *Res Miranda*: thing to be marveled at; *Pares forma*: equal in nature; *Gaudeamus*: let us rejoice; *Transeamus*: let us go hence.

lost his right hand for defending icons in the great controversy of long ago. He offered the Virgin his severed hand and prayed to her for its restoration. She appeared to him and did as he asked. His hand was reattached to his body, as capable as ever; in thanksgiving, the saint made a silver hand and hung it on the icon. Now the icons are written with the third hand included, a reminder that the Holy Mother can restore to us what seems lost forever: love, hope, peace, wholeness. She is abundantly able. *Miraculous, restoring Mother, whispering wholeness and understanding to your children: heal our wounds, renew our hearts, and allow us to lay our burdens into your all-encompassing hand. Take what is broken in your daughters and make it new.*

It's March. The sky is gray this evening, and behind the clouds the sun is setting fast. Despite the equinox, the wind paints frost pictures across the window and the stoves burn hot all day. I have dinner boiling away on one of them, a sneezy toddler up in arms about something, and a dog trying intently to sneak one of the rolls behind my back. Inside my head, it feels as though the sounds are all pressing on my brain, behind my eyes. Distracted, I drop a roll and the dog pounces.

My evening feels shredded now; my poor, sick boy is crying for the lost roll while his sister tells the dog just how bad she is for stealing. The wind is howling, the stoves need tending, and all I want is quiet and solitude for hours and hours. But in the lamplight, I can see the Three-Handed Mother, glowing like a moon in green, gold, and red from her perch on the north wall. She whispers wholeness and healing and aid, and with her hands she shows the way.

The icon of the Three-Handed Virgin is always holding Christ, always directing us toward him, and yet always able to reach out another hand, a hand that is doing nothing, holding nothing, simply waiting to serve. It is as though she's saying to each of us, *Here is my Son; contemplate him, love him, and focus on him for a while. I will hold your burdens and distractions, guard your bread, and comfort your child while you spend a moment or two with him.*

— Emily Goepel, Maine

BLESSED MOTHER

The dictionary defines the word "blessed" as "worthy of veneration" and "made holy, consecrated". As a noun, "blessed" is defined as "one who lives in heaven with God". For Catholics, the reality of Mary as a worthy, highly favored, and venerable mother in heaven is easy to accept, almost as much as we accept that the grass is green. For non-Catholics, or maybe for those Catholics who struggle with our relationship with Mary, Our Lady under the title Blessed Mother may be a perfect starting place to get to know her. In a mother is where we all start.

I remember a beautiful story told by a girl who was at one time a missionary from the United States to Belize, in Central America. This girl had recently converted to Catholicism. She deeply loved and devoutly revered her new religion. But there was still one aspect of the Catholic faith that she kept wrestling with: the Church's veneration of Mary. Oh, she understood Mary's profound fiat, the bearing of God-made-man. She understood that Catholics don't worship Mary and that Mary's role in salvation history was integral. But what she didn't understand was the personal-relationship part. She felt that God had already given her a mother in Massachusetts. That was it, one mom. And this girl had a fierce devotion to her mom. No one, no matter how holy, courageous, grace filled, humble, beautiful, or strong, was ever going to slip into her heart to replace or compete with the love she already had for her dearly beloved earthly mother.

But then one night, she and a group of fellow missionaries were traveling back to the mission from a weekend at the Cayes, the resort islands of Belize. An oncoming car swerved and slammed head-on into the van. Everyone was shaken and in some way hurt, but one girl in particular suffered serious head trauma. She was hanging in the balance between life and death.

The very next car on the scene was that of the mom and dad of the mission, the couple who had sacrificed their lives of comfort in the States to move their family of nine to Belize. The mission mom immediately got out of her truck and, being a nurse by profession, went directly to minister to and comfort the girl with head trauma. On that night, she was wearing an all-white dress. The recent convert said that at one point she looked over to the front of the truck. There, in the midst of light pouring down from the beams of the headlights, she saw the mission mom, whose white dress was covered in red blood, caressing the wounded girl. As the convert saw that image and witnessed that love, her heart was flooded in an instant with the realization of who Mary, her Blessed Mother—mother to us all—truly is. And she began to weep.

Dear Blessed Mother, pray for us!

— Ursula Crowell, Oregon

OUR LADY OF THE BROOM

Our Lady of the Broom was one of Catherine de Hueck Doherty's favorite devotions, and she is the reason I learned of it. From the get-go, pages of *Soul Gardening Journal* have been filled with Catherine's spirituality, for I love and yearn to share this amazing woman's heart, spirituality, and story with others. A native of Russia, she was raised Orthodox and married quite young. She loved God passionately and lived life with complete conviction in the gospel. A young nurse on the front lines of WWI and then caught up in the Russian Revolution, she was imprisoned with her husband in their summer home in Finland and left to starve to death. She told God that if he saved her, she would give her entire life to him. Beautiful, rich, and a baroness, she had lost everything. Yet God did save her, and she never turned back.

It is fitting that mothers meditate on Mary in her role of Our Lady of the Broom. Does not a broom epitomize the virtue of patience? When we see a mountain of laundry, we must take to it one step at a time with love for Christ. So, too, with the dishes, the floors, and all the little everyday tasks we do over and over again. Mary can model for us (and pray for us to have) such patience.

With her husband, Catherine made her way to England, where she was received into the Catholic Church. Later she emigrated to North America, a penniless refugee, but in time she regained a wealthy lifestyle. Remembering her promise to God, she gave up everything and united herself to the poor. She set to work and gave each day to God. In New York City, she spent a few months with her good friend, the hardworking Dorothy Day of the Catholic Worker. Catherine then moved to Harlem, where she helped establish Friendship House. She eventually moved to Canada, where she founded the community of Madonna House in rural Ontario. She died in 1985, and many believe she was a saint.

Madonna House still operates as a lay community of people living a life of work, poverty, and prayer. Growing their own food and living off donations, they sacrifice a great deal, but their life is very rich. Most important, their days are formed by love, putting into practice Catherine Doherty's philosophy that little things must be done well, for love of God.

At Madonna House, there is a beautiful bronze statue of Our Lady, her loving mantle flaring about her like fire as she runs to embrace us, her children. I prayed beneath this statue at the impressionable age of fifteen with my friend Mary. I prayed and adopted for my own the Litany of Our Lady of Combermere. After commissioning the construction of the statue, Catherine composed this litany containing the very simple titles of Mary that encompass the sacredness of an incarnational life and the importance of living it with intention.

Let us learn to let love transform our days so that by giving Jesus the mundane job of sweeping and doing it with utmost love and care, we can store up our treasure in heaven.

Our Lady of the Broom, pray for us!

— Sia

LITANY OF OUR LADY OF COMBERMERE

God the Father of heaven, *have mercy on us.*
God the Son, Redeemer of the world,
God the Holy Spirit,
Holy Trinity, one God,

Our Lady of Combermere, *pray for us.*
Our Lady of the Trinity,
Our lady of Tenderness,
Our Lady of Blessings,
Our Lady of the Towel and the Water,
Our Lady of the Wilderness,
Our Lady of Nazareth,
Our Lady of Unity in Christ,
Our Lady, calm for troubled waters,
Our Lady of the thousand joys,
Our Lady of the heights and the depths,
Our Lady of the Visitation,

Questing Madonna of all God's children,
Questing Madonna of thirsty hearts,
Questing Madonna of hungry souls,
Questing Madonna of all who search,

Mother and consoler of the sick,
Mother and consoler of the disabled,
Mother and consoler of those distracted in mind,
Mother and consoler of the poor,
Mother and consoler of the lonely,
Mother and consoler of the hopeless and abused,
Mother and consoler of the lost sheep,
Mother of Christ's Body, the Church,

Refuge of the afflicted,
Homemaker of Nazareth,
Teacher of everyday wisdom,

Guide to the great silence of God,
Icon of the total fiat,
Iconographer of Christ's love among us,

Golden door to the secret chambers of the King,
Gate to the Father, Son, and Holy Spirit,
All-loving Mother of her Son's priests,
Companion of all mothers and wives,
Consolation of widows and orphans,
Icon of womanhood to husbands and fathers,

Protection of Christians,
Protection of all God's children,
Protection of the tempted,
Protection of all who work,
Protection of all God's handiwork,

Star of hope,
Womb for the unwanted and rejected,
Home of the homeless,
Patroness of artists and scholars,
Wisdom of scientists,
Guardian of truth and morality,
Wayfarer with all pilgrims,
Companions to all cross-bearers,
Visitor to all prisoners,

Queen of the humiliated and rejected,
Queen of fools for Christ,
Queen of the servants of God,
Queen of the Madonna House Apostolate,
Queen of the history of salvation,
Queen of heaven and earth,

Lamb of God, who takes away the sins of the world,
have mercy on us.
Lamb of God, who takes away the sins of the world,
have mercy on us.
Lamb of God, who takes away the sins of the world,
grant us peace.

Let us pray:

> Father of our Lord Jesus Christ, we thank you and praise you for giving us Our Lady of Combermere to be our Mother, Guide, and Director. May we entrust our wills to her so that your divine will may be accomplished in us, namely, that each of us may become another Christ, and that all of us together may become a living icon of love, reflecting the love you share with your Son and the Holy Spirit. We ask this confidently through Jesus Christ our Lord. Amen.[4]

MARY'S TRUST

I used to be better at trusting in God, or at least it feels that way. Maybe it was the fact that my life was a blank slate and anything was possible. Or that as a classic youngest child with few opportunities to voice my opinion, I was pretty good at being along for the ride. But somewhere along the way I started losing these skills and became less comfortable with not being in the driver's seat. As an adult, and especially as a mother, so many things are in our control: what to make for dinner; which Mass to attend; how to educate our children; what color to paint the kitchen; and whether or not to spank, circumcise, sign up for cable, register as a Republican, or make the kids wear shoes. It's ridiculous the amount of decisions we make in just one day; if we're not careful, we might wake up one morning and look in the mirror to find a middle-aged control freak.

I've been thinking about Mary's trust. It seems that for many of us grown-ups, something happens in adult life when we are faced with a real trial, sometimes even

[4]Used with permission from Madonna House Publications.

a crossroads. It's as if the devil waits, offering us the illusion that everything is fine and in control, and then ambushes with a challenge we did not expect. The trials vary from person to person, but for all, the temptation is the same: doubt. And for all, the remedy is likewise the same: trust.

Trust is the antidote of our times. It is Jesus' concrete message to our world through Saint Faustina, a humble Polish nun who died in the 1930s and whose message became the crown jewel of Pope Saint John Paul II's pontificate. John Paul II labored for years to bring Faustina's diary and devotion to Divine Mercy out of a twenty-year ban (due to mistranslations) and into the heart of the living Church. The message of Divine Mercy permeated the teachings of John Paul II and acted as both the apex and the bookends of his papacy. He began his pontificate with the words "Be not afraid!" He instituted Divine Mercy Sunday and canonized Saint Faustina, proclaiming on that day, "This is the happiest day of my life."[5] He died on the vigil of the fifth anniversary of the feast, right after receiving Holy Communion. The Divine Mercy image is now seen and revered throughout the world—few Catholics have not seen the familiar image of Jesus, clad in white, with rays of red and white pouring from his heart, framed with the caption "Jesus, I trust in you!"

Do you ever find yourself struggling to give your life to God? I mean really give it. Do you fear what his plan might mean for you? I do sometimes. When I look at how some of the saints suffered, I'm tempted to hide in the corner and be a mediocre Catholic. You know, stay in the state of grace but ignore the further promptings of the Holy Spirit—maybe the devil won't see me as too much of a threat and he'll leave me alone! But we fool ourselves if we think this would be the case. Fear does not protect us from harm; it just makes us miss out on all that God has in store.

Let's look at Mary's life for inspiration. First, God asked her a question, of sorts, and gave her the freedom to refuse. Mary's acceptance made her the heroine of mankind. God literally saved the world through the Yes of one country girl who surrendered her life to God and

trusted that his plan was greater than her own. Surely she had friends who she knew would scorn her for being pregnant out of wedlock, especially since she couldn't just sit down and explain everything over a few tears and a cup of tea. Yet whatever she may have had planned for her life, she knew God's plan was greater. She probably had no clue just how much greater.

I keep thinking about the sacrifices she made compared to the rewards God lavished on her because of her obedience and trust. She was transformed in the following ways:

- from being unpopular to being the most popular person in the world
- from being a mother of one to being the mother of all
- from being a perpetual virgin and experiencing a lack of physical union to having the most amorous and intimate human-God relationship that exists
- from being a humble small-town girl to being the Queen of Heaven and Earth

Wow. There is nothing more God could have done to exalt the woman! After her fiat (or Yes), her trusting wasn't over, and I imagine the devil didn't leave her alone either—especially now that she carried around the key to heaven. Her trust continued through all this:

- being away from home with a full-term pregnancy and not knowing where she was going to deliver her baby or who would help her
- being on the run during a holocaust of infants, when hers was the one being pursued

---

[5] "The Great Mercy Pope", The Divine Mercy, https://www.thedivinemercy.org/message/john-paul-ii.

- losing the preadolescent Jesus for three whole days (you know how slowly time goes when you can't find your child)
- watching her Son be defamed by high priests and religious leaders
- watching her Son suffer and die, and waiting for his Resurrection
- mothering the frightened apostles and the infant Church and waiting for the Holy Spirit to come as promised

Mary had said, "Behold, I am the handmaid of the Lord; let it be to me according to your word" (Lk 1:38). I imagine she didn't say that only once, but over and over again, through every trial, constantly surrendering her will and putting her trust in God alone. Imagine our loss if she had not said those words!

Our loss is also significant if we do not echo those words ourselves. The point of all this is that our Lord is good and is worthy of our trust. Not only that, but he also has a burning desire for our trust, and it is the one thing that consoles his heart more than anything else. So much of our duty as mothers entails decision-making and being in control, but so much of our vocation as mothers entails letting it be done. The very nature of a woman's role in the sexual act, as receiver, echoes *Let it be done unto me*. Conception is not something we can control or force or something we should artificially prevent, so we say without words, *Let it be done unto me*. Labor pains come upon a pregnant woman whether she is ready for them or not: *Let it be done unto me*.

I once heard it said, "The only thing you can count on in life is that you will be surprised." Like us, Mary was not exempt from the blindfold of the present moment. She treasured within her heart the surprises God had in store for her and surrendered her will with trust through her many trials. Let us rouse the feminine receptivity, which was Mary's gift and is ours as well, to receive God's mercy and in return to give him our trust so that when we wake up one day and find that seasoned woman in the mirror, the lines in her face might be not from years of worrying but from too many days in the sunshine.

— Hope

MORNING STAR

O Mary, Morning Star, guide us and comfort us as we go about our days. Through our work, rest, and play may we be vessels of peace and love, as you were. May we be reflective of Christ's light. Lead us closer to your Son, Jesus, through all things. Mary, bright Star shining, guide us through the dark, guide us through the stormy seas.

The image of Mary as the morning star brings to mind morning dewfall, sunrise, and first birdsong, emphasizing so much hope. It is similar to her title Star of the Sea, which brings with it the reflection on her being the light in the darkness, the guide for one in stormy waters. But Morning Star emphasizes the *morning*: a *new* day, a *new* start, a *new* opportunity to begin again.

Morning Star is of course a beautiful, ancient title found in the Litany of Mary. Venerable Father Casimir Wyszyński, one of the founders of the Marians,[6] wrote, "[Mary] is the noble Star rising from the House of Jacob whose rays illuminate the whole world.... Let us, then, watch attentively the ascent and motions of this brightest star. Let us follow her. Let us rise up from the sleep of death by sin."[7] A ten-pointed star symbolizes

---

[6] The Congregation of Marians of the Immaculate Conception.

[7] Andrew R. Mączyński, M.I.C., *Father Casimir Wyszyński: His Life and Mission*, trans. Marina Batiuk (Stockbridge, Mass.: Marian Heritage, 2020), 68–69.

for them Mary's ten gospel virtues, each ray representing one virtue.

In imitating Mary, we are encouraged to put into practice her ten virtues:

1. Her *purity*: all physical aspects of her being were ordered toward God; she was "full of grace" (Lk 1:28).

2. Her *prudence*: in the Annunciation, Mary carefully considered the situation and her options, leading to her *fiat*, her Yes to God.

3. Her *humility*: reflecting God in all things, she became the handmaid of the Lord.

4. Her *faith*: in all things, Mary was able to surrender herself to God's will.

5. Her *devotion*: Mary was a devout woman, drawing nearer to God in every way possible. "Mary kept all these things, pondering them in her heart" (Lk 2:19).

6. Her *obedience*: as she said to the servants at the wedding of Cana, "Do whatever he tells you" (Jn 2:5), she, too, does just that.

7. Her *poverty*: she gave birth in a stable; she was detached from all material things, simple of heart.

8. Her *patience*: trusting in God through all that life brought her, she endured all things patiently and trustingly.

9. Her *charity*, or *mercy*: we see this demonstrated in the journey Mary, with child, took through the hill country to visit her cousin Elizabeth to help her for three months.

10. Her *sorrow*: this virtue lies in the offering up of her sorrow, in union with her Son's Crucifixion. Sorrow pierced her heart like a sword, but she gave it to God. "As Pope John Paul II taught in his apostolic letter on the meaning of human suffering, *Salvifici Dolores*: Our unavoidable sufferings and sorrows can find meaning in Christ, and can be put to good use. We are not only to do good to the suffering, he wrote, we are also to be good by our sufferings."[8]

Mary, model of virtues, pray for us, that we might be better disciples!

— Sia

Bright morning stars are rising,
Day is breaking in my soul.
——American Folk Song

Brightest and best of the sons of the morning,
Dawn on our darkness, and lend us thine aid;
Star of the East, the horizon adorning,
Guide where our infant Redeemer is laid.
——Traditional Shape-note Carol

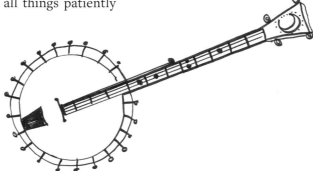

[8] Robert Stackpole, S.T.D., "Mary, the Morning Star Who Lights Our Way", The Divine Mercy, January 30, 2016, www.thedivinemercy.org/articles/mary-morning-star-who-lights-our-way#:~:text=As%20Pope%20John%20Paul%20II,be%20good%20by%20our%20sufferings.

> Everyone is in love with an ideal love, a love that is so far beyond sex that sex is forgotten.... That ideal love ..., to which we instinctively turn when flesh-love fails, is the same ideal that God had in His Heart from all eternity—the Lady whom He calls "Mother." She is the one whom every man loves when he loves a woman—whether he knows it or not. She is what every woman wants to be, when she looks at herself. She is the woman whom every man marries in ideal when he takes a spouse; she is hidden as an ideal in the discontent of every woman with the carnal aggressiveness of man; she is the secret desire every woman has to be honored and fostered; she is the way every woman wants to command respect and love because of the beauty of her goodness of body and soul. And this blueprint love, whom God loved before the world was made; this Dream Woman before women were, is the one of whom every heart can say in its depth of depths: "She is the Woman I love!"
>
> —Venerable Fulton Sheen
> *The World's First Love*

OUR LADY, UNDOER OF KNOTS

Susan died last May. She was a young seventy-two, vibrant, with a big personality and lots of style. Insatiably curious, Susan explored life from corporate New York to Mother Teresa's convent. She was smart, witty, and too full of life to die. But die she did. She called uncharacteristically late one weekday evening and told me that she'd just spoken to her doctor. Her acute indigestion was actually pancreatic cancer that had metastasized to her liver. With sacraments poured out, with her family and friends around her, Susan died an enviable death a mere six weeks later.

Susan loved to chat and gave sage advice, so it should come as no surprise that she would visit me one night in November, in dreams, to chat. She was wearing the very clothes in which she'd been buried, looking radiant and happy to see me. We held hands, I asked her how she was doing, and she told me she was working hard. Working? How can that be? She explained that where she is, one begins a process of undoing knots, all the knots that have burdened us in life. She explained that we have to go back to the very beginning of our lives and undo every difficulty, forgive every trespass; we have to make the path smooth before we can see the face of God.

To illustrate her point, she explained that there was a man with her, in purgatory, who had been her high school teacher and that he had been particularly unkind to her. She'd forgotten about him entirely until she encountered him again, and there it was: bitterness, anger—a knot. I begged her to forgive the man so that she would go to Christ, and while we embraced, she whispered, "You untie every knot too so that we can be in eternity together."

The next morning, the vivid dream lingered, as did the strange image of undoing knots. A few days later, I told the story to my confessor, and he asked me if I knew that Pope Francis' favorite Marian devotion was to Mary, the Undoer of Knots. I had never heard of such a thing.

And so it is, I believe, that I was visited by my friend, who's met Mary, the Undoer of Knots. From eternity, she continues to teach me. Such is the love of a true friend.

We have to untie every knot, every single one, so let's get busy.

— Cathy Schneir, California

OUR LADY OF PROMPT SUCCOR

Need help and need it quickly? This title of Our Lady is for you.

Have you ever wondered why New Orleans has such Catholic roots in a very Protestant Deep South? Well, the city happens to have a very special and powerful patroness. Several missionaries accompanied the French explorers and pioneers who settled there in the late seventeenth century, and the Catholic stronghold was only made stronger when French Ursuline nuns established a monastery in the city in 1727. When the restrictions of the French Revolution made sisters scarce, the bishop of Montpelier was unable to spare a single nun to help Mother Saint Michel, who was running a new and struggling boarding school for girls in 1803. He told her that only the pope could grant her request for more sisters, and as Pope Pius VII was a prisoner of Napoleon at the time, communication and help seemed impossible. Mother Saint Michel didn't give up. She gave it to Our Lady. She wrote a letter to the Holy Father anyway and sealed it with a prayer: "O most holy Virgin Mary, if you obtain a prompt and favorable answer to my letter, I promise to have you honored in New Orleans under the title of Our Lady of Prompt Succor."[9]

Just a month later, she received a positive response granting her request and several postulants were added to their numbers. After commissioning a statue—the crowned Virgin holding the crowned Infant Jesus—Mother Saint Michel had it placed in the monastery chapel, and the people of New Orleans hold it in special veneration to this day.

Several miracles have been attributed to Our Lady when her intercession was sought under the title of Prompt Succor. During a great fire in New Orleans in 1812, the convent seemed certain to burn, as it was in the direct path of the fire. One nun placed a small statue of Our Lady of Prompt Succor in the window and prayed feverishly, "Our Lady of Prompt Succor, we are lost if you do not come to our aid!" Suddenly the wind

shifted, and the monastery was saved. She interceded again during the famous Battle of New Orleans when General Andrew Jackson was far outnumbered by British troops. Several of the Ursuline sisters, along with soldiers' wives and daughters, gathered in vigil before the statue on the eve of the great battle. And the next day, January 8, at the very moment of Communion, a courier rushed into the chapel to inform all present that the British had been miraculously defeated.

In our own lives, and in the life of our nation, we sometimes need immediate and decisive help. Let us turn to Our Lady of Prompt Succor:

> Oh Virgin so gracious,
> Oh Virgin, who saved France,
> Oh Virgin, who beckons New Orleans,
> Oh Virgin, who can save our own nation,
> Oh Virgin of quick response,
> Oh Virgin, who instills charity,
> be with us.
> Our Lady of Prompt Succor, be ever and quickly
>   attendant to our needs!

— Ellie

---

[9] "Our History", The National Shrine of Our Lady of Prompt Succor, accessed July 6, 2024, www.shrineolps.com/history.

STELLA MARIS

Come to Mary, Star of the Sea. Pointing to Christ, she is a beacon of light in a dark world. This title of Mary is as ancient as the hills, going back to the ninth century. Mary is a shining light "lest we capsize amidst the storm-tossed waves of the sea".[10] The old Gregorian chant hymn "Ave Maris Stella" ("Hail, Star of the Sea") is such a gorgeous, mystical melody. Pray with the lyrics and the music; they are beautiful!

> Hail, bright star of ocean,
> God's own Mother blest,
> Ever sinless Virgin,
> Gate of heavenly rest.
> Taking that sweet Ave
> Which from Gabriel came,
> Peace confirm within us,
> Changing Eva's name.
> Break the captives' fetters,
> Light on blindness pour,
> All our ills expelling,
> Every bliss implore.
> Show thyself a Mother;
> May the Word Divine,
> Born for us thy Infant,
> Hear our prayers through thine.
> Virgin all excelling,
> Mildest of the mild,
> Freed from guilt, preserve us,
> Pure and undefiled.
> Keep our life all spotless,
> Make our way secure,
> Till we find in Jesus,
> Joy forevermore.
> Through the highest heaven
> To the Almighty Three,
> Father, Son and Spirit,
> One same glory be.
> Amen.
> 　　—attributed to Saint Bernard of Clairvaux

I have long loved this image of Mary being the guiding star to those at sea, to those who seek a livelihood in the coastal waters. Many fishing villages, naval ports, and coastal communities have sought her patronage in naming their churches. But Star of the Sea has a figurative meaning as well. Like a lighthouse, she shines as a beacon of light on the rough waters of hard times. She tenderly calls all voyagers to Christ. She is our guide, calling all pilgrims, all pagans, all Christians, all Gentiles home. In the words of Saint Bernard of Clairvaux, "If the winds of temptation arise; If you are driven upon the rocks of tribulation, look to the star, call on Mary; If you are tossed upon the waves of pride, of ambition, of envy, of rivalry, look to the star, call on Mary. Should anger, or avarice, or fleshly desire violently assail the frail vessel of your soul, look at the star, call upon Mary."[11]

— Sia

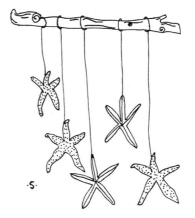

·S·

---

[10] Father Johann Roten, S.M., "Star of the Sea", *All about Mary*, Marian Library, University of Dayton, accessed July 6, 2024, https://udayton.edu/imri/mary/s/star-of-the-sea.php.

[11] Bernard of Clairvaux, *Homilies on the Gospel "Missus Est"*.

MARY'S HOMESCHOOL

Perhaps you are like me and the older you get, the more you realize how little you've learned and how much you still need to learn. It's humbling and often so discouraging. Yet despite our faults, that's the trap we must never fall into—discouragement. I've always had a strong devotion to Mary, but in the past few years that devotion has been challenged. While I'm accustomed to viewing Jesus as my Beloved, my boyfriend of sorts, lately I've been tempted to view Mary as my mother-in-law instead of my mother. I can become frustrated at my Lover's aloof ways, his mystery that I can't seem to penetrate, the veil that separates us. And when I offend him, I imagine her disapproval. While I know that Jesus' divine heart is capable of forgiving without tiring, I'm not always so sure about his mother. Surely *she* must be sick of it. With all the graces and privileges I've been given, how could I hurt her beloved Son, over and over?

I spoke to a priest about this and, thankfully, he assured me that this is not the correct way to view Mary. And I know he's right. So this year I'm taking a different approach to my relationship with these two, Jesus and Mary, and inserting myself, small as I am, into the Holy Family itself.

When he taught us the Our Father, Jesus made it clear that he is our big brother. This sibling relationship that he grants us is what makes us heirs to the throne; it's what gives us a right to call God "Abba" and turn to him with our smallest of needs. I once heard it said that every Catholic heresy comes from a lack of belief that God's love is that big—big enough to bring us inside the magic circle he's in, the Trinity, his family. A love this great is audacious and can seem scandalous to some, but I think half the time our problem with not reaching sanctity is not believing it's possible. He gave us his mother, and he gave us his Father. We are meant to be *that* intimate with the Divinity. I've never had a brother, though I've always wanted one, and for now, instead of being his pining and needy lover (which hasn't been going so well on my part) I'm going to be his dweeby kid sister who is excited just to follow him around. If he's aloof

with me, or withdrawn, I'll accept that, because that's what older brothers do sometimes—though when it comes down to it, a good brother will do anything for his baby sister, and this one would even sacrifice his life. And Mary? She will see me as her smallest child, not as an in-law or an outlaw, but as bone of her bone and flesh of her flesh. All the time she is taking care of the baby Jesus, I'll be floating in the womb of Mary, safe. When she is tending to Jesus as a child, I'll be in her sling, going where she goes. As he grows and she instructs him in the home, I'll be in her arms, peering over her shoulder and watching. I will homeschool at her table and attend to the lessons (however small) she has prepared for me that day. She'll put Band-Aids on my scrapes and make me lunch and teach me how to wipe down the counters and say my prayers, and she'll make me laugh. And there will likely be days when I will be obstinate, and Mary will have to speak very ... slowly ... and repeat herself often, in order to get things through my thick head. But she will, and she won't mind because she's my mom. She will help me get to know Jesus and become more like him, which of course I'll want to do because that's how little sisters are with their big brothers. When Jesus is big and strong, working outside with Saint Joseph, or when he leaves the holy home of Nazareth to go out and accomplish his mission, I will stay behind with Mary, the deadbeat kid who never leaves the house. But that's okay, I think. I'm pretty sure I will never graduate from her homeschool, now that I've enrolled.

Each year, during the month of January, I choose a particular title of Mary to which I dedicate my year. You should try it. Our Lady of Nazareth is my choice this year, and she is teaching me all these things and helping me rediscover the genius of the hidden and domestic life, which I was starting to lose. *Our Lady of Nazareth, pray for us! And teach us, your daughters, everything we need to know as homemakers and daughters of God. Love us with your perfect maternal heart, and stay close, so close, to us.*

— Hope

TABLE

When we were growing up, we deeply valued family mealtimes; they provided a foundation for conversation, connectivity, and consistency in our days. The meals we now share with our own children can be hectic, even unruly at times, but still we gather, and we invite them into the art of it all: the seasoning and tasting, the simmering and boiling, the searing and sautéing, the reading of cookbooks over a good cup of tea, the work of scrubbing, chopping, and peeling. In the kitchen, soul gardening is at play in the formation and feeding of the whole person: beauty for the eyes, nourishment for the body, and refreshment for the spirit, bringing a true communion and joy that is a foretaste of the heavenly banquet.

The digital world contains a sea of recipes for every possible culinary interest, but sometimes it's hard to know where to start. Most mothers love to try trendy new recipes, but those that follow are a sampling of staples: the dog-eared, the requested, and the shared: parent to child, friend to friend, mother to mother. Some of these recipes read more like conversations; they might feel like your mother's voice encouraging your exploration and confidence in the kitchen. We've included measurements where necessary but have placed a greater emphasis on the art of cooking rather than the science of it. We have steered away from exact measurements and toward flexible, forgiving recipes for the busy woman who would rather not have to count the garlic cloves and measure out the quarter cups of olive oil but instead throw ingredients into a pot with confidence. The working mother, the homeschooling mother, the tired mother, the solo parent—we all must make time to nourish ourselves and those in our care despite the challenges of life, yet we must do so in a practical way that fits with daily living. This brief, unique collection contains, for the most part, only recipes that are nourishing, delightful, and uncomplicated, with a few labor-intensive exceptions for the sake of tradition and joy.

The working home is a splendid place of blessed busyness. Although the kitchen can invoke feelings of warmth, it can also be a site of tedium and tiredness. We invite you to put your heart into the repetitive motions and live fully the adventure of domestic life. Let us seek and find joy in the labors of hearth and home, passing on traditions for generations to come and making the world a more beautiful place, beginning with our tables.

APPLE CAKE
FOR AUTUMN AFTERNOONS

A late-night Internet search led me to this recipe, and alas, I don't remember the source. I'd like to track down the originator of this apple cake and cover her with gold and costly perfumes, because it's genius. Quick and simple to make, and so very appley-delicious. Everyone should have this recipe.

Sia would like to add that this makes a lovely afternoon snack for teatime, pairing well with a strong cup of black tea with whole milk and your favorite puzzle or book. For a healthier alternative, swap out the vegetable oil for coconut, avocado, or olive oil.

2 eggs
1 cup white sugar
⅔ cup vegetable oil
6 Tbsp. apple juice
2 tsp. vanilla
1½ cups flour
2 tsp. baking powder
A large pinch of salt
2 tsp. cinnamon
Brown sugar, maybe ½ cup
8 small apples, sliced

In a bowl, cream together the eggs, sugar, oil, apple juice, and vanilla. Sift and add the flour, baking powder, and salt. Beat until the mixture forms a smooth batter. In a separate medium-sized bowl, combine the cinnamon and brown sugar. Reserve a few tablespoons of this mixture for topping; toss the rest with the apples until fully coated. Place apples in a greased 9 × 9-inch cake pan and cover with batter. Sprinkle the top with the reserved brown sugar and cinnamon. Bake at 350° F until cake is firm and pulls away from the sides, 35–40 minutes.

— Mary

APPLE CHICKEN BREAKFAST SAUSAGE

My father makes these a few times a year and stores them in the freezer. Even though I generally have no time to make my own sausage, fifteen years of craving these brought me one day to the act of dropping everything to turn my kitchen into a sausage factory. The results were everything I had hoped for, and it wasn't as hard as I thought. Everything tastes better homemade, and sausage is no exception. I hope there is something like this in heaven.

Note: The chicken must be cut, then frozen, so allow for that in your preparations.

About 7 lbs. chicken thighs (boneless with skin and fat)
3–4 cups dried apples
1 cup boiled cider reduction (look for this online or in specialty stores)
2 Tbsp. salt
1½ Tbsp. black pepper
4 Tbsp. ground sage or poultry seasoning

> At the table with good friends and family you do not become old.
>
> — Italian proverb

TABLE   241

Cut thigh meat into strips or chunks and freeze on a cookie sheet. Then chop in a food processor. Chop dried apples into coarse chunks in food processor. Mix all ingredients well. Test (pan fry) a small amount and adjust seasoning. Form into patties and freeze. Cook slowly, fresh or from frozen, in lightly greased pan on low heat.

— Hope

THE ART OF SALAD

To make a beautiful salad is to be an artist and to wear the crown of domesticity. One secret I've learned is to sprinkle a bit of salt and some freshly ground pepper directly into the salad bowl as a finishing touch; the salad always disappears faster. Generally, a good homemade dressing uses equal parts oil and acid (vinegar, citrus, or both). The best lunches, in my opinion, consist of a crunchy salad with some leftover meat from a previous night's dinner.

Here are my favorites; add any of these combinations to a bowl full of salad greens.

Greek
Feta cheese, diced red onion, cucumber, cherry tomatoes, chopped basil, kalamata olives
Dressing: Olive oil, red wine vinegar, fresh garlic, chopped rosemary

California
Sliced avocado, peeled and sliced oranges or grapefruit, sliced almonds, red onion
Dressing: Olive oil, orange juice, apple cider vinegar, fresh garlic

Sia's Lemon-Parsley
Coarsely chopped Italian parsley (without stems), sliced celery, coarsely shredded Parmesan
Dressing: Olive oil, lemon, salt, pepper

Please note: Parsely salad is not for nursing mothers! Too much parsley can inhibit milk production.

Fall Favorite
Leftover roasted vegetables (squash, sweet potato, etc.), pomegranate seeds, pears, pecans
Dressing: Balsamic (See Sia's recipe!)

Beet and Goat Cheese
Beets (boiled, peeled, cooled, and sliced), goat cheese, candied walnuts (toasted walnuts with honey or maple syrup), arugula (optional)
Dressing: Balsamic

Hispaniola
Cooked meat of choice (leftover taco meat, chicken, etc.), diced tomatoes, green onions, black beans, avocado, cilantro, crushed tortilla chips
No dressing, just salsa and sour cream on top

Quick-and-Easy
Grapes, pine nuts, feta cheese
Dressing: Balsamic

North Country
Diced apples, dried cranberries or raisins, lightly toasted walnuts (cook in pan with butter on low for 10 minutes, stirring occasionally), grated sharp white cheddar
Dressing: Lemon juice, garlic, olive oil

— Hope

BALSAMIC VINAIGRETTE, CALIFORNIA STYLE

Ode to Garlic!

Salad dressings are in abundance on the shelves of conventional health food grocery stores. But they are often full of unnecessary fillers and unhealthy oils and are far too sweet. I've also never tasted a store-bought vinaigrette this vinegar-y and garlic-y, with the perfect thickness.

Having spent my childhood in Northern California, I find the taste of garlic is as natural to me as the taste of salt. I led a busy life as a child, plugged into public schools, tennis, swimming, music lessons, and art classes. The evenings were consistently a time of order, tasty food, and music as my parents unwound from their busy days with Dave Brubeck or Patsy Cline on the record player. There were sliced carrots, tamari almonds, and Kalamata olives on the dining room table as we all bathed and got ready for dinner. The kitchen was the most central part of our family life—even the reading nooks, bookshelves, and piano were "in" the kitchen (which was actually one long room).

My mother loved garlic. I remember even apple slices having the scent and taste of garlic because every cutting board was naturally seasoned with it!

While I could probably create an entire cookbook of all the homemade recipes that came from my childhood kitchen, for now I'm sharing with you this very simple salad dressing. My mother used to whip it up in a flash and heavily dress our leafy green salads of romaine and red leaf lettuces (sometimes from our city backyard garden), and in time, my sisters and I learned to make it too. I consider it fundamental for any salad, whether it's brown rice salad, beet salad, leafy green salad, quinoa salad, leftover zucchini salad—you name it! It's even great on pasta, if you like extra zest in addition to sauce. This takes about five minutes to make, so it's every busy mother's best friend.

4–6 cloves garlic, minced or crushed
2 Tbsp. honey mustard or Dijon mustard
2 Tbsp. honey
Half an orange, squeezed, or about
    3 Tbsp. or so of orange juice
A pinch or two of sea salt
Freshly ground pepper to taste
Balsamic vinegar
Extra virgin olive oil

Place first six ingredients in a quart-sized Mason jar. Then pour balsamic vinegar into this jar about three inches high. Whisk vigorously and add extra virgin olive oil the rest of the way up (leaving an inch or so at the top.) Place the lid on top and shake well. Store in the pantry for up to three months or in the fridge, like … forever.

— Sia

BEST COOKIE-CUTTER COOKIES

These melt-in-your-mouth cookies are made from just five ingredients. They are delicious as is but are extra tasty and delightful to look at when topped with a powdered-sugar glaze. Every year for over twenty-five years this recipe has been pulled out in different seasons as our children cut out cookies—Christmas trees and stars, Valentine hearts, and butterflies for a shower or baptism, all created by little hands.

TABLE   243

⅔ cup sugar
1 cup butter (room temperature)
2 eggs
½ tsp. vanilla
2½ cups flour

Cream sugar and butter. Add eggs and vanilla. Beat until creamy. Add flour and mix. When well mixed, form dough into 2 disks, wrap each in plastic, and chill in the refrigerator for 30 minutes.

After chilling, roll out dough on a lightly floured board to ¼-inch thickness and cut out with cookie cutters. (My only caution is to keep the shapes modest in size since this cookie is a bit delicate when the shape is large. We tried using a giant gingerbread-boy cutter and the cookies fell apart.) Place on ungreased baking sheets (or parchment paper if you have some, but it's not necessary—they are very buttery). Bake at 375° F for 8–9 minutes. They should be a very light golden brown. Let cool for a couple of minutes and transfer to cooling racks.

After cooling, you can enjoy the cookies as they are or add a simple glaze. Our favorite is made with powdered sugar. For one batch of cookies, we combine one cup powdered sugar with a splash of almond extract and a small amount of milk (a tablespoon or so), adding slowly while mixing to a good spreading consistency. A tiny amount of food coloring in the glaze makes a yellow star, a charming lavender butterfly, a pink heart, or a green shamrock.

Makes 3 dozen cookies or so, depending on the size of the shapes.

Enjoy both the taste and the beauty of these cookies!

— Laura Langley, California

BONE BROTH'S HEALING POWER

No matter our budget or life situation, bone broth is an affordable and doable pot of gold that all of us can make on the stovetop in a huge stockpot, in a regular old pasta pot (my go-to), or in a Crock-Pot. I usually don't buy boneless chicken breasts or other favorite American cuts of meat; instead, I buy meat with the bones so that I can save them for broth. My own extended family cracks up when I'm around at potlucks and reunions because I make it known that there is a bowl on the counter for everyone's bones, from their chicken wings and drumsticks to their ribs. "Collect the bones for Sia! She'll turn them into broth." Yes, I'm a bit of a spectacle, always taking home those bones.

Broth is one of my all-time favorite foods because it helps heal the gut flora within a few weeks, boosts the immune system, and feeds the soul. The other advantage to consuming the precious glycerin in bones is that it's a built-in collagen booster! (Healthier milk for nursing babies? Heck, yeah! A more youthful face and fewer stress wrinkles? Yes, please! The potential to reverse cavities? Anything to restore the calcium, right?)

He will regard all utensils and goods of the monastery as sacred vessels of the altar.

— *The Rule of Saint Benedict*

In making bone broth from scratch, one becomes connected to the past, to our heritage as human beings. It is the practice of utilizing the animal down to its last bit. In Native American and hunter-gatherer traditions, it is revering the animal to its core. We give thanks for the chicken (or cow, or fish, etc.), eat the meat, then utilize the nutrients from the bones. Granted, if I were homesteading, I could also be using animal skins, feathers, and so forth, but I think that in our urbanized, consumer, fast-paced Western culture, the best we can do is use the parts we can buy. Though homesteading or farming may be an ideal, many of us are simply getting through each week of work, school, grocery shopping, driving the children to extracurriculars, and gathering for family meals.

Here is my own delicious, everyday recipe for homemade chicken broth, which I credit fully to my mother, who gave me the tips I needed to achieve the full flavor that my original home concoction had been missing. I have since learned, from a bone broth maker in Portland, Oregon, that the apple cider vinegar helps to pull the beneficial nutrients from the bones.

1–2 cooked chicken carcasses, or the bones from your family's dinner, equaling about 10 chicken thighs or drumsticks

10 peppercorns
5 whole cloves
A dash of raw apple cider vinegar (or about 2 tsp.)
2 tsp. or more of sea salt
1 tsp. dried thyme
2–4 bay leaves

Place bones in a Crock-Pot or pasta pot, fill with water, add the rest of the ingredients, and heat on low. Let it simmer; try not to bring it to a boil. Simmer gently this way for 24–48 hours. If you have a larger quantity of bones, use a stockpot or freeze bags of bones for future use. Halfway through the simmering process, use tongs to pull the bones out of the broth. Cool for 15 minutes on a plate or cookie sheet. When bones are cool enough to handle, break each bone in a couple of places so that the marrow is thoroughly released during the simmering process. Return the bones to the pot and continue to simmer. When broth is finished, strain and use for soup or freeze for later. Or drink it as is, adding whatever additional seasoning or salt that is needed. I usually use it on the second night for soup, or I cool it and put it into a couple of Tupperware containers for freezing.

— Sia

OF BRIOCHE AND THE BLESSED "LEANING IN"

Gluten-Free Brioche Cinnamon Rolls

It is currently midwinter. My heart and intentions have gone into hibernation mode, and every fiber of my being longs for my softest blanket, my giant mug of loose-leaf oolong, one more gluten-free brioche cinnamon roll on my blue tin plate, and my children squashed in about me, hanging on to my every word as I read aloud from our latest selection, *Anne of Green Gables*.

The reality, however, is that we are all coming down off of a beautiful and blessed festal season. We are a bit people-weary. We are trying to find our rhythms again with one another and the everyday tasks and our home education.

It isn't easy, no matter our rose-colored intentions, to step out in love. To say "I'm having a rough day and everything is hard. Let's put on the brakes and bake." (Because the last thing I want to do when I'm feeling angsty and poured out is to lean in and physically say "I love you" by welcoming my children into my culinary domain.) But baking is a way I can love

TABLE   245

people well—especially *my* people. And God in his rich mercy gave me a gift I could cultivate in order to bless others: to be a physical representation of his love and the love of his Blessed Mother.

Our time is so very precious. There isn't a lot of it. In the wearying moments that feel like eternity has been balled up into twenty-four hours, and when our instinct is to pull away and protect ourselves, if we make the choice instead to lean in, to embrace, to lay down our time and our instinct to pull away, we gain connection. We gain the opportunity to bring order and balance and depth to relationships with our families and those we open our hearts and homes to.

So, what happens when we decide to lean in to our spouse's love and friendship, to lean in to the balance and connection our children are craving, to bring our tribe of mama hearts closer together? It isn't just our own souls that gain a holy flame through these dark and quiet months. We spread that luminous love to the hearts of our people—like a light on a hill, like a spark that says "You are welcomed here. You are safe here. You are loved here." We carry a fire that nourishes and refines and tells our roots to grow deeper so that when the warmth and light come again, we can grow and bear fruit in the tender garden of our hearts.

So, without further ado, I give you these gluten-free brioche cinnamon rolls. The kind of soft, springy, rich cinnamon rolls that beg to be accompanied by a good cup of French press or your darkest tea. They take time, a lot of love, and a bit of patience. I like to start this dough in the afternoon so that the rolls can rise overnight in the fridge and be popped into the oven in the morning. You'll want to make sure your butter and eggs are at room temperature before diving in. It is what makes this dough rich and springy. Blessed baking!

Brioche dough:
  1 Tbsp. dry yeast
  5 Tbsp. unbleached sugar
  ¼ cup warm water
  ⅔ cup brown rice flour
  1 cup tapioca starch or flour
  4 tsp. xanthan gum

  ¾ tsp. kosher salt
  4 eggs (room temperature)
  9 Tbsp. butter (room temperature)

Filling:
  1 cup brown sugar
  1 Tbsp. cinnamon
  2 Tbsp. butter (room temperature)

Frosting:
  8 oz. cream cheese, softened
  1 stick of butter, softened, *not* melted
  Dash of vanilla
  3–4 cups powdered sugar
  Milk, enough to get the right consistency

In a small bowl, combine yeast, 1 Tbsp. of the sugar, and warm water. Whisk and let it sit until foamy and bubbly. In a large bowl, combine the remaining sugar, flours, xanthan gum, and salt. Add yeast mixture and eggs, one at a time. Add butter, 1 Tbsp. at a time, mixing well in between. Cover the bowl with plastic wrap or beeswax wrap and let dough rise for 1–2 hours, till nearly double in size. Scrape down, then chill dough for 30 minutes or so (it will make dough easier to handle).

To make the filling, combine brown sugar and cinnamon. The butter will be spread on the dough separately.

Cut a large piece of parchment paper and sprinkle generously with tapioca flour. Scrape chilled dough onto the parchment, sprinkling with more flour (and on rolling pin as needed). Gently roll out into a large rectangle (about the size of the parchment paper). Spread the soft butter onto the dough using your fingers. Sprinkle the cinnamon/sugar mix as evenly as possible and then gently pat it down with your palm. Starting with the long end closest to you, slowly roll the dough away from you into itself, lifting the parchment to give you the momentum. When rolled up, gently press the seam into the roll. Using a serrated knife, quickly cut into desired "pucks" (about 1 to 1½ inches thick) and arrange in a greased pan a couple of inches apart. Cover with beeswax wrap or plastic wrap and place in the fridge overnight.

The next morning, preheat oven to 350° F, remove rolls from fridge, uncover, and let rest for about 30 minutes. Bake for 30 minutes or until lightly browned and done in the middle.

While the rolls are baking, use mixer to combine cream cheese and butter, and whip well. Add in vanilla, half of the powdered sugar, and 2 Tbsp. of milk. Whip until consistency is spreadable but thick. Add in the rest of the powdered sugar and a dash of milk until consistency is right. You can either spread frosting over the entire pan of cinnamon rolls or dollop them individually when plated.

Makes one 8 × 8-inch pan of rolls. I usually like to double this recipe so we have extra!

— Ita McIlvain, Washington

BUSY-MAMA PROTEIN CASSEROLE

A note from Sia: *A friend of mine made this for us after the birth of our first baby girl. Sarah served it to me hot and fresh out of the oven, with a huge spinach salad on the side. I devoured it gratefully and felt instantly nourished. This is relatively quick, super easy, and packed with protein for those nursing or pregnant busy mamas out there who too often find themselves famished, even between meals. You may want to cook the beef and rice in the morning so they are ready to go. (Brown rice takes about 45 minutes to cook.) The measurements below are a good starting point, but you can improvise if you want to make it easy on yourself. Whatever you have in your pantry will work just fine: a can of refried beans here, a jar of salsa there, a handful of spinach—you get the idea. I've given it a practical name, but the original recipe is from Sarah Doll, who takes such good care of everyone in her community.*

This Mexican-style brown rice casserole is very flexible. Substitute whatever ingredients you like or add more spices. I add more of everything to make a *huge* casserole and split it with a family in need. It also freezes well, so I make a big batch and save some for later.

4 cups cooked brown rice
16 oz. fresh salsa
1 lb. ground beef, cooked
1 tsp. ground cumin
15 oz. refried or whole beans
10 oz. frozen corn, thawed
4 oz. mild green chile peppers, diced (optional)
1 Tbsp. chile powder
10 oz. chopped frozen spinach or collard greens, thawed and drained (optional)
2 cups shredded cheese

Preheat oven to 375° F. Coat a 2-quart dish with coconut oil or butter. In a bowl, combine rice, salsa, ground beef, and cumin. Spoon half of the mixture into a 9 × 13-inch baking dish and spread evenly. In another bowl, combine beans, corn, chile peppers, and chile powder. Spread bean mixture on top of rice layer and smooth out. Squeeze any water from the spinach and then spread on top of bean layer. Sprinkle with 1 cup of the cheese. Top with remaining rice mixture and sprinkle with the rest of the cheese. Bake until heated through and cheese is bubbling, about 30 minutes.

— Sarah Doll, Oregon

TABLE   247

CAFFEINE-FREE CHAI

Spiced chai is one of my family's favorite cool-weather drinks, and we can easily drink one or two gallons a day between all of us. We love to share this with anyone who comes over to our house, and we try to keep a pot ready on the stove. We make it six to eight quarts at a time, so it lasts for a while—well, at least for a day!

Here's the basic recipe. Feel free to innovate by trying different spices and different proportions. We have encountered lots of chai recipes, but this is the one that works best for our tastes. We buy all our organic spices whole (not ground) and in bulk. The main two companies we use are Starwest Botanicals and Frontier, which are both available online.

About 6 quarts water (optionally add 4–8 cups almond milk too)
4 oz. fresh ginger, cut into slices

6–8 cinnamon sticks
⅓ cup whole cardamom pods
⅓ cup whole anise seeds
⅓ cup whole fennel seeds
1 Tbsp. black peppercorns
1 Tbsp. whole cloves
1 Tbsp. whole coriander seed

Boil the entire mixture and then reduce to a simmer for an hour or longer. Strain with a sieve to make sure whole spices don't end up in someone's cup. You can leave the whole mixture on the stove overnight and just reheat it the next day. Serve with a ladle. You can either sweeten the whole pot with honey or simply sweeten individual cups as you serve them. A little cream or almond milk added to the cup makes it just perfect.

— Deirdre Becher, Maine

CARNITAS

Carnitas make a delicious and satisfying dinner—true comfort food! Carnitas are chunks of roasted pork that are used to make tacos or burritos, or even breakfast tacos. They can also be a stand-alone meat dish served with sides and warm flour tortillas. This recipe is for tacos for lunch or dinner, and I personally prefer to serve them on corn tortillas. During the process of cooking carnitas, the pork fat is rendered, making lard. Lard is high in vitamin D, nourishes the nervous system, and aids in keeping depression and Seasonal Affective Disorder (SAD) at bay. Lard is even mentioned in the *Roman Ritual, Volume III: The Blessings* (the pre-Vatican II book of blessings said by priests), where there is a "Blessing of Lard" (and bacon!). This recipe serves a large family.

2 lbs. pork shoulder
Tortillas

Toppings:
  1 onion, minced
  ½ cup cilantro, chopped
  Hot sauce
  4 limes, quartered
  Salsa
  Salt

You will need a large pot with a lid, such as a Dutch oven. Place the pork shoulder fat side down in the pot

> I was thirty-nine when I started cooking; up until then, I just ate.
>
> —Julia Child

(you'll notice that one side of it is white—that is the fat side). Cover and heat on lowest setting.

Cook for two hours or so, checking it every half hour. If it appears to be drying out on the bottom, put a half cup of water in it. The meat is finished cooking when the pork is tender enough to be pulled apart easily with a fork and the meat is somewhat detached from the bone.

Remove the cooked meat from the pot and put into a baking dish or a dish with a rim to catch any juices. (If you're making this meal ahead of time, this is the stage to let it cool and store, then fry when ready to eat).

To make carnitas, turn up the heat under the pot to frying temperature (somewhere around medium to high—adjust temperature as needed). Break off pieces of meat by hand and fry in the lard. Turn the meat with tongs to fry all sides, a few minutes each. Remove pieces from pot to a serving dish. Once all the meat is fried, shred it with a fork.

To make tacos, put a small amount of the meat in a corn tortilla and top with any of the suggested toppings. The limes, for squeezing, are served on the side.

Save the bone from the cooked pork shoulder and use it to make broth. And be sure to store the lard (the fat at the bottom of your pan) in a jar in the fridge for cooking.

Corn tortilla note: We love to make simple and delicious homemade corn tortillas with masa (corn flour) and water. Or fry store-bought corn tortillas in a touch of olive oil.

— Kerensa McKnight, Texas

CHICKEN LIVER PÂTÉ

I never thought of pâté as being a thing I'd ever make, for me or for my kids, until I went to a talk by Sally Fallon, acclaimed health expert and author of *Nourishing Traditions*. It was a fascinating presentation with an eclectic group of farm-to-table foodies, and at the end they served a feast based on local fare and the superfoods our ancestors ate. On the menu was a pâté similar to this, and what happened to me when I first ate it has happened again every time I've had it since: I can feel my body thanking me. It's like some deep nutrition—the real food-based iron, vitamins D and K, and Lord knows what else—is penetrating my bones. I can feel them satisfying deep deficiencies I didn't know I had until I took my first bite.

Iron-rich organ meats were once prized by native cultures and were reserved for the young and child-bearing. Sadly, organ meat consumption has fallen out of practice, and as Fallon points out, our overall health and vitality is not equivalent to that of our great-grandparents. It would benefit us all, but especially if you have growing children and are in your childbearing years, to think about ways to add liver to our diets. In my house, I aim to whip up a batch of this once a season. My teenagers actually love it.

The best way to eat pâté is on already buttered sourdough toast, with a final sprinkle of salt on top. I've built a nourishing but simple poor-man's dinner around this recipe and served bowls of pâté and hummus (for the fussy ones) with fresh carrots and cucumbers, sliced baguettes, and some fresh fruit or fig jam. Pâté also makes a great after-school snack. If you are hesitant, I strongly recommend trying it at least once. See if you can feel in your body what I'm talking about.

8 Tbsp. unsalted butter

2 chopped shallots

1 lb. chicken livers (can be purchased
   from Whole Foods)

1 Tbsp. fresh thyme

⅓ cup port

3 Tbsp. heavy cream

Kosher salt

TABLE   249

Sauté butter and shallots in a medium-sized pot until shallots are translucent. Add chicken livers and continue to sauté until browned on the outside. Add thyme and port; cook 5 minutes more. The insides of the livers should still be pink. Blend in food processor with cream and salt to taste. Refrigerate in a quart-sized Mason jar for up to 7 days. You can also store in small individual jars with buttered seals. Just melt some butter, pour a thin layer on top of the paté in each jar, seal, and refrigerate; it will last longer and prolong your experience of fresh pâté.

— Hope

CHRIST OF THE WEARY AND THE SOUP BOWL

Where do we go when we need comfort? When all we can manage to pray is *Lord, have mercy* on repeat as we slide our prayer ropes and rosaries through our fingers? What can a mother do when her own heart is wearied and worried and her children need that peace that passes understanding? As Saint Brigid teaches concerning the sacrificial hospitality of the home, it is in the hearth and on the table that we find the sustenance of Christ and the comfort of his mother as we serve our families. Tangible comfort for my family is our favorite soup, soft blankets strewn about our sofa and chairs, beeswax tapers, and our leafed twinkly lights. We most often play Scottish music as we dance our way around our family spaces—decorating and filling the home with the things that bring us delight.

In the simple act of drawing the comforts of home around us, God refreshes our hearts and fills us with peace and hope in his mercy. God is in the making, the weary heart—and the soup bowl!

Saint Brigid's Soup (Feast Day: February 1)

2 medium onions, diced
1 stick of unsalted butter
1 leek, thinly sliced
2 heads broccoli, chopped
4 quarts broth
6–8 potatoes, peeled and cubed
2 bay leaves
1 cup water mixed with 2 Tbsp. tapioca starch or flour
8 oz. extra-sharp cheddar cheese

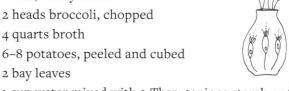

Salt and pepper to taste
Suggested toppings: crumbled bacon, sour cream, chives

In a 6-quart Dutch oven, brown onions in butter over medium heat. Add leek and broccoli and sauté for 5 minutes. Add broth and bring to a rolling boil until broccoli and leek are tender. Add potatoes and bay leaves and cook, stirring occasionally, until potatoes are done (15–25 minutes). Reduce heat to medium low, remove bay leaves, and add tapioca starch and water mixture to soup, stirring until soup thickens. Turn off heat, add cheese, and stir until melted, finishing off with salt and pepper to taste. Divide into bowls and top with bacon, sour cream, and chives. Serve with your favorite Waldorf salad and crusty, warm bread slathered in butter. Serves 8–10.

— Ita McIlvain, Washington

COTTAGE PIE

Introducing: a British classic—the cottage pie. The dish has been around since at least 1791, when potatoes were first introduced to the working poor (who often lived in cottages) as a crop that was cheap and versatile. Originally the dish was made up of leftover meat from a roast, which was encased in mashed potato and then baked till a golden crust formed on the top.

Generally, in Europe it is now accepted that cottage pie refers to a dish that has ground beef in it, often with a variety of home-grown vegetables as well, whereas shepherd's pie is the same dish but using lamb mince. There is also fisherman's pie (using any type of fish, but often white fish) and shepherdless pie, the veggie or vegan alternative.

Versions of this dish exist around the world in various guises—from the Chilean *pastel de papa*, which also contains hard-boiled eggs and olives, to the French *hachis Parmentier*—but however it is known, it is most certainly comfort food at its finest: simple, hearty, and perfect for a chilly winter's eve. My family loves to eat this after a day of hiking across the moors or along the coastline near our home—it's perfect for warming you up from the inside out.

2 Tbsp. oil
2 lbs. ground beef
1 onion, peeled and chopped
1 carrot, peeled and chopped
2 Tbsp. tomato paste
1 tsp. thyme
2 Tbsp. fresh parsley (or use a smaller amount of dried herbs)
2½ cups beef stock
Salt and pepper to taste
2 lbs. potatoes, peeled and cut into chunks

Heat oil in a large pan and brown ground beef on high heat. Remove meat from pan. Sauté onion and carrot until the onion is translucent and both are softening. Return meat to the pan, add tomato paste, thyme, and parsley. Pour stock over all, season with salt and pepper to taste, and simmer for 15–20 minutes.

Meanwhile, boil potatoes for 20 minutes or until soft. Drain and mash. Spoon meat mixture into a deep dish and then pile the mash on top. Note: The previous steps can be carried out in advance and the dish left in the fridge for up to 24 hours, if required. Cook in a preheated oven at 400° F for 20 minutes or until the potato topping is golden brown. Serve with cabbage or green beans. Serves 6.

— Julie Churcher, Devon, England

TABLE   251

CRANBERRY ORANGE BISCOTTI

I remember my mom baking these biscotti. She would give them away as gifts around the holidays, and on many mornings they would accompany our kitchen table coffee moments. Now that I am a coffee roaster myself, I can't imagine a better accompaniment to a well-crafted cup of joe.

½ cup butter (room temperature)
¾ cup sugar
2 eggs
2 Tbsp. orange zest
1¼ tsp. baking powder
1 tsp. vanilla
1 tsp. almond extract
2 cups flour
1 cup almonds (slivered and slightly toasted)
1 cup dried cranberries
Raw sugar, for dusting

Preheat oven to 350° F. Cream together butter, sugar, eggs, orange zest, baking powder, vanilla, and almond extract. Stir in flour, almonds, and cranberries. Form dough into two balls and place on a greased cookie sheet. Flatten each ball into a rectangular log about 1½ inches thick. Dust the tops with raw sugar. Bake for 10 minutes at 350° F. Remove from oven and allow logs to cool slightly. Slice each into 10–12 individual biscotti. Place the biscotti on their sides and bake for another 10 minutes until lightly browned. Makes about 2 dozen.

— Samantha Flanders, California

CULINARY MAC AND CHEESE WITH BÉCHAMEL SAUCE

Vermont is a food-y place, with plenty of vegetarians, but my dad was a fisherman and a hunter, so fresh trout and venison were frequently on our dinner table when I was growing up. One staple cookbook, however, was Anna Thomas' 1972 edition of *The Vegetarian Epicure*, an earthy, impressive collection that *almost* makes one consider a meatless life.

The page that broke the binding, splattered and dog-eared, held a version of this recipe, and my fondest food memories revolve around it. It's a dish that seems like it's always been with me; my father brought a large, hot baked bowl of it to me as a gift of comfort the day my best friend, Tree, died, and as a newlywed I proudly served it as the only thing I knew how to make. My friend Christine remembers me delivering it to her after her third baby. My husband and kids still get excited when I start the sauce, and I almost cry when I eat it because it takes me back.

Note: Little ones who are used to box macaroni and cheese might not appreciate the more mature flavors of this dish. Best to call it something *other* than macaroni and cheese around them, else they may scoff and tell you it's nothing of the sort.

1½ sticks of butter
1 onion, chopped
3 Tbsp. flour or a gluten-free flour alternative
6 cups milk
2 bay leaves
2 tsp. thyme (fresh or dried)
Fresh cracked pepper
Salt

2 lbs. short pasta like penne, bowtie, shells, or macaroni (you can also use gluten-free rice noodles)

1 loaf of good quality bread

2 cups grated sharp white cheddar cheese

2 cups grated Swiss cheese

1 cup freshly grated Parmesan cheese

If you have them, use two large oven-safe bowls for this recipe. (You could adapt to casserole dishes using fewer layers, but it's pretty fabulous baked in a colorful clay or ceramic bowl.) Melt 6 Tbsp. of butter in a 2-quart saucepan, add onion, and sauté on low until onion is translucent. Whisk in the flour (or flour alternative) and cook for a few more minutes. Slowly add milk, stirring with a wire whisk as you go. Add bay leaves, thyme, and a few rotations of fresh cracked pepper and cook for 10–20 minutes on low, regularly stirring with wire whisk. Sauce will thicken. Meanwhile, bring 4 quarts of salted water to a boil, add pasta, and cook *al dente* (taking it out just before it's fully done). Drain. Cube bread, place on buttered sheet pan, and toast in the oven at 325° F for 10 minutes. Remove bread cubes from the oven but leave the oven on. Combine cheeses. Grease the bowls with butter and layer the ingredients as follows: noodles, cheese medley, béchamel sauce, salt, and pepper. You should have room for two layers in your bowls. Top with buttered bread cubes and bake for 30–40 minutes, until the tops are brown and bubbly. Serve with a bright green salad.

— Hope

DOUBLE THE GOOD STUFF!

My approach to baking sweets, and even savories, is to double the good stuff and cut the sugar, because sugar is *not* the good stuff. The following recipes reflect that. The brownies are adapted from *Betty Crocker's Cookbook*, which I received as a wedding shower present thirty-three years ago.

Brownies

2 oz. unsweetened chocolate

½ cup (1 stick) butter

½ cup unsweetened cocoa

¼ tsp. espresso powder (optional)

2 eggs

¾ cup sugar

1 generous tsp. vanilla

¼ tsp. salt

¾ cup flour

Coarse ground salt (optional)

Melt the chocolate and butter over low heat in a medium-sized saucepan. Remove from heat. Stir in cocoa and espresso powder. Combine eggs and sugar and stir into chocolate mixture. Add vanilla, salt, and flour. Stir till smooth. Spread in a greased 9 × 9-inch pan, dust with coarse ground salt, if desired, and bake at 350° F for 12–13 minutes, until just done.

Peanut Butter Chocolate Chip Cookies

½ cup (1 stick) butter

1 cup peanut butter

¼ cup granulated sugar

¼ cup brown sugar

1 egg

1¼ cups flour

¾ tsp. baking soda

½ tsp. baking powder

¼ tsp. salt

1 cup chocolate chips

> Let us always meet each other with a smile, for the smile is the beginning of love.
>
> — Saint Teresa of Calcutta

TABLE   253

Cream together butter, peanut butter, and the sugars. Mix in egg. Add flour, baking soda, baking powder, and salt. Beat until smooth. Fold in chocolate chips. Shape into 1-inch balls, place on an ungreased cookie sheet, and flatten in crisscross pattern with fork. Bake at 375° F for 8–10 minutes, until just done. (Variation: Increase brown sugar to ½ cup, keeping granulated sugar at ¼ cup. Experiment to see what texture and taste you prefer. Sugar does increase the density and, of course, the sweetness of this cookie.)

— Kathleen Tomassi, Oregon

EASY SAUSAGE AND LENTIL SOUP

When I was recovering from the birth of my third baby, a dear friend stopped by with this soup and a loaf of crusty bread. It has been a family favorite ever since— the perfect midweek meal that comes together so quickly. All you need is a simple side salad or bread to go with it.

½ cup onion, chopped
1 carrot, chopped
1 large stalk of celery, chopped
1 Tbsp. olive oil
½ lb. Italian sausage, casings removed
5 large mushrooms, chopped
4 cups beef broth or stock

1 cup dry lentils, green or brown
1 tsp. garlic, crushed
15-oz. can diced tomatoes
1 tsp. salt
½ tsp. pepper
1 cup spinach or kale, freshly chopped

In a Dutch oven or large soup pot, sauté onion, carrot, and celery in olive oil for 5 minutes. Add sausage and brown for about 5 minutes. Add the rest of the ingredients and stir. Cover and simmer for about 25 minutes.

— Mary Millington, Montana

EGGPLANT PARMESAN

This is my go-to recipe to bring to a friend who's just had a baby. Containing particular enzymes that are known to promote circulation, eggplant is very toning and healing to the cervix (perfect for postpartum). This hearty vegetarian meal is a true crowd pleaser for the whole family. If you're postpartum yourself, have someone on your support team make it for you.

Approximately ¼ cup or more of olive oil, depending on pan size
1–2 medium to large eggplants, sliced
2–3 eggs, beaten

¾ cup whole wheat flour
1 jar (about a quart) marinara sauce
10–12 oz. fresh mozzarella cheese

Grease a 9 × 13-inch baking dish with olive oil and heat the rest in a large frying pan until hot. Dip slices of eggplant in the beaten eggs, then in the flour to coat. Fry 3–4 slices at a time until lightly brown on one side, then flip. Lightly brown on second side. They may not be fully tender in the middle but will finish cooking in the oven. Once all slices are browned, layer ingredients in baking dish as follows: eggplant, marinara sauce, mozzarella. Repeat 2–3 times. Reserve a small amount of marinara sauce and mozzarella cheese for the topping.

At this point, the dish can be refrigerated until you take it to be baked at the new momma's home (so it's hot and fresh). Or, to simplify things for her, bake it at your place at 350° F for 20–30 minutes, until it's bubbling well and browning on top. This will serve 4–6 people. Serve with a delicious salad and bread.

— Madeleine Pidel, Connecticut

FAST FOOD

Knock, knock! I wonder who can possibly be at the door at 5:00 P.M.? I heave my third-trimester body off the couch, where I have been lying like a sun-bathing walrus. "Oh, it's you, dear! How was work today?" A vague memory of the skinny, energetic twentysomething newlywed who used to cook meals for her husband flits through my mind. *He must be hungry. It's suppertime. The kids are full of apples and cheese, I'm full of preterm baby, but a hungry man needs supper. Why, oh why didn't I think of this two hours ago?*

This, and many other predicaments, are the real-life scenarios of my kitchen. I know women who swear by their meal planners, color highlighted and sticky noted, but I go by an organic process called "spillover". It works like this. You make lots of food—yummy, filling food the whole family loves, even the toddler, and you put the leftovers in the fridge. That's lunch for tomorrow. You do this often, and you never run short.

That is, until you do.

So I've had to rely on food that can be pulled out of the fridge and served without preparation (or less than ten minutes prep, which is almost as good) and can satisfy a hungry man (or teenager or child) or be packed quickly into a picnic basket for impromptu picnics and road trips.

- **Grilled sandwiches:** Well, they're sandwiches. What could be faster? But there's something about *hot* food that makes a meal. Butter the outsides and place the sandwiches on cooling racks on top of cookie sheets and put them in the oven for 10 minutes or so. It's surprising how tasty all-veggie sandwiches can be when heated.

- **Stovetop caramelized onions:** Slice two or three onions (or more, since they shrink) and toss in a pan with salt and butter. Fry until brown. *Everything* tastes better with fried onions.

- **Sourdough bread:** I include it because it's the only kind of bread we can eat, with our wimpy digestive tracts, and because it's just plain beautiful. Rip and share! If you can make your own, I recommend it for its wild flavor. With butter and honey or caramelized onions and mushrooms, it's a hearty snack.

- **Prewashed salad:** Forget the farmers' market lettuces caked with dirt. There will be a time for those, someday. Today, go for bags you can rip open for a salad in seconds, like spring mixes or arugula.

- **Boiled potatoes:** The much-maligned potato is your best friend for quick but filling breakfasts, especially for gluten-free families. Fill your biggest pot with whole potatoes: red, Yukon Gold, or peeled russet. Boil until tender, allow to cool, and then refrigerate without draining. Cooked potatoes left in their water reabsorb water, making them the perfect refrying consistency. Make lots and store them in the fridge, slicing and frying as you need.

TABLE   255

- **Kimchi and sauerkraut:** Kitchen probiotics—so simple and so fun! One hour of glorious mess, chopping and packing vegetables into jars with salt (incidentally, a great activity for children), equals weeks of instant salads. Salt preserves them, and they eventually turn sour and create the most amazing flavors. Find a good recipe that excites you and give it a try. Truly, gourmet artisan pickles!

- **Yogurt jars:** We make our own yogurt because it's more economical for us. If this sounds impossible, don't worry, I won't make you. Store-bought yogurt is fine. We fill small jars with plain yogurt, berries, syrup, and even leftover oatmeal. It stores well in jars, and it's an instant snack.

- **Sausages and hot dogs:** Your children will adore you. I was raised in an anti-hot-dog house; homeopathic remedies were on hand in case one inadvertently passed our lips. But new hot dogs are on the market with more meat and fewer entrails. They might ease your conscience, even if they don't win you points for your gourmet palette.

— Mary

FESTIVE POTATOES

This recipe is a favorite in our family and has become a universal must-have on Easter and Christmas. For Christmas it is a rich and creamy accompaniment to a rib eye roast or turkey, with fresh green beans. For Easter it is marvelous with lamb or pork roast, with asparagus. I guarantee it will be a dish that will be savored and perhaps added to your future feasts or special occasions. This is a pretty simple recipe and an especially welcome one on a holiday when a mother is so often sleep-deprived. If you have children old enough, don't forget to delegate the potato peeling and slicing to a capable child or two.

3½ cups heavy whipping cream
5 cloves garlic, thinly sliced
12 or more fresh sage leaves, chopped
1½ tsp. salt
1 tsp. freshly ground pepper
¼ tsp. ground nutmeg
8 extra-large potatoes, sliced (or enough potatoes of varying sizes to fill a 3-quart or 12-cup baking dish, oblong or round)

Makes 8 servings; can be doubled.

Preheat oven to 375° F. Butter baking dish. In a saucepan, bring the cream to a boil with the garlic and sage. Lower the heat and simmer for 15 minutes, occasionally stirring. (Be sure to watch the heat, as it can easily begin to boil over.) Season with salt, pepper, and nutmeg. Set aside.

Peel and slice the potatoes ¼-inch thick. Layer the potatoes in the baking dish and pour the cream over them. The cream should just cover the potatoes. If it does not, add a bit more cream. Cover with aluminum foil and bake immediately, or set aside for up to 2 hours. Bake for 30 minutes covered with foil; then remove the foil and continue to bake until the potatoes are tender but still hold their shape, about 20 minutes longer. The tops of the potatoes should just be turning golden brown.

— Laura Langley, California

FISH TACOS

A FAMILY FAVORITE

Years ago, in our first apartment in Southern California, we lived next door to a humble culinary genius. He made these tacos for us one night, and I wanted to drink the sauce, but instead I committed the recipe to memory.

This meal is a mother's dream. It is simple and complete with four elements: fish, cabbage salad, tortillas, and a magic sauce. It's especially great in the summer, but we make it all year long, even on Fridays in Lent, though it's anything but penitential.

Rice, beans, and watermelon make great sides, and hot sauce is welcome to some, but the meal stands alone without these additions. Any recipe that becomes a staple in a family of ten must be uncomplicated and satisfying. Quantities below feed a large family, or a small family with guests, but feel free to halve the recipe if desired. (Assemble salad and sauce while the fish bakes, or beforehand if grilling.)

Fish:
   3–4 lbs. any fresh or frozen white fish, such as tilapia
   ½ stick of butter or ⅓ cup avocado oil
   Any all-purpose seasoning
   Lemons or limes

To bake: Place fish in a glass baking dish, dot with butter, sprinkle with seasoning, and bake at 350° F for 30 minutes. Remove from oven when it's juicy and flaky and squeeze some fresh citrus on top.

To grill: Marinate fish in avocado oil, seasoning, and a few squeezes of fresh citrus for 10 minutes or more. Grill for 5 minutes on each side over a medium flame.

Cabbage salad:
   1 green or red cabbage, shredded
   3–5 Tbsp. apple cider vinegar
   3–5 Tbsp. olive oil
   Salt to taste

Combine all ingredients in a medium to large bowl.

Sauce:
   ½ cup mayonnaise
   ½ cup sour cream
   1 bunch cilantro, chopped
   2 jalapenos, seeded and diced
   Juice of 4 limes
   ½ tsp. cumin
   1 tsp. chile powder
   Salt and pepper to taste

Combine all ingredients in a small to medium bowl.

On your favorite warmed tortillas, layer fish, cabbage salad, and sauce. Or skip the tortillas and enjoy as a low-carb salad.

— Hope

FRANCISCAN WEDDING SOUP

Our good friend Sean Wood is a fabulous chef (you will find recipes from his mother and his sister within these pages). Before discerning with the Community of the Franciscan Friars of the Renewal (CFR) in New York, he lived next door to us and would sometimes cook for our family. This meal was our favorite. A spinoff of Italian wedding soup, we jokingly called it Sean's Wedding Soup, wondering whether he would become a friar or marry some beautiful, holy woman. Its new name, Franciscan Wedding Soup, is a nod to

TABLE   257

the Italian celebratory nature of the dish, his time of formation with the CFRs, and his lovely soon-to-be wife, Elizabeth.

Prepare yourself for satisfaction. With broth, sausage, basil, peppers, spinach, and cheese, it's one of the most nourishing and deeply satisfying foods ever served from a ladle.

For best results, make your stock the night before "Italian style", with the addition of parsley, basil, oregano, and garlic. (See our bone broth recipe for basic instructions.) This recipe served our large family for two nights, so adjust quantities if you prefer.

About ¼ cup olive oil
8 onions, chopped
Salt and pepper to taste
4–6 red bell peppers, sliced
1½ cups white wine
2 heads garlic, peeled and crushed
Zucchini, mushrooms, or other vegetables (optional)
Fresh thyme, oregano, and fresh basil

3 lbs. Italian sausage links
27 oz. coconut milk
Juice of 2–3 lemons
2 lbs. spinach
Red pepper flakes
Freshly grated Parmesan

Sauté onions in olive oil in a large soup pot. Add salt and pepper. Add red bell peppers, wine, some more olive oil as needed, and garlic. Add some zucchini, mushrooms, or other vegetables, if desired. Add thyme, oregano, and basil.

Slice sausage links and sauté in a pan. Then combine everything with broth and bring to a boil. Reduce heat and simmer for 20 minutes.

Add coconut milk, lemon juice, spinach, and lots of red pepper flakes.

Garnish with Parmesan, basil, and more red pepper flakes if desired.

— Hope

HAPPY MORNING BREAKFAST COBBLER

I can't remember exactly when this became a regular in my house, but it was probably from eating the leftovers from last night's dessert for breakfast and realizing that in some cases, dessert for breakfast is completely okay. Now we make it most weekends, and I can sit and drink my coffee while it bakes away, instead of flipping flapjacks. This recipe is simple, and my kids assemble it more often than I do. It's a great beginner recipe for anyone eight years old and up, and it's free of gluten, refined sugar, and eggs (but you'd never know). Fresh berries are wonderful and easy to come by in the summer months, but still we rarely have large quantities on hand. Most of the time I make this with frozen blackberries or raspberries. Berries are some of the healthiest foods known to man and child. Full of antioxidants, they have anti-cancer and anti-inflammatory properties, and unlike beets or kale, they require zero coercion when it comes to small children. Serve this dish with some bacon or breakfast sausages for a more balanced start to the day. This also makes a great side dish for company brunch.

Happy morning 99 percent guaranteed. Serves a crowd—halve the recipe if you have a small family.

4-lb. bag frozen berries or fruit, or 6–8 cups fresh
¼ cup arrowroot powder or another thickening powder
2 sticks of melted butter
½ cup maple syrup

1½ cups oats
1 cup almond meal
½ cup flax meal
1 tsp. vanilla
1½ tsp. cinnamon
1½ tsp. salt

Fill a 9 × 13-inch pan with fresh or frozen fruit of your choice. Blackberries, raspberries, blueberries, pears, peaches, and apples all work well. Mix arrowroot powder into the fruit. (This helps thicken the fruit base so it's more like pie.) In a bowl, combine butter, syrup, oats, almond meal, flax meal, vanilla, cinnamon, and salt. Pour mixture over the fruit and bake until top is golden brown, about 50 minutes.

— Hope

HIGH-PROTEIN GRANOLA

Are you looking for a quick, crunchy breakfast or an afternoon or bedtime snack? Boxed breakfast cereal bars need not apply. After trying this recipe, you might not want to go back! Besides amazing, it is also grain-free and paleo.

You will need 20 minutes, a really large mixing bowl (if you want to make it only twice a month, which is what I do), and baking trays. A food processor is also helpful for chopping the nuts. In this recipe I never measure anything; I just dump a bunch of things together and it always turns out great. I realize, however, that you'll need a starting point, so it goes something like this.

3½ cups chopped pecans
3½ cups other chopped nuts, the more the better
    (cashews, almonds, walnuts, and brazil nuts are
    all good)
1½ cups pumpkin seeds
1½ cups unsweetened shredded coconut
2½ cups melted coconut oil
1–1½ cups honey or maple syrup or a combo
    (preferred)
2 Tbsp. vanilla
2 Tbsp. cinnamon

2 Tbsp. salt
Raisins, chia seeds, flax seeds, sunflower seeds, or
    anything else that suits you (optional)

Mix it all up and give it a taste. See if it needs more sweetening (as tastes differ.) Spread out on baking trays and bake at 250° F for 15 minutes. Let it cool on the trays and then store in a large sealed container. Serve it with whole milk, almond milk, or whole yogurt, and may I suggest some frozen blueberries on top?

— Hope

TABLE   259

LEMON CURD

Lemon curd is one of those delicate, ambrosial foods of the gods that you should make only once or twice a year, except that it is so ridiculously easy to make, and we do so love to eat it by the spoonful. You could also bake it in tart shells or slather it on crêpes. It is a perfect Easter breakfast food.

1 stick of butter, cut into pieces
½ cup granulated sugar
2 large eggs, lightly beaten
½ cup freshly squeezed lemon juice (will require
   3–4 medium lemons)
2 tsp. lemon zest

Melt butter in a saucepan over low heat. Stir in sugar and eggs. Add lemon juice and zest. Whisk vigorously on high heat until just about boiling and mixture begins to thicken. Force through a fine sieve set in another bowl. Serve warm or cooled to room temperature. Refrigerating lemon curd gives it a slightly grainy texture.

— Mary

LEMONY TUNA SALAD

During a visit to Phoenix years ago, my dad took me to his favorite deli. (My parents eat out a lot, so I knew this place must be something special to earn the title of "favorite".) I asked him what to order, and without any hesitation he recommended the tuna salad. I don't get a chance to eat out a lot, and I wasn't sure I wanted to blow this opportunity on a boring tuna salad. He told me to trust him, and I'm so glad I did because I've been making a similar tuna salad ever since. The game changer is *lemon*. It brightens and lightens the salad, which can otherwise feel quite heavy.

I don't measure any of the ingredients but rather give the mixture a stir after every addition to see whether I have the proportions right. For example, when I add the celery, I stir it in, see whether it looks like I have enough, add more if needed, stir again, then move on to the next ingredient. This way, you can add more or less of what your family prefers.

Albacore tuna (canned)
Celery, small diced
Red onion, small diced
Dill pickle relish
Dijon mustard
Mayonnaise
Salt
Pepper
Lemon zest
Lemon juice

Tip: You really want to taste the lemon, so chances are you're going to need more than you think you will. I add the juice and zest last so I can taste and adjust the lemon flavor until I get it just right.

— Amy Dragoo, California

MAMA'S PHỞ

I first tasted pho when I was in need of something warm, comforting, and nourishing. I was staying in the Intensive Care Unit with our oldest daughter, three years old at the time, who was struggling for her life with viral pneumonia. Her godmother came bearing this apparently popular Vietnamese fare, and, needing sustenance, I savored every bite.

Being a guest around another friend's table and experiencing her own simple version of this meal later inspired me to make my own pho from my already-established pots of chicken broth frequently simmering on the stove of my kitchen.

This traditional soup, pronounced "fuh", is now a regular favorite in our home, and I have since taught our oldest son to make it from scratch, broth and all, as he is the one to request this, his favorite comfort food, throughout the year.

While traditional Vietnamese pho broth is made using beef bones (a combination of marrow bones and meaty bones), I keep it simple using any kind of bone broth I've already made—usually chicken. It's tricky to make a flavorful beef-bone broth from scratch, as a rich flavor is hard to achieve with beef bones, which have to be carefully hand selected. (However, finding brisket and meaty "soup bones" at one's local market is not too difficult.) The broth is flavored with cinnamon, anise, onion, and beef. Additional broth ingredients, such as a dash of sugar or coriander, can be added for a more traditional flavor. While I sear my beef and immediately add it to the table for optional toppings, it is traditional to use sliced raw beef in the bowls, ladling the very hot broth over it, cooking it within seconds. The rice noodles can be found in the Asian aisle of your store; I use pad Thai–style noodles.

The aesthetics of this meal are a joy to pursue if you've got the time. If you can afford to buy beautiful ramen bowls, happy shopping! If you know local potters and can afford to patronize them, do. And commission them to make you deep Japanese-style bowls with strong, nontippy feet for family meal ease. If not, any large soup-style bowl will do. The table set with large bowls and the center filled with an abundance of fresh green toppings is a delight to gather around. Call the family to the table, light a candle, give thanks and praise, singing your song. Savor aromas and warmth. Breathe in. Slurp. Inhale. Connect. You will need napkins to wipe your chin.

Below is my own way of making this dish, without many of the traditional ingredients that are harder and more time-consuming to gather.

4–6 quarts chicken or beef bone broth
2 cinnamon sticks
5 anise stars
Salt to taste
Some peppercorns
1 or more lbs. beef (sirloin tip, thinly sliced, or flanken ribs)
3 boxes (about 1 lb.) fresh or dried Thai-style rice noodles

Toppings:
  Cilantro sprigs, rinsed
  Fresh basil stalks laden with an abundance of large, healthy basil leaves
  Fresh mung bean sprouts
  Lime wedges
  Hoisin and sriracha sauces

To achieve pho's unique flavor, simmer cinnamon sticks, anise, salt, and peppercorns in broth for an hour or two. Strain out bones and spices and discard. Set broth aside. Chop beef into bite-sized pieces and sear. Cook the rice noodles in a separate pot of salted water. Err on the side of almost done as opposed to very done, as you will be pouring hot broth over them and they may continue to cook a little. Strain. Put cooked rice noodles and meat into each bowl, ladling broth over the top. Place toppings in the middle of your table in serving bowls or on long serving boards. Add the toppings and sauces to your own liking, being sure to squeeze a lime wedge or two into your bowls.

— Sia

TABLE   261

MARIE'S JEWISH COFFEE CAKE

I almost always make this for Christmas Eve so I can have it for Christmas morning with some leftover quiche, a mug of mocha, and a flute of mimosa. It starts the day right for me. It goes without saying, though, that a good coffee cake can be enjoyed all year (and all day) long. This recipe comes to me from my dad, but a lot of his sisters make it as well. My dad says it's called "Jewish" because of the sour cream. Somehow, I don't believe that's right, but it is delicious, regardless.

1 cup chopped walnuts
1 Tbsp. cinnamon
½ cup brown sugar
2 sticks of butter, softened
2 cups sugar
4 eggs
2 tsp. vanilla
4 cups flour, sifted
1 Tbsp. baking powder
1 tsp. baking soda
½ tsp. salt
1 pint sour cream

Preheat oven to 350° F. Grease Bundt pan. Combine walnuts, cinnamon, and brown sugar in a small bowl and set aside for filling. With a mixer, cream together butter and sugar until fluffy (about 5 minutes). Reduce speed to low and beat in eggs, one at a time until well mixed. Add vanilla and mix in. In a separate bowl, combine flour, baking powder, baking soda, and salt. With mixer on low, slowly add flour mixture to the batter, alternating with the sour cream. Pour ⅓ of the batter into the Bundt pan. Sprinkle ½ the filling over the batter. Add another ⅓ of the batter over the filling, then the rest of the filling, and, finally, the remainder of the batter. Bake in the oven for about an hour. The top of the cake should be brown, and a knife inserted in the center should come out clean.

— Jessica Haggard, California

MEATBALLS ARE FOR LOVERS

Why is it that after many years of being in charge of "What's for dinner?", I still get stumped at the question? "Didn't I just make you dinner twenty-four hours ago? Why are you asking me again already?"

Yes, of course we can plan menus, freeze meals, and employ all sorts of other tricks that prevent this question from inspiring dread. Still, how often are we humbled by this one question alone? It's like a conspired attack on our personhood; our minds go blank as if we had never known a spatula, and somehow we feel personally offended by the fact that our family has even broached the subject.

One underutilized strategy is having the kids do the cooking for you. Admittedly, with homework and sports this isn't always possible, yet if it is, consider giving your kids over the age of ten this recipe; you will enjoy a night off, and I think you'll be pleased with the outcome. (If your children are still small, this is a nice recipe to make along with them, if you have any patience left at 5:00 P.M.)

Late have I loved thee, homemade meatballs! If I had known the homey feeling you bring to the table, your versatility, your frugality, your old-world charm, I'd have made friends with you much sooner.

This recipe is gluten- and egg-free, and you won't miss either one. It's a great universal base to suit the various diet restrictions in a large family. You can pair with rice pasta or regular pasta, French bread, cauliflower rice, or zucchini noodles, or just eat it solo. But do serve with a bright, fresh green salad. (Sia's garlic salad dressing would be perfect.) Complete the experience with freshly grated Parmesan on the plate and Dean Martin on the stream. "Memories Are Made of This" will make you want to kiss your children all evening long.

This recipe feeds a large family with leftovers; halve the recipe for a smaller family, or freeze extras. Dried or fresh herbs can work; just triple the amount if you're using fresh.

4 lbs. ground beef

2 onions, diced

10 garlic cloves, chopped

2 tsp. oregano

2 tsp. parsley

2 tsp. basil

2 tsp. garlic powder

4 tsp. salt

2 tsp. pepper

1 tsp. any or all of the following spices: sage, rosemary, marjoram, thyme (optional)

2–3 (24-oz.) cans plum tomatoes

2 Tbsp. salt

1 Tbsp. oregano

Preheat oven to 425° F. In a mixing bowl, place beef, onions, garlic, oregano, parsley, basil, garlic powder, salt, pepper, and optional spices if desired. Mix with hands till smooth. Form into meatballs. Heat a large skillet on medium-high. Cook meatballs for 10 minutes, turning once halfway through.

To make the marinara sauce, blend tomatoes with salt and oregano. Pour 2–3 cups of marinara sauce into a 9 × 13-inch baking dish. Transfer meatballs to baking dish and pour more sauce on top. Cover dish with foil and bake for 20 minutes.

— Hope

MINESTRONE MONÁSTICO AND CROÛTES, FOR LENT

During Lent, our parish has soup suppers every Friday following the Stations of the Cross. This is one of my favorite liturgies, not because of the actual prayers in the little prayer booklets we all follow but because I simply like to be in church, thinking about just one thing: our Lord's Passion. It's physically involved, with all the kneeling and standing and turning our heads toward each station, and it keeps me focused. The *Stabat Mater* (in which the Passion is being felt and lived through our mother Mary) is lovely, and we dwell on the great mystery of our faith: that Christ became *one of us*, that *his* mother was also *our* mother. He tasted the dirt on the ground each time he fell; he shed sweat,

blood, and tears just as we do. He recoiled from pain. Each Friday when I pray the Stations, I try (while at the same time bouncing my babies and reminding my older ones to sit still and look up at the stars on the ceiling) to unite myself to his pain, his emotions, and, most importantly, his great love for us. And I love the end of Stations, when everyone in the church makes his way downstairs, where hot soup and bread are waiting.

As Catholics we are encouraged to abstain from meat throughout all of Lent, but it is mandatory on Fridays. This discipline strengthens the spirit, and one comes to love the simplicity of Lenten meals

TABLE   263

when they are paired with such an enriching liturgical time in the Church. The peasant, meatless foods with only water to drink is a fitting meal for a Lenten Friday. The simplicity brings to mind the dry, hot, barren land where our Lord carried his Cross to Calvary. It is a good journey, and full of hope. And so we gather together to share a meal, with joy in our hearts, for our faith continually nourishes us and feeds our hungry souls, as does the hot food on our tables.

One of the soups we annually serve at our parish is a delicious tomato minestrone soup. The recipe we use is a slightly more time consuming one than this, taken from *A Continual Feast* by Evelyn Birge Vitz. I've provided a shorter, simpler recipe, which I find to be less intimidating on a busy day, while not compromising freshly prepared ingredients. Almost any minestrone soup is delicious, especially if topped with homemade garlic croutons, a big handful of Parmesan cheese, and a smattering of fresh parsley! I have included a variation of this recipe too, if one prefers the more traditional red minestrone with more kinds of beans and added greens. Happy Lenten mealtimes!

Wash and peel the vegetables and cut them into small pieces. Pour the water into a large soup pot and add vegetables and white beans. Cook slowly over medium heat for 1 hour. Sauté the onions in a bit of the olive oil in a large frying pan. (I use a cast-iron skillet.) When the onions start to become golden, remove from heat. To the soup, add the onions, wine, the rest of the olive oil, macaroni, tarragon, salt, and pepper and continue cooking for 15 minutes. Cover the pot and allow the soup to simmer for another 10 minutes. Serve hot, topped with Parmesan cheese. Makes 6–8 servings.

Variation:
For a Minestrone soup with tomatoes and more beans (and that will feed more people), add this to the soup along with the sautéed onions:

8-oz. can kidney beans
1 or 2 (8-oz.) cans crushed or diced
   tomatoes
More salt and pepper to taste
1 tsp. basil
½ to 1 head of green cabbage, finely
   shredded
A few handfuls of fresh spinach

Minestrone Monástico
Adapted from *Twelve Months of Monastery Soups* by Brother Victor-Antoine d'Avila-Latourrette

3 carrots
3 potatoes
1 cup green beans
2 celery stalks
3 quarts water
1 cup dry white beans
3 onions
1 cup olive oil
1 cup dry white wine
1 cup uncooked macaroni
Tarragon, minced
Salt and pepper to taste
Freshly grated Parmesan cheese

Croûtes
1 loaf Italian bread (preferably stale)
Olive oil

Preheat oven to 400° F. Slice bread into ½-inch slices. Cut off the crusts. Brush with olive oil. Place the slices on a baking sheet and bake for approximately 5–8 minutes on each side, or until golden brown.

Variation:
Use butter instead of olive oil, though this is more French than Italian. Rub the croûtes with a peeled clove of garlic for a little added flavor. For smaller croûtes—croutons—cube slices of bread and proceed with the recipe.

— Sia

MONTANA BURRITOS

Dinner should be, as often as possible, made from scratch—something you can whip together for your family, for company, and for the unexpected guest. It should be of high quality but not expensive, and it should taste good: real food with a whole lotta soul mixed in. Use what you have, with what you know: simple ingredients, flavorful spice, and the freedom to invent. I have few "recipes" because I cook by intuition and to feed and gather people. I'm a mother of nine, and these burritos always feed the tribe! Enjoy with cilantro, salsa, and salad. Don't stress and make sure it's blessed.

2 Tbsp. oil
1 onion, chopped
5–6 cloves garlic
1 green bell pepper, diced, or 4-oz. can chiles
2 lbs. chicken or ground beef (optional)
15-oz. can kidney, pinto, or black beans, drained
14.5-oz. can diced tomatoes (I often use up the rest of a jar of leftover salsa in place of this)

1 Tbsp. chile powder
1 tsp. cumin
Salt and pepper to taste
12 flour tortillas, 10 inches or larger
10-oz. can red or green enchilada sauce
2–3 cups shredded Monterey Jack, Pepper Jack, or cheddar cheese

Heat oil in a large cast-iron skillet. Sauté onion, garlic, and green peppers or chiles until aromatic. Add chicken or ground beef if desired and cook through. Add beans, diced tomatoes or salsa, chile powder, cumin, salt, and pepper. Using a slotted spoon, fill each tortilla, roll, and place in a baking pan. Top with enchilada sauce and cheese. Bake at 375° F until the cheese is bubbly and browning.

— Maggie Eisenbarth, Montana

MUSSELS IN TOMATO AND GARLIC BROTH

Sally Fallon, one of my favorite dietitians and author of *Nourishing Traditions*, comments on how a significant part of the degradation of American health has to do with the removal of shellfish from the American family diet. High in vitamin D, zinc, and omega 3s, shellfish should be eaten *regularly*, she says.

This recipe is a great place to start. I first tried it on the feast of Our Lady of Lourdes, looking for a French dish that seemed different and doable. Now I make it for guests, for any French feast day, and just because. It's such an impressive meal requiring such little effort that it wins big for me. The most surprising part about this recipe is how much my little kids love it, as if something deep inside of them was longing for that dose of nature-made zinc. Be sure to put a big bucket or bowl in the middle of the table for the shells, and serve with toasted garlic bread or baguettes and a simple salad to round out the meal.

1–2 onions, diced
¼ cup olive oil
5 (14.5-oz.) cans diced tomatoes
A few sprinkles of red pepper flakes
Some thyme, fresh or dried

TABLE   265

2–3 Tbsp. fresh parsley, chopped
Salt to taste
4 lbs. fresh or frozen mussels (in shells)
Freshly ground pepper

In a large pot, sauté onions in oil for 5 minutes until translucent. Next add tomatoes, red pepper flakes, thyme, parsley, and salt. Reduce heat and simmer, partially covered, for 20–25 minutes. Add mussels, stir, cover, and cook an additional 3–5 minutes. Add pepper.

— Hope

POSOLE

IN HONOR OF OUR LADY OF GUADALUPE

In northern New Mexico, running north to south from Taos to Santa Fe, is a rugged, narrow section of the Rocky Mountains called the Sangre de Cristo range. This translates as "Blood of Christ". In the fall, aspen groves dot the land in golden hues and sunshine glitters from rapids in the waters of the Rio Grande. This country is cold and bright in the winter, and piñon smoke trails from the chimneys into the bright blue sky. Snow lies on the ground, and hand-tied chile ristras hang from porch roof timbers, vibrant splashes of red on the earth-hued adobe. Some doors are painted turquoise, and there is snow on the peaks above. On Christmas Eve, paths and roof parapets are dotted with luminarias, lit candles inside little paper bags weighted with sand.

Eating posole reminds me of my childhood table because my father grew up in Albuquerque and the meals he ate as a child were not forgotten in our home. The cuisine in that part of the country is famous for its heat, flavor, and simplicity. Nothing fancy, posole  is a simple dish made from hominy, chile, garlic, and pork and made quite distinctive in flavor by the addition of juniper berries and limes. I recently dodged outside at dusk to harvest some berries straight off my own little juniper tree to put into my soup. They bring the flavor of the scrubby, pungent evergreen right into the bowl. If you don't have a tree and you don't live where juniper trees grow, you can order the berries or find them at specialty stores.

Hominy is a food produced from dried field *maize* (corn) kernels. Canned hominy can be found in the Mexican aisle in the supermarket and comes in very large cans. Using canned hominy will cut off at least an hour of the cooking time. Just simmer for about an hour to let the flavors meld. Dried hominy can be ordered from your food co-op or Mexican supply store. If you live near an international food supply store in a bigger city, you're in luck! Posole made with dried hominy is always better. It is also good to find pure chile powder—just ground chiles, not chile powder mixed with salt and "other flavors". You can order Hatch chile powder straight from New Mexico.

Posole improves over time, so if you're planning on serving guests, keep in mind that it may be all the more delicious if you make it one or two days beforehand and then heat and reheat the soup. The flavors become richer as the days go by. I love to serve this on Christmas Eve or the feast of Our Lady of Guadalupe, paired with *The Lady of Guadalupe* by Tomie dePaola. (My children love the roses and the rainbow.)

This recipe for posole is our own family's way of cooking it, but there are as many versions of posole as there are regions of Mexico and New Mexico. (My father cooks it one way, my uncle another.) For further reading, you may want to pick up the cookbook by Diane Kennedy, *The Cuisines of Mexico* (1972).

2 lbs. dried hominy or 105-oz. can hominy

2 lbs. pork shoulder, fat removed, cubed

A few Tbsp. olive oil

5 garlic cloves

2 onions, chopped

6–10 limes, quartered

A pinch of turmeric (optional)

½ tsp. coriander

Dried juniper berries

1 tsp.–2 Tbsp. hot New Mexico chile powder, according to taste

Sides:

    Radishes, thinly sliced

    1–2 bunches fresh cilantro

    Corn tortillas

    Grated Monterey Jack or Colby cheese

    Refried beans

If using dried hominy, rinse, place in a large soup pot, and cover with water. Bring to a rolling boil and continue boiling for about an hour until kernels open. They should still be hard-ish and chewy. If using canned hominy, heat in your soup pot on the side, just enough to get hot. In the meantime, sear the pork on high heat in the olive oil until browned. Mince garlic and add it to the pork. Stir another 5 minutes, lowering the heat so the pork doesn't burn. Add to the pot of hominy along with the chopped onions. Add a few limes, turmeric, coriander, about 10 juniper berries, and chile powder to taste. Simmer for a few hours until everything is done. Don't worry about overcooking the pork; the limes make it so tender. (If you do not simmer the limes in the soup, be sure to serve them on the side—the flavor they provide is, to me, essential!) Serve with bowls of juniper berries, chile powder, lime wedges, radishes, and freshly chopped cilantro so guests can season their bowls as desired. For kids, provide a big platter of corn tortillas rolled up with melted cheddar or Monterey Jack cheese and refried beans. (I lay tortillas on a cookie sheet, top with cheese and refried beans, bake at 350° F until cheese is melted, and then roll them up.)

— Sia

If an ear is to grow or a flower blossom, there are times which cannot be forced; for the birth of a human being, nine months are required; to write a book or a worthy piece of music, years must often be spent in patient searching.... To encounter the mystery takes patience, inner purification, silence and waiting.

— Pope Saint John Paul II
General Audience, July 26, 2000

RAISIN SCONES

If you spend time with the Wood family, you will be offered steaming hot tea, either Assam or Irish Breakfast, poured into a heated bone china tea cup. We serve the tea with a small pitcher of half and half. At Sunday brunch the tea will often be accompanied by raisin scones right out of the oven, served with Irish butter and raspberry jam. Nothing is more delicious! I made the scones for our grandchildren recently, and upon biting into one, our three-year-old granddaughter exclaimed with a big smile on her face, "I love scones!" Later on, when the grandchildren were leaving, I said to the five-year-old, "I will give you some scones to take home. How many should I put in the bag?" Matthias said, "Grannie, if I were you, I would put all of them in." We like our food to be both delicious and healthy, so I use spelt flour or whole wheat flour for the scones. I have been making this recipe for as long as I can remember.

3 cups flour (either whole wheat or spelt)
3 Tbsp. sugar
1 tsp. baking soda
½ tsp. salt
6 Tbsp. chilled butter
⅓ cup raisins (or currants or dried cranberries)
1 egg
1 cup buttermilk
A little milk for brushing on top of the scones

Optional: sugar, finely grated lemon peel, and ground ginger, combined in a small container to sprinkle on top of the scones

Preheat oven to 425° F. Grease a large cookie sheet with a little butter. In a large mixing bowl, combine flour, sugar, baking soda, and salt. Cut butter into pieces with a knife and add to dry ingredients; then cut in with a pastry cutter until mixture resembles fine crumbs. Add raisins (or currants or dried cranberries) and gently mix. In a medium-sized mixing bowl, mix egg and buttermilk until well combined. Pour egg and buttermilk mixture into the large bowl, combining with a large spoon just until all dry particles are combined with liquid. Batter should just be wet enough to absorb all the dry parts. If you still have any dry bits, you can add a tiny bit more buttermilk. Using a large spoon, measure out equal child-fist-sized portions (about 12 total) that you can shape into balls and flatten slightly. Place on cookie sheet, leaving about an inch between each scone. Lightly brush each top with a little milk, and if you would like, sprinkle on either a little sugar or sugar, fine lemon peel, and ginger combined together. Bake for about 18 minutes. They should be slightly golden on top.

— Mary Wood, California

RAW CACAO, COCONUT, AND DATE ENERGY BALLS

A few years ago, when I was at a stress-filled crossroads of work and motherhood, I realized just how much I relied on added sugars and caffeine to power through my full life. I did a series of cleanses and learned to enjoy life with less sugar, which improved my health dramatically. These are easy and energizing without any sugars: a paleo treat that is rich, scrumptious, and so healthy. It stores well in the fridge, so it makes a perfect instant snack for ravenous toddlers, school-aged children, or breastfeeding mommas or an indulgent treat for a friend dropping by for coffee. Makes 12–18.

2 cups whole organic Medjool dates, pitted
¼ cup water
½ cup organic almond butter
2 cups unsweetened shredded coconut (plus more for rolling balls in, if desired)
1 tsp. vanilla
2 Tbsp. raw cacao powder (plus more for rolling balls in, if desired)
2 Tbsp. chocolate protein powder of choice (optional)
¾ tsp. cinnamon
Pinch of salt

Soak dates in ¼ cup water for 5 minutes. Then pour dates and water into a food processor or Vitamix blender. Add the rest of the ingredients and pulse to combine, making sure all dates are fully processed. Scoop out small amounts of the mixture to roll into balls, and roll gently in raw cacao, coconut flakes, or both, depending on how you want them to look. Place on a serving platter and refrigerate until serving, 30 minutes or more.

— Madeleine Pidel, Connecticut

ROASTED EGGPLANT SALAD

I wasn't a fan of eggplant until I discovered this salad. Now we're besties. I could eat bowls of it! I serve it at dinner parties and it's the first thing to disappear.

3 small eggplants, peeled and medium diced
2 Tbsp. olive oil
Salt and pepper to taste
¼ cup red onion, small diced
4–5 tsp. balsamic vinegar
6–8 leaves fresh basil, cut chiffonade style
⅓ cup feta cheese, crumbled

Preheat oven to 375° F. Toss diced eggplant with olive oil, salt, and pepper and spread evenly on a baking sheet. Roast eggplant in the oven for 30–40 minutes or until tender, turning once halfway through for even browning. While the eggplant is roasting, put onions and balsamic vinegar in a bowl with a little salt and pepper for 10–15 minutes. When the eggplant is done, transfer it into the bowl with onion and vinegar. Coat the eggplant with the mixture and let it cool to room temperature. Once the eggplant has cooled, add the basil and feta cheese. Toss and serve.

— Jessica Haggard, California

> It's easy to halve the potato where there is love.
>
> — Irish proverb

TABLE   269

ROASTED VEGETABLE SHEPHERD'S PIE

Even in the hottest and driest days of early fall in Southern California, I start craving the warmth and comfort that cold-weather meals bring to the home. We've worked hard to establish the tradition of a family meal each evening, and while there are date nights and pizza nights and friends over on the weekends that come as regular interruptions, I'm grateful we are able to sit around the table together most weekday evenings. Meals are still an amalgamation of reminding little ones (and big ones!) of their manners, making sure we are all listening as we take turns sharing the best parts of the day, and getting up one too many times to refill the four-year-old's water. There are tears over denied desserts, interruptions, and fights over the better seat, but there is also laughter and poetry recitation and the baby polishing off everyone's leftovers while we all look on with doting affection. I see us growing into dear friends around our family table, and I hope we always come back to it.

The seasons have shaped our meals together and helped established our traditions. The long, hot days of summer are refreshed by ice-cold watermelon and herbs and citrus over grilled meats, while the colder months call for stews, soups, and hearty bakes. Sausage and onions in the bottom of the cast-iron skillet will bring my kids in from the yard, saying things like "It smells like fall!" and "I've missed this dish!" and "It's been ages since the kitchen smelled this way." For years, establishing tradition felt like such a slog, but it's beginning to come together so naturally now, and with such happiness, that even the smallest ones anticipate the rhythm. Our senses are all united with the turn of the season, and we intuitively feel the importance of gathering together at the table over days and months and seasons and years.

One of our favorites for the colder months is a hearty shepherd's pie. As long as you make sure each layer is tasty, you cannot mess this up. You can opt for a flavor pairing of pork sausage with sweet potatoes or Yukon Golds with beef—whatever you have around!

We plop a large pan of this in the center of the table with a big wooden spoon and have at it (with manners). Make it in a big enough pan, and a few lucky kids might even have leftovers to sneak into their lunch boxes the next day. My kids all love it, and I'm sure yours will too.

To darker days, colder nights, and the soul-warming comfort of a family meal!

Assorted roasting vegetables (e.g., onion, Brussel sprouts, carrots, sweet potatoes, etc.)
Salt
Pepper
Thyme
Olive oil
2 lbs. sliced sausage or ground beef or pork
4–5 lbs. potatoes of choice
1 stick of butter
½ cup heavy cream (or more)
2 cups shredded cheddar cheese

Use enough vegetables to fill the bottom of a large roasting pan. Sprinkle generously with salt, pepper, and thyme and drizzle with olive oil. Roast at 400° F for about 35 minutes, until vegetables are caramelized. In the meantime, brown the meat, seasoning generously with salt and pepper while it cooks.

At the same time, place potatoes in a pot of cold water. Bring to a boil and cook until you can pierce them with a fork. Drain and mash with butter, salt, and pepper. Add cream a little at a time until potatoes are a desired consistency.

Layer meat over roasted vegetables in the roasting pan. Spread mashed potatoes evenly on top. Using a fork, swirl peaks into the potatoes. These will brown well and get crispy. Sprinkle with cheese. Return to oven and continue baking until cheese is melted and potatoes have a nice toasty look.

— Blythe Fike, California

SALSITA MEXICANA

This recipe comes from my grandmother and mother from Zacatecas, Mexico. It can be customized in a variety of ways, but I present it here in its simplest form to be used on taco night! It can be used with pork, beef, chicken, and fish. Your home will smell like a Mexican kitchen! If your family can't handle any spice but would love a little Mexican flavor, you can omit the peppers completely. Just add a little extra tomato. (My mom used to make it that way for us when we were kids.)

Easy-peasy! *Provecho!*

2 large fresh jalapeños (can substitute with serrano peppers or habanero peppers to make it spicier)
1 large tomato
2–3 garlic cloves (can substitute with 1 tsp. garlic powder)
Half of a large onion
A dash (or two) dried oregano
1½ cups water (can use less if you want it thicker)
Salt to taste

Cut the stems off the chile peppers. If using serrano or habanero peppers, you can tame the flavor by taking out the seeds, but rinse your hands thoroughly afterward or use gloves. Place the peppers, tomato, and garlic in a pan over medium heat and bring skin to a char (the tomato should be a bit mushy when you touch it). Note that roasting the chile peppers may cause coughing. Mix all ingredients together using a blender.

— Lorena Robles Towle, California

SALTWATER CLAMS WITH FETTUCCINE

If you have ever been to a saltwater shoreline, you know the scent of salt. At low tide there is an especially briny and pungent smell to the air, mingled with the aroma of nearby bushes and wild weeds. There are hours of treasure hunting for the children, who find pretty shells, feathers, and pebbles as they turn over the rocks looking for crabs, which scurry away out of the light. When the tide is out, that is also the chance to scavenge for dinner. We make our way, barefoot, following the freshwater stream from the grassy shoreline, down and out onto the mudflats to look for clams. We are grateful for the ease on our feet as we walk on the pebbly areas of the ground, for as we make our way farther, we have to be careful of the barnacle-covered rocks and the sharper shells sticking up all around. The terrain that we walk on is an underwater floor when the tide is high. My family digs for clams; I've got the baby on my hip and my jeans rolled up, and there in my bare feet with the wind on my face, the seagulls crying above and the smells so intoxicating, I'm just as happy as a clam! We bring in the clams, being careful as we pour them onto the soft grass so as not to break the shells or harm the living creatures inside; using the hose, we rinse the mud off and gently place them back into the bucket, refilling it to keep them cold and alive and to soak them for as long as possible to get the sand out. We discard any cracked or open clams. The hose makes puddles on the lawn, and we submerge our bare feet in the clear, fresh water to wash off the mud. Fill the bucket; gently pour it out; fill again …

Our good friend who lives here on this saltwater inlet taught us how to dig up and bring in the clams, and she taught us how to cook them too. It is a fun and memorable family event! Before you harvest, be sure that the area you choose has clean water and that you are not right on the shores of a big city. To harvest them, all you need to do is search amid the mud to find them and place them in your bucket. There are

TABLE   271

different types of clams; here in the Puget Sound in Washington, we harvest what I think are Manila clams: compact, pebbly mollusks, gray in color. Depending on where you live or go on vacation, a clam rake may be helpful. Here in the inlet, all we need are our hands; we scrape the mud with just our fingers and find that the clams are right under the surface, some spitting water! Have you ever read the children's book *One Morning in Maine*, written and illustrated by Robert McCloskey? If you have, I'm sure you remember that page with the delightful illustration of the clams spitting up water that spouts up out of the mud like a fountain!

In the evening hours as the tide is coming in, we all change into our swimsuits. The water that now covers the mudflats glistens in the evening sun. Now that the heat of the day is over, we welcome this evening swim at high tide. The squeaky, soft saltwater succulents shine a beautiful bright green, waving in the clear, moving waters. We slip in and swim way out, finding pockets of cool and warm water. There are always seals here; if you look you can spot them. It is a wonder to see them at eye level as you tread water quietly, their little gray heads with dark eyes staring right back at you not far away. I teach my children the breaststroke and plunge the baby in. He hugs me, holding on tight as he watches and learns. We taste saltwater on our lips, and the swimming is delicious; it is just the thing before a fresh clam meal. These experiences are already so saturated in refreshment and delight that we might as well bottle them up and put them in our mouths!

Back at the house we are sticky with the salt, and we feel alive and energized. It is cocktail hour now and time to cook …

Pasta of choice (however much you need to feed your household)
Sea salt
3–6 fresh garlic cloves, chopped
½ stick of butter
½–1 cup any white wine or mild beer
Fresh clams (enough for each person to have about 10) (seaside markets often have fresh clams for sale, and you can still find them in the seafood section of most large grocery stores)

Dash of cream
2 cups fresh coarsely grated Parmesan cheese
2–3 lemons, cut in wedges
Fresh cracked pepper
Fresh parsley, chopped

Fill a pot of water to cook the pasta; add some sea salt to flavor the water and speed the boil. My favorite pasta for this dish is fettuccine, but you can use any kind, really. While the pasta is cooking, sauté the garlic in a few tablespoons of butter in a cast-iron pan over medium heat. I add a splash of Columbia River Gorge chardonnay or some beer from the Benedictine Brewery in Oregon, in addition to some water, and then add the clams. Cover and steam them until the shells open, about 5–10 minutes. Say cheers to your loved one and take your first sip of your cocktail of choice. Lift the lid and inhale! Let your little ones see the clams in the pot and smell the reduction. The minute those clam shells open up, the clams are cooked and ready to eat. By now hopefully your pasta has cooked and been strained. *Al dente* is ideal! Toss the pasta in a little butter, which will melt if you do it quickly, and cream, just enough to moisten the pasta. Serve the clams atop or on the side, using a slotted spoon to lift them, shell and all, out of the pot and onto your plate. Use a regular serving spoon to ladle some of the flavorful clam broth onto your plate as well. Top with Parmesan cheese and season to taste with freshly squeezed lemons, pepper, sea salt, and parsley. Pairs beautifully with saltwater kisses and more night swims once the sun goes down.

— Sia

SPANISH OMELET

My husband used to travel quite often for his job, so I found myself regularly needing to make meals for one adult and one young child. I tried to find dishes that were fairly quick and easy or could at least be neglected periodically if I had to attend to his needs. This Spanish omelet became one of our go-to meals, as it's both nourishing and satisfying and reheats well for lunch the next day. Even now it remains my son's favorite dish, and despite the fact that I make it every few weeks, he always requests it on his birthday. It makes my heart glad to know I can nourish his body with wholesome food and nourish his soul with something he enjoys just by cooking him a simple meal.

4 Tbsp. ghee or butter
1 lb. red potatoes, thinly sliced
1 medium onion, peeled and thinly sliced

6 eggs
½ tsp. thyme
1 tsp. sea salt
Pepper to taste (optional)

Preheat oven to 350° F. In a cast-iron skillet (or other oven-safe pan), melt ghee (or butter) and sauté potatoes until golden, about 15 minutes. Remove potatoes from the pan and add onions to the ghee (adding more if needed). Fry until translucent, about 5 minutes. While the onions are frying, whisk eggs with thyme and salt. Add egg mixture to the onion and potato mixture and continue cooking for another 5 minutes. Place the skillet in the oven and bake for 5–10 minutes, just until the egg sets. Let cool for 5 minutes and then cut into wedges.

— Rebecca Zipp, Colorado

SUMMER HARVEST CASSEROLE

Looking for *another* way to use up your zucchini and other garden veggies? Want to satisfy your craving for Italian food without filling up on the starches that are in pizza or pasta? Now that squashes and nightshades are abundant, I've been making this more regularly, and it's as close to a family favorite as anything, with a 70 percent approval rating. I wish I could say I'm throwing in all the vegetables from my own box gardens, but somehow I can't keep the toddler from letting the chickens loose on our garden beds! Thank goodness for our awesome Community Supported Agriculture (CSA) weekly produce bin, which is where I source most of my ingredients. Like anything, the fresher the better. So, if you're not a gardener, do try to frequent your farmers' market or seasonal roadside veggie stand, and this dish will taste even more flavorful. Don't worry about following this recipe to a tee;

I make it differently every time, and it always turns out great. I usually double this recipe so I can freeze one or share with another family, but if your family is small, you'll likely have some leftovers to look forward to. Using the quantities below, this recipe serves 8–10.

½ lb. Italian sausage
½ lb. ground beef (optional)
1–2 eggplants
Olive oil
Salt to taste
1 onion
2 bell peppers
About 5 zucchini or 1 spaghetti squash, or a combo of the two
28-oz. can diced tomatoes, homemade tomato preserves, or 24 oz. jar marinara sauce

TABLE   273

Garlic powder
Oregano
Red pepper flakes
Salt
Pepper
Fresh basil
1 lb. sliced mozzarella
Cayenne pepper (optional)
½ lb. Parmesan (optional)

Preheat oven to 375° F. Brown meat and drain. Place in a large mixing bowl. Cut up eggplant in 1-inch cubes (no need to remove skin) and roast on a cookie sheet with olive oil and salt for 20 minutes. Cut up onions, peppers, zucchini, and squash. Sauté on the stove in olive oil until softened (you may need to do this in batches), or place in a roasting pan and roast alongside the eggplant. (If you use spaghetti squash, halve the squash, remove the seeds, dash with oil, and roast for 30 minutes until the cooked squash can flake off the peel with a fork, in spaghetti-like form.) Add cooked veggies to the meat. Add enough of the selected tomato product to form a thick and chunky sauce. Season to taste with garlic powder, oregano, red pepper flakes (go easy for the children's sake), salt, and pepper. Add lots of fresh chopped basil if you have it.

Fill 1–2 casserole dishes, depending on how much you've made, and top with sliced mozzarella. If you are saving for later, cover tightly before putting in the fridge or freezer. To bake immediately, reduce oven temperature to 350° F. Bake for 30–40 minutes until the cheese has golden-brown bubbles. Serve with a large, fresh green salad, a small bowl of freshly grated Parmesan, and another of red pepper flakes.

— Hope

SUNNY MORNING GERMAN PANCAKE

This recipe is a blast to make with kids. Like a popover, it magically poofs up in the oven while sweet little faces try to make it out through the dirty oven glass.

You will need a good cast-iron pan. An 8-inch one works well. One German pancake serves 3–4. I recommend making 2 or 3 at a time to serve your family.

3 eggs
½ cup all-purpose flour
½ cup whole milk
½ tsp. vanilla
½ tsp. salt
2 Tbsp. butter
Fruit jam or berry sauce (made with about 3 cups
    frozen berries and 2–3 Tbsp. arrowroot powder)
Juice from half a lemon
2 Tbsp. powdered sugar

Preheat oven to 350° F. Whisk eggs in medium-sized bowl. Add flour; stir to combine. Add milk, vanilla, and salt; stir to combine. Melt butter in cast-iron pan. Pour batter into pan. Bake in oven for 10–15 minutes until puffed up and golden.

While baking, prepare fruit topping. (Jam needs no preparation, but I highly recommend cooking down a few cups of frozen berries with arrowroot powder into a thick, warm berry topping. This takes about 10 minutes.)

Squeeze lemon juice on cooked pancake, cover with fruit topping, and sprinkle with powdered sugar. Slice into wedges and serve immediately.

— Hope

TARTA DE SANTIAGO

This tart is a traditional accompaniment to the Camino de Santiago, the ancient pilgrimage of Saint James. It makes for a light dessert fit for the simplest to the grandest of feasts, either on its own or topped with berries and whipped cream. It's also the perfect way to celebrate the feast of Saint James on July 25.

6 large eggs, separated
1¼ cups superfine sugar
Grated zest of an orange and a lemon
¼ tsp. almond extract

2½ cups ground almonds
Powdered sugar for dusting

Beat yolks and sugar to a pale cream. Add zest, almond extract, and ground almonds. Whip whites to a stiff peak. Fold into egg and almond mixture. Pour into prepared 11-inch springform pan. Bake at 350° F for 40 minutes. Cool and dust with powdered sugar.

— Melanie Ryland, Ohio

TEA RECIPES

These recipes can be mixed in bulk by hand, tossed gently in a big bowl, and stored in jars. I use my own abundance of lemon balm and rosemary, which I cut and dry myself, but any bulk herbs that you don't have in your garden can be bought from Frontier or other natural food co-ops. To make a mug of loose-leaf tea, use about 1 tsp. dried herbs in a fine-mesh tea strainer or bulb. Boil water; pour over tea strainer and let steep for 4 minutes. Add honey if desired and enjoy sipping while hot. The titles say it all. Do not oversteep the Mother's Perk, for it will become bitter.

Mother's Calm
1 cup dried lemon balm leaves, crushed
1 cup dried German chamomile flowers
½ cup dried rosehips
Scant ¼ cup crushed dried hibiscus

Mother's Perk
1 cup dried lemon balm leaves, crushed
½ cup dried rosemary needles
½ cup dried peppermint leaves

— Sia

VANILLA CAKE

This is the most basic of basic cakes. It fills the role of the boxed-mix cake in that it is quick and easy and answers the following questions: Which cake to sandwich between layers of whipped cream and strawberries? Which cake to cut into pieces and reassemble as a "robot" cake? Which cake to whip up and cover with buttercream and spring flowers for grandma's surprise visit? It is light, firm, and plenty *vanilla*.

4 eggs
2 cups sugar
2½ cups flour

TABLE   275

2¼ tsp. baking powder
¾ cup oil
1 cup milk
2 tsp. vanilla

Preheat oven to 350° F. Grease and flour a Bundt or 9 × 13-inch cake pan. Beat eggs and sugar for 1 minute, until thickened. Add the rest of the ingredients and beat 1 more minute. Do not overbeat. Pour batter into cake pan. Bake for 30–40 minutes, or until edges are golden brown and the fork comes out clean.

— Mary

WALDORF KALE SALAD

Here in Vermont we have lots of local honey, artisan cheese makers, and crisp, rosy apples in the fall. It's a land of local food pride, where roadside farm stands and farmers' markets are scattered over the whole of the state. But even if we pick up the ingredients at the conventional grocery store, this salad is a family favorite: easy, unfussy, healthy, and delicious. It gets my pickiest of children to eat kale, and the cheese gives it a maturity that adults enjoy. As an added benefit, it keeps nicely in the fridge overnight.

Adjust quantities according to your family size. Start with a bowl of chopped kale, large or small (depending on how many people you are feeding) and go from there. For the toppings, no need to measure. Just eye it according to taste. A cup of the honey dressing is enough for one large salad bowl.

Kale, chopped
Apples, chopped
Blue or Gorgonzola cheese, crumbled
Pecans or walnuts
Sweet potatoes, cubed and roasted (optional)
Warm honey
Olive oil
Kosher salt to taste

In a big bowl, combine kale, apples, cheese, nuts, and sweet potatoes. To make the dressing, whisk about equal parts of warm honey and olive oil (more oil than honey if you don't want the salad too sweet). Add salt and coat salad well with dressing.

— Brooke Wright, Vermont

WEEKNIGHT ROASTED CHICKEN

I once saw in a magazine a recipe called Engagement Chicken, which claimed that a girl could increase the chances of her boyfriend proposing to her if she simply cooked him a whole roasted chicken. I'm not sure what I think about that, but I do think it's a good thing to confidently and regularly pull a whole roasted chicken out of your oven for the people you love.

This recipe uses 8-inch cast-iron pans, and if you have a big family, you should have at least two cast-iron pans, says I. We roast two whole chickens most Wednesday nights, turn the bones to broth, and look forward to soup on Thursday.

This method was adapted from *Cook's Illustrated Magazine*. The high temperature gives the chicken a nice crispy outside, and the slowly cooling oven seals in the juices and makes the inside nice and tender rather than dried out.

You can turn this meal into anything you want. Greek night? Waldorf chicken salad? Roasted chicken tacos? And the leftover chicken is a much tastier choice for sandwiches than pricey, processed deli meats.

Here's a trick: if you can remember the number 45, you will never need to read this recipe again.

1 whole chicken
Oil
Salt
Pepper
Lemon, rosemary, or other seasonings (optional)

First, put your cast-iron pan in the oven and preheat to 450° F. Next, rinse your bird, discard any unwanted innards, and cover the outside with oil, salt, and

> Cooking and sharing food is central to the human condition. The fire. The pot. The knife. The table.
>
> — Christopher Kimball
> *Milk Street*

pepper. (If you want to season with lemon, rosemary, or other seasonings, go ahead, but I like it simple!) Place chicken on the hot pan breast side up; it should sizzle and sear the bottom. Close the oven and leave it alone for **45** minutes. After 45 minutes, turn the oven off and leave it alone for another **45** minutes.

— Hope

WHITE BEAN STEW FOR WINTER EVENINGS

In the cold months, we spend the days curled up beside the woodstove watching the snow fall, drinking tea, and blessing the fire. It's easy for me, in these slow days, to pour together white beans and chicken broth early in the day and let them simmer. The recipe is fluid: chicken broth is replaced with vegetable broth on Fridays, cheese is grated in when we'd like something thicker, and carrots or potatoes can be added when they're available. But at its heart, white bean stew is an easy, hearty, low-maintenance dinner for snowy days at home. It's especially tasty with rye bread, broken and buttered, and cold beer or hot milk steamed with spices.

4–5 cloves garlic
¼ cup butter
3–4 quarts chicken or vegetable broth
2½–3 cups dry white beans, such as great northern

3–4 cups vegetables, such as chopped carrots or cubed potatoes (optional)
Salt and pepper to taste
1–2 cups grated cheese (optional)

The garlic is simmered in butter for a while before adding the broth and beans, to give the garlic a chance to release its flavor. When everything is combined, I cover the pot and leave it on the woodstove for hours while I go about my day. Every now and then (when I remember and have a moment), I stop to check the beans, stir them, and make sure there is enough broth to keep them from burning. If they seem to be soaking up the broth too quickly, I add more. If I don't have chicken broth, I add water. When the beans are about half done, I add whatever roots and vegetables I have handy and re-cover the pot. After the beans have softened and the

TABLE   277

stew is thick and creamy, I add salt and pepper. If I'm adding cheese, this is when I grate it in.

For those without a woodstove, set the stove on a level that allows the beans to simmer slowly. It might take a little more focus throughout the day, turning the stove to the lowest setting once the beans are moderately soft.

This recipe, with bread, makes more than enough to feed a very hungry man, his wife, and a toddler who loves beans more than anything.

— Emily Goepel, Maine

WINDFALL APPLESAUCE

Just as berries and peaches are easy to come by in the summer, it's easy to find apples aplenty during the fall months. At farmers' markets or bulk co-ops you can often find discounted "windfall" or "second quality" apples for juicing or baking. In cooler weather, nothing feels as homey as homemade applesauce simmering on the stove. My father used to make the prettiest pink applesauce, but I think he peeled the apples, and with nine children I have no time for that. Thankfully my neighbors can't look in my windows, because I give my small children knives and cutting boards and we all have at it. We stick all the odd shapes of apple pieces with their peels (minus the cores) into a big pot until it's about half full, add a few inches of water, cover, heat on low, and then go about our lives. If you

have cinnamon sticks, excellent. Throw some in. A dash of freshly grated nutmeg? Yes. Ground spices are fine too. After 30 minutes or more of simmering, the apples will be ready for your hand blender, or you can have it chunky if you like. Some like a squeeze of fresh lemon to brighten the flavor, but there is no need to sweeten! This makes a brilliant snack and a wonderful side to pork chops, roasted chicken, or even Thanksgiving dinner, and your children will feel like home is a wonderful place to be.

— Hope

YORKSHIRE PUDDING WITH CRANBERRY SAUCE

For the Christmas Season
In England, the winters are dark, rainy, and damp. Here in the Pacific Northwest where I make my home, the climate is quite similar. Being 75 percent English, I have some very British likings: cups of strong black tea and a finely set table, complete with candles, silver, cloth napkins, and china. This may have something to do with the home of my upbringing. At special meals,

my parents sometimes made Yorkshire pudding. And at some point in my own raising of children, I decided Yorkshire pudding would be a part of every Christmas. This is my adapted (tripled and simplified) recipe from the *Joy of Cooking*, my favorite handbook for every Western European recipe under the sun.

Yorkshire pudding is a moist, fatty, bready side dish that is traditionally made to accompany roast beef, because the drippings from the meat are needed to cook it. In our family, it serves as the starch for the meal. Unlike for many of the other recipes in this book, which are more forgiving, it is important to be attentive to the timing, the ingredient calculations, and the mixture's temperature. But don't let this deter you! It is well worth the effort. Served straight out of the oven, piping hot, it should be the final dish to grace your table for your special occasion. It pairs well with roast beef, tender baby green beans gently steamed (to bright green only), a flavorful beef gravy, and my cranberry sauce, which should be made mid-day or even the day before your festive meal, as it gives the sauce time to thicken a bit. Enjoy and make merry, relishing the dipping, pairing, and feasting that this traditional dish brings to your table.

Cranberry Sauce

This can be stored in your serving bowls or in jars in the fridge, or on the counter for a few hours just sitting in the saucepan you cooked it in. (I do recommend procuring a canning funnel, which can be found in the jam-making section of your grocery store, for easy pouring into jars.) If a thicker garnishing cranberry sauce is desired, the sugar and water can be halved. I like ours to have plenty of sauciness, as it complements the salty flavors of the rest of the meal while also providing more sauciness to dip our Yorkshire pudding into.

2 cups water
2 cups sugar
2 bags cranberries
1 orange, peeled and chopped with serrated knife, seeds removed

In a medium-sized saucepan, whisk water and sugar over medium heat, bringing to a boil. Add cranberries and stir, turning heat down a bit. Let simmer until cranberries begin to pop. Immediately remove from heat. Stir in orange pieces. Serve warm or cold but not piping hot.

Yorkshire Pudding

Four hours before dinner, set out all ingredients so they will be at room temperature at time of assembling. Make the batter two hours before the roast will be coming out of the oven, being sure to budget enough time for the mixture to refrigerate properly.

2½ cups plus 2 Tbsp. all-purpose flour
1½ tsp. salt
1½ cups milk
1½ cups water
6 eggs
¾ cup hot beef drippings or 1½ sticks of butter, divided

Whisk flour and salt together in a large bowl by hand or use a stand mixer. Make a well in the center. Pour milk and water into it and beat until fluffy. Add eggs and continue to beat until large bubbles form on the surface. Cover and refrigerate for at least 1 hour.

Remove from the fridge and let stand almost another hour, returning to room temperature. When the mixture is close to room temperature, pour about ¼ cup of hot beef drippings into the bottoms of three 9 × 13-inch pans (or place half a stick of butter into the bottoms of the pans). Preheat oven to 400° F and place these pans into the oven while it is preheating (the butter will take only a minute to melt, so be attentive). When the pans are hot, take them out of the oven and line them up on your stovetop. Beat the batter again and pour it into the prepared pans. Batter should be about ½-inch high in each. Bake for 20 minutes at 400° F. Reduce heat to 350° F and bake for another 10–15 minutes.

Remove cooked pudding by flipping pans and tapping them on the counter to release (a hard spatula may also be needed). Place pudding on a serving platter that can be passed around for immediate serving. Guests can tear off pieces as the dish is passed.

— Sia

TABLE   279

Lord give bread to the hungry

and hunger for you to those who have bread

☩

Catherine Doherty